British Cinema in the 1980s

KENT·INSTITUTE
OF·ART·&·DESIGN
LIBRARY

0198 742568   791. 430942

Book No.................... Class No./Mark 4IL

This book is to be returned on or before the last date
stamped below.

23. OCT. 2000

2 4 SEP 2001

-7 JAN 2002

25. NOV 03.

23. APR 10

23. APR 10

10 MAY 10

WITHDRAWN
from the University Library

D1354444

C40282

British Cinema in the 1980s
issues and themes _____

John Hill

Clarendon Press · Oxford
1999

Oxford University Press, Great Clarendon Street, Oxford OX2 6DP

Oxford New York

Athens Auckland Bangkok Bogotá Buenos Aires Calcutta
Cape Town Chennai Dar es Salaam Delhi Florence Hong Kong Istanbul
Karachi Kuala Lumpur Madrid Melbourne Mexico City Mumbai
Nairobi Paris São Paulo Singapore Taipei Tokyo Toronto Warsaw

and associated companies in
Berlin Ibadan

Oxford is a registered trade mark of Oxford University Press

Published in the United States
by Oxford University Press Inc., New York

© John Hill 1999

The moral rights of the author have been asserted

First published 1999

All rights reserved. No part of this publication may be reproduced,
stored in a retrieval system, or transmitted, in any form or by any means,
without the prior permission in writing of Oxford University Press.
Within the UK, exceptions are allowed in respect of any fair dealing for the
purpose of research or private study, or criticism or review, as permitted
under the Copyright, Designs and Patents Act, 1988, or in the case of
reprographic reproduction in accordance with the terms of the licences
issued by the Copyright Licensing Agency. Enquiries concerning
reproduction outside these terms and in other countries should be
sent to the Rights Department, Oxford University Press,
at the address above

This book is sold subject to the condition that it shall not, by way
of trade or otherwise, be lent, re-sold, hired out or otherwise circulated
without the publisher's prior consent in any form of binding or cover
other than that in which it is published and without a similar condition
including this condition being imposed on the subsequent purchaser

British Library Cataloguing in Publication Data
Data available

Library of Congress Cataloging in Publication Data
Hill, John (W. John)
British cinema in the 1980's : issues and themes / John Hill.
Includes bibliographical references and index.
1. Motion pictures—Great Britain—History.   2. Motion picture
industry—Great Britain—History.   3. Motion pictures—Social
aspects—Great Britain.   4. Motion pictures—Political aspects—
Great Britain.
PN1993.5.G7H549   1999   791.43'0941'09048—dc21   98–3901
ISBN 0–19–811984–4
ISBN 0–19–874256–8 (pbk.)

1 3 5 7 9 10 8 6 4 2

791. 430942
HIL

Typeset by Graphicraft Limited, Hong Kong
Printed in Great Britain
on acid-free paper by
Bookcraft Ltd,
Midsomer Norton, Somerset

Acknowledgements

Ed Buscombe and Colin MacCabe first suggested that I do a book on British cinema in the 1980s (albeit of a rather different kind). Pamela Church Gibson encouraged me to carry on with the idea and Andrew Lockett at OUP nursed the project over a period of years. The Faculty of Humanities at the University of Ulster helped me with a period of leave of absence and the British Academy provided me with financial support at an early stage. My colleagues in the School of Media and Performing Arts—especially David Butler, Dan Fleming, and Martin McLoone—also helped to lighten my workload at strategically important junctures. My thanks to them all.

I would also like to thank Pam Cook, Claire Monk, and David Pattie for making unpublished work available to me as well as all those who read and commented on parts of the draft manuscript—David Butler, Pamela Church Gibson, Kelly Davidson, John Deeney, Sarah Edge, Cheryl Herr, Birgit Kellner, Andrew Lockett, and Noel McLaughlin. Thanks too to Mick Belson at OUP for his determination that I should finish!

Finally, I have tested out a number of ideas in the book with students who have enrolled on my British cinema courses. I am grateful to them for the liveliness of their responses and their insistence that I make myself clear.

Contents

List of Plates

Introduction _____

This is a book about British cinema in the 1980s. It is not, however, a straight-forward history nor an exhaustive account of films and events. What it seeks to do is raise a number of themes and issues to which filmmaking in this period gives rise. In this sense, it is a book that is primarily about 'cultural politics': about the ways in which the practice of filmmaking in the 1980s both grew out of, and responded to, the social, economic, and cultural circumstances charac-teristic of the period. In this respect, the book may be regarded as a species of 'contextual history', in which the primary aim is to examine how (some of) the meanings 'spoken' by films during this period connected to broader patterns of social and cultural life.

In doing so the book is concerned to avoid what Annette Kuhn has described as a 'text-context dualism' in film studies, whereby the analysis of texts and con-texts is kept distinct.[1] Although recent critical debates have emphasized the multiplicity of ways in which texts may be 'activated', the focus of this discussion is on how texts are activated in relation to specific socio-historical contexts and, therefore, how particular films may be read in relation to the specific circum-stances in which they were first produced and circulated. However, while it is argued that films may be profitably understood in relation to their context of production and dissemination, it is also recognized that a film has its own specificity (and semiotic productivity) that cannot be reduced to context. In this respect, many of the book's arguments are related to questions of film form and how a text's own internal operations structure the ways in which meanings are produced. In this respect, the book attempts to combine a sensitivity to the specificities of film texts with a consciousness of the contexts in which they are located.

As such, two major themes inform this book. The 1980s were very much the Thatcher years. A Conservative government was elected to office in May 1979 and Mrs Thatcher continued as Prime Minister right through the 1980s until her eventual resignation as party leader in November of 1990. As Chapter 1 argues, the Thatcherite project exerted a significant influence over all aspects of social life, including cinema. It is therefore impossible to talk about British cinema in the 1980s without taking some account of how it was engaged in an ongoing dialogue with Thatcherite ideas, meanings, and values. Indeed, much of what was distinctive about British cinema in the 1980s was precisely the way

---

[1] Annette Kuhn, *Cinema, Censorship and Sexuality, 1909–1925* (London: Routledge, 1988), 5.

in which it responded to the social changes around it and sought to address contemporary social and cultural developments.

A key aspect of the cinema's response, in this respect, was its exploration of questions of 'identity'. The economic and political changes of the 1980s were played out in terms of changing, and contested, versions of social and political identities and the cinema was an active participant in the defining and reworking of these. In this respect, the book is concerned to explore the ways in which the cinema became involved in a cultural politics of 'identity' and 'difference' and, in doing so, sought to negotiate the complex terrain of class, gender, sexual orientation, 'race', and nationality during this period.

The structure of the book is as follows. Part One is concerned with contexts. Chapter 1 discusses what is meant by the term 'Thatcherism' and explores the economic, political, and ideological characteristics of the Thatcherite 'project'. It then examines whether the period could be said to have seen the emergence of a 'Thatcherite' cinema, using *Chariots of Fire* as a specific case-study. The general conclusion, however, is that, for various reasons, the British cinema in the 1980s was largely unsympathetic to Thatcherism and challenged many of the values associated with it. Ironically, it was, in large measure, as a result of the implementation of Thatcherite policies that this 'anti-Thatcherite' cinema emerged in the way that it did. As Chapter 2 indicates, the consequences of the Thatcher government's policies towards the British film industry was to enfeeble it economically and make it increasingly dependent upon the support of television. Chapter 3 examines how the film and television industries effectively merged during this period and how this, in turn, encouraged the development of a British 'art cinema' which combined the concerns of a 'national cinema' with those of public-service television. Much of the distinctiveness, and socially critical character, of British cinema in the 1980s may therefore be accounted for by the role which television played.

The rest of the book is taken up with a discussion of the films themselves and the issues which they raise. It is common to see British cinema in the 1980s as split between those films which looked to the past and those which addressed the present. Part Two looks at the kinds of images of the past which the first group of films provided. Chapter 4 looks at what has become known as 'heritage films' and assesses how these both constructed and challenged particular versions of national, class, gender, and sexual identities. These films, it is argued, reveal a degree of ideological ambivalence, characterized by elements of both social critique and social conservatism. This is an argument that is developed further, in Chapter 5, in relation to films and 'empire'.

Films such as *A Passage to India* and *Heat and Dust* are seen to raise specific questions concerning 'race' that are absent from the other heritage films, and the ways in which these films enact dramas of 'inter-racial' connection are considered. As with the heritage film more generally, it is argued that there is a degree of ideological tension in the way in which these films both question and reinforce conventional social and cultural divisions. Finally, the section on representations of the past ends with a short case-study of *Dance with a Stranger*.

In comparison to the heritage film, this is set in a more recent historical period —the 1950s—and in a more ordinary social milieu. This chapter looks at how the 1950s are remembered in this film and assesses how far its formal approach, and social attitudes, may be seen to differ from those of the heritage film.

Part Three is concerned with representations of the present. Although there is a degree of implied contrast between these and the representations of the past, discussed in Part Two, the distinction is not rigid. So while the films concerned with the present are generally seen to be more successful in challenging the fixities of inherited identities than the heritage film, it is also necessary to distinguish individual films in both camps. Chapter 7 looks at what became known as the 'state-of-the nation' film and explores the ways in which a strategy of 'national allegory' was employed to pass comment on the current state of Britain. Although some of these films grew out of a British filmmaking tradition that has characteristically combined social criticism with realism, this chapter identifies the increasingly diverse and hybrid aesthetic strategies which 1980s British films employed when dealing with social issues. These arguments are developed in Chapters 8 and 9 which deal with issues of class and gender and Chapters 10 and 11 which deal with 'race'. These distinctions are not hard and fast, however, as it is the ways in which different 'identities' are articulated together that is of interest in all four chapters. Chapter 8 looks at how the tradition of working-class realism in the 1980s was characterized by the decline of the working-class male hero and discusses the emergence of a new kind of working-class heroine. Chapter 9 continues the discussion by taking two films —Mike Leigh's *High Hopes* and Ken Loach's *Riff-Raff*—as case-studies of the way in which issues of class politics were worked out in relation to questions of gender in the work of these two important British directors .

Chapters 10 and 11 continue to examine how traditional conceptions of national, 'racial', and class identities were explored in British films of this period. Chapter 10 focuses on the work of Hanif Kureishi and Stephen Frears—particularly *My Beautiful Laundrette* and *Sammy and Rosie Get Laid*—and considers the ways in which they challenge traditional conceptions of 'race' and celebrate the emergence of new kinds of hybrid identities. This interest is developed further in Chapter 11 in relation to the black workshops, and the films of Isaac Julien in particular. This chapter looks at the ways in which a politics of 'race', gender, and sexuality, rooted in the specific circumstances of Britain, was combined, in films such as *The Passion of Remembrance* and *Looking for Langston*, with a politics of form in order to explore some of the cultural complexities of contemporary black, British identities. Finally, the book concludes with some remarks on 'nationality' and a short examination of the ways in which British cinema in the 1980s increasingly put into question the idea of a shared 'Britishness'.

Although the book discusses a fair number of films, there are inevitably omissions and I am conscious that there are important films and directors who have not been given the full attention they deserve. The selection has, of necessity, been governed by the interests which have underpinned the study.

This has meant that my choice of films has been selective but not, I think, in a way that is significantly out of step with the main trends of the period. As Richard Dyer observes, film studies has been characterized by different principles of 'mattering', of assumptions about why the study of film matters.[2] In my own case, the study of film is important not simply because of its 'intrinsic' value but also because of its socio-cultural character, its relationship to larger concerns about how we live. In this respect, this is not only a book about film in the 1980s but also a book about the contribution of cinema to more general political and cultural currents.

[2] Richard Dyer, 'Introduction to Film Studies', in John Hill and Pamela Church Gibson (eds.), *The Oxford Guide to Film Studies* (Oxford: Oxford University Press, 1998), 3.

part one

Contexts _____

chapter 1

The British Cinema and Thatcherism _____

Defining the 1980s

Despite the appeal of periodizing the past in terms of decades, it is rare that social and political developments, or indeed cinematic trends, conform to neat ten-year patterns. There is, however, some justification for attributing a degree of basic coherence to Britain of the 1980s. At a political level, this was provided by the premiership of Margaret Thatcher and the related phenomenon of 'Thatcherism'. As the Introduction indicated, a Conservative government was elected to office in May 1979 and Mrs Thatcher continued as Prime Minister right through the decade (finally resigning as party leader in November 1990). While the remnants of the Thatcherite project may have survived her, there is still no doubting that this was the end of an era.

In the case of the British cinema, it is less easy to pinpoint dates although the Oscar-winning success of *Chariots of Fire* in March 1982 undoubtedly signalled what at least popularly became known as a 'renaissance' of British filmmaking. As with previous revivals (in the mid-1930s, during the Second World War, and in the early 1960s), this renaissance was, almost inevitably, destined to prove short-lived. None the less, the British cinema which emerged in the 1980s did contain a number of genuinely novel and distinctive aspects and did, at least temporarily, overcome some of the difficulties which beset British filmmaking in the 1970s. However, if it makes sense to view the 1980s as a relatively coherent period, is it the case that the cinema and the politics of the period were in some ways connected? The answer is almost undoubtedly 'yes' although the connections were not necessarily straightforward. In order to identify some of the links which existed, therefore, it is necessary to begin with a discussion of what is meant by the concept of 'Thatcherism'.

Thatcherism

Thatcherism is not, of course, an uncontested term and it is one which has been the subject of considerable debate. Andrew Gamble has suggested that the term has been used in three main ways: in relation to Margaret Thatcher's political style, to the ideological doctrines of the New Right, and to the policies of the Thatcher government.[1] Gamble himself opts for the idea of Thatcherism as a 'political project', one which he sees as emerging in the wake of the Conservative election defeats of 1974.[2] In particular, the Thatcherite 'project' is regarded as evolving in response to the problems besetting the British economy in the 1970s (and which were in turn related to a more general crisis in the world economy): a low rate of growth, a high level of inflation, and a deterioration in industrial relations, culminating in the so-called 'winter of discontent' of 1978–9 when over one million low-paid public service workers were on strike for nearly three months. The new Conservative government of 1979 was elected on the basis of a commitment to reverse the long-term decline of the British economy and, in attempting to do so, embarked upon a course which is often taken to represent a significant departure in post-war political life.

Since the election of a Labour government in 1945, British politics had been characterized by a degree of 'consensus' in terms of both political approach (an emphasis on consultation and compromise) and political policy (a commitment to a mixed economy, Keynesian economics, full employment, and public welfare provision). Although the precise character of Thatcherite policies changed over the Conservatives' three periods of office, they none the less retained a basic coherence. In line with the precepts of economic liberalism, the new Thatcherite Conservatives were committed to the strengthening of market forces in all areas of society and to 'rolling back' the frontiers of state as a means of securing economic efficiency. In doing so, they have also been seen as being committed to a restructuring of the British economy along more 'flexible', international lines (or what is often characterized as the establishment of a new 'post-Fordist' regime of accumulation).[3] As a result, the Conservatives abandoned many of the policies which had been a feature of the post-war consensus. The main planks of the Thatcherite programme, in this respect, were as follows:

[1]   Andrew Gamble, 'The Thatcher Decade in Perspective', in Patrick Dunleavy, Andrew Gamble, and Gillian Peele (eds.), *Developments in British Politics*, 3 (Basingstoke and London: Macmillan, 1990), 333–4.
[2]   Ibid. 336. Thatcherism, none the less, was never a unitary phenomenon and went through a number of stages. Frank Gaffikin and Mike Morrissey, for example, identify four main 'phases' associated with different economic and political emphases: 1979–82, 1982–7, 1987–9, 1989–90. See *Northern Ireland: The Thatcher Years* (London: Zed Books, 1990), 12–14.
[3]   This is an argument found in Andrew Gamble, *The Free Economy and the Strong State: The Politics of Thatcherism* (Basingstoke and London: Macmillan, 1988) amongst others. For a good account of the transition from a Fordist to post-Fordist regime of accumulation, see David Harvey, *The Condition of Postmodernity* (Oxford: Basil Blackwell, 1989) esp. Part 2. For some useful points of reservation regarding the theoretical underpinnings of this debate, see Karel Williams *et al.*, 'The End of Mass Production?', *Economy and Society*, vol. 16, no. 3 (Aug. 1987).

- the prioritization of the control of inflation as a policy objective;
- a reduction of public expenditure;
- a reduction of taxation as a means of restoring 'incentives';
- an abandonment of the commitment to full employment;
- trade union reforms designed to weaken the power of the unions, deregulate the labour market, and make industry more competitive;[4]
- the increasing deregulation of the private sector (especially banking and financial services culminating in the City of London 'Big Bang' of 1986);
- the privatization of publicly owned corporations, the selling of public assets such as housing, and the 'marketization' of the public sector through the imposition of market disciplines and contracting-out of services.[5]

Despite claims that this programme was responsible for an 'economic miracle', its results were decidedly mixed. Following a dramatic rise to 18 per cent in 1980, the rate of inflation did begin to fall, reaching as low as 3.4 per cent in 1986. However, there was a steady rise in inflation for the rest of the 1980s and, at the time of Mrs Thatcher's departure from office, inflation was actually higher, at 10.9 per cent, than when she became Prime Minister. Much the same is true of the figures for economic (GDP) growth. After the recession of 1980–1 (which the government's policies had largely precipitated), there was a period of sustained growth but this too slowed down towards the end of the 1980s and, by 1990, the growth rate was again lower than in 1979. Moreover, by international standards, Britain's record for the period was undistinguished. Howard Vane, for example, compares Britain's economic performance for the period 1979–88 with six other major industrialized countries (Canada, France, Germany, Italy, Japan, and the United States) and reveals that four of these had a superior record on economic growth. He also indicates that Britain's rate of growth was no better than for the period 1973–9 and worse than for the periods 1951–64 and 1964–73.[6] It was, therefore, only the figure for economic productivity which

---

[4] The government's determination to break trade union power was symbolized by its confrontation with the National Union of Mineworkers over pit closures in 1984–5. The NUM strike lasted a year but ended with the miners going back to work without a settlement.

[5] A useful summary and discussion of the Thatcher government's main economic policies may be found in Stephen Edgell and Vic Duke, *A Measure of Thatcherism: A Sociology of Britain* (London: HarperCollins, 1991). In the discussion which follows I have also drawn upon *Economic Trends Annual Supplement* (London: HMSO, 1993); Chris Hamnett, Linda McDowell, and Philip Sarre (eds.), *The Changing Social Structure* (London: Sage, 1989); Michael Ball, Fred Gray, and Linda McDowell, *The Transformation of Britain: Contemporary Social and Economic Change* (London: Fontana, 1989); Peter Riddell, *The Thatcher Era and its Legacy* (Oxford: Basil Blackwell, 1993); John Wells, 'Miracles and Myths', *Marxism Today*, May 1989, 22–5; Christopher Huhne, 'From the Horn of Plenty to the Poisoned Chalice', *The Independent on Sunday* (25 Nov. 1990), 10–11; and 'Eleven Years of Thatcherism: Audit of Her Era', *The Independent* (23 Nov. 1990), 4.

[6] 'The Thatcher Years: Macroeconomic Policy and Performance of the UK Economy, 1979–1988', *National Westminster Bank Quarterly Review* (May 1992), 26–43. One explanation for Britain's poor economic performance is the lack of investment. Investment as a proportion of GDP during the 1980s was considerably down on previous decades and again compared unfavourably with international competitors. See Nicholas Costello, Jonathan Michie, and Seumas Milne, *Beyond the Casino Economy* (London: Verso, 1989), 86–7.

showed a, more or less, consistent increase over Mrs Thatcher's period of office and which compared favourably with Britain's industrial competitors.

However, one of the prices to be paid for this growth in productivity was a dramatic rise in unemployment. In the period 1979–82 unemployment more than doubled and unemployment stayed at over 3 million from 1982 until 1986. Although this figure then dropped (helped by some massaging of the statistics), the rate of unemployment was not only significantly higher at the end of Mrs Thatcher's term of office than at its start but also growing again (reaching well over 2 million in 1991). This rise in unemployment was linked, in turn, to a decline in British manufacturing. In the period June 1979–January 1981, manufacturing output fell by 19.6 per cent and 23 per cent of all manufacturing jobs were lost. Manufacturing output did subsequently improve but by 1987 was still no higher than in 1973. Overall, during the period between 1979 and early 1991, manufacturing employment fell by more than 2 million and this was reflected in a deteriorating trade position. In 1983, the balance of trade in manufactured goods went into deficit for the first time and this was not compensated for by trade in services. Thus, by 1989, the overall trade deficit had escalated to almost record heights of £19.6 billion. This did subsequently fall but Britain was still badly in deficit at the end of Mrs Thatcher's period of office and in a worse position than when she had taken over.

Unemployment also had consequences for the Conservatives' ability to control public expenditure. Although public expenditure under Mrs Thatcher's government did fall relative to GDP, from 44 per cent to 39 per cent, it also increased in real terms by 16 per cent. As a result, the government became heavily dependent upon revenues from North Sea oil and privatization in order to finance public spending and to keep down public borrowing. This failure to reduce significantly public expenditure was in part the result of the extra demands which the unemployed put on the state and, despite the various changes to entitlement for benefits which the government made, social security expenditure still grew by 38.4 per cent between 1978 and 1988. However, changes in public expenditure were not uniform and expenditure on housing, for example, declined by 59.9 per cent, thus contributing to the increase in homelessness that was a feature of the late 1980s.[7]

The Conservatives' record on taxation was also a mixed one. There is no doubt that the Tories were successful in lowering rates of direct taxation and that this contributed greatly to their repeated electoral successes. The basic rate of income tax was dropped, in stages, from 33 per cent to 25 per cent and the top rates from 83 per cent to 40 per cent. These cuts in direct taxation, however, were more than offset by increases in indirect taxation which meant that the average tax burden (including income tax, national insurance, VAT, excise duties, and poll tax) actually increased during the Thatcher period (from 35 per cent to

---

[7] In 1990, local authorities in Great Britain accepted 156,000 households (two-thirds of which contained dependent children) as homeless. This was nearly three times the figure for 1978. See Central Statistical Office, *Social Trends 22* (London: HMSO, 1992), 150.

38 per cent of earnings). Indeed, there was only one group who clearly benefited from the Conservatives' tax reforms and this was the very rich. This constituted a reversal of the redistributive attitude which had been a feature of previous post-war governments and contributed to greater inequality in the UK during the 1980s. Thus, between 1979 and the early 1990s, the share of income, after housing costs, of the top fifth of households increased by 23 per cent (and the top tenth by over 60 per cent) while the income of the bottom 10 per cent dropped by 40 per cent.[8] As a result the number of people living in poverty at the end of the 1980s was significantly larger than at the beginning. In 1979, 5 million (or 9 per cent of the population) were living below half-average income. By 1992–3 this had risen to 14.1 million (or 25 per cent of the population).[9]

Indeed, for Bob Jessop *et al.*, the significant feature of Thatcherism was its shift from traditional Conservative 'one nation' policies to what they call a 'two nations' strategy.[10] This, they suggest, created a division between those who were the beneficiaries of the Thatcher years—not only the very rich but also the new 'service class' in the private sector and core workers in the growth industries—and the losers—especially 'peripheral' workers, the long-term unemployed and the new poor. These inequalities were, in turn, linked to other kinds of division. The decline of manufacturing and the rising importance of the service sector accentuated divisions between north and south, insofar as it was the north where manufacturing jobs were most often lost and the south where private sector services were primarily concentrated. As Denis and Ian Derbyshire sum up,

the decline of the 'smokestack' and second wave industries in the traditional industrial regions of the northeast, northwest, central Scotland, South Wales and West Midlands and the growth of the new high-tech and service sector industries in southern and eastern England . . . widened regional economic differentials, as reflected in unemployment, average income, home ownership and even health statistics.[11]

The restructuring of the labour force along more 'flexible' lines also had consequences for gender divisions, creating a pool of long-term unemployed males while drawing increasing numbers of women into the workforce. As Elizabeth Wilson explains,

---

[8] Central Statistical Office, *Social Trends 24* (London: HMSO, 1994), 77. Although rising inequality was a feature of a number of countries during the 1980s, according to a report for the Joseph Rowntree Foundation, 'the UK was exceptional in the pace and extent of the increase in inequality in the 1980s'. See Joseph Rowntree Foundation, *Inquiry into Income and Wealth*, vol. 1, chaired by Sir Peter Barclay (New York: Joseph Rowntree Foundation, 1995), 14.

[9] Department of Social Security, *Households Below Average Income: A Statistical Analysis, 1979–1993/4* (London: HMSO, 1996), 155. Half the average income is normally taken as the unofficial poverty line.

[10] See Bob Jessop, Kevin Bonnett, Simon Bromley, and Tom Ling, *Thatcherism*, (Oxford: Polity Press, 1988) and Bob Jessop, Kevin Bonnett, and Simon Bromley, 'Farewell to Thatcherism? Neo-Liberalism and "New Times"', *New Left Review*, no. 179 (Jan./Feb. 1990), 81–102.

[11] J. Denis Derbyshire and Ian Derbyshire, *Politics in Britain: From Callaghan to Thatcher* (Chambers, 1988), 182. See also Doreen Massey, 'A New Class of Geography', *Marxism Today* (May 1988), 12–17.

the decline of the manufacturing sector, the increase of part-time work in the service sector, and changes in technology and in consumption patterns . . . combined . . . to create a situation in which more and more women became wage workers, yet as an increasingly vulnerable part of the workforce.[12]

Thus, in 1990, women represented over 43 per cent of the labour force. However, 76 per cent of these were in part-time work and, as such, were more likely to face low pay, diminished employment rights, and limited opportunities for advancement.[13] Ethnic minorities also suffered a disproportionate share of low-paid jobs and unemployment. Thus, in 1991, unemployment rates for Pakistanis, Bangladeshis, and Black-Africans were nearly three times, and for Black-Caribbeans twice, the average UK rate.[14] In the case of Caribbean men aged between 18 and 19, the unemployment rate was a staggering 43.5 per cent.[15]

Social Neo-Conservatism

This widening of economic inequalities and social divisions inevitably had consequences for another aspect of the Thatcherite project. For as numerous commentators have observed, Thatcherism was not simply fuelled by economic neo-liberalism but also by a more traditional brand of social neo-conservatism. As Margaret Thatcher explained in the wake of her initial election: 'The mission of this government is much more than the promotion of economic progress. It is to renew the spirit and solidarity of the nation.'[16] Thatcherism, in this respect, may be seen not simply to be responding to the economic travails of the 1970s but also the perceived breakdown in social authority and standards which the 'permissiveness' of the 1960s had set in motion and which had carried over into the 1970s. As a result, it sought to harness, as Stuart Hall suggests, the neo-liberal economic precepts of 'self-interest, competitive individualism, anti-statism' with the organic conservative themes of 'tradition, family and nation, respectability, patriarchalism and order'.[17] As such, Thatcherism was only committed to the rolling back of the state in the interests of market freedom; otherwise it was quite prepared to strengthen state power, and restrict freedoms, in the interests of national regeneration, social order, and discipline. It was these 'politico-legal' aspects of Thatcherism which Stuart Hall sought to account for

[12] Elizabeth Wilson, 'Thatcherism and Women: After Seven Years', in Ralph Miliband, Leo Panitch, and John Saville (eds.), *The Socialist Register 1987* (London: Merlin Press, 1987), 208.

[13] Central Statistical Office, *Social Trends 24* (London: HMSO, 1994), 59. Linda McDowell argues that because of the concentration of women's jobs in the service sector, and the numbers of women working on a part-time basis, women's earnings were on average about two-thirds those of men. See 'In Work', in Michael Ball *et al.*, *The Transformation of Britain*, 159–60.

[14] Ceri Peach, 'Introduction', in Ceri Peach (ed.), *Ethnicity in the 1991 Census Vol. 2 The Ethnic Minority Populations of Great Britain* (London: HMSO, 1996), 17.

[15] Peach, 'Black-Caribbeans: Class, Gender and Geography', in Peach (ed.), *Ethnicity in the 1991 Census, Vol. 2*, 34.

[16] Speech in Cambridge, 6 June 1979 quoted in *The Independent* (23 Nov. 1990), 4.

[17] Stuart Hall, *The Hard Road to Renewal: Thatcherism and the Crisis of the Left* (London: Verso, 1988), pp. 48 and 2.

with his concept of 'authoritarian populism'.[18] For Hall, Thatcherism was able to feed upon genuine popular discontents with the state of Britain (economic decline, state bureaucracy, increasing crime) and mobilize support for right-wing, or 'authoritarian', solutions to them.

These political and ideological aspects of Thatcherism were manifest in a number of ways:

- a commitment to a 'strong' defence policy (partly fuelled by an intense anti-Soviet rhetoric), involving a real increase in public spending on defence, investment in new nuclear missiles (such as Trident) and a strong identification with US foreign policy (which included allowing the Americans to site Cruise missiles at Greenham Common and Molesworth and to use British bases for their air attack on Libya in 1986);
- an accompanying obsession with 'official secrecy' and determination to use the Official Secrets Act against various targets such as the civil servants Sarah Tisdall (who passed documents to *The Guardian* concerning the installation of nuclear bases) and Clive Ponting (who leaked documents concerning the sinking of the General Belgrano, during the Falklands war, to Labour MP Tam Dyell), the BBC's *Secret Society* (1987) series (which included a programme on Zircon, a satellite surveillance system developed by the Ministry of Defence), and the ex-MI5 officer Peter Wright's book, *Spycatcher* (1987);
- a programme of spending on law and order (the biggest increase in public expenditure during the period), increases in police and judicial powers under the Criminal Justice Acts of 1982 and 1988, the Police and Criminal Evidence Act of 1984, and the Public Order Act of 1986, changes to policing methods (including national co-ordination), and an increased use of political surveillance;[19]
- a tough line on 'terrorism', including refusing to grant 'political' status to republican prisoners in Northern Ireland or to bow to hunger strikers;[20]
- a tightening of the control of immigration through the British Nationality Act of 1981 (which, by dividing UK and Commonwealth citizenship into

---

[18] Ibid., esp. chap. 8.

[19] Colin Leys suggests the Thatcher government was responsible for an acceleration of changes in the following areas: the bureaucratization of the police and elimination of popular control, a shift from 'community policing' to 'fire-brigade policing', the development of police technology, the expansion of secret police surveillance of political opposition, and the militarization of policing. See *Politics In Britain: From Labourism to Thatcherism* (London: Verso, 1989), 356–7. The national coordination, and politicization of the police, was particularly evident during the coal dispute when the National Reporting Centre was used to orchestrate and direct police operations at coalfields.

[20] For a history of the 1981 hunger strike in Long Kesh (The Maze) prison, in which ten prisoners (beginning with Bobby Sands) died, see David Beresford, *Ten Men Dead: The Story of the Irish Hunger Strike* (London: Grafton Books, 1987). Beresford sees Margaret Thatcher's refusal to make concessions to the prisoners as an early example of 'the politics of confrontation' that would later be pursued in relation to Argentina during the Falklands war and the National Union of Mineworkers during the coal dispute (p. 428). However, despite this 'victory' for the Thatcher government, the polarization and instability in the north of Ireland that it created led, in the longer term, to a more politically pragmatic approach to the conflict. Thus, in 1985, Mrs Thatcher signed the Hillsborough, or Anglo-Irish, agreement, which, by setting up an Intergovernmental Conference involving the Republic of Ireland, brought the Conservatives into conflict with their 'natural allies', the Ulster Unionists.

three categories, restricted both nationality and immigration rights) and the Immigration Act of 1988 (which reduced the rights of those who had settled in the UK to bring their dependants into the country);[21]
- a reduction in local democracy, including the abolition of the Greater London and other metropolitan councils;[22]
- an abandonment of the 'arms-length' principle in dealings with public bodies (such as the BBC and the Arts Council) combined with an increasing use of political appointees to non-governmental agencies (such as health boards and development agencies);
- a rhetoric of familialism and anti-permissiveness and an increased intolerance of sexual difference, as manifest in the notorious Section 28 of the 1988 Local Government Act which prohibited local authorities from the intentional promotion of homosexuality.[23]

However, as with economic policy, the actual results were mixed. Thus, despite the commitment to fighting crime, the amount of recorded crime actually rose by 60 per cent during the Thatcher years.[24] In this respect, there was a certain tension between the economic and the politico-legal aspects of Thatcherism, and the ideological rhetoric of Thatcherism was often at odds with its economic effects. Thus, despite the Thatcher regime's appeal to order, unity, and social cohesion, it was evident that Thatcherite economic policies were contributing to an increase in social divisions and conflicts. This became most apparent in what Ian Taylor has described as a 'quite unprecedented series of urban riots' that occurred during the Thatcher years. Writing in 1987, he observes:

A country which throughout the entire post-war period to 1979 has experienced a total of about three discrete sets of urban disturbances, (the Notting Hill and Nottingham riots of 1958, the Mods and Rockers confrontations of 1962–4 and the Vietnam demonstrations of 1968–70) has since witnessed at least a dozen major riots in a period of only seven years: beginning in St Paul's, Bristol, one year into the first Thatcher Government, further major insurrections and/or riots have occurred in Brixton

---

[21] Although Home Office Minister Timothy Renton argued that the Immigration Act of 1988 was necessary to avoid 'mass immigration on a vast scale', immigration was already in decline and only 47,800 were accepted for settlement in the UK in 1986 (of which the vast bulk were relatives or dependents). See Central Statistical Office, *Social Trends 24* (London: HMSO, 1994), 29.

[22] Peter Riddell estimates that no less than fifty separate acts were passed during the Thatcher years aimed at reducing the independence of local authorities. See *The Thatcher Era*, 177.

[23] Michele Barrett describes 'familialism' as an 'ideology of family life' which extends beyond the realities of actual families in *Women's Oppression Today: Problems in Marxist Feminist Analysis* (London: Verso/New Left Books, 1980), 206. Thus, it was the 'family', along with the 'individual', that was often invoked as the key social and economic unit in the rhetoric of Thatcherism. Thatcherism is often seen, in this respect, to have involved an assault on 'intermediary' institutions such as local authorities and public corporations that stood between the state and individuals and their families. It is this attack on 'civil society' that underpins Margaret Thatcher's notorious claim, in an interview for *Woman's Own*, that: 'There is no such thing as society. There are only individual men and women, and there are families.' Quoted in Riddell, *The Thatcher Era*, 171.

[24] Ibid. 234. Ian Taylor argues that this increase in crime was distinctive to the UK and was not paralleled in North America where crime rates in the US and Canada were falling. See 'Law and Order, Moral Order: The Changing Rhetorics of the Thatcher Government', in Ralph Miliband *et al.* (eds.), *The Socialist Register 1987*, 303.

(April 1981), in Toxteth and Moss Side (July 1981), St Paul's again (January 1982), Notting Hill Gate (April 1982), Toxteth (April 1982 and July 1982), St Paul's once more (June 1983), Handsworth, Birmingham (9–10 September 1985); Brixton (23 September 1985) and Tottenham (October 1985).[25]

Although the Conservative government was reluctant to accept that such disturbances were linked to either unemployment or the rundown of the inner cities, it was evident, as the Scarman Report on the 1981 riots recognized, that the disorders could not be understood outside of 'the context of complex political, social and economic factors which together create a predisposition towards violent protest'.[26] For Scarman, these factors included unemployment, poor housing, discrimination and, especially amongst young blacks, 'a sense of frustration and deprivation'.[27]

This tension between rhetoric and reality was also in evidence in the Thatcher government's discourses surrounding the family and sexuality. Thus, despite the emphasis upon the family and 'family values' the rate of divorce continued to increase and a record number of 192,000 petitions for divorce were filed in 1990.[28] The number of births outside of marriage also increased dramatically (rising from 12 per cent of all births in 1981 to 23 per cent in 1987).[29] Moreover, as a result of the increasing numbers of people living alone, in single-parent families or without children, the conventional nuclear family, involving a married couple with dependent children, represented a declining proportion of households (only 25 per cent in 1991).[30] Many of these households, moreover, consisted of 'reconstituted' families (involving previously married partners or children from different marriages) and failed to correspond to the 'normal family' model of a working father and non-working mother. If these factors are taken into account, the 'normal family' probably accounted for less than 10 per cent of all households.[31] Indeed, as in the case of crime, it can be seen how Thatcherite economic policies actually contributed to the undermining of the

---

[25] Ian Taylor, 'Law and Order, Moral Order: The Changing Rhetorics of the Thatcher Government', 304. The ending of Margaret Thatcher's period of prime ministerial office was also characterized by major social disturbances in response to plans for the introduction of the controversial community charge (or 'poll tax') in Scotland in April 1989 and in England and Wales in April 1990. The introduction of the tax led to nationwide protests, including serious rioting in London on 31 March 1990.

[26] Lord Scarman, *The Scarman Report: The Brixton Disorders 10–12 April 1981: Report of an Inquiry by the Rt Honourable The Lord Scarman OBE* (London: Pelican Books, 1982, orig. 1981), para 8.7, p. 195. For a general discussion of the issues raised by the disturbances, see John Solomos, *Race and Racism in Contemporary Britain* (Basingstoke: Macmillan, 1989), esp. chaps. 5 and 6.

[27] *The Scarman Report*, para 2.23, p. 29.

[28] Central Statistical Office, *Social Trends 23* (London: HMSO, 1993), 30. Ironically, the *Matrimonial and Family Proceedings Act 1984* made divorce easier by permitting couples to file for divorce after their first wedding anniversary.

[29] David Willetts, 'The Family', in Dennis Kavanagh and Anthony Seldon (eds.), *The Thatcher Effect* (Oxford: Clarendon Press, 1989), 262.

[30] Central Statistical Office, *Social Trends 26* (London: HMSO, 1996), 51.

[31] See Jon Bernardes's breakdown of census figures for the family in 'In Search of "The Family"— Analysis of the 1981 United Kingdom Census: A Research Note', *Sociological Review*, vol. 34, no. 4 (Nov. 1986), 832. Given the decline in numbers of married couples with dependent children between 1981 and 1991 (a drop of six per cent) and the increase in working wives, Bernardes's figures for the 'normal family' will have actually decreased during the decade.

very 'family values' that the government claimed to represent. The encouragement of 'enterprise' and 'flexible' labour markets, as has been seen, not only led
to high rates of male unemployment that deprived families of the traditional
male bread-winner but also propelled increasing numbers of women into the
labour force (including about 60 per cent of married women).[32] Thus, far from
women being returned to the home, women's work became a crucial element in
the restructuring of the economy. As Angela Coyle suggests, the use of women
as cheap, flexible labour put women workers at 'the forefront of a Government
strategy' to dismantle 'the regulation and control of employment' and 'free' the
employer/employee relationship.[33] In the same way, strong rhetoric concerning
the family, did not protect women from the effects of public expenditure cuts.
As Sarah Franklin, Celia Lury, and Jackie Stacey put it, 'the severe cut-backs in
welfare benefits and services' (including cuts in housing benefits and the freez-
ing of child benefit) that the Thatcher governments implemented 'had a profoundly negative effect on women overall, particularly in their long-established
roles as carers, nurturers, and homemakers', helping to relegate increasing
numbers of families, especially single-parent families, to poverty.[34]

Moreover, although the Thatcher government adopted a strong moral tone,
it was, in fact, reluctant to intervene legislatively in areas of 'moral' concern.
As Elizabeth Wilson points out, legislation concerning moral issues such as
divorce, the death penalty, homosexuality, and abortion has traditionally been
treated as a 'matter of conscience' and has often come about through a private
member's bill and a free vote.[35] Thus, despite the government's 'law and order'
stance (and Margaret Thatcher's own personal support for restoration), the
reintroduction of the death penalty was rejected on three occasions (in 1979,
1983, and 1988) by a free vote in the House of Commons. Likewise, the efforts
of Liberal MP, David Alton, to amend the 1967 Abortion Act (by reducing the
permitted period for terminations to 18 weeks) also proved unsuccessful. An
amendment to the 1990 Human Fertilization and Embryology Act, setting a
new limit of 24 weeks, was subsequently supported by the government but this
was already conventional medical practice and, politically, commanded the
kind of 'consensus' that the Conservative government would not normally have
sought. Maureen McNeil also suggests that, while the Thatcher government
clearly disassociated themselves from the sexual 'permissiveness' of the 1960s, it
did not do so though 'an explicit stand', or the implementation of clear policies,

---

[32] Willetts, 'The Family' in Kavanagh and Seldon (eds.), *The Thatcher Effect*, 264. This growth of
women in the workforce was to lead the government—the government of the 'family'—to introduce
separate taxation for married women in 1990.

[33] Angela Coyle, 'Going Private: The Implications of Privatization for Women's Work', *Feminist
Review*, no. 21 (Winter 1985), 6–7. Elizabeth Wilson points out, however, that the policies of the
Conservative government did not affect women uniformly and, just as inequalities increased generally
under Thatcherism, so the gaps between 'better off women and those at the bottom of the employment
hierarchy' also became greater. See 'Thatcherism and Women: After Seven Years', 206.

[34] Sarah Franklin, Celia Lury, and Jackie Stacey, 'Feminism, Marxism and Thatcherism', in Sarah
Franklin, Celia Lury, and Jackie Stacey (eds.), *Off-Centre: Feminism and Cultural Studies* (London:
HarperCollins, 1991), 26.

[35] 'Thatcherism and Women: After Seven Years', 227.

but simply by refusing 'to articulate the discourse of sexuality'. Thus, despite its 'strong moralistic image', she argues that the Thatcher regime, unlike the Reagan administration, was hesitant 'to enter the discourse of the sexual since . . . such engagement might have proliferated, rather than eliminated, that which it wished to destroy'.[36] This, in fact, turned out to be the case in the government's involvement in the notorious Clause 28 of the Local Government Bill (which prohibited the 'promotion of homosexuality'). Like other 'moral' issues this was initially an initiative of backbenchers and failed to secure government support. When it subsequently did so, this was as much the result of the government's determination to bring Labour local councils to heel as a concerted assault on lesbian and gay rights and led to effects that were entirely contrary to those that had been intended. As Jackie Stacey argues:

Rather than silencing and marginalizing lesbians and gays, the introduction of Section 28 set in motion an unprecedented proliferation of activities which put homosexuality firmly on the agenda in Britain in 1988–9. The terms of the public debate may have been set by the right, but the widespread resistance to the Section and its implications brought about greater visibility, a strengthened lesbian and gay community and a politicized national and international of lesbian and gay activists.[37]

Evidence of such overt resistance to the Thatcher government's policies not just by lesbians and gays but trade unionists, peace campaigners and anti-nuclear groups, supporters of local government, students, anti-poll tax campaigners, and so on inevitably raise questions about the ideological successes of Thatcherism. For a while, for Stuart Hall, Thatcherism was both populist and 'hegemonic' in character, Thatcherism did not in the end secure either full hegemony or, in empirical terms, clear popular support. The winning of the Falklands/Malvinas war in 1982 certainly rescued the Tories from the massive unpopularity of their early years of office (when, according to opinion polls, Mrs Thatcher was the most unpopular Prime Minister since polling began) and seemed to encourage the temporary expression of the kind of 'national-popular' sentiments that Thatcherism sought to orchestrate. However, as Raymond Williams argued, the Falklands affair relied upon 'a certain artificial, frenetic, from-the-top, imagery of the nation' and did not suggest any deep-seated growth of 'Thatcherite consciousness'.[38] So, although the 'Falklands factor' undoubtedly helped to win the Conservatives a second term of office in June 1983, their share of the vote was none the less down.

---

[36] Maureen McNeil, 'Making and Not Making the Difference: The Gender Politics of Thatcherism', in Sarah Franklin *et al.* (eds.), *Off-Centre: Feminism and Cultural Studies*, 233. Her argument, in this respect, draws on Foucault's critique of the 'repressive hypothesis' concerning discourses of sexuality and his recognition of how prohibitive discourses may incite other discourses of sex. See Michel Foucault, *The History of Sexuality, Vol. 1* (London: Allen Lane, 1978).

[37] Stacey, 'Promoting normality: Section 28 and the regulation of sexuality', in Sarah Franklin *et al.* (eds.), *Off-Centre: Feminism and Cultural Studies*, 302. Once the Local Government Act was passed, Clause 28 became Section 28.

[38] Raymond Williams, 'Problems of the Coming Period', *New Left Review*, no. 140 (July–Aug. 1983), 9–10.

It was, indeed, one of the paradoxes of the Thatcher years that while the Conservatives, under Mrs Thatcher, were elected three times and embarked upon a radical economic and social programme, they do not appear to have at any time commanded majority political support. Thus, in the 1979 election, the Tories' share of the vote was only 44 per cent while in the following two, in 1983 and 1987, it was even less at 42 per cent. Moreover, the evidence from opinion polls and social surveys also suggests that the electoral successes of the Thatcher government were not accompanied by any major shifts in public attitudes. Thus, while Conservative policies towards trade unions were undoubtedly popular, there was no similar support for the government's efforts to reduce welfare provision.[39] It has therefore been suggested that pragmatism and economic calculation on the part of voters were more responsible for keeping the Conservatives in power than ideological commitment.[40] This seems to have been particularly so of skilled manual workers whose defection from Labour to Conservative was crucial in maintaining the Thatcher government in power. Thus, while the majority of the semi-skilled and unskilled working class continued to support Labour in the 1983 and 1987 elections, the majority of skilled workers—or C2s—voted Conservative.[41]

Support for Thatcher was also overwhelmingly in the south of England. As David McCrone points out, 'less than 10 per cent of Conservative MPs elected in 1979 and 1983 came from Scottish and Welsh seats, the smallest proportion since the 1920s, and only 16 per cent from the north of England, the smallest proportion for over a hundred years'.[42] These discrepancies were even more marked following the 1987 election when Scotland returned only ten Conservative MPs and Wales only eight (out of a total of 358). In Scotland, there was little acceptance of the Thatcher government's break with consensual, social-democratic government and, as McCrone explains, 'the attack on state institutions—the nationalised industries, the education system, local government, the public sector generally, even the church, institutions which carried much of Scotland's identity—was easily perceived as an attack on "Scotland" itself'.[43] Thus, for all of its rhetoric of 'national unity', the nationalism of the Thatcher government

---

[39] See, for example, the essays by Ivor Crewe 'Has the Electorate Become Thatcherite?', in Robert Skidelsky (ed.), *Thatcherism* (Oxford: Basil Blackwell, 1988) and 'Values: The Crusade That Failed', in Dennis Kavanagh and Anthony Seldon (eds.), *The Thatcher Effect*, 239–50. The survey data provided by the annual reports of *British Social Attitudes* also suggest how resistant popular attitudes have been to Thatcherite nostrums. Indeed, Frances Cairncross goes as far as to suggest that Mrs Thatcher's electoral 'success was in spite of, rather than because of, her economic philosophy' in *British Social Attitudes: the 9th Report* (Aldershot: Dartmouth Publishing, 1992), 47–8.

[40] See, for example, Stephen Hill, 'Britain: The Dominant Ideology Thesis after a Decade', in Nicholas Abercrombie, Stephen Hill, and Bryan S. Turner (eds.), *Dominant Ideologies* (London: Unwin Hyman, 1990). Joel Krieger also argues that Thatcherism depended on an 'arithmetic politics' characterized by 'particularistic appeals' to electorally significant sections of the population. See *Reagan, Thatcher and the Politics of Decline* (New York: Oxford University Press, 1986), 86.

[41] See Massey, 'Heartlands of Defeat', *Marxism Today* (July 1987), 23. Also Peter Jenkins, *Mrs Thatcher's Revolution: The Ending of the Socialist Era* (London: Jonathan Cape, 1987), 317–18.

[42] David McCrone, *Understanding Scotland: The Sociology of a Stateless Nation* (London: Routledge, 1992), 173.

[43] Ibid. 172.

was less British (or unionist) than (southern) English and pivoted, moreover, upon a particularly narrow and exclusivist version of 'national' identity. As Andrew Gamble explains, the Conservatives learnt that they no longer had 'to project themselves as the party of the Union in order to win elections'. The appeal of 'the Conservative Nation', in this respect, was 'directed much more towards England, and towards certain regions of England, the old metropolitan heartland of the Empire'.[44]

This growth of a narrow English nationalism was also apparent in the government's 'populist' response to 'race' and immigration in which 'Englishness' was characteristically associated with 'whiteness'.[45] Indeed, Mrs Thatcher's rise to political success was undoubtedly assisted by her willingness to make the politics of race respectable.[46] It could also be seen in the Thatcher government's relationship with Europe. The Thatcher government was always a half-hearted member of the European Community, committed only to a deregulated 'free' European market but not to greater political or economic union which it regarded as a threat to national sovereignty. However, Europe was an issue that divided Conservatives and matters came to a head over plans for increased political and monetary union (including a single European currency and a central European bank). Following the Rome summit of October 1990, at which Mrs Thatcher had stood out against plans for European integration, the Deputy Prime Minister, Geoffrey Howe, resigned, thus setting in motion the events that were to lead to Thatcher's own resignation as PM not long afterwards. In a sense, the seriousness of the split amongst Conservatives over Europe revealed some of the fragility of the alliance between free economic thinking and nationalist ideas that characterized the Thatcher years. For, at an economic level, the Thatcherite project was clearly to internationalize the economy and integrate it into a global system (in a way, moreover, that severely circumscribed the ability of national government to exercise control over the 'national economy'). Yet, at a political level, the government remained firmly attached to 'Little England' notions of national sovereignty and identity that increasingly stood at odds with the realities of globalizing economic and cultural forces.

What, however, helped to keep the Tories in power during the 1980s, despite the divisions within their ranks and their relative unpopularity, was the divided nature of the political opposition that they faced. In 1981, a number of Labour MPs, concerned at the apparent drift of the main opposition party towards the left, broke away to form the more 'centrist' Social Democratic Party, or SDP.

---

[44] Andrew Gamble, *The Free Economy and the Strong State*, 214.

[45] The association of English/British identity with 'whiteness' is explored by Paul Gilroy, *There Ain't No Black in the Union Jack: The Cultural Politics of Race and Nation* (London: Hutchinson, 1987).

[46] On television in January 1978, Mrs Thatcher claimed that 'people are really rather afraid that this country might be rather swamped by people with a different culture and . . . that if there is any fear that it might be swamped, people are going to be really rather hostile to those coming in'. See Melanie McFadyean and Margaret Renn, *Thatcher's Reign* (London: Chatto and Windus, 1984), 85. Andrew Gamble describes this as 'one of her most successful political interventions before she became Prime Minister', reporting how the Conservative party's rating in the polls rose by nine points. See Andrew Gamble, *The Free Economy and the Strong State*, 136–7 and 250.

Although never able to 'break the mould' of British politics as initially claimed, the new party (in electoral alliance with the Liberals) did none the less do sufficiently well, especially in the south of England where the Labour vote was weak, to split the opposition and ensure that no one party was then able to mount an effective challenge to the Conservatives during the 1980s. Thus, in the first election following the formation of the SDP in 1983, more electors voted against the Conservatives than for and the Tories' share of the vote fell. However, thanks to opposition splits and the 'first past the post' electoral system, the number of Conservative seats in parliament still managed to rise.

However, if claims for the ideological success of the Thatcher government have undoubtedly been overstated, it would also be wrong to dismiss the ideological impact of Thatcherism altogether. The policies of the Thatcher government left few areas of social life untouched and if the majority of the population did not actively support the changes which these policies wrought they did not remain unaffected by them and were often required to accommodate to them. As Stuart Hall suggests, the institutional reforms which the Thatcher government implemented were able to bring about changes in conduct without necessarily winning over 'hearts and minds'.[47] Moreover, if Thatcherism did not always succeed in mobilizing popular assent for its policies it did undoubtedly succeed in presenting itself as the most viable political option. Labour's failure at the polls, in this regard, was not simply the result of a split opposition but also an inability to offer a credible alternative remedy for Britain's economic difficulties. As Colin Leys puts it, 'for an ideology to be hegemonic, it is not necessary that it be loved. It is merely necessary that it has no serious rival'.[48]

Thus, in an effort to improve their electoral prospects, Labour, following their initial swing to the left, were forced to move rightwards, adopting many policies similar to those of the Conservatives and reversing their initial hostility to such measures as privatization and the sale of council houses (which had proved an undoubted vote-winner for the Conservatives).[49] Thus, if the Conservatives began their first term of office by departing from the old 'social-democratic consensus' they had, by the end of the 1980s, forged something of a new 'consensus' amongst political parties around the acceptable limits of economic and political action. This convergence of political policies then became even greater when John Major replaced Mrs Thatcher as Prime Minister in 1990 and John Smith, followed by Tony Blair, succeeded Neil Kinnock to the Labour party leadership (and, in the case of Blair, to ultimate electoral victory).

[47] Stuart Hall, 'Thatcherism Today', *New Statesman and Society* (26 Nov. 1993), 14–16. Hall uses the example of higher education where, despite a continuing commitment to old social democratic values, academics learnt to adapt to new entrepreneurial and managerial imperatives.

[48] Colin Leys, 'Still a Question of Hegemony', *New Left Review*, no. 181 (May/June, 1990), 127.

[49] Whereas the majority of council tenants consistently voted Labour, the majority of home-owners, amongst both the working and middle classes, voted Conservative. See Massey, 'Heartlands of Defeat', 23.

British Cinema and Thatcherism _____

However, if Thatcherism may be seen to have dominated the politics of the 1980s, the study of Thatcherism has not had much to say about the cinema. In terms of the history and analysis of the politics of the period, the role of cinema has not been regarded as important and most studies of Thatcherism have ignored it. Thus, in a well-known collection of essays on the effects of the Thatcher government on British social life there is no mention of the British cinema despite chapters devoted to both the mass media and the arts.[50] While this may reflect an assumption, on the part of the authors, that the British cinema is no longer a 'mass medium' nor an 'art', it more probably indicates just how minor an impact Thatcherism is assumed to have had upon British filmmaking (and, by corollary, how marginal the study of British cinema is to an understanding of Thatcherism).

However, from the perspective of studies of the British cinema, the relationship between the politics and the cinema of the 1980s does not appear so negligible. Indeed, it is the links with Thatcherism that are often taken to be one of the most significant aspects of the cinema of the period. This relationship has largely been thought of in terms of the ideas, and ideologies, which the films of the period suggest. However, while in the case of Hollywood cinema of the 1980s, it is often argued that a rightward turn is detectable this is not so evident with British cinema of this period.[51] Arthur Marwick lists what he regards as the most important films of the 1980s and concludes that 'it cannot be said that these films conform to one particular ideology, certainly not that of Thatcherism'.[52] Kenneth MacKinnon explicitly compares British and American films of the 1980s but is also reluctant to identify an explicitly Thatcherite cinema.[53] So, while the rightward turn of American cinema in the 1980s has been associated with a revival of morally conservative, entrepreneurial, and militaristic themes, it is difficult to identify an equivalent trend in British cinema.

Thus, unlike Hollywood, there is little evidence of a significant grouping of 'backlash' movies that sought to roll back the gains of feminism by debunking career women or attempting to return women to the home. *The Good Father* (Mike Newell, 1986) does make common cause with a conservative movement towards the 're-assertion' of the paternal 'rights' of divorced fathers and links this with a degree of criticism of 1960s radicalism, the women's movement,

---

[50] Kavanagh and Seldon (eds.), *The Thatcher Effect*, chaps. 22 and 23.

[51] See Michael Ryan and Douglas Kellner, *Camera Politica: The Politics and Ideology of Contemporary Hollywood Film* (Bloomington: Indiana University Press, 1988), Robin Wood, *Hollywood From Vietnam to Reagan* (New York: Columbia University Press, 1986), and Andrew Britton, 'Blissing Out: The Politics of Reaganite Entertainment', *Movie*, nos. 31/32 (Winter 1986). Britton uses the term 'Reaganite entertainment' to refer to 'a general movemment of reaction and conservative reassurance in the contemporary Hollywood cinema' (p. 2).

[52] Arthur Marwick, *Culture in Britain Since 1945* (Oxford: Basil Blackwell, 1991), 153.

[53] Kenneth MacKinnon, *The Politics of Popular Representation: Reagan, Thatcher, AIDS and the Movies* (London: Associated University Presses, 1992).

and lesbianism. However, the logic of the film's attack is not fully worked through and the ending involves a degree of 'compromise' whereby Roger (Jim Broadbent) wins exclusive custody of his son in the courts but, shocked by the judge's ruling that his son should never stay with his mother (who is living with another woman), works out his own informal arrangements for joint custody. Roger also distances himself from Bill (Anthony Hopkins), the divorced father who had encouraged Roger (as a way of vicariously working out his own anger) to give his wife a 'tug on the lead' by fighting her in the courts. Bill himself is revealed as a deeply flawed character who has an ambivalent relationship with his own son (there is a fantasy scene in which he is seen strangling him) and shows himself incapable of sustaining a relationship with either his wife or his girlfriend. At the film's end, he is on his own, 'imprisoned' in his newly fenced backyard. In this way, the film tempers the criticism of the women characters by criticizing the cynical and deceitful manner in which Roger is encouraged to gain custody of his son (not just by Bill but by a self-seeking, money-making barrister typical of the new commercial culture) and by bringing out how Bill's war against 'castrating' women has its roots in his own psychological inadequacies.

A similar ambivalence is also evident in films that address the growth of an 'enterprise culture'. Adam Barker, writing in 1989, suggested that *How To Get Ahead in Advertising* (Bruce Robinson, 1989) and *Dealers* (Colin Bucksey, 1989) marked a new development for British cinema in which filmmakers began 'to take seriously the social formations which have emerged from a newly created culture of commerce'.[54] However, neither of these could be regarded as straightforwardly endorsing this new culture. Tracing the obsession of advertising executive Dennis Bagley (Richard E. Grant) with finding a new way of selling pimple cream (and his subsequent development of a malignant boil), *How To Get Ahead* mobilizes a fairly well-worn critique of the idiocies of advertising and the emptiness of commercial culture. The film ends with Bagley, his head now replaced by the boil (which has assumed his facial characteristics), rushing through the countryside ('England's clean and pleasant land') on his horse while preaching his creed of limitless consumerism to the accompaniment of 'Jerusalem' on the soundtrack. As he clambers onto a plinth on the top of a hill and holds his arms aloft in a traditional Christ-like pose, the demented mix of fundamentalist religion, nationalism, and boundless entrepreneurialism ('I'll give them anything, and everything they want') that the film associates with Thatcherism is clearly apparent.

The critique of the new commercial culture in *Dealers* is more muted but has elements of overlap. Set in the City, the film deals with the yuppie lifestyles of financial traders and the ups and downs of the 'casino economy'. However, at the film's end, the film's risk-taking young trader Daniel Pascoe (Paul McGann)

[54] Adam Barker, 'Business as Usual? British Cinema in an Enterprise Culture', *Monthly Film Bulletin* (Aug. 1989), 228. These were hardly the first films to comment on the enterprise culture—as films such as *My Beautiful Laundrette* (1985) and *Empire State* (1987) would indicate—but they were unusual, as Barker suggests, in being set almost exclusively in the world of business.

leaves the bank, followed by his fellow trader and girlfriend Anna (Rebecca De Mornay). Like Bagley's wife, Julia (Rachel Ward), in *How To Get Ahead* who leaves her husband because she wants something 'that can't be bought', so Anna, and by implication the film, question whether she and Daniel have 'got it all' (a book on Keith Richards entitled 'Emotional Rescue' is clearly visible behind the characters in the final scene in the bank). Admittedly, the film's attack on the new entrepreneurial culture is less than wholehearted given the extent to which the film is itself seduced by the glamour and wealth of the world it condemns. However, unlike Oliver Stone's *Wall Street* (1987), to which it is indebted, or Caryl Churchill's play *Serious Money* (1987), set at the time of the Big Bang in 1986, the film is so lacking in substance that it is effectively prevented from investing the world of financial trading with any degree of real complexity or fascination.

In terms of a resurgence of militarism, probably the only overtly militaristic film of the period was *Who Dares Wins* (Ian Sharp, 1982), made in the wake of the siege of the Iranian embassy in 1980, which demonizes the anti-nuclear movement as a front for internationally financed terrorism and celebrates the military prowess of the SAS (Special Air Services). However, there was no film made celebrating the Falklands/Malvinas war (despite Margaret Thatcher's wish for one) and those films that did touch on the topic—such as *For Queen and Country* (Martin Stellman, 1988) and *Resurrected* (Paul Greengrass, 1989)— did so from a critical perspective. Both of these films concentrate on the experiences of the returning soldier. In the case of *For Queen and Country*, the black soldier Reuben (Denzel Washington), who has served in both the Falklands and Northern Ireland, returns 'home' to a depressed council estate in south London beset by poverty, racial divisions, and heavy-handed policing. He also discovers that, despite his military service, he is no longer eligible, under the 1981 British Nationality Act, for British citizenship (having been born in St Lucia).

In *Resurrected*, the central character Kevin Deakin (David Thewlis) went missing during the advance on Port Stanley and has been presumed dead. Based on the case of the Scots Guardsman Philip Williams, the film explores the reactions to his subsequent return to Britain when he is discovered, seven weeks later, with amnesia. The actual 'truth' of the matter is left ambiguous but what the film dissects is the anguish, ostracism, and eventual violence (at the hands of his regiment) which Deakin suffers because he is unable to live up to the role of 'national hero' which the media, his home community, and the army has bestowed upon him. This is underlined in the film's final scene in which a television set in the military hospital to which Kevin has been admitted (following his beating) shows the return home to his wife of Second World War hero, Douglas Bader (Kenneth More) in the 1950s war movie *Reach for the Sky* (1956). The camera moves off the television set, and across a ward of wounded soldiers to reveal Kevin lying dejected in bed, the victim not only of a squalid and unpleasant war (which was far from the 'game of cricket' referred to by Bader's wife on the television) but also the 'patriotism' and false expectations of those who had supported the war 'back home'. However, it was a film that was not about war at all—*Chariots of Fire*—which is often seen to have most embodied the Falklands spirit and, in doing so, to have given one of the most eloquent expressions to Thatcherite values. Given the importance of the film during this period, it is worth examining, in rather more detail, just how far this was actually the case.

Chariots of Fire: A Thatcherite Film?

'If there is one moment at which the idea of a "British film renaissance" took shape, it is that Oscar night, 23rd March 1982,' writes Nick Roddick.[55] The Oscar night to which he refers is, of course, the now infamous occasion on which *Chariots of Fire* won four Oscars (including for 'Best Picture') and Colin Welland, accepting the award for 'Best Original Screenplay', declared that 'the British are coming!' Whatever was intended by the remark (and Welland has subsequently claimed he was misinterpreted), there is no doubt that his confident claim was destined to assume a more general significance. Shortly after the Oscars ceremony, on 2 April 1982, the Argentinians invaded the Falklands/ Malvinas islands and, on 5 April, the Thatcher government dispatched a naval task force from Portsmouth which successfully retook the islands in June. There can be little doubt that the Falklands victory revived the political fortunes of the Thatcher government (as Hugo Young reports, 'the prime minister's rating in the opinion polls, which stood at rock bottom in late 1981, soared to 51 per cent in June 1982') and that the 'Falklands factor' played a major role in securing the Conservatives a second term of office.[56] Mrs Thatcher herself identified the Falklands victory with a new national spirit. 'We have ceased to be a nation in retreat' she told Cheltenham Tories in July 1982. 'We have instead a new-found confidence, born in the economic battles at home and tested and found true 8,000 miles away.'[57]

In a sense, the coincidental timing of military victory in the Falklands and Oscar-winning success in Los Angeles seemed to link the two events together and, following its re-release, *Chariots* showed successfully across Britain during the entire Falklands episode. It is this connection which is so vividly suggested in Alan Parker's polemical 'documentary' on British cinema, *A Turnip-head's Guide to the British Cinema* in which shots of the runners and cheering crowds at the Olympics in the film are intercut with actual footage of similar crowds welcoming home the Falklands task force (along with images of social disturbance) to the accompaniment of the *Chariots* theme tune by Vangelis.[58] Indeed, in the film itself, a newspaper hoarding announcing 'Our boys are home' is

[55] 'The British Revival', in Gilbert Adair and Nick Roddick, *A Night At The Pictures: Ten Decades of British Film* (Bromley: Columbus Books, 1985), 76.

[56] Hugo Young, *One of Us: A Biography of Margaret Thatcher* (London: Pan Books, 1990), 280.

[57] Quoted in ibid. 281.

[58] *A Turnip-head's Guide to the British Cinema* (Wr./dir. Alan Parker, Thames Television (12 Mar. 1986)).

clearly visible when the runners return to England, seemingly anticipating the way in which the tabloids were to celebrate the return of 'our boys' from the Falklands. Hugo Young also reports that David Puttnam, the producer of *Chariots*, was a subsequent guest of the Prime Minister's at Chequers and that there was 'much talk in the Thatcher circle about the desirability of something similar being put on to celluloid to celebrate the Falklands victory'.[59]

This was possibly a rather curious fate for a film which had struggled to find financial backing and which, according to Welland, told the story of a 'couple of fellows who put their fingers up to the world'.[60] The film, set in the wake of the First World War, is also aware of the high cost of war—the Master of Caius (Lindsay Anderson) pays tribute at the freshman's dinner to the Cambridge men who had 'died for England'—and the war itself is linked, by the Duke of Sutherland (Peter Egan), to 'guilty national pride'. As this would suggest, *Chariots of Fire* is a rather more complex piece of work than its reputation often suggests and, if it became identified with refurbished national sentiment and a Thatcherite outlook, this was undoubtedly related to the special circumstances in which it was received. There are, nevertheless, a number of elements within the film which facilitated this particular response.

For, clearly, *Chariots* is a film which celebrates British success and which, in doing so, evokes a number of the 'traditional' values similar to those that Thatcherism was itself seeking to revive. The focus of the film is, of course, sport and it is sporting success and the values traditionally associated with sport which are its main subject of celebration. The original script had apparently begun with an explicit reference to what was perceived as the break-up of the Olympic ideal in the face of business and political interests (the US had, in fact, boycotted the 1980 Moscow Olympics because of the Soviet invasion of Afghanistan).[61] In choosing to return to 1924, therefore, the film is evidently seeking to resurrect what it regards as the original Olympic spirit of competitive sportsmanship and the ideals which this represents.

In this respect, the film may be linked to a certain 'return of the hero' which also characterized American cinema in the 1980s. As various writers have noted, the 'new Hollywood' of the late 1960s and early 1970s gave rise to a number of films characterized by loose, episodic plots, alienated or 'unmotivated' heroes, and pessimistic resolutions.[62] From the mid-1970s onwards, however, there was an increasing return to much more linear narratives involving goal-oriented action and positive heroes. In some respects, *Chariots* may also be seen to represent a reaction to the breakdown of traditional models of British filmmaking that occurred in the 1960s and to involve a return to a more conventional kind

---

[59] *One of Us*, 277. In addition to Mrs Thatcher's admiration for the film, it was also reported that it was one of President Reagan's favourite films of 1981. See *Screen International* (10 Apr. 1982), 7.

[60] Quoted in Anon. 'Chariots Begins At Home', *AIP & Co.*, no. 35 (Nov./Dec., 1981), 12.

[61] 'These are sour days in Olympic history. The bureaucracies of big business and nation states have finally demanded more of the original slender ideal than it can possibly bear and it's fatally beginning to crack' is quoted in 'Chariots Begins at Home', 11.

[62] See, for example, Thomas Elsaesser, 'The Pathos of Failure. American Films in the 1970s: Notes on the Unmotivated Hero', *Monogram*, 6 (1975), 13–19.

of British cinema. It is significant, in this respect, that the trailer for *Chariots* self-consciously promoted it as 'a British film about British heroes' and linked it to an earlier tradition of 'wonderful' British films.[63]

Thus, despite some play with temporal relations, *Chariots* employs a relatively straightforward narrative structure, organized around the desire for sporting victory on the part of its central characters: the runners Harold Abrahams (Ben Cross) and Eric Liddell (Ian Charleson). Inevitably, this emphasis upon male sporting success also has implications for the film's portrait of gender roles. It is no accident that the film begins with the words, from Ecclesiastes, 'Let us now praise famous men', for it is men who occupy the active roles and whose desires structure the film's forward movement. The roles performed by the women characters, in contrast, are narratively subordinate and peripheral. Thus, Jennie Liddell (Cheryl Campbell) functions largely as a—temporary— obstacle to her brother's pursuit of sporting glory while Abrahams's girlfriend Sybil Gordon (Alice Krige) provides patient support for the sporting activity to which she is required to take second place (hence, there is a significant scene in which the embrace of Abrahams and Sybil is interrupted by the coach Sam Mussabini (Ian Holm) who literally comes between the couple in the frame). Indeed, such is the marginality of women to the main business of the film that the film's emphasis upon male bonding, images of physical prowess and looking verges, as Neale suggests, on the homo-erotic.[64] As has been noted, it has been common in discussion of the American cinema of the 1980s to associate the return of the hero with a reaction to the challenges of feminism and a desire to return women to their 'proper' place. Although male anxieties about changing female roles are not overtly dramatized in *Chariots*, its celebration of a social world which is unashamedly masculine and, in which, there is very little room for women certainly suggests a certain longing for a more traditional division of labour between the sexes.

However, if the heroism of *Chariots of Fire* is linked to sporting achievement and traditional versions of masculinity, it is also linked to the theme of nationality as well. As Anthony D. Smith suggests, in his discussion of 'golden ages', the hero is 'never solitary' but a vessel for national virtues and qualities.[65] To this extent, criticism of the film's distortion of historical fact (including, for example, identifying Abrahams as breaking the record for the Caius college dash, exaggerating his battle against anti-Semitism—when he subsequently converted to Catholicism—as well as his commitment to a professional ethic of sporting) may miss the point. For, as Smith argues, the actual 'historicity' of heroes is less significant than their thematization of national qualities.[66] The

---

[63] See Sheila Johnston, 'Charioteers and Ploughmen', in Martyn Auty and Nick Roddick (eds.), *British Cinema Now* (London: BFI, 1985), 103.

[64] Steve Neale, '"Chariots of Fire", Images of Men', *Screen* vol. 23 nos. 3/4 (Sept./Oct. 1982), 47–53. Neale goes on to argue, however, that the film's narrative resolution is dependent upon a repression of the male homosexual desire which has, at least implicitly, been suggested during the course of the film and that this confirms the film's status as a conservative film.

[65] Anthony D. Smith, *The Ethnic Origins of Nations* (Oxford: Basil Blackwell, 1986), 195.

[66] Ibid. 200.

film's licence with history, in this respect, not only permits a clearer delineation of dramatic conflicts (as in the fictionalized encounter between Liddell and the Prince of Wales (David Yelland)) but also a sharpening of the issues at stake in the film's celebration of 'national' virtues.

It is therefore to be expected that, in the film, athletics and sporting achievement are identified with a traditional 'English' education and with traditional English virtues. Thus, the Master of Trinity (John Gielgud) explicitly links athletics with 'the education of an Englishman' and the capacity not only to 'create character . . . (and) . . . foster courage, honesty, and leadership' but also encourage a 'spirit of loyalty, comradeship and mutual responsibility'. Although the film may take its distance from the character who says this (due to his snobbishness and bigotry), it none the less endorses (perhaps, more than the character himself) the values to which his speech lays claim. However, while sporting endeavour provides a loose allegory of national effort and achievement it also does so in a way that is quite complex. This is the result of the different models of sporting hero which the film portrays and the varied religious and ethnic allegiances which they embody.

For although the characters share a desire for sporting success, they do not all run for the same reasons. Harold Abrahams regards himself as at odds with the establishment and runs, as he puts it, as a 'weapon' against being Jewish. Eric Liddell runs for the glory of God while the aristocratic Lord Lindsay (Nigel Havers) runs because he enjoys it (as he explains to Sybil, 'the whole thing's fun'). The film, in this respect, may be seen to offer somewhat different versions of the 'manly ideal': what Paul Hoch has referred to as the 'playboy' and the 'puritan'.[67] Lindsay clearly represents the 'playboy' hero linked to a gentlemanly ethic of gallantry, leisure, and enjoyment (one of the film's most memorable scenes consisting of Lindsay practising hurdling by jumping over full glasses of champagne). Abrahams and Liddell are, by contrast, 'puritans' characterized by self-discipline and a commitment to work and duty over pleasure. However, although it is the 'puritans' who secure victory, the success of Liddell is none the less dependent upon the intervention of the 'playboy' whose gallantry in withdrawing from the 400 metres allows him to compete.

The main characters are also distinguished by their religious and ethnic affiliations. Indeed, for a film which is reputedly so nationalist, it is surprising how conscious it is of the complexities of national allegiance. Hence, Abrahams is identified not only as a Jew but one of Lithuanian extraction. His coach, Mussabini (Ian Holm), is part Italian and part Arab and possesses a Geordie accent. Eric Liddell was born in China but is fiercely proud of his Scottishness, announcing in his first scene in the film: 'I am and will be while I breathe—a Scot!' In this respect, Abrahams, Mussabini, and Liddell are all 'outsiders' who stand apart from the English establishment by virtue of their social status, religious affiliations, and ethnic backgrounds. In order for these characters to

[67] Paul Hoch, *White Hero Black Beast: Racism, Sexism and the Mask of Masculinity* (London: Pluto Press, 1979), 118–20.

function as 'national heroes', therefore, the film seeks to overcome these differences and forge an image of 'national' unity out of the multiple identities which
it reveals. The film, in this respect, may usefully be regarded as 'mythical' in
impulse. This is not simply, as Ed Carter suggests, because the film deviates so
dramatically from actual history but also because of the way in which it seeks
to resolve the social tensions and contradictions that its different characters
represent.[68]

It does so, primarily, through an attempted integration of the film's outsiders
into the 'national' community represented by the Olympic team. In contrast to
the more accentuated individualism of American cinema, the heroic values
which the film celebrates are allied with team effort and the *esprit de corps* to
which Aubrey Montague (Nicholas Farrell) refers at the film's start. Former
competitors Abrahams and Liddell end up running under the 'same flag' and
Lord Lindsay's sacrifice on behalf of Liddell, in effect, cements an alliance across
class and nationality (as well as fusing different versions of masculinity). However, although this may be linked, as one writer puts it, to a view of the 'nation'
in which 'difference constitutes rather than fragments national unity', it also
involves a certain suppression of differences as well.[69]

This may be seen in the film's treatment of Eric Liddell. For although the
timely intervention of Lord Lindsay permits him to run for both God and country, this is less a resolution of a conflict than an evasion of it. Indeed, Liddell's
religious fervour continues to remain at odds with national duty as the
sequence intercutting scenes from the Olympics with his sermon to the Paris
congregation attests, relying, as it does, on a text from Isaiah: 'All nations before
him are as nothing; and they are counted to him less than nothing, and vanity.'
Indeed, insofar as neither Abrahams or Montagu enjoy success while running
on a Sunday, the film itself appears to show some sympathy towards Liddell's
sabbatarianism. Liddell's Scottishness also remains problematic. For while a
number of commentators have noted the apparent disappearance of Liddell's
Scottishness as an issue, there is a sense in which the very version of 'Scottishness' which the film constructs makes it difficult for it to be incorporated
into the film's final celebration of 'national' characteristics. This is most evident
in the film's use of images of nature. For although this has been seen as reinforcing the mythic and transhistorical character of the film's story, it is also apparent that it is in the Scottish scenes in which this imagery is most pronounced
(and Liddell's declaration of his love of Scotland is clearly identified with his
father's 'wee home in the glen' and with the rural Highlands where we first see
him run). Even the scenes set in the Scottish capital, Edinburgh, are linked to
nature (Liddell and Jenny converse on a hill above the city) and although we are
informed that Liddell runs for Edinburgh University (a university almost as old
as Cambridge) it is never actually shown or offered as a marker of Scottishness

    [68] Ed Carter, '*Chariots of Fire*: Traditional Values/False History', *Jump Cut*, no. 28 (1988), 15.
    [69] Tana Wollen, 'Over Our Shoulders: Nostalgic Screen Fictions for the 1980s', in John Corner and
Sylvia Harvey (eds.), *Enterprise and Heritage: Crosscurrents of National Culture* (London: Routledge,
1991), 181.

PLATE 1.   Forging an image of 'national' unity: *Chariots of Fire*

in the way that Cambridge is associated with Englishness. To this extent, the film's use of imagery reproduces a romantic conception of Scotland in terms of the rural and the 'primitive' and the qualities of Liddell himself become linked to these terms: he is a sporting 'natural' (seen training in the glens) who runs 'like a wild animal' and also a 'primitive' whose religious fundamentalism defies the urbanity and reasonableness of the English upper classes. Thus, when he finally wins for 'country' at the film's end, the film is obliged to suppress the 'otherness' of the 'Scottishness' with which he has previously been associated and effectively convert him into a symbol of Englishness. Thus, while the newspaper hoarding informs us that it is Abrahams who is 'the toast of England', it is, in fact, Liddell whom we have seen held aloft by his English team-mates at the Olympic stadium and cheered by the English crowds at the railway station.

So if the conclusion of *Chariots of Fire* involves a eulogy to the nation, it is—as it is in the Thatcherite version of the nation—primarily England and Englishness which it celebrates. This is, perhaps, clearest in the film's use of the memorial service which is shown at the film's beginning and end and which is used to frame the Olympics story. Although a commemoration of Abrahams in particular, it involves a tribute to his fellows as well ('all these men were honoured in their generation and were a glory in their days'). What is of note, however, is that this is clearly a 'Christian and Anglo-Saxon' Church of England service. So while Liddell was a Scottish Presbyterian and Abrahams was a Jew (and therefore, as the porter at Caius points out, unlikely to join the chapel choir) they have, by the film's conclusion, been effectively appropriated by both a religion and an establishment to which neither initially belonged. The film's 'solution' to the national and religious differences which it has identified, therefore, is to subsume them within a dominant version of 'Englishness'. It is not surprising then that the service should conclude with a rendition of William Blake's *Jerusalem* (from which the film's title is taken) and an invocation of the strong sense of English patriotism which this carries with it.[70] It is also notable that this is invested with a degree of solemnity and seriousness at odds with the more ironic attitude towards Englishness (and its 'constructed' character) implied by the use of Gilbert and Sullivan (and their lines that 'despite of all temptations to belong to other nations, he remains an Englishman').

The ideological resolution which the film provides, in this respect, not only represents the incorporation of its outsiders into the establishment but also a fusion of the old and the new. This may be seen in relation to Abrahams in particular. For although the film invokes traditional sporting values, it also, through Abrahams, subjects them to a degree of criticism. Thus, when the Masters rebuke Abrahams for his use of a professional coach, he remains unrepentant and criticizes their values as 'archaic'. 'I believe in the pursuit of excellence', he declares, 'and I'll carry the future with me.' In a sense Abrahams's rebellion against the establishment is not simply related to his Jewishness but also his willingness to break with an ethic of gentlemanly amateurism and adopt a more professional approach to his sport. In this respect, while the film appeals to traditional values it also seeks to invest them with a more entrepreneurial (or, as the Master of Caius would have it, tradesmanslike) spirit. It is, perhaps, in this way that the film links most directly with Thatcherite ideology. For, as has already been noted, it was a central characteristic of Thatcherism that it combined economic neo-liberalism with social neo-conservatism. As such, Thatcherism assumed a certain Janus-faced quality: ideologically looking backwards to past imperial glories and 'traditional' values but economically looking forward and attempting to restructure the British economy along more competitive lines. Indeed, it is this mix of tradition and modernity within Thatcherism which Stuart Hall sought to account for in his use of the phrase 'regressive modernization'.[71] Something of a similar combination may be seen to be provided by the heroes of *Chariots of Fire*. Eric Liddell's traditional religious fervour and aversion to compromise (the 'language of the devil' according to his father) not only has links with the social and moral conservatism of Mrs Thatcher but also her faith in 'conviction politics'. Similarly, Harold Abrahams's aggressive individualism and philosophy of self-help suggests

---

[70] Sophia B. Blaydes notes how Blake's anti-industrial and utopian poem 'became associated with nationalistic causes' during the First World War after it had been set to music by Sir Hubert Parry. See 'Blake's "Jerusalem" and Popular Culture: *The Loneliness of the Long-Distance Runner* and *Chariots of Fire*', *Literature/Film Quarterly*, vol. xi, no. 4 (1983), 212.

[71] Hall, *The Hard Road to Renewal*, 2.

something of the entrepreneurial values of Thatcherism while his conflict with a complacent aristocratic establishment contains more than an echo of Mrs Thatcher's own rise from a petty bourgeois background (she was a shopkeeper's daughter) and her battles with the traditional Tory grandees.

The modernizing project of *Chariots*, however, only goes so far. It does not stretch, for example, as far as the well-drilled 'Fordist' approach to athletics employed by the Americans whom we observe in training. It is also less than fully meritocratic and occurs on a terrain which remains that of (aristocratic) social privilege. It is notable, for example, that the lower-class professional Mussabini remains an outsider at the film's end. Thus, he is unable to join the Olympic crowd and, in a telling scene, learns of Abrahams's victory from the distance of his hotel room. As a result, at the very moment the Union Jack is raised and the British national anthem is played, the film's focus is on the character who has made the victory possible but is none the less excluded from the society to which it brings glory. He also remains impervious to the claims of national pride and, in a drunken celebration with Abrahams following the race, declares his conviction that the win was a personal one for himself and Abrahams (a claim that derives some added force by the way in which Abrahams—'the toast of England'—remains apart from his team and the waiting crowd on his return from Paris).

The other character who makes victory possible is, of course, the aristocratic playboy Lord Lindsay. While his standing aside may represent a certain giving way of the old aristocratic order to a new, more meritocratic one, it also encourages affection for the ethic which he represents. He emerges as a much more sympathetic character than either Abrahams and Liddell whose goals, rather than personalities, we are encouraged to admire. The film, in this respect, displays a singular ambivalence to the aristocratic traditions which it displays. On the one hand, particularly as represented by the Masters, the establishment is berated for its archaism and hypocrisy. On the other hand, it is admired for the strength of its traditions and the elegance it maintains (and, despite their conflicts with Abrahams, the Masters, as the film shows, have no difficulty at all as claiming his victory as theirs). A significant factor, in this respect, is the film's use of visual style.

For at the very moments the film overtly criticizes the establishment, it also appears to relish the visual pomp and splendour with which it is associated. This may be seen in the sequence in which Abrahams makes his most outspoken criticism of the establishment's anti-Semitism. This begins in his rooms at Cambridge where he discusses with Montagu his father's relatively humble origins. As the conversation continues there is a cut to a Cambridge chapel. 'Here I am setting up shop in the finest university in the land', Abrahams declares, 'but the old man forgot one thing—this England of his is Christian and Anglo-Saxon and so are her corridors of power and those who stalk them guard them with jealousy and venom.' However, at the same time as Abrahams makes this speech, the camera encourages us to relish the splendour of the buildings, as it moves slowly down from a view of the ceiling to where the two men are standing. As the men leave the chapel, the camera captures them in long shot and, as they move off, pans to the right and then moves slightly upwards to take in more of the surrounding architecture. So while the film may be highlighting the permanence and grandeur (as well as the power) of the tradition to which Abrahams sees himself opposed it is, at the same time, making use of the setting to provide the audience with a visually pleasing spectacle.

This is also the case in the scene involving Abrahams's confrontation with the Masters in which Abrahams's objections to the Masters' 'archaic' values is none the less presented in a manner that renders the physical benefits of their privilege attractive. Thus, when Abrahams stands up to make his speech he is seen surrounded by the accoutrements of the Masters' lifestyle: the portraits, candles, and dinnerware.[72] The camera then pulls back to reveal more of the table, bringing Abrahams's central positioning within the frame to an end and emphasizing further the environment in which he is located. At this point, Abrahams concludes his remarks by announcing his claim to the future. However, the camera does not follow Abrahams but holds on the Masters as he departs from the frame. It is for reasons such as these that one critic was to claim that *Chariots* was 'a film whose subtext contradicts its text'.[73] Ostensibly critical of an archaic establishment, it is a film which none the less presents it, in the words of Monagu, as a 'sumptuous affair'. Thus, while the film shares with Thatcherism a certain nostalgia for English 'greatness', it also reveals a certain tension between the culture of individual enterprise, on the one hand, and a cultural fascination with the aristocratic *ancien régime*, on the other.

Conclusion: British Cinema and Anti-Thatcherism

Chariots of Fire was one of a number of 1980s films, such as the heritage films and films of empire (discussed in Chapters 4 and 5) that looked to an aristocratic past. Although, as will be seen, these incorporated a number of conservative elements, they were also ideologically ambivalent and were, in some ways, critical (from a liberal-humanist perspective) of the nationalist and commercial values associated with Thatcherism. Indeed, what is often argued as most distinctive about British cinema in the 1980s is not its support for Thatcherite ideas but rather its distance from, and even overt criticism of, Thatcherism and its effects. Hence, Lester Friedman argues that what united the bulk of British directors during the 1980s was 'their revulsion, to one degree or other, for the ideology of Thatcherism' while Leonard Quart claims that the 'film renaissance'

---

[72] In his discussion of 1990s heritage films, Paul Dave notes how aristocratic 'heritage time', which is 'spatializing, pre-modern and classificatory', is opposed by 'the progressive time of plot and the experience of an indefinite future' which is associated 'with the middle class'. This is also a good description of the tension manifest in *Chariots of Fire*. See 'The Bourgeois Paradigm and Heritage Cinema', in *New Left Review*, no. 224 (July/Aug. 1997), 117.

[73] Stuart Byron, *Village Voice* (21 Oct. 1981), 50, quoted in Ed Carter, 'Chariots of Fire', 14.

of this period was 'one of the more positive by-products of the Thatcher ethos, though in an almost totally oppositional and critical manner'.[74] There is, however, a danger that this reading of the British cinema of the period is too quick to homogenize the films concerned and to attribute a political significance to them.[75] Not all British films of the period are obviously linked to Thatcherism and not all can be seen as straightforwardly critical of the Thatcher regime. However, it is undoubtedly the case that it is much easier to identify an anti-Thatcherite cinema than a pro-Thatcherite one.

There seem to be a number of reasons why this was so. It has already been argued that Thatcherism, as a project, did not command popular ideological appeal and managed to secure economic and institutional change without necessarily winning over 'hearts and minds'. In this respect, many of the ideological themes of Thatcherism did not achieve the currency or effectivity within British society that its supporters wished and so failed to exert a significant influence upon filmmakers. This is particularly evident in the case of the social and moral themes associated with the New Right which have conventionally been taken as informing a series of Hollywood films in the 1980s.[76] For while it has been common to link the emergence of the 'New Rights' in Britain and the US, there were also significant differences between them. As Lynne Segal suggests, Thatcherism was both 'ambivalent' and 'less than successful' in its battle against 'permissiveness' and, as a result, was '*unlike* the moral right in the USA, supported by Reaganism, which (was) directly anti-feminist, explicitly against abortion and equal rights for women, as well as anti-gay'.[77] As such, Britain did not experience quite the same kind of 'backlash' (against feminism and women's rights) that occurred in the US nor the emergence of a similar kind of 'backlash' movie.

The extent of hostility to Thatcherism, during the 1980s, has also been noted. In this respect, the British filmmaking community was clearly associated with some of the social groups least sympathetic to the Thatcherite vision. Although the professional middle class voted for the Thatcher government in substantial numbers, there were significant sections within the middle class who did not, especially amongst the university-educated and the intelligentsia.[78] Indeed, for Martin Holmes, a supporter of the Thatcher project, one of the 'limits of Thatcherism' was precisely its failure to win over 'centrist intellectual opinion'

[74] See Lester Friedman (ed.), *British Cinema and Thatcherism* (London: UCL Press, 1993), pp. xix and 17.

[75] This is particularly evident in the Friedman collection, *British Cinema and Thatcherism*, where even the most unlikely of 'British' films (e.g. *Altered States, Insignificance*) are interpreted in relation to Thatcherism.

[76] See, for example, Susan Faludi, *Backlash: The Undeclared War Against Women* (London: Chatto and Windus, 1992) and Elizabeth G. Traube, *Dreaming Identities: Class, Gender and Generation in 1980s Hollywood Movies* (Boulder, Colorado: Westview Press, 1992).

[77] Segal, 'The Heat in the Kitchen', in Stuart Hall and Martin Jacques (eds.), *The Politics of Thatcherism* (London: Lawrence and Wishart, 1983), 213.

[78] Massey, 'Heartlands of Defeat', 18.

which he associates in particular with the universities, the arts, and the BBC.[79] In this, he agrees with Sir Peter Hall, the then director of the National Theatre, who claimed, in 1988, that 'well over 90 per cent of the people in the performing arts, education and the creative world' were 'against' Mrs Thatcher.[80] The opposition to the Thatcher government displayed by the educational and arts communities arose, in turn, from their specific dislike of the government's apparent philistinism, and hostility to public provision for the arts, as well as a more general liberal-left, 'intellectually centrist' disdain for the socially and culturally divisive consequences of Thatcherite economic policies. In this respect, the filmmaking community in Britain, with its links to the other arts (especially theatre) and public-service television, formed part of a grouping which could be expected to be out of sympathy with Thatcherite ideas. And, while it is not possible to 'read off' the ideological dispositions of film texts from the social and political attitudes of their makers, many of the films of the period were, none the less, quite self-consciously informed by the anti-Thatcherite sentiments of their producers, directors, and writers.

Finally, it may be argued that one of the key factors encouraging the emergence of an anti-Thatcherite cinema was the impact of Mrs Thatcher's policies upon the industry itself. For while discussion of the relationship between Thatcherism and the British cinema has characteristically focused on ideological outlook, much less attention has been paid to the more direct consequences of the Thatcher government's policies upon the film industry itself. As the following chapter indicates, the most immediate impact of Thatcherism on the cinema was the extension of its economic policies to the conduct of the film industry. These had seriously damaging consequences for the economic viability of the British cinema which became increasingly dependent upon television, and Channel 4 in particular. Given the public service remit of Channel 4 and its commitment to relatively low-budget contemporary British filmmaking, it provided both the cultural space, and the economic basis, for many of the films most critical of Thatcherism to emerge. In this way, the economic policies of the Thatcher government, when applied to the film industry, actually helped to stimulate the production of films which, at an ideological level, were typically hostile to Thatcherite beliefs. It is to these policies that I will now turn.

[79] Martin Holmes, *Thatcherism: Scope and Limits* (Basingstoke: Macmillan, 1989), chap. 8. The Conservative government clashed with the BBC over a number of issues including the transmission of an episode of the *Real Lives* series, 'At the Edge of the Union', dealing with Northern Ireland politicians Martin McGuinness (of Sinn Fein) and Gregory Campbell (of the Democratic Unionist Party) in 1985, and the reporting of the US bombing of Libya in 1986. For an overview of these events and the general threat to the impartiality and 'public service' status of the BBC, see Steven Barnett and Andrew Curry, *The Battle For the BBC* (London: Aurum Press, 1994).

[80] Quoted in Hugo Young, *One of Us*, 411.

chapter 2

Film Policy and Industrial Change ____

Thatcherism and the Film Industry

On 15 June 1990 more than twenty representatives of the UK film industry arrived at No. 10 Downing Street to attend a seminar on the future of the industry, chaired by Mrs Thatcher herself. The seminar had been arranged in response to approaches from Sir Richard Attenborough, the then chairman of both the British Film Institute and British Screen Advisory Council as well as a successful producer and director, and he was evidently pleased with the outcome. '[T]he government is demonstrating that films are back on the agenda', he commented afterwards, 'and the Prime Minister is responsible. She's not only committed; she has demonstrated her interest.'[1] This was, perhaps, a surprising remark. There had been little evidence of the Prime Minister's enthusiasm for the film industry during her previous years of office and the record of her government with respect to film was not impressive. Only the previous year, UK feature film production had dropped to thirty films, the lowest figure since 1981 and the second lowest since 1914, and, according to the then Chief Executive of the Producers Association, it was 'a matter of fact' that a series of government policy decisions had 'brought the UK film and television production industry to its knees'.[2] It was all the more ironic, therefore, that Mrs Thatcher's departure from office should have followed on so soon after in November. Without Mrs Thatcher's personal interest, the momentum for change slowed and many of the proposals which had emerged from the Downing Street seminar were delayed, amended, or rejected. Thus, nearly one year later, in May 1991, the trade newspaper *Screen International* felt sufficiently let down to run an uncharacteristically robust editorial, denouncing the government's continuing lack of commitment to the British film industry and commenting sourly that 'there is barely a promise made by this government that is not reneged upon shortly afterwards'.[3]

[1] Quoted in 'An Active Agenda', *Screen International* (23–9 June 1990), 8.
[2] John Woodward, 'Cinema 1989–90—Production Focus', *Film and Television Yearbook 1991* (London: British Film Institute, 1990), 25
[3] 'One Ahead, Two Back', *Screen International* (17–23 May 1991), 9.

However, if Mrs Thatcher's departure had left the industry unhappy, her arrival in office had hardly been welcomed either. For it was clear from the very beginning that the policies of the Thatcher government—with their attachment to free market economics and hostility to subsidy—would be unlikely to bring the industry much comfort. Although it was not until their second term of office, and after considerable dilly-dallying, that the Thatcher government's solitary White Paper on the industry, *Film Policy* (1984), finally appeared, their approach to the film industry was apparent from an early stage.[4] What this involved, in the first instance, was the bringing to a halt of those policies which had been gradually evolving under the previous Labour administration and which had been due to be incorporated into the forthcoming film legislation of 1980. As Dickinson and Street observe, government film policy had traditionally been conceived within the framework of commercial considerations irrespective of the party in power.[5] During the 1970s, however, Labour had begun to move towards a more cultural stance. In the wake of the slump that had followed the massive withdrawal of US finance from British production at the end of the 1960s, the Labour Prime Minister Harold Wilson had set up a committee, under the chairmanship of John Terry, to investigate the future of the British film industry. This, in turn, was followed by the first and second reports of the Interim Action Committee on the Film Industry, chaired by Harold Wilson himself after his resignation as Labour leader. What is evident in all of these reports is the new turn in government thinking. 'A positive and constructive' film policy, the Terry report (1976) argued, 'should not be based exclusively on considerations of commercial profitability' but also 'on the benefits to be derived by the community as a whole.'[6] This was a point echoed in the second of the Interim Action Committee's reports in 1979. 'The object of government policy for films', it suggested, was not simply economic and to create employment, encourage investment, and increase exhibition; it was also cultural and to provide aid for 'an art form' and 'films which reflect British life'.[7] This concern to develop a policy which would encourage both the economic and cultural aspects of film was manifest in the Terry report's recommendations for substantially increased funding for film production as well as its proposal for the establishment of a British Film Authority which would coordinate and be responsible for the various activities undertaken by government. Although the proposal was accepted in principle by the Labour government, and Wilson's first report in 1978 laid out specific recommendations for its constitution, the

[4] *Film Policy*, Cmnd. 9319 (London: HMSO, 1984). Although the government announced its review of the film industry in August 1982 this report did not appear until nearly two years later in July 1984. This was due, in part, to the general election of June 1983 and the loss of his seat by the minister responsible for the review, Iain Sproat. The review was concluded under his successor, Kenneth Baker, and the White Paper laid the basis for the 1985 *Films Act*.

[5] Margaret Dickinson and Sarah Street, *Cinema and State: The Film Industry and the British Government, 1927–84* (London: British Film Institute, 1985), 1–3.

[6] *The Future of the British Film Industry*, Report of the Prime Minister's Working Party, Cmnd. 6372 (London: HMSO, 1976), 10.

[7] *The Financing of the British Film Industry*, Second Report of the Interim Action Committee of the Film Industry, Cmnd. 7597 (London: HMSO, 1979), 5.

plan was abandoned by the new Conservative regime.[8] During the 1980s, government policy continued to suffer from a lack of overall integration and responsibility for film remained divided amongst various departments: the Department of Trade and Industry (with a responsibility for commercial matters), the Treasury (with a responsibility for fiscal affairs), the Home Office (with a responsibility for censorship, cinema licensing, and the regulation of television, cable, and satellite), the Foreign Office (with a responsibility, via the British Council, for the promotion of films abroad), and finally the Office of Arts and Libraries, created out of the Department of Education and Science in 1980 (with a responsibility, via its funding of the British Film Institute, Arts Councils, and Regional Art Associations, for the more cultural and educational aspects of film). The proposal to make one minister responsible for all of the government's film activities was revived at the time of the Downing Street seminar but still met with no favour.[9]

More generally, however, the whole tenor of the government's approach to film was to alter. This was hardly surprising of a government whose approach towards the arts in general involved cutbacks and the encouragement of business sponsorship and economic self-sufficiency.[10] However, in the case of film, the new Conservative government was reluctant to conceive of it in artistic and cultural terms at all with the result that its policies were almost entirely concerned with the commercial aspects of the industry. This change in perspective was evident in the Board of Trade review of the industry written shortly after the election of the new government in response to the Wilson committee's second report on film financing. It queried how far the committee's proposals were compatible with 'the government's general policy of reducing public expenditure and the scope of the public sector' and asked what role, if any, the state should have in supporting the film industry.[11] A clear answer was provided by the government's White Paper which, in line with 'the government's approach to industry generally', sought to set the film industry 'free' by doing away with 'the paraphernalia of Government intervention' and an 'intrusive regulatory framework'.[12] What this meant, in practice, may be seen in relation to the three

---

[8] *Proposals for the Setting Up of a British Film Authority*, Report of the Interim Action Committee on the Film Industry, Cmnd. 7071 (London: HMSO, 1978).

[9] See Terry Ilott, 'Film-makers Say Thatcher Meeting Could Spark Recovery for Film Industry', *Screen Finance* (14 June 1990), 2. After the April 1992 election, the new Conservative administration did, however, reorganize the responsibility for film, along with the arts and sport, into a new Ministry of National Heritage.

[10] For a discussion of the government's general approach to the arts and arts funding, see Brian Appleyard, 'The Arts', in Dennis Kavanagh and Anthony Sheldon (eds.), *The Thatcher Effect* (Oxford: Clarendon Press, 1989), Robert Hewison, *The Heritage Industry: Britain in a Climate of Decline* (London: Methuen, 1987), esp. chap. 5, and 'United Kingdom', in Andrew Feist and Robert Hutchinson (eds.), *Cultural Trends*, no. 5: 'Funding the Arts in Seven Western Countries' (London: Policy Studies Institute, 1990).

[11] *Review of Policy on Film Finance* (London: Department of Trade, mimeo, June 1979), 1.

[12] *Film Policy*, pp. 12 and 18. As was the case more generally, it was the economic aspects of Thatcherism which predominated in the implementation of film policy. The 'moral' aspects were, however, in evidence in the wake of a moral panic surrounding 'video nasties' and the passing of the 1984 Video Recordings Act. For a discussion of the role of the British Board of Film Censors (BBFC) during the 1980s, see Tom Dewe Mathews, *Censored* (London: Chatto and Windus, 1994).

main planks—or 'props' as the White Paper puts it—of government support for films up to this point: the quota, the Eady levy, and the National Film Finance Corporation.

Government Policy

The quota dates back to the Cinematograph Films Act of 1927 which, in response to the decline in the number of British films in British cinemas, had required distributors and exhibitors to handle a minimum percentage of specifically British films. The government did initially extend the life of the quota but in January 1982 reduced the quota of 30 per cent for feature films by half before suspending the quota altogether from 1 January 1983. Announcing the measure to the Commons, the then 'films minister' Iain Sproat claimed that the industry would thereby be 'relieved of a formidable and unnecessary administrative burden'.[13]

Similar thinking also underlay the government's abolition of the Eady levy. This was originally devised by the Treasury official Sir Wilfred Eady and was introduced on a voluntary basis in 1950 before being made compulsory under the Cinematograph Films Act of 1957. Designed to return a proportion of box-office takings back to production, it consisted of a levy upon exhibitors' earnings and was administered by the British Film Fund Agency. Under the Films Act of 1980 and the Film Levy Finance Act of 1981, the government extended the life of the levy but, in a plan designed to reduce public expenditure, required the BFFA to allocate a proportion of its funds to the NFFC as well as the BFI and Children's Film Foundation. The 1985 Films Act which followed, however, abolished the levy completely. According to the preceding White Paper, the levy—like the quota—represented 'an unreasonable burden on the cinema exhibition industry' and had also failed to provide 'an efficient way of encouraging an economic activity that should be essentially oriented towards the market'.[14]

A similar line of reasoning was also applied to the NFFC. Originally designed as a temporary measure to help alleviate the then crisis in British production, the National Film Finance Corporation was established in October 1948 as a specialized bank to make loans in support of British film production and distribution. Subsequent legislation ensured a continuing role for the NFFC and, by the end of the 1970s, the NFFC had invested in over 750 British feature films. Largely as a result of growing financial difficulties, the NFFC's activities during

[13] Quoted in *Screen Digest* (Jan. 1983), 10. Although not official, the title of 'Films Minister' was commonly applied to the minister at the Department of Trade and Industry whose responsibilities included film. One measure of the government's apparent lack of regard for the film industry is the large number of occupants of this post: no less than twelve between 1979 and 1991. This lack of continuity added to the industry's difficulties in dealing with government, including the period after the Downing Street meeting when the 'Films Minister' changed twice: Lord Hesketh replaced Eric Forth in July 1990 and Lord Reay replaced Hesketh in May 1991.

[14] *Film Policy*, pp. 12 and 11.

the 1970s had become limited and between 1972 and 1979 it was involved with only twenty-nine features. However, with the appointment, by Labour, of Mamoun Hassan as the new managing director of the NFFC in January 1979 the organization's fortunes looked set to change. The corporation had a statutory duty to make loans on 'a commercially successful basis' but historically had failed to do so. This was because the low level of funds at its command had forced it to adapt to the prevailing methods of raising production finance whereby it was called upon to provide, in the form of 'end money', the riskiest proportion of a film's budget. Under the proposed changes it was now expected that not only would the Corporation receive increased funding but that it would also be encouraged to support less obviously commercial films of a type which the NFFC had only recently begun to assist (e.g. *Radio On* (1979), *Babylon* (1980)). 'The Corporation's brief', explained its annual report, 'should be to make not only films that appeal to a popular audience, but also films that will feed ideas and invention.'[15] Following the general election, however, such plans were to change. 'I was taken on to lead the charge', Hassan commented afterwards, 'and very soon was mounting a siege.'[16]

As with the Eady levy, the Conservatives did initially lengthen the life of the Corporation. However, in doing so, they sought, not to extend its cultural mandate, but rather to put it on an even more commercial footing than hitherto. Under the 1980 Films Act and the 1981 National Film Finance Corporation Act it wrote off the Corporation's debts to the government and awarded it a final grant of £1 million. As already indicated, subsequent funding was to be derived from the Eady levy and commercial borrowing. With the decision to abolish the Eady levy, however, the government went one step further and, in effect, sought to 'privatize' the Corporation. This involved the replacement of the NFFC by the British Screen Finance Consortium which, according to the White Paper, was to continue to fulfil 'the positive functions of the NFFC, while at the same time being enhanced by the dynamic of private enterprise'.[17] To encourage private investment in the new company, the government was prepared to provide £7.5 million over a five-year period at the end of which it was expected that the company should have become self-supporting. Three private investors —Channel 4, Cannon, and Rank—agreed to provide (in the form of loans) £300,000 per annum for five years, £300,000 per annum for three years, and £250,000 per annum for three years respectively. Neither Cannon nor Rank renewed their commitment after the initial three-year period. Granada then agreed to provide £750,000 over a two-year period in 1989 but it too did not renew its commitment. Channel 4 alone continued with its investment during this period.

In assessing these measures, it would be wrong to regard them as simply misguided and destructive. Thus, in the case of the quota and the Eady levy, it was

[15]   National Film Finance Corporation, *Annual Report and Statement of Accounts for year ended 31/3/79* (London: HMSO, 1980), 5.

[16]   Quoted in Raymond Snoddy, 'Mamoun Hassan: Not Going Quietly', *Stills* 13 (Oct. 1984), 8.

[17]   *Film Policy*, 15.

not their abolition which presented a problem so much as the absence of any alternatives to them. It was already evident in the 1970s, for example, that the quota was not being enforced and that a number of cinemas, especially independents, were failing to meet their quota of British features. One of the reasons for this was the decline in British feature production, such that the number of films registered as British for purposes of quota fell by over half, from 98 to 48, between 1971 and 1979. If the original purpose of the quota had been to stimulate British film production the evidence suggested that it was now failing to do so and that its objective might be better fulfilled by other means.

This was also true of the Eady levy which, by the 1980s, represented in real terms only one-seventh of its original value. Moreover, it had been a recurring criticism of the levy since its inception that its allocation on the basis of box-office success characteristically rewarded those least in need of it. This was amply demonstrated when the details of the levy's distribution were made public from 1979 onwards and revealed the extent to which the most commercially successful 'British' films such as *The Wild Geese* (1977), *Superman* (1978), *Alien* (1979), and *Flash Gordon* (1980) accounted for the lion's share of the pay-out.[18] The other shortcoming of the system was that payments were made without regard to merit, however defined, and the Interim Action Committee in particular had complained of the way in which the fund was being used to help the makers of soft-porn (or 'films that exploit sex' as the Committee preferred to put it).[19] Moreover, with the decline in cinema attendances that was a feature of the late 1970s and early 1980s there was certainly some justice in the exhibitors' claims that the levy was not only an increasingly onerous burden upon them but also an unfair one given the extent to which films were viewed on television and increasingly videotape.

As early as 1973, the Cinematograph Films Council recommended, as part of its strategy for reviving the British film industry, that a levy be imposed on the showing of films on television in order to support film production.[20] Underlying this proposal was a recognition that while films were increasingly important to the television schedules (in terms of both proportion of programming and audiences attracted), this was not reflected in the returns to filmmakers from television screenings and there was a suspicion that prices were being kept artificially low as a result of the BBC and ITV broadcasting duopoly. The prices paid for features by television continued to be a bone of contention during the 1980s and both the Association of Independent Producers

---

[18] Thus, for example, for the period ending 17 Oct. 1981, the biggest Eady payments were to *For Your Eyes Only* (£500,000), *Superman II* (£500,000), and *Flash Gordon* (£405,205). In contrast, more genuinely British films such as *Babylon* (1980) received £13,069, *Memoirs of a Survivor* (1981) £1,694, *Rude Boy* (1980) £429, and Ken Loach's *Black Jack* (1979) only £138. See 'Two Tie for Top Eady Slot', *Screen International* (17 Apr. 1982), 8–9.

[19] *The Financing of the British Film Industry*, 10. It had, in fact, been a recommendation of the Terry report that the proposed British Film Authority should study 'the feasibility of a system of financial support for films of outstanding artistic merit'. See *The Future of the British Film Industry*, 30.

[20] Cinematograph Films Council, *Thirty-sixth Annual Report for the year ended 31 March 1974* (London: HMSO, 1975), 6.

(AIP) and the Association of Cinematograph Television and allied Technicians (ACTT) lobbied for change.[21] A much-cited example, in this regard, was that of *Chariots of Fire* (1981). This was seen by $3\frac{1}{2}$ million people in the cinema who paid £7 million in order to do so. When the film was first screened on television it attracted four times this audience but at a cost to the BBC of £1 million. This sum, moreover, was high by television standards and covered more than one showing.[22]

It was for all of these reasons that many accepted that the Eady levy should go but that it should be replaced by a different form of levy, either on television or videotape. Indeed, in April 1985, the House of Lords went so far as to vote in support of an amendment to the Films Bill which would have introduced this change. The amendment, however, was subsequently rejected by the Commons for reasons that had already been made clear in the White Paper. Maintaining the levy, but changing its source, it had argued, would only be appropriate should it be wished 'to recycle reasonably substantial sums into British production'.[23] It was apparent that the Conservative government did not wish to do so and it was this unwillingness to find means to support British filmmaking, rather than the abolition of the Eady levy in itself, which represented the real problem for the production sector of the British film industry.

This unwillingness was also evident in the government's approach to fiscal matters. Following the recommendation of the Interim Action Committee's second report, the Inland Revenue had ruled in 1979 that films could be treated as 'plant' which were eligible for 100 per cent capital allowances in the first year. As a result of this ruling the financing of film production became more attractive to City institutions which, through the operation of leaseback deals, became increasingly involved in the support of British films (including, for example, *Chariots of Fire*, *Educating Rita* (1983), and *Local Hero* (1983)). Despite this boost to production, the scheme was not permitted to survive. The scheme underwent a number of amendments before the Chancellor announced in 1984, the same year as the White Paper, that he was abolishing it altogether and that the first-year allowances would be phased out by 1986. Although the White Paper argued that these changes would 'encourage efficiency and enterprise' the evidence suggested otherwise.[24] Investment in film which had been rising steadily during the 1980s fell dramatically from 1986 onwards, dropping from £270.1 million to £135.7 million in 1988 and to only £49.6 million in 1989. Although the withdrawal of capital allowances was not solely responsible for this fall, it was sufficiently important a factor for the industry to continue to lobby for

[21] See, for example, *A.C.T.T.'s Response to the Government White Paper 'Film Policy'* (London: undated) which advocates a levy on films shown on TV as well as on prerecorded and blank videocassettes (17–18).

[22] These figures are cited by Guy Phelps in 'A Degree of Freedom: Simon Relph at British Screen', *Sight and Sound* (Autumn 1987), 269.

[23] *Film Policy*, 11.

[24] Ibid. 12. For a discussion of the capital allowance scheme see two articles by Alan Stanbrook, 'The Land of the Rising Sun?', *Stills* (July–Aug. 1983), and 'When the Lease Runs Out', *Sight and Sound* (Summer 1984).

tax incentives which would at least match those of other European countries. This campaigning looked like it might meet with some success following the Downing Street seminar when two working parties, one on the structure of the industry and one on tax reform, were established. The second of these, under the chairmanship of then BFI director Wilf Stevenson, reported later that year and made three main recommendations: tax relief for foreign artists working in the UK, accelerated write-offs against tax, and the establishment of a new tax vehicle, modelled on the French SOFICAS, which would entitle shareholders to tax exemption or deferral. All of these proposals were rejected, however, by the Chancellor Norman Lamont in his 1991 Budget.[25]

The major form of state support for film production to survive, in this respect, was the annual allocation of £1.5 million to British Screen. Despite the low levels of funds at its disposal, the company, under its first Chief Executive Simon Relph, managed to defy the gloomy forecasts of its early critics. Indeed, in both the quantity and range of the films which it supported it actually did rather better, during the 1980s, than its predecessor the NFFC had been able to (operating albeit under inauspicious circumstances). Thus, while the NFFC was involved in only seventeen completed features between 1980 and 1985, British Screen had a stake (in the form of investments and guarantees) in forty-four features in the period 1986 to 1989. Admittedly, in doing so, Relph was required to adopt a more commercial approach than Hassan: providing a lower proportion of a film's budget, insisting upon faster returns on his investments, and making finance conditional upon a sales agreement. Unlike Hassan, Relph was also reluctant to either commission scripts or be the first to commit to a project. The support of the company for 'quality British film' was, however, sustained and the projects in which it was involved were impressively diverse including, for example, *The Belly of an Architect* (1987), *The Last of England* (1987), *Stormy Monday* (1987), *Venus Peter* (1989), and *Hush-a-Bye Baby* (1989).[26] Indeed, in one particular case, British Screen proved more adventurous than the NFFC insofar as it was able to provide support for Mike Leigh's *High Hopes* (1988) despite the absence of a script.

However, although British Screen achieved a generally respectable return on its investments and won some notable commercial success (especially in the case of *Scandal* (1988)), it did not succeed as a profit-making enterprise and failed to become self-supporting by the end of the 1980s as the government

[25] See Neil McCartney and Mark Le Fanu, 'Treasury Ponders Return to Eady Levy as Industry Awaits Budget Explanation', *Screen Finance* (17 Apr. 1991), 1–3. According to the authors it was felt by government that accelerated write-offs were too like the capital allowances which had been scrapped and that the SOFICAS (Sociétés de Financement de l'industrie Cinématographique et Audiovisuel) were insufficiently different from the UK Business Enterprise Scheme (BES) which had failed to stimulate investment in film. The BES scheme allowed tax relief to individuals investing in film companies but was restricted to £40,000 per year and was thus unlikely to have been a major source of film finance. The BES regulations also limited the amount raised by a single company to £500,000 in any one year. British Screen had sought an exemption from this rule but were refused by the government. See 'British Screen Drops BES Plan', *Screen International* (2 July 1988), 2.

[26] For an assessment of British Screen's early performance, see Adam Dawtrey, 'British Screen Pushes for Private Cash to Match Renewed Government Support', *Screen Finance* (26 July 1989).

had hoped. As a result, Relph negotiated a postponement of loan repayments (subsequently converted to equity) due to the initial investors in 1989 and the Department of Trade and Industry also agreed to a continuation of funding.

British Screen, in this respect, benefited from the government's apparent reluctance to follow through fully its commitment to the logic of the market-place. Some of this reluctance undoubtedly derived from a belated recognition of the almost impossible demands that had been made upon the organization. For while British Screen was required to be run on 'a commercially successful basis' it was not free to operate as a purely commercial enterprise insofar as it was also obliged to encourage specifically British film production and foster British talent.[27] Moreover, what must also have become apparent was how important a role British Screen played in this regard. In 1984, the White Paper had expected the contribution of the company to British film production to be 'modest'. However, by the end of the decade, British Screen had, in fact, become a major source of British production finance, as was demonstrated by its involvement in 25 per cent (i.e. fourteen out of fifty-six) of all British pro-duction starts in 1988. It occupied, in this respect, such a key position within the industry that even a Conservative government must have had reservations about simply abolishing it, particularly given its own failure to stimulate the commercial sector of the industry in the way it had promised.

Failing Production

Some indication of this failure is provided by a comment found in the second report of the Interim Action Committee. Writing in 1979, the Committee observed that there were only three British film companies which invested in film to 'a material extent': Rank, Associated Communications Corporation (ACC), and EMI.[28] Seven years later, however, the involvement of all these com-panies in production had largely ended. The first to pull out was Rank. Rank's investment in film production during the 1970s had in fact been quite modest (around £1.5 million a year) until it decided to embark upon a new production programme in 1977 (involving an estimated investment of about £10 million). However, the company was uncertain about what films to make and what audi-ences to address with the result that it oscillated uneasily between playing safe (a television spin-off, *Wombling Free* (1978), re-makes of *The Thirty-Nine Steps* (1978), and *The Lady Vanishes* (1979)) and taking risks on films which it was then unsure how to handle (Anthony Harvey's western *Eagle's Wing* (1979), Nicholas Roeg's *Bad Timing* (1980)). Significant commercial success proved

---

[27] Thus, in addition to 'encouraging the production of British films on a commercially successful basis' the policy of British Screen is 'to encourage British talent and original high quality British film work, especially from younger less established producers and directors'. See British Screen Finance Limited, *Report and Accounts for the year ended 31 December 1987*, 2.

[28] *The Financing of the British Film Industry*, 2.

elusive and the company's enthusiasm for production soon waned. In June 1980 it announced that it was pulling out altogether. In the event, Rank Film Distributors did continue to invest—on and off—in some films (in return for non-US distribution rights) but this was confined almost entirely to 'safe' American films for which US distribution deals were already in place. Thus, apart from its initial loan to British Screen (a small sum compared to what the company saved from the abolition of the Eady levy), its contribution to British production for the rest of the decade was negligible (e.g. *The Fourth Protocol* (1985) and *Dealers* (1989)).

If Rank's production policy of the late 1970s had lacked direction, the strategies of ACC, under Lew Grade, and EMI, chaired by his brother Bernard Delfont, were much clearer. Impressed by the huge earnings of the 'big' US films of the mid-1970s (such as *Star Wars* (1977)) and emboldened by the commercial success of EMI's own *Murder on the Orient Express* in 1974, both companies set their eyes firmly on success in the US market. In the case of ACC, they were responsible for about fourteen films a year between 1976 and 1981, most of which were self-consciously tailored to appeal to what was imagined to be American taste (e.g. *The Cassandra Crossing* (1976), *The Boys from Brazil* (1978), *The Medusa Touch* (1978)). Although no major hit was forthcoming, some of the films did at least do reasonably well (e.g. *The Eagle Has Landed* (1976)) and, because of Lord Grade's skills at pre-selling, ACC's losses were kept to manageable levels. However, with ACC's expansion into both exhibition (the acquisition of the Classic cinema chain) and distribution (the setting up, with EMI, of a US distribution arm, AFD) the company became overstretched and was unable to carry the scale of losses incurred by such an expensive flop as *Raise the Titanic* (1980), a film which for a time became synonymous with the collapse of the British film industry. In June 1981 it was revealed that ACC's film division had lost £26.4 million. The Classic chain was put up for sale, Grade's film programme was brought to a halt and Grade himself departed his own company the year after following a takeover by the Australian businessman, Robert Holmes à Court. As part of the Bell Group, ACC's filmmaking division ITC survived but with the exception of the occasional film (e.g. *Whoops Apocalypse* (1986)) its contribution to film production was, like Rank's, negligible.

ACC's attempts to compete with Hollywood were taken one step further by EMI when, in 1976, it acquired British Lion and with it the services of Barry Spikings and Michael Deeley. During the 1970s, EMI had maintained a revolving fund of about £5 million which it had invested in films oriented primarily towards the domestic market (comedies, TV spin-offs, horror). With the arrival of Spikings and Deeley, the company were persuaded not only to aim for the US market but to do so by actually making American films in America. *The Deer Hunter* (1978) and *Convoy* (1978) provided this policy with some initial success but subsequent films, made after Deeley had left, proved financially disastrous. *Can't Stop the Music* (1980) and *Honky Tonk Freeway* (1981), EMI's most expensive film ever, cost the company particularly dear and the attempt to beat Hollywood at its own game was ended.

A financially enfeebled EMI had by now been taken over by the electrical giant Thorn for whom Spikings embarked upon a new production programme. Although this was again American in orientation it was much more modest in scale (*Frances* (1982), *Tender Mercies* (1982), *Handgun* (1982)) and also included two British films: David Gladwell's *Memoirs of a Survivor* (1980), and Lindsay Anderson's *Britannia Hospital* (1982) which were both made in association with the NFFC. The films division, however, continued to sustain losses and, following the arrival of Verity Lambert in late 1982 as the new head of production, Spikings left. In contrast to the last project to be initiated by Spikings, *Slayground* (1983) which was partly shot in the US with an American star, Lambert now committed the company to a policy of medium-budget British filmmaking. *Comfort and Joy* (1984), *Morons in Outer Space* (1985), and *Clockwise* (1986) were amongst the films that followed but they failed to do sufficiently well to win the renewal of Lambert's contract at the end of three years. The Chief Executive of Thorn EMI Screen Entertainment (TESE), Gary Dartnall then in effect closed down the company's in-house production division and announced in its place a system of development deals with independent producers. However, before these arrangements were to show any tangible results TESE was sold, in March 1986, first to the Australian Alan Bond and then, only one week later, to Cannon. In the face of considerable hostility, Cannon's owners, Menahem Golan and Yoram Globus, declared their commitment to British film production and established a fund to assist first-time directors. *Business as Usual* (1987), and *The Kitchen Toto* (1987) were made under this scheme but Cannon, whose financial affairs had been the subject of much speculation, faced mounting debts, leading not only to an end to their British production activity but also the controversial sale of the studio at Elstree (which eventually passed into the hands of Brent Walker). The Cannon Corporation was then itself acquired by the Italian Giancaro Parretti's Pathé Communications which in turn faced financial difficulties following its surprise acquisition of MGM/UA.

The demise of Thorn EMI was also a blow to the credibility of the government's film policy. In November 1984, the then Films Minister Norman Lamont had cited Thorn EMI as an illustration of the 'impressive strength' of the British film industry when addressing objections to the government's Film Bill in the Commons.[29] What was even more ironic, however, was that his other two 'notable examples' of companies successfully investing in film—Goldcrest and Virgin—should also have ceased their involvement in production so soon afterwards as well.

The collapse of Goldcrest was particularly striking in this regard given the way in which the company had come to symbolize such a large part of the much discussed 'renaissance' of the British cinema of the early 1980s. This was particularly so following the Oscar-winning successes of *Chariots of Fire* in 1981 and *Gandhi* in 1982, two of the films in which the company had been involved

[29] *Parliamentary Debates (House of Commons)*, Sixth Series, vol. 68, col. 29 (19 Nov. 1984).

(although, in the case of *Chariots*, nothing like to the extent to which it was commonly assumed).[30] Indeed, the government's White Paper cited the success of these two films specifically when justifying their proposals to reduce state support for British filmmaking. Goldcrest had been founded by the Canadian Jake Eberts and had evolved from a small film development company (involved in such projects as *Watership Down* (1978), *Black Jack* (1980), and *Breaking Glass* (1980)) into a major production company responsible for a number of successful features, including not only *Gandhi* but also *The Killing Fields* (1984), *Local Hero*, *The Ploughman's Lunch* (1983), and *Another Country* (1984). Although a number of these were expensive productions, Eberts pursued a policy of financial prudence, keeping his films' budgets tight and spreading the risks as far as possible through co-investment deals and pre-sales. Following Eberts' departure from the company in 1984 and his replacement by James Lee as Chief Executive, Goldcrest embarked upon a much more ambitious policy, becoming involved simultaneously in three high-budget projects: *Revolution* (1985), *Absolute Beginners* (1986), and *The Mission* (1986). This production programme was, according to Eberts, 'wrong on every level': 'the scripts were not good . . . all the films were too expensive, and . . . too much risk was spread across too few productions'.[31] These problems were added to when the films overran their already inflated budgets (in the case of *Revolution* by £4 million), promised equity finance did not materialize, and the company was faced with a cash-flow crisis. The films then did badly at the box office and together lost the company over £15 million. Ironically, the much more modestly budgeted productions in which Goldcrest had been involved, such as *Dance with a Stranger* (1985) and *A Room with a View* (1985), were to turn a profit. *A Room with a View*, moreover, outperformed all three films at the US box office despite only costing a fraction (£2.3 million) of the budgets of *Revolution* (£19 million) and *The Mission* (£17.6 million). Although Eberts returned to the company in 1985 (replacing the ousted Lee), his job was basically to mop up the mess so that when Goldcrest was sold in 1987 to Brent Walker it amounted to little more than a sales and distribution company. The new Goldcrest did subsequently return to production but only on a small scale and with the US market primarily in mind (e.g. Mike Hodges' *Black Rainbow* (1989)).

A further casualty of the Goldcrest débâcle was the third company cited by Lamont: Virgin. Virgin Films had been formed in 1980 to distribute *The Great Rock 'n' Roll Swindle* featuring the Sex Pistols who had been a profitable source of income for Virgin Records. Under Al Clark, the company moved into

---

[30] Goldcrest had, in fact, provided initial development money of £17,700 for *Chariots of Fire*. The actual production finance was provided by Allied Stars, the film company of Egyptian shipping millionaire Mohammed Al Fayed, and Twentieth Century-Fox. It was no small irony that such a quintessentially British film, and the harbinger of the British cinema's 'renaissance', should have been funded from Egyptian and Hollywood sources.

[31] *My Indecision is Final: The Rise and Fall of Goldcrest Films* (with Terry Ilott) (London: Faber and Faber, 1990), 654. Terry Ilott argues, on the basis of profitability forecasts, that the company's investment of £35 million was based on the expectation of a 'probable' return of £6 million but at a risk of losing £23 million (ibid. 530).

production, providing support for Richard Eyre's *Loose Connections* (1983), Zelda Barron's *Secret Places* (1984), and Steve Barron's *Electric Dreams* (1984), one of a number of films with a musical cross-over interest for Virgin. The company, however, sustained losses with *1984* (1984) (a film spoken of approvingly by Lamont) and, as a result, became more cautious about film investment. The company believed it was on relatively safe ground when investing, along with Goldcrest, in *Absolute Beginners*. The failure of this film, however, proved to be the last straw and a few months after the opening of *Absolute Beginners*, the company announced, in October 1986, that it was withdrawing from equity financing.

The effects of Goldcrest's collapse were also more widespread. One of the company's successes had been to make use of the capital allowance scheme and attract normally reluctant City investors (insurance companies, investment trusts, and pension funds) into film production. The failure of the company, however, reminded the City just how risky film investment could be and undermined confidence in the industry as a whole. With the simultaneous removal of capital allowances by the government, it was not surprising that City funding declined dramatically with the result that it became virtually impossible, as Ilott observes, 'to raise finance outside the entertainment industry itself'.[32] However, by the end of 1986 (following the withdrawal of Rank and others from production), there was virtually no British film company involved in financing production either.

One consequence of this lack of British funding was an increasing tendency to look to the US for finance. This was not, however, a reliable substitute. The US majors were generally reluctant to invest in indigenous British features, preferring to use Britain as a base for their own productions (shooting, for example, *Batman* at Pinewood and *Indiana Jones and the Last Crusade* at Elstree in 1988). British production companies did, in the mid-1980s, succeed in securing good deals with US independent distributors such as Cinecom, Atlantic, and Orion Classics (who enjoyed considerable success with films such as *A Room with a View*, *My Beautiful Laundrette* (1985), and *Wish You Were Here* (1987)). However, in the face of increasing competition from the majors, many of these companies began to encounter severe financial difficulties and subsequently became much more cautious about investing in British productions. As a result, there was a certain pressure on UK producers 'to adopt transatlantic production values in order to sell their films to US film distributors' and this became manifest in the way that a number of companies such as Handmade, Palace, Zenith, and Working Title began to reorientate themselves towards the US market at the end of the decade.[33] However, the degree of risk involved in this approach was substantial and led, in most cases, to an exacerbation, rather than easing, of the financial problems that British production companies faced.

[32] Ibid. 652.

[33] Adam Dawtrey, 'US Distribution Crisis: UK Producers Have to Look Harder for New Ways to Raise Production Finance', *Screen Finance* (5 Oct. 1988), 19.

Like Virgin, Handmade Films was initially conceived with a specific purpose in mind: the production of *Monty Python's Life of Brian* (1979) which EMI had developed but subsequently pulled out of because of its controversial subject-matter. Ironically, in the light of EMI's production policy of the time, *Life of Brian* went on to become the United Kingdom's fourth biggest earner of 1979 and to take more than $124 million at the United States box office. Emboldened by such success, Harrison and his then business manager, Denis O'Brien, proceeded with a policy of producing low-budget comedies, often involving members of the Python team (*The Missionary* (1981), *Privates on Parade* (1982), *A Private Function* (1984)). Terry Gilliam's *Time Bandits* (1981) proved particularly successful in the United States and later films such as *Mona Lisa* (1986) and *Withnail and I* (1986) also did well there. A shift towards more American projects was begun with the Sean Penn and Madonna vehicle *Shanghai Surprise* (1986) and was followed by a series of American or American-based projects such as *Five Corners* (1987), *Track 29* (1987), *Powwow Highway* (1988), *Checking Out* (1988), and *Cold Dog Soup* (1989). These, however, performed badly: the company cut back on its production and, despite some belated success with *Nuns on the Run* (1990), pulled out of feature production altogether in 1990 (eventually selling up in 1994). In 1984 the company had narrowly failed to finalize a deal with City investors (Prudential) and had continued to finance production through a mix of its own resources and pre-sales. Despite O'Brien's reputation for financial prudence, the company became overstretched when success in the US market proved elusive. Faced with such poor returns, George Harrison's enthusiasm for (and willingness to finance) film production faltered and the company's production policy went into decline.

Indifferent performance in the US also contributed to the difficulties of Palace. Ironically, Palace had survived the financial débâcle of *Absolute Beginners* which had cost both Goldcrest and Virgin so heavily. However, this reprieve was destined to be shortlived. The company had begun in video distribution (where it scored significant successes with films such as *Diva* (1981) and *The Evil Dead* (1982)) before moving into film distribution (with Neil Jordan's *Angel* (1982)) and then into production (Neil Jordan's *Company of Wolves* (1984)). It was also a Neil Jordan film (made for Handmade)—*Mona Lisa* (1986)—which helped to re-establish the company's credibility as a producer after the bad publicity of *Absolute Beginners*. The company opened an American office and also succeeded in securing City investment (in the form of a revolving credit loan from the merchant banks Guinness Mahon and Pierson, Heldring and Pierson). Results, however, were mixed. Palace's first all-American film, *Siesta* (1987) and Neil Jordan's *High Spirits* (1988) (made with US money but shot in England and Ireland) did badly while the company's second American project *Shag* (1987) along with *Scandal* both performed well. In 1989, Palace then went into production with *The Big Man* (1990) and *Hardware* (1990) followed, the following year, by *The Miracle* (1990), *The Pope Must Die* (1991), and *A Rage in Harlem* (1991) (another all-American project). Although none of these were comparable in cost to those that had brought down Goldcrest (the most expensive of the group being *A Rage in Harlem* at £5.6 million), the budgets were high relative to prospective earnings and represented a substantial investment for a small company with few capital reserves. In March 1990, a strategy review, undertaken by the consultant Stoy Hayward, reported that the company was suffering from 'an excessive spread of activities' and 'an inadequate level of financial resources'.[34] This was apparent not only across the Palace Group as a whole (which, in addition to production, was involved in film and video distribution, video retail, television production, recorded music, and software) but also the programme of production embarked upon by Palace Productions. Thus, when the returns on these films proved poor, the company lacked the resources to cover its losses and faced a growing mountain of debt. A rescue package was negotiated with Polygram (then owned by the Dutch electronics company Philips) but this fell through when Polygram realized the full extent of Palace's debts. As a result, in May 1992, Palace Productions went into administration. Unfortunately, the company's biggest success, *The Crying Game* (1992), which earned over $62 million at the US box office in 1992–3, came too late to make any difference to the company's fate.

Ironically, Steve Woolley of Palace had justified the move towards bigger-budgeted films aimed at the US market as a way of breaking out of low-budget British production and ensuring financial viability.[35] However, without the resources to ride failure, there is, as the examples of Palace and Handmade both reveal, little guarantee of success. This is also demonstrated, in a different way, by the experience of Working Title. Working Title was formed by Sarah Radclyffe and Tim Bevan in 1984 and scored an early success with *My Beautiful Laundrette* (1985). This was then followed by a series of films including *Caravaggio* (1986), *Sammy and Rosie Get Laid* (1987), *Wish You Were Here* (1987), *A World Apart* (1987), and *For Queen and Country* (1988) which earned the company a reputation for producing low-budget dramas with a political edge. As with other companies, there was then a certain reorientation towards the US market (and bigger budgets) when they became involved in *The Tall Guy* (1989) and *Chicago Joe and the Showgirl* (1989) towards the end of the 1980s. Although neither of these films was especially successful, the attempt to succeed in the US market gained momentum when Polygram acquired a stake in the company in 1991 as part of its strategy to become a 'European major'. However, while Polygram and Working Title subsequently enjoyed great success with *Four Weddings and a Funeral* (1994), many of their other projects did poorly and Polygram's film division as a whole lost money.[36] In this way, Working Title, unlike Handmade and Palace, benefited from the protection

---

[34] Quoted in Angus Finney, *The Egos Have Landed: The Rise and Fall of Palace Pictures* (London: Heinemann, 1996), 225.

[35] Cited in Duncan Petrie, *Creativity and Constraint in the British Film Industry* (Basingstoke: Macmillan, 1991), 104.

[36] Writing in 1997, Martin Dale points out that Polygram's film division 'has lost $20–40 million in every year since starting'. See *The Movie Game: The Film Business in Britain, Europe and America* (London: Cassell, 1997), 156.

of a large multinational corporation that was prepared (and able) to sustain short-term losses in the interests of a longer-term strategy (involving not just production but also distribution).

Declining Profitability

When introducing the government's Film Bill to the Commons the then Films Minister Norman Lamont predicted that the British film industry was on 'the threshold of a strong commercial future'.[37] In line with the government's general economic policies this was to be achieved by the reduction of state support for film and a resulting exposure of the industry to the bracing winds of market forces. By the end of the decade it was clear that Lamont's optimism had been misplaced. Far from thriving, the traditional commercial sector of the industry had all but collapsed. That it did so illustrates one of the major shortcomings of the Conservative government's commitment to the virtues of the free market. For as a number of commentators have observed of the government's economic policies more generally, a reliance on the free play of market forces does not in itself reverse industrial decline but only reinforces existing market strengths and weaknesses.[38] This was particularly so in the case of the film industry where state intervention was historically based upon a recognition that the British film industry did not, and could not, compete on equal terms within the international film market. By withdrawing its support, therefore, the government did not revive the industry, only enfeebled it further.

The weakness of the British film industry in this respect derives from the pre-eminent position enjoyed by Hollywood within the world market. Filmmaking is, of course, a particularly high-risk industry. Indeed, to describe even mainstream film production as 'commercial' can be misleading insofar as a substantial percentage of films do not, in fact, make money. Within the West it is only the Hollywood majors that have been able to spread the financial risks of production in such a way as to make filmmaking, more or less, consistently profitable. That they have been able to do so is the result of a number of factors: the scale of their production (in terms of both quantity and cost); the size of the US home market and the returns which this provides;[39] the ability, through control of distribution, to restrict foreign access to the US market; and the ownership or control of an international network of distribution and exhibition

---

[37] *Parliamentary Debates*, vol. 68, col. 38 (19 Nov. 1984).

[38] See Colin Leys, 'Thatcherism and Manufacturing', *New Left Review*, no. 151 (May–June 1985), and Perry Anderson, 'The Figures of Descent', *New Left Review*, no. 161 (Jan.–Feb. 1987), who both argue for the importance of the state adopting a 'developmental' (Leys) or 'regulative' (Anderson) role in reversing economic decline.

[39] Box-office returns from the US and Canada were, in 1990, about ten times those of the UK and accounted for around 40 per cent of world box-office. See figures in Ilott, *Budgets and Markets: A Study of the Budgeting of European Film* (London: Routledge, 1996), 13.

interests.[40] On the basis of these economic advantages, the Hollywood majors are not only in a privileged position to make money out of their films but also to dominate other national markets. Britain and the United States do not compete on equal terms in this respect and, with the abolition of the quota, Hollywood's domination of the British market was strengthened. Thus, in 1990, US films accounted for 88 per cent of UK box-office revenues.[41]

In this respect, the British film industry found itself in a position similar to that of the 1920s when the government had first introduced a quota for British films as a result of dwindling market share. The responses to US domination which were open to the production sector of the British film industry in the 1980s were, however, different from this earlier period. Historically, British cinema had been faced with the choice of attempting to compete directly with Hollywood in the international market, or relying primarily on the domestic market for commercial viability. Direct competition with Hollywood at an international level involved the attempt to secure success in the US market by emulating the Hollywood model (and cost) of filmmaking. This was attempted at various junctures in the history of British cinema: by Alexander Korda in the 1930s, by Rank in the 1940s, and, of course, by EMI, ACC, and Goldcrest in the 1970s and 1980s. In all cases, these attempts proved financially disastrous and the collapse of Goldcrest marked something of a retreat from what one writer has described as 'the traditional kamikaze assault on the American theatrical . . . markets'.[42] Some companies such as Handmade and Palace did subsequently aim for the US market with a different style of cheaper 'independent' production but even this policy proved impossible to sustain. It is therefore the second strategy—competition in the domestic market—that has traditionally formed the bedrock of British cinema.

As a result of the quota (and later some additional forms of state support), the existence of a commercial British cinema which did not compete with Hollywood internationally but only in the home market proved possible from the 1930s to—just about—the 1970s (when Hammer horror, the *Carry Ons*, and the *Confession* films all ceased production). The basis of this cinema, however, was an audience of sufficient size to sustain its economic viability. In the 1980s, this viability became increasingly threatened by falling audience figures. Since their peak of 163.5 million in 1946, cinema admissions fell steadily until they

---

[40] This last point is particularly emphasized by Nicholas Garnham who argues that 'the power and prosperity of the majors is based upon control of worldwide distribution networks which give them alone the possibility to balance, on world scale, production investment with box-office revenue'. See 'The Economics of the US Motion Picture Industry', in *Capitalism and Communication: Global Culture and the Economics of Information* (London: Sage, 1990), 203. For a more general discussion of the competitive advantage enjoyed by Hollywood, see Steve McIntyre, 'Vanishing Point: Feature Film Production in a Small Country', in John Hill, Martin McLoone, and Paul Hainsworth (eds.), *Border Crossing: Film in Ireland, Britain and Europe* (Belfast and London: Institute of Irish Sudies/BFI, 1994).

[41] See 'UK Film, Television and Video: Statistical Overview', *BFI Film and Television Yearbook 1993* (London: BFI, 1992), 41.

[42] Ian Christie, 'National Cultural Identity in Television and Film—European Methods of Subsidising National Production and Protection against Multinational Penetration', in *The European Film in the World Market* (Wien: Austrian Film Commission, 1989), 18.

reached an all-time low of 54 million in 1984. Although this figure subsequently rose (largely as a result of the opening of muliplexes from 1985 onwards), the 94.5 million admissions recorded in 1989 was still lower than any figure recorded during the 1970s (when the lowest was 103.5 million in 1977).[43] Although gross box-office levels were in part maintained through increases in ticket prices, it was clear that the returns which a British film could expect from the domestic market were considerably lower than in previous decades. Thus, whereas it was once possible for a British film to recoup its costs on the home market this proved virtually impossible for the vast majority of British movies during the 1980s. Thus, in 1989, only five 'British' films earned over £1 million and two of these—*Wilt* and *The Tall Guy*—earned less than their costs of production. Even those that did 'cover' their costs were not necessarily guaranteed a profit, however. Given that only a small proportion of box-office revenues actually return to the producer rather than the exhibitor and distributor, even such an apparent success as *Scandal* would only have recovered a fraction of its production costs—of £3.2 million—from its UK takings of £3.7 million.[44]

Hollywood did, of course, have to contend with falling audiences as well. However, by the end of the 1980s, the major studios—Warner Bros, Disney/ Buena Vista, Paramount, MCA/Universal, 20th Century-Fox, Columbia/TriStar, and MGM/UA—were more profitable than ever as a result of their ability to take advantage of the new market for video, the revenues from which grew from 1 per cent of studio income in 1980 to over 45 per cent in 1990.[45] The video market also grew substantially in the UK so that, in 1989, the spending on film on video (both rental and retail) was four times greater than the UK theatrical box office.[46] However, the growth of this market for film has largely been to the benefit of Hollywood films which have dominated video sales and rentals even more than theatrical box office. As a result, the return to the British film industry from video during the 1980s was relatively insubstantial. Thus, while Hollywood studio films were able to compensate for the drop in audiences at cinemas by generating revenues from video (and pay-TV), this was not generally the case with British films. There was also little evidence of a willingness on the part of British video companies to invest in British film despite the increasing size of the video market. The large Parkfield Group did invest in

---

[43] 'UK Film, Television and Video: Overview', *BFI Film and Television Handbook 1998* (London: BFI, 1997), 42. The first purpose-built multiplex was opened in Milton Keynes in 1985. By 1989 the total number of muliplexes was twenty-nine and, by 1990, forty-one (or 24 per cent of all UK screens). See Monopolies and Mergers Commission, *Films: A Report on the Supply of Films for Exhibition in Cinemas in the UK* Cm. 2673 (London: HMSO, 1994), 96. The multiplexes were particularly responsible for encouraging more cinemagoing on the part of the over-35s, women, and the better off (social groups ABC1). See Karsten-Peter Grummitt, *Cinemagoing*, 4 (Leicester: Dodona Research, 1995), 1.

[44] According to Monopolies and Mergers Commission figures for 1990, exhibitors' and distributors' costs and profits accounted for 84.8 per cent of box-office takings. See *Films: A Report on the Supply of Films for Exhibition in Cinemas in the UK* Cm. 2673 (London: HMSO, 1994), 118.

[45] These percentages are based on calculations made by Goldman Sachs which appear in *Screen Finance* (5 May 1993), 8.

[46] Sara Selwood (ed.), *Cultural Trends 1995: Cultural Trends in the '90s, Part 1*, Issue 25 (London: Policy Studies Institute, 1996), 61.

The Krays but its collapse in July 1990 meant few others were tempted to follow its example.

Changing Structures

This declining profitability of British film also led to a restructuring of the British film industry. In the wake of the 1927 Cinematograph Films Act, and its establishment of a British film quota, the British film industry moved steadily, during the 1930s and 1940s, towards an integration of production, distribution, and exhibition interests. This, in turn, led to the domination of all aspects of the industry by two organizations, Rank and ABPC, by the end of the Second World War. It also lay the basis for a modest domestic version of the Hollywood studio system whereby these two companies ensured a regular supply of films for their cinemas through production in their own studios. As cinema audiences began to decline, however, the economic basis of this system began to be threatened, and the two British majors increasingly devolved responsibility for actual production onto independent producers. This process of devolvement then reached its conclusion in the mid-1980s when the withdrawal of Rank, Thorn EMI, and Cannon not only from direct involvement in production but also investment in production led to an almost complete divorce within the industry between producers on the one hand and distributors and exhibitors on the other.

This meant that British film production during the 1980s was largely carried on by independent production companies who typically put together projects on an irregular or one-off basis. Thus, no less than 342 production companies were involved in film production during the decade and the majority of these—250—were involved in only one film (many, in fact, having been set up solely for this purpose).[47] Few of these companies were involved in production on a continuing basis and only a handful—such as Handmade and Goldcrest—made more than ten films. And, as has been seen, even these were unable to sustain a secure position within the industry. Although Hollywood underwent a similar process of restructuring production, adopting what Storper and Christopherson describe as a 'vertically disintegrated' system of 'flexibly specialized production', the US majors, none the less, continued to be the key players in the financing of Hollywood productions.[48] Insofar as this was not the case in the UK, the split between producers and distributors and exhibitors necessarily added to the problems of the production sector which not only lost a stable source of finance but also the security of a guaranteed outlet which a vertically integrated industry had once provided.

[47] See Richard Lewis, *Review of the UK Film Industry: Report to BSAC*, mimeo (London: British Screen Advisory Council, 1990).

[48] Michael Storper and Susan Christopherson, 'Flexible Specialization and Regional Industrial Agglomerations: The Case of the US Motion Picture Industry', *Annals of the Association of American Geographers*, vol. 77, no. 1 (1987).

The exhibition and distribution sector, moreover, had no particular interest in the showing of British films and increasingly drew its income from Hollywood products. This was a position exacerbated by the continuing concentration of exhibition interests in the UK as well as the growing power of US distributors over UK cinemas. In 1983 the Monopolies and Mergers Commission found against both Rank and EMI, and their aligned distributors, which they estimated controlled some 60 per cent of the film exhibition market and an even greater share of the film distribution market in Britain.[49] Despite its commitment to the free market, the government was reluctant to take remedial action, especially as it was dependent upon the goodwill of Rank and EMI in the founding of British Screen. The Office of Fair Trading subsequently undertook an experiment to investigate how distribution and exhibition could be made more competitive but it was not until the end of 1987 that it reported and a further year before it actually came up with some proposals regarding barring.[50] During this time the duopoly extended its control of exhibition and distribution even further so that, when Cannon took over the ABC chain (as part of its acquisition of Thorn EMI), the two leading companies accounted for two-thirds of all UK box-office revenue. Patterns of exhibition did, of course, alter following the opening of multiplex cinemas, mainly by US exhibitors, from 1985 onwards.[51] However, MGM Cinemas (following MGM Pathé's acquisition of Cannon) and Rank still remained the largest exhibitors at the end of the decade and accounted for substantially the same amount of box-office share as previously reported by the Monopolies Commission.

As these chains (along with the new US-owned multiplexes) were closely tied to Hollywood distributors, this inevitably added to the problems of film producers. MGM Cinemas was aligned with United International Pictures (UIP), jointly owned by MCA/Universal, MGM, and Paramount, as well as with Warners while the Odeon chain was aligned with Fox, Columbia, and Buena Vista (a subsidiary of Disney). As the Monopolies and Mergers Commission argued, in a further report in 1994, this practice of alignment represented 'a form of market sharing' and clearly restricted competition.[52] It also helped to ensure the dominance of Hollywood films in the UK market insofar as UIP, Warner Distributors, Columbia, Buena Vista, and Fox—all distribution

---

[49] Monopolies and Mergers Commission, *Films: A Report on the Supply of Films for Exhibition in Cinemas*, Cmnd. 8858 (London: HMSO, 1983), 73.

[50] See Richard Gold, 'Why Film Industry Does Not Like Barring Proposals', *Screen Finance* (7 Sept. 1988). One of the central problems of the Conservative's commitment to a market free of controls and restrictions was that this did not necessarily increase competition but, as with film distribution and exhibition, reduce it. A similar contradiction was evident in the 'free market' policies of the Reagan administration in the US whose lax enforcement of anti-trust legislation allowed the Hollywood majors to move back into exhibition. See Thomas Guback, 'The Evolution of the Motion Picture Theatre Business in the 1980s', *Journal of Communication*, vol. 37, no. 2 (Spring 1987).

[51] The most significant of these exhibitors has been United Cinemas International (UCI), jointly owned by MCA and Paramount, which entered the British market at the end of 1988 and soon became the third largest exhibitor in the UK.

[52] Monopolies and Mergers Commission, *Films: A Report on the Supply of Films for Exhibition in Cinemas in the UK*, 12.

subsidiaries of Hollywood majors—commanded the lion's share of the UK box-office (a striking 84.6 per cent in 1989).[53] As a result, the Commission found evidence of both a 'scale monopoly' (i.e. market share of over 25 per cent) in the case of MGM Cinemas and a 'complex monopoly' (i.e. the operation of anti-competitive practices) in the case of the leading distributors and exhibitors. Although they were reluctant to link this monopoly situation to the low percentage of British films on British screens, it seems clear that the alignment between major distributors and the leading exhibition circuits (either tied to or owned by US interests) made it much more difficult for independent British films to secure an adequate release. As Simon Relph reported in his paper for the Downing Street seminar, while 'big budget popular British films' were generally able to gain access to the main circuits, 'cheaper films with a smaller but still clearly identifiable audience'—in effect the bulk of British films—had much more 'difficulty in getting sufficient access to the market place'.[54] Thus, even two successful films such as *My Beautiful Laundrette* and *Letter to Brezhnev* (1985) were turned down by both Rank and EMI. Moreover, as Relph also observes, while the UK majors may have dropped out of production, the 'internal pricing structures' which had been a feature of a vertically integrated industry remained. These arrangements had been designed to accelerate returns from exhibition and distribution rather than production. Hence, when the UK majors left production they were able (along with US distributors) to hold on to the most profitable sectors of the film business while pushing the greater financial risks onto the producer and production financier. This is then reflected in the low proportion of revenues returned to producers which make it possible for both exhibitors and distributors to make money out of a film even if the producer makes a loss.

Conclusion

In its discussion of 'how UK producers finance their features', *European Filmfile* described the situation at the beginning of the 1990s:

Since companies such as Rank, Thorn EMI and Handmade stopped producing films directly, no company in the UK has operated on a sufficiently large scale to finance the production of features without outside money. The UK can be described as a nation of small producers each producing few films, with no powerful integrated companies as in most other big European countries. As a result, the role of UK producers is rather different from that of their counterparts in the rest of Europe. Rather than finding one source which can majority-back a project . . . the UK producer is forced to assemble a web of sources, resulting in a more complicated pattern of financing than elsewhere.[55]

---

[53] Ibid. 82. With only a 3.9 per cent share of box-office in the same year, Rank was playing a decreasingly significant role in distribution but remained a major force in exhibition.

[54] *A Review of UK Film Production: For the Prime Ministers Seminar, 15 June 1990* (London, mimeo, 1990), 5.

[55] *European Filmfile*, vol. 3 (Winter 1993–4), 103–4.

While this has led to the importance of pre-sales (and, correspondingly, the role of the sales agent who pre-sells territories on a commission basis), it has also meant that, in the absence of traditional sources of finance, producers have increasingly had to look to government-backed agencies and television for support. Thus, for all of the government's determination that it should 'stand on its own feet', it is apparent that what stability the British film industry enjoyed during the 1980s largely derived from a continuing dependence upon the state —either directly in the form of help from state-funded agencies such as British Screen or indirectly through television, and Channel 4 in particular, for which, through licence and regulation, the government possessed a statutory responsibility. Indeed, so important had the relationship between film and television become by the end of the 1980s that, in 1990, the Policy Studies Institute suggested that 'the only factor which appears to have prevented the wholesale collapse of the British film production industry has been the increasing involvement of UK television companies'.[56] It is this role played by television with which the following chapter will now deal.

[56] Andrew Feist and Robert Hutchison (eds.), *Cultural Trends*, no. 6 (London: Policy Studies Institute, 1990), 33.

chapter 3

Film and Television
A New Relationship _____

Towards a Fourth Channel

As a result of the economic problems that faced the film industry in the 1980s, it was television that was destined to play an increasingly significant role in the maintenance of British film production. The origins of this relationship between film and television may be traced back to the Annan report on the future of British broadcasting which was published in 1977.[1] The influence of this report, however, was indirect rather than direct. For although the report considered a number of proposals to require television to finance the film industry—including a levy on film transmission, a rise in the cost to television of films shown, use of the levy on excess profits of the Independent Television companies to support filmmaking, and the encouragement of BBC and ITV production funds—it rejected them all on the grounds that the development of a formal relationship between film and television was unlikely to lead to 'the rejuvenation of the British film production industry'.[2] Despite this pessimism concerning the role that television could play in supporting film production, it was, none the less, the Annan report that paved the way for the relationship between film and television that was to develop during the following decade.

It did so by virtue of its recommendations for a fourth channel. The idea of a fourth television channel had been in circulation since the 1960s but it was not until the 1970s that it really gained momentum.[3] With the Annan report, however, its precise character began to take shape. The report was concerned that the new channel should not simply be an extension of the BBC/ITV duopoly and rejected the proposal for an ITV2. Instead it proposed a new fourth channel which would 'encourage productions which say something new in new ways'.[4]

---

[1] *Report of the Committee on the Future of Broadcasting*, Cmnd. 6753 (London: HMSO, 1977).
[2] Ibid. 342.
[3] A useful overview of the pre-history of Channel 4 is provided by Sylvia Harvey, 'Channel 4 Television: From Annan to Grade', in Stuart Hood (ed.), *Behind the Screens: The Structure of British Television in the Nineties* (London: Lawrence and Wishart, 1994).
[4] *Report of the Committee on the Future of Broadcasting*, 482.

This would be run by a new Open Broadcasting Authority and financed from a variety of sources including advertising, sponsorship, and grants. The Labour government largely accepted these recommendations but, before it found the time to pass the relevant legislation, it lost the 1979 general election. There were then fears that the incoming Conservative government, under Mrs Thatcher, would simply revert to the idea of ITV2 but the old-style Tory Home Secretary, William Whitelaw, persevered with the proposal, albeit in somewhat modified form, and Channel 4 was successfully launched as the fourth national television channel on 2 November 1982.

Channel 4

Instead of the Open Broadcasting Authority envisaged by the Annan report, the new channel became a subsidiary of the Independent Broadcasting Authority (IBA) which also regulated the ITV companies. However, although within the IBA's ambit, the channel was none the less charged with a clear 'public service' remit to provide a distinctive television service. This meant that, under the Broadcasting Acts of 1980 and 1981, the channel was obliged to appeal to tastes and interests not generally catered for by the existing television services as well as to 'encourage innovation and experiment in the form and content of pro-grammes'.[5] The channel was also provided with a clear set of financial arrange-ments which avoided some of the difficulties to which Annan's proposals for the OBA might have led. Thus, while its programme-making was to be financed purely by advertising, it was to be done so indirectly in the form of a subscrip-tion paid by the ITV companies as a percentage of their net advertising rev-enues. In return the ITV companies had the right to sell and collect the income from Channel 4's own advertising time. This arrangement provided particu-larly important financial protection for Channel 4 in its early years as it was not until 1987 that the channel's advertising revenue exceeded its income from the television companies.[6]

The other significant feature of the channel was its adoption of the 'publish-ing model' of broadcasting envisaged by Annan which, in the context of British broadcasting, was to prove its most notable innovation. Thus, unlike the exist-ing BBC and ITV companies, Channel 4 did not itself operate as a production house but either purchased or commissioned work from independent produc-tion companies, the ITV companies, or foreign sources. Its role in sustaining an independent production sector was especially significant and, for the year ending 31 March 1990, 54 per cent of the channel's output was provided by 526 different independent production companies.[7] In fact it was this development which was probably at the heart of the channel's survival during the Thatcher

---

[5]   *Broadcasting Act 1981* (London: HMSO, 1982), 13.

[6]   Channel Four Television Company Ltd., *Report and Accounts for year ending 31 March 1990* (London, 1990), 44.

[7]   Ibid. 14 and 17.

years. For although it is often regarded as a paradox that the channel was able to support television programming which was so often at ideological odds with prevailing government attitudes, its ability to do so was partly reliant upon its role as a 'Trojan horse' in the restructuring of the economic basis of British television towards a more 'flexible', 'post-Fordist' mode of production that other television companies were then obliged to follow. Thus, in 1987, the government was sufficiently happy with the pattern of independent production, reduced overheads, and flexible labour that the Channel had encouraged to announce that it expected the BBC and ITV to follow suit and to commission 25 per cent of their output from independent production companies by 1992 (a quota subsequently enshrined in the Broadcasting Act of 1990).

It is this combination of public-service principles and a commissioning model of broadcasting that provided the context for the channel's support for film. The channel's first Chief Executive, Jeremy Isaacs, was aware of the role which German and Italian television had played in encouraging film and, in his application for the post in 1980, he expressed his desire 'to make, or help make, films of feature length for television here, for the cinema abroad'.[8] At this stage, he did not envisage a theatrical release for Channel 4 films in Britain. This was partly because union agreements made 'TV only' films cheaper to produce and partly because a cinema showing would make an early television transmission difficult. Under a barring policy operated by the Cinematograph Exhibitors Association (CEA), such films could only be shown three years after their initial cinema exhibition and this made television investment much less attractive than it might otherwise have been. Despite this obstacle, the channel persevered in providing some of its first commissions with a cinema release. Colin Gregg's *Remembrance* was the first of these and received a short theatrical run in June 1982, a few months prior to the channel beginning transmission. Further 'Film on Four' began to appear in cinemas on a selective basis and the channel also reached an agreement, in 1986, with the CEA that the bar would not apply to films costing under £1.25 million (a figure subsequently increased to £4 million in 1988). However, because of the channel's pressing requirements for programming, many of the early films enjoyed only a short cinema run. Thus, even successful films, such as *The Ploughman's Lunch* (1983) which kicked off the second season of 'Film on Four' in November 1983, were unable to enjoy as full a cinema release as they might have deserved.[9] Subsequently, as the channel built up a backlog of films, it became normal to allow those films which merited it a proper cinema (and sometimes video) release and a longer television holdback.

This use of a theatrical platform by Channel 4 was not entirely without precedent: London Weekend Television, for example, had shown Peter Hall's *Akenfield* in cinemas in 1975. However, what was new was the level of commitment to supporting film production and the numbers and range of 'television

---

[8] Jeremy Isaacs, *Storm Over 4: A Personal Account* (London: Weidenfeld & Nicolson, 1989), 25. Isaacs also indicates that his experience as chairman of the British Film Institute Production Board made him conscious of the needs of independent filmmakers for an additional television outlet.

[9] See Chris Auty, 'Films in Boxes', *Stills*, 8 (Sept.–Oct. 1983), 40–1.

films' subsequently provided with a cinema release. Thus, according to the channel's own calculations, between 1982 and 1992, it invested £91 million in 264 different works.[10] During the 1980s the budget for 'Film on Four' rose from around £6 million to £12 million and the funding of films took three main forms: full funding, co-investment, and the pre-purchase of television rights. Full funding was most common in the early days when the track record of the channel was as yet unproven but it continued to be an option for the channel. Thus, in the case of Ken Loach's *Riff-Raff* (1990), the channel put up the whole of the £750,000 budget. Perhaps, the most notable example of full funding, however, was *My Beautiful Laundrette* (1985), a film which initially looked quite uncommercial but subsequently proved to be one of the channel's biggest successes of the 1980s and virtually became identified as the 'archetypal' 'Film on Four'. However, such successes notwithstanding, the vast bulk of films with which the channel were involved depended upon co-funding. This usually involved the channel providing a combination of equity investment and payment for TV rights, although in some cases—such as *A Room with a View* (1985) and *Mona Lisa* (1986)—the channel simply pre-bought the television licence.[11] The practice of pre-purchasing was, however, a significant development in its own right insofar as television had, in the past, generally bought the rights to television transmission after a film was made rather than before.

For David Rose, Senior Commissioning Editor for Fiction, the policy of 'Film on Four' was to make films 'on comparatively modest budgets . . . written and directed by established filmmakers and introducing new writing and directing talents'.[12] Although the channel displayed a commendable internationalism in its choice of investments, providing backing, for example, to films such as Wim Wenders' *Paris, Texas* (1984), Agnès Varda's *Vagabonde* (1985), and Andrei Tarkovsky's *The Sacrifice* (1986), its main commitment was to indigenous British productions, especially original screenplays on contemporary social and political topics. This was certainly characteristic of many of the most popular or critically successful of the films such as *The Ploughman's Lunch* (1983), *Wetherby* (1985), *My Beautiful Laundrette* (1985), *Letter to Brezhnev* (1985), *No Surrender* (1985), *Sammy and Rosie Get Laid* (1987), *Rita, Sue and Bob Too* (1986), *High Hopes* (1988), and *Riff-Raff* (1990) although it by no means exhausts the range of films which 'Film on Four' supported which also included 'heritage' costume drama (e.g. *Heat and Dust* (1982), *A Room with a View*, *A Month in the Country* (1987)), comedy (e.g. *She'll Be Wearing Pink Pyjamas* (1984)), crime drama (e.g. *Mona Lisa*, *Stormy Monday* (1987)), and the British 'arthouse' film (e.g. *Comrades* (1986), *Fatherland* (1986), *Caravaggio* (1986), the work of Peter Greenaway).

---

[10] Monopolies and Mergers Commission, *Films: A Report on the Supply of Films for Exhibition in Cinemas in the UK* Cm. 2673 (London: HMSO, 1994), 151. These figures, however, cover more than just 'Film on Four' and seem to include some titles acquired after completion.

[11] As a result, the contribution of the channel to individual films varied enormously, ranging from as little as £17,000 to over £1.3 million and from 2 per cent to 100 per cent of the budget. See John Pym who provides financial information on virtually all 136 films transmitted as part of the 'Film on Four' slot between 1982 and the end of 1991 in *Film on Four: A Survey 1982/1991* (London: BFI, 1992).

[12] Quoted in Nigel Willmott, 'The Saviour of the Silver Screen', *Broadcast* (28 Oct. 1983), 13–14.

However, although it is 'Film on Four' with which the channel has been most associated, it was not the only way in which film production was supported. This was also done through the Department of Independent Film and Video which, under its first senior commissioning editor Alan Fountain, was responsible for financing rather more experimental work than 'Film on Four' would generally have contemplated.[13] Given the growth during the 1980s of a primarily commercial independent sector, the term 'independent' can be misleading. In the case of the Department of Independent Film and Video, however, the idea of independence was specifically linked to a tradition of social and aesthetic radicalism, outside of the mainstream of film and television production.[14] As Fountain explained, the department was concerned to support 'the sort of work unlikely to be taken up elsewhere in the television system' and which would 'represent the alternative, oppositional voice'.[15] The main outlet for this material was *The Eleventh Hour* which supported work both from outside the UK (especially the 'Third World') as well as more unorthodox work from within, particularly political documentaries which defied the conventional TV norms of 'balance' and 'impartiality'. As a part of its policy, the department also supported low-budget independent cinema which typically deviated from the norms of mainstream cinema and sought to combine aesthetic self-reflexivity with political radicalism. Thus, films supported included Ken McMullen's *Ghost Dance* (1983) and *Zina* (1985), Sally Potter's *The Gold Diggers* (1983), Mick Eaton's *Darkest England* (1984), Derek Jarman's *The Last of England* (1987), Peter Wollen's *Friendship's Death* (1987), Lezli-An Barrett's *Business as Usual* (1987), and Ron Peck's *Empire State* (1987).

The department also provided support to the independent film and video workshop sector which had first emerged in the late 1960s. Under the Workshop Declaration—agreed initially in 1982 with the ACTT, the British Film Institute, the Regional Arts Association, and the Independent Filmmakers Association— Channel 4 committed itself to the financing of a number of 'franchised' non-profit-making workshops. Such workshops were to be run co-operatively and were to be committed to 'integrated practice', i.e. not only production but exhibition, distribution, and the development of 'audiences, research, education, and community work' more generally.[16] Although only a proportion of all UK workshops benefited from the franchise system it, none the less, helped to bring stability and financial security to those (about a dozen) which did. In return the channel was provided with a supply of programming for both its *Eleventh Hour*

---

[13] In addition to the Drama Department and the Independent Film and Video Department, the channel also supported film through the Multicultural Affairs Department (which provided pre-purchase moneys for films such as *Salaam Bombay* (1988) and *Mississippi Masala* (1991)) and the Films Acquisition Department (which pre-bought a number of films including, for example, *Drop Dead Fred* (1991)).

[14] A good overview of the history of independent cinema is provided by Simon Blanchard and Sylvia Harvey, 'The Post-war Independent Cinema—Structure and Organisation', in James Curran and Vincent Porter (eds.), *British Cinema History* (London: Weidenfeld & Nicolson, 1983).

[15] Alan Fountain quoted in *AIP & Co.*, no. 51 (Feb. 1984), 18.

[16] *ACTT Workshop Declaration* (ACTT: London, 1984), 1.

and *People to People* slots, including a number of notable film features such as Trade Film's *Ends and Means* (1984), Frontroom's *Acceptable Levels* (1984), Amber's *Seacoal* (1985) and *In Fading Light* (1989), Cinema Action's *Rocinante* (1986), Sankofa's *The Passion of Remembrance* (1986), Derry Film and Video's *Hush-a-Bye Baby* (1989) and, the first video feature designed for theatrical release, Birmingham Film and Video Workshop's *Out of Order* (1987). The particular importance of this work was its strong connections to the regions and concern to give a voice to those communities (blacks, women, the working class) which traditionally lacked access to filmmaking. The growth of black British filmmaking, in particular, was a key development of the 1980s (see Chapter 11) and was largely nurtured by the workshop movement.

Channel 4 also contributed to British filmmaking by providing support to other organizations involved in film production. In the case of British Screen, the channel was not only one of the original funders but also a major co-investor. Thus, in the period 1987–90, Channel 4 was involved in thirty-two of the forty-nine films backed by British Screen.[17] From 1985 onwards, Channel 4 also became the British Film Institute Production Fund's most consistent source of outside finance. Towards the end of the 1970s, the Production Fund, under Peter Sainsbury (who was Head of Production until 1985 when he was succeeded by Colin MacCabe), had shifted its focus towards low-budget features, providing support for films such as Chris Petit's *Radio On* (1979), Menelik Shabazz's *Burning an Illusion* (1981), Pat Murphy's *Maeve* (1981), Edward Bennett's *Ascendancy* (1983), Sally Potter's *The Gold Diggers* (1983), and most successfully of all, Peter Greenaway's *The Draughtsman's Contract* (1982). The Production Board was supported by the British Film Fund Agency but with the abolition of the Eady levy (which funded the BFFA) its future was put at risk. A deal was negotiated with Channel 4 which provided, in return for television rights, around £500,000 per year towards features, the production of shorts, and development. This money permitted the Board to continue to support a number of 'innovative' features including *Caravaggio* (1986), *Distant Voices, Still Lives* (1988), *Venus Peter* (1989), *Play Me Something* (1989), *Melancholia* (1989), *Fellow Traveller* (1989), and *Young Soul Rebels* (1991).[18]

The BFI Production Board also provided the model for the Scottish Film Production Fund which was established in 1982 with financial backing from the Scottish Education Department and the Scottish Arts Council. Channel Four and BBC Scotland provided additional funding later. Operating on an overall budget of about £214,000 by the end of the 1980s, the fund was committed to the promotion of Scottish cinema and was involved in supporting a range of shorts, documentaries, and features. While it did not have the means to become a major investor in feature production, it did, none the less, play an important

---

[17]   See *Screen Finance* (6 Oct. 1993), 13–14. Subsequent to this, however, cooperation between the two declined due to a deal which British Screen struck with the satellite broadcaster BSkyB in April 1994.

[18]   The policy of the the BFI's production division is described at this time as involving a commitment to 'work which is innovative in form, content, production method or use of film and video technology'. See British Film Institute, *Annual Report, 1988–89* (London: BFI, 1989), 18.

role in the development and making of *Venus Peter* (1989) and provided consistent support for the work of Timothy Neat, including his first feature *Play Me Something* (1989).[19] Channel 4 itself also invested directly in a number of Scottish features during the 1980s including *Ill Fares the Land* (1982), *Another Time, Another Place* (1983), *Living Apart Together* (1983), *Heavenly Pursuits* (1986), and the first film feature in Scots Gaelic, *Hero* (1982).

In the case of Wales, the most significant contribution of Channel 4 was the establishment of its Welsh-language television service, Sianel Pedwar Cymru (S4C). S4C was responsible for about twenty-five hours a week of Welsh-language programmes and commissioned around five films or 90-minute documentaries per year. While most of these were for television transmission, some did receive a theatrical release, most notably in the case of Stephen Bayly's *Coming Up Roses* (1986) and Karl Francis's *Boy Soldier* (1986).[20] As for Northern Ireland, Channel 4 probably had less impact than in the other 'national regions'. Nevertheless, its support for the workshop movement did make possible the production of the first film features to be made in Northern Ireland since the 1930s, most notably Frontroom and Belfast Film Workshop's *Acceptable Levels* (1983) and Derry Film and Video's *Hush-a-Bye Baby* (1989).

ITV and BBC

However, if Channel 4, by a variety of means, was the most consistent and committed of television companies involved in film production it was not completely on its own. Indeed, the very success of its film policies, and the kudos it enjoyed as a result of them, encouraged other television companies to become involved in film production as well. One company, Thames Television had, in fact, established its own filmmaking subsidiary, Euston Films, as far back as 1971 but, apart from the occasional TV spin-off such as *Sweeney!* (1976), had mainly been involved in the production of television series, shot on film. During the mid-1980s the company decided to return to film production, financing in part *Bellman and True* (1987), *A Month in the Country* (1987), *Consuming Passions* (1988), and *Dealers* (1989) and financing in full *The Courier* (1987).

Central Television also established its own film subsidiary, Zenith Productions, in October 1984. Central had previously financed Stephen Frears' *The Hit* (1984) and Zenith continued with a policy of medium-budget feature investment, producing amongst others *Wetherby* (1985), *Sid and Nancy* (1986), *Wish*

[19] For a discussion of the Scottish Film Production Fund by its first chairman, see Ian Lockerbie, 'Pictures in a Small Country: The Scottish Film Production Fund', in Eddie Dick (ed.), *From Limelight to Satellite: A Scottish Film Book* (Glasgow and London: Scottish Film Council and BFI, 1990). For a different assessment, critical of the Board's move into features (built on in the 1990s), see Colin McArthur, 'In Praise of a Poor Cinema', *Sight and Sound* (Aug. 1993).

[20] More recently, films such as *Elenya* (1992), *Gadael Lenin/Leaving Lenin* (1993), and the Oscar-nominated *Hedd Wyn* (1992) have increased awareness of the films which S4C has supported. See David Berry, *Wales and Cinema: The First Hundred Years* (Cardiff and London: University of Wales Press and BFI, 1994), esp. Section Four 'Television and a Welsh Film "Mini-boom"'.

You Were Here (1987), *Prick Up Your Ears* (1987), and *Personal Services* (1987). In October 1987 the company was sold to Carlton Communications who then merged it with their own production unit, The Moving Picture Company. This had been acquired the previous year and, under producer Nigel Stafford-Clark, had been responsible for a number of early 'Films on Four' such as *The Bad Sister* (1983, shot, in fact, on video), *Parker* (1984), and *The Assam Garden* (1985). The new Zenith embarked upon a further slate of productions (including *For Queen and Country*, *The Wolves of Willoughby*, *Patty Hearst*, and *Paris By Night*, all 1988) but ran into financial difficulties as a result of problems with US distributors. In November 1989, Carlton sold 49 per cent of the company to Paramount, following which there was a greater emphasis on television production.

The third television company to establish a filmmaking subsidiary was Granada which set up Granada Film Productions in 1987. The company invested in three productions (all made, in fact, for transmission on Channel 4)— *Joyriders* (1988), *Tree of Hands* (1988), *Strapless* (1988)—before it was merged, in 1989, with Granada's production division which, under Steve Morrison, was responsible for *The Magic Toyshop* (1986), *The Fruit Machine* (1988), and the Oscar-winning *My Left Foot* (1989). Other companies made smaller but, none the less, significant contributions. London Weekend Television put money into *A Handful of Dust* (1987), *The Tall Guy* (1989), *Wilt* (1989), and *Under Suspicion* (1991); TVS co-produced *The Innocent* (1984), *The Dawning* (1988), and *Queen of Hearts* (1989) (all sold to Channel 4); Scottish Television was involved in *Gregory's Girl* (1980), *Ill Fares the Land* (1982), *Comfort and Joy* (1984), *Killing Dad* (1989), and *The Big Man* (1990); Grampian made a small investment in *Play Me Something* (1989) as did Ulster Television in *December Bride* (1990).

As for the BBC, it had a long tradition of shooting drama on film but specifically for TV transmission. During the 1980s, however, the BBC too began to become involved in films intended for cinema release. It did so initially, through the Film Acquisitions Department, which was involved in pre-buying television rights for films such as *Gandhi* (1982), *The Shooting Party* (1984), *The Bostonians* (1984), and *White Mischief* (1987). In the late 1980s, the drama department, under Mark Shivas, also began to invest in films with a view to theatrical release. Four films (*War Requiem* (1988), *Dancin' in the Dark* (1989), *Fellow Traveller* (1989), and *The Reflecting Skin* (1990)) backed by the drama department were given a cinema release and others followed, including *The Object of Beauty* (1991), *Truly, Madly, Deeply* (1990), *Edward II* (1991), and *Enchanted April* (1991).

Television Economics

However, if television—and Channel 4 in particular—became the most significant source of British film finance during the 1980s, it should be clear that this was not simply for commercial reasons. Although Channel 4 has been party to a number of spectacular box-office successes (especially in the 1990s), the main benefit of theatrical release to the channel (and television more generally) has not been the revenues that have been generated. The channel has, of course, benefited from the critical attention and publicity that a showing in cinemas has encouraged as well as the better viewing figures which films, rather than single television dramas, can generate. It has also gained considerable prestige and a reputation for 'quality' as a result of the support for filmmaking that it has provided. However, when measured according to conventional commercial criteria, most of the channel's films have actually made a loss. Indeed, in their submission to the Monopolies and Mergers Commission, the channel openly acknowledged that 'in ten years only a handful of films had actually made a profit for the channel'.[21] While Channel 4 has not, of course, depended upon direct financial returns in the same way as conventional film production companies, it may, nevertheless, be seen to have 'subsidized' film production insofar as the relatively high percentage of the channel's overall budget (6.2 per cent between 1982 and 1992) devoted to 'Film on Four' has not been matched by the number of programme hours or audience ratings which it has provided. As Jeremy Isaacs explained in the early days of 'Film on Four', he regarded such films as having 'a socio-cultural provenance and purpose' which went beyond their financial returns or contribution to the ratings.[22] In this respect, the channel has been content (and able) to carry the 'losses' of film production because of its belief in its cultural value. However, as broadcasting entered a more commercial environment at the start of the 1990s, the willingness of television to provide this support underwent a degree of change.

Under the 1990 Broadcasting Act, Channel 4 was responsible, from the start of 1993, for selling its own advertising. Although there were initial fears about how the channel might fare, it actually did far better than many predicted. Nevertheless, the channel was forced to compete much more strongly for both ratings and advertising revenue and this inevitably had consequences for the channel's ability to fulfil its original programming remit, including its ability to support film. As has been argued, the channel's investment in film production in the 1980s was, to some extent, 'underwritten' by the arrangements between the channel and the independent television companies concerning the sale of advertising. With the channel no longer guaranteed its income, and in competition with the other television companies for advertising, there was increased pressure not only to make programming more 'popular' but also to take less artistic and financial risks. Thus, the 'deficit-financing' of feature films that was a characteristic of Channel 4 in the 1980s, and which was critical in getting some of the more unorthodox films of the period made, came under increasing threat.[23]

[21] Monopolies and Mergers Commission, *Films: A Report on the Supply of Films for Exhibition in Cinemas in the UK*, 151.

[22] Quoted in Stephen Lambert, 'Isaacs: Still Smiling', *Stills*, no. 6 (May–June 1983), 26.

[23] For a fuller discussion of these changes, see John Hill, 'British Television and Film: The Making of a Relationship', in John Hill and Martin McLoone (eds.), *Big Picture, Small Screen: The Relations Between Film and Television* (Luton: John Libbey Media/University of Luton Press, 1996).

This was particularly evident in the case of the Department of Independent Film and Video which, during the early 1990s, ended its ongoing support for the workshops and moved away from the production of film features. As with 'Film on Four', the channel's support for the workshops rested upon a belief in the social and cultural value of this sector insofar as the number of programme hours the workshops provided (fifteen to twenty per year) was relatively low in proportion to their budget allocation (£1.7 million for the year ending March 1990). Given these economics (and the decline in support for the workshops from local and metropolitan authorities), the Department of Independent Film and Video sought to move towards a more project-based system of funding for the workshops at the end of the 1980s.[24] In 1991 the Department abandoned its separate budget for the workshops altogether, since when the workshops have been forced to compete for resources in the same way as conventional producers. At the same time, the Department moved away from the low-budget feature work which had been one of its distinguishing characteristics: for while such work was cheap in terms of cinema it was still relatively expensive for television.

Similar commercial pressures also affected the willingness of the ITV companies to involve themselves in film production. As has been seen, a number of ITV companies were tempted to invest in feature film towards the end of the 1980s. Altogether, ITV companies were involved in about twenty productions between 1985 and 1989. However, in 1988, the government altered the way of collecting the ITV levy (in effect a tax paid by the ITV companies for the right to broadcast) by imposing it on advertising revenues rather than, as from 1974, on profits. This had the effect of increasing the amount of levy which the broadcasters had to pay (an increase of £17 million in two years) as well as closing off a form of 'tax shelter' whereby ITV companies had written off up to 30 per cent of their production costs against the levy.[25] As a result, the making of features became much less attractive than before and ITV involvement in feature production fell by one-third between 1989 and 1990.

This drop in production was also related to the anxiety surrounding the allocation of television franchises due to be announced in 1991 (and which did, indeed, result in two companies involved in film production—Thames and TVS—losing their licences). The now notorious system of competitive bidding used to decide the new franchise-holders also reduced the amount of money available for programme-making, and, given its high cost, feature production was destined to be less appealing. Disputes over the involvement of Granada Television in film production were, for example, one of the factors which led to the resignation of Granada Chairman David Plowright in February 1992 while,

[24] See Adam Barker, 'Film Workshops Face Pressure from C4 and BFI', *Screen Finance* (8 Feb. 1989), 9–10, and Alan Lovell, 'That was the Workshop that Was', *Screen*, vol. 31, no. 1 (Spring 1990), 102–8. A similar economic logic was also at work in the Department's changing relationship to the BFI which involved a move away from long-term funding and an increased emphasis on case-by-case funding for its film features (*Screen Finance* (19 May 1993), 5).

[25] For the details, see Neil McCartney, 'Change in UK Levy System Threatens ITV Film Deals', *Screen Finance* (29 June 1988), 9–11.

more generally, ITV investment in British films began to dry up. This was also true of new 'commercial' sector of satellite television. Launched belatedly in April 1990, British Satellite Broadcasting (BSB) had taken a leaf out of Channel 4's book and committed itself to a substantial investment in film, including *Chicago Joe and the Showgirl* (1989), *The Big Man* (1990), *Hardware* (1990), *Hidden Agenda* (1990), and *Memphis Belle* (1990). However, following its merger with Sky less than a year later, the company's investment plans for film were brought to a halt and the new British Sky Broadcasting (BSkyB) confined itself to the occasional pre-purchase of satellite rights.[26]

In this respect, it can be seen that the support of film provided by television during the 1980s was largely unplanned and was not an explicit goal of government film and broadcasting policy. In such circumstances, the delicate ecology between film and television which evolved in the UK during the 1980s was always vulnerable to changes in government policy or increasing financial pressures. Indeed, rather perversely, the first policy document to appear since the White Paper on film in 1984, *The British Film Industry* (1995) argued that the dependence of British film on television actually represented a part of 'the problem' faced by the film industry rather than a part of the solution to the difficulties that had been encountered by the industry in the 1980s.[27] In this respect, the document appeared, despite all the lessons of the 1980s, to be hankering after precisely the kind of 'international' big-budget cinema that precipitated the downfall of Goldcrest and others. If such a cinema had proved viable, however, the British film industry would not, of course, have become so dependent on television in the first place.

Television Aesthetics

Inevitably, this coming together of film and television during the 1980s generated considerable debate concerning the kind of films that were then produced. Thus, while many observers acknowledged the economic importance of television to film, they were also sceptical of whether the resulting films were properly 'cinematic'. Thus, in her introduction to a series of discussions of the relations between film and television, Penelope Houston, the then editor of *Sight and Sound*, argues that 'no one wants to look the Channel 4 gift-horse in the mouth ... but ... there remains a nagging feeling that what we've got ... isn't quite enough: that the movie movie, as opposed to the TV movie, enjoys not only a wider vitality, but the power to probe more deeply'. This, in turn, is related to what she describes as both 'crucial aesthetic differences, as well as differences in the quality of the experience' between film and TV.[28]

---

[26] Partly in an effort to improve the European content of its channels, BSkyB did, however, conclude a three-year deal with British Screen in April 1994 for pay-television rights to its films.

[27] Department of National Heritage, *The British Film Industry*, Cm. 2884 (London: HMSO, 1995), 5 and 18.

[28] Penelope Houston, 'British Cinema: Life Before Death on Television', *Sight and Sound* (Spring 1984), 115.

However, whether it is possible to distinguish cinema from television in such a clear-cut way as this is open to question. For all cinema, and not just that in Britain, has become dependent upon television (and video) both for funding and revenues. This has meant that all films are now watched more on the small screen than in the cinema and that the 'quality' of experience associated with cinema in the 'classical' period (large screen, darkness, shared public space, relative immobility, concentrated viewing) can no longer be regarded as the cinematic norm. In the same way, the recognition that the ultimate destination of all cinema is the small screen has led to varying strategies (from sticking to 'safe-action' areas when filming to the adoption of more 'segmentalized' narrative forms) that have led inevitably to a blurring of the boundaries between film and TV aesthetics.[29] As a result, discussion about film and television in Britain has tended to reflect critical preferences for particular kinds of cinema rather than any 'essential' differences between the two mediums. As Martin McLoone suggests, there has been a tendency, especially in Britain, to champion 'cinema in its big picture, "event" mode' as the only 'real' form of cinema while downplaying, or failing to acknowledge, the qualities of other kinds of 'smaller' non-Hollywood cinemas.[30]

As such, it may be argued that what was at stake in discussions of British cinema in the 1980s was often not so much its status as cinema *per se* as the particular *type* of cinema that British films had come to represent (and which marked a certain break with British cinema of an earlier era). In the last chapter, it was argued that the conventional strategies of British cinema—competition with Hollywood in the international market or production primarily aimed at the home market—had proved unsustainable. In this respect, British film production in the 1980s was pushed in the direction of a different form of production aimed at more specialized markets—both in the cinema and on TV, and at home and abroad. In doing so, the character of British filmmaking also began to alter and moved much more decisively towards what might be called an 'art cinema'.

'Art' Cinema

Writing in 1969 Alan Lovell argued that, unlike its European counterparts, the British cinema had failed to develop an art cinema (or at any rate that the documentary film had served in its place).[31] During the 1980s, however, it could

---

[29] For an overview of these debates, see John Hill, 'Film and Television', in John Hill and Pamela Church Gibson (eds.), *The Oxford Guide to Film Studies* (Oxford: Oxford University Press, 1997).

[30] Martin McLoone, 'Boxed In?: The Aesthetics of Film and Television', in Hill and McLoone (eds.), *Big Picture, Small Screen*, 81. Not all critics of television-supported British cinema, however, judged it by the standards of Hollywood. James Park argues, for example, that, in comparison with a tradition of European filmmaking, the 'television film' lacks 'fantasy' and the capacity 'to dream'. In doing so, however, he tends to draw 'essentialist' distinctions between cinema and television rather than relate these to the historical uses to which the two mediums have been put. See James Park, *Learning To Dream: The New British Cinema* (London: Faber and Faber, 1984), esp. chap. 5.

[31] Alan Lovell, *The British Cinema: The Unknown Cinema*, mimeo (London: BFI, 1969), 2.

be argued that it was the 'art cinema' tradition that became pre-eminent within British filmmaking. As Steve Neale suggests, art cinema has traditionally offered, to European countries especially, a way of occupying 'a different space' from Hollywood within the film market. This has involved a process of 'differentiation' whereby a national cinema marks itself as distinct from Hollywood, by drawing upon features of either 'high Art' or nationally specific 'cultural traditions'.[32] A certain form of differentiation has, of course, always been a feature of British film production. Andrew Higson, for example, suggests how British cinema has traditionally sought to distinguish itself from Hollywood films through local variations of popular genres or the creation of 'prestige' drama.[33] Such films, however, still depended upon the 'mass' market at home for their viability. As British cinema became more dependent upon television on the one hand and specialist international outlets on the other, so the parameters of its narrative and stylistic practices also began to alter.

David Bordwell attempts to identify the defining features of art cinema in terms of a particular set of formal conventions which distinguish it from both classical narrative cinema and the avant-garde. These include the loosening of narrative structures, a concern with 'realism' (both 'objective' and 'subjective'), authorial expressiveness, and textual ambiguity.[34] His categorization, however, mainly covers the specific moment of art cinema characteristic of European cinema in the late 1950s and 1960s (and the work of such directors as Antonioni, Bergman, Fellini, Truffaut, and Resnais) and only goes so far in capturing the full range of ways in which European cinema has subsequently circulated as 'art' rather than 'popular' cinema.[35] In the case of British cinema, two main considerations are of relevance.

As has already been noted, 'art cinema' has never simply been a matter of textual characteristics but has also been allied to a particular system of production (typically state or television subsidy) and distribution (festivals and a specialist arthouse circuit). As the outlets for British films in Britain have contracted and films have become more dependent upon international audiences, so even relatively conventional, or artistically conservative, works have tended to circulate as 'art cinema'. This has been the case, for example, with the 'heritage film' which has successfully carved out a niche in the US market by

---

[32] Steve Neale, 'Art Cinema and the Question of Independent Film', in Rod Stoneman and Hilary Thompson (eds.), *The New Social Function of Cinema: Catalogue: British Film Institute Productions '79/80* (London: BFI, 1981), 42.

[33] Andrew Higson, *Waving the Flag: Constructing a National Cinema in Britain* (Oxford: Clarendon Press, 1995), 11. For Higson, the process of 'differentiation' involves distanciation from a relatively unvarying Hollywood norm. However, since the 1960s, Hollywood itself has undergone a certain transition from 'classical' to 'post-classical' forms of narration. British cinema of the 1980s, therefore, may be distinguished not only from the tight-knit patterns and functional style characteristic of 'classical' Hollywood but also from the more spectacular, 'post-classical' 'event' movie. For a helpful overview, see Peter Kramer, 'Post-classical Hollywood', in Hill and Church Gibson (eds.), *The Oxford Guide to Film Studies*.

[34] David Bordwell, 'The Art Cinema as a Mode of Film Practice', *Film Criticism*, vol. 4 no. 1 (Fall 1979).

[35] Bordwell himself defines the 'apogee' of art cinema as the years 1957–69 in *Narration in the Fiction Film* (London: Methuen, 1985), 230–1.

providing 'highbrow', 'quality' drama which is clearly distinguishable from mainstream Hollywood (see Chapter 4).[36] More generally, the involvement of British cinema within an international system of arthouse distribution has encouraged an increasing emphasis upon a 'branding' of British cinema in terms of its directors. As Bordwell argues, the art film has traditionally relied upon viewing procedures which regard it as 'the work of an expressive individual'.[37] However, while 'authorship' may be visible as a textual property (in the form of an overt inscription of the authorial voice into the text), it is also, as Bordwell recognizes, the product of an elaborate infrastructure of critical writing and reviewing, education, promotion, and marketing. Thus, as British cinema has increasingly occupied the terrain of art cinema at the level of production and distribution, so it has also become more common for British cinema to be characterized, and promoted, in terms of personal approaches and styles. As a result it is not just the overtly 'authored' films of directors such as Derek Jarman and Peter Greenaway that have circulated internationally as 'art' films but also the less artistically self-conscious work of Stephen Frears, Mike Leigh, Ken Loach, and, even, James Ivory.[38]

As a result, it is difficult to map the range of British films that circulated as 'art cinema' in the 1980s directly onto the textual strategies of art cinema identified by Bordwell's model. This is not simply because of the way the institutional apparatus of art cinema mobilized discourses surrounding British cinema, however, but because the British cinema itself manifested a new hybridity and blurring of aesthetic boundaries. A significant development, in this respect, is described by Christopher Williams. For Williams, a key trend of the 1980s was the emergence of a British 'social art' cinema in which the traditional 'social' interests of British cinema—debate on 'issues of present social and media concern', the use of 'elements of observational, cultural, and stylistic realism' and an 'interest in group rather than individual entities and identities'—were combined with the more individualistic and stylistically self-conscious concerns of the European art film (which, as Bordwell points out, seldom involved an analysis of 'groups and institutions').[39] This was not an entirely new phenomenon. The British 'new wave' of the 1960s had already accomplished a degree of *rapprochement* between social realism and art-cinema narration in films such

---

[36] See Martin A. Hipsky, 'Anglophil(m)ia: Why Does America Watch Merchant-Ivory Movies?', *Journal of Popular Film and Television*, vol. 22 no. 3 (Fall 1994).

[37] Bordwell, 'The Art Cinema as a Mode of Film Practice', 59.

[38] A good example of this is provided by the British Council's promotional booklet *British Filmmakers of the 1980s* (London: British Council) which provides thumbnail sketches of no less than thirty-seven 'British' directors. Books surveying British cinema of this period such as Jonathan Hacker and David Price, *Take 10: Contemporary British Film Directors* (Oxford: Clarendon Press, 1991) and Lester Friedman (ed.), *British Cinema and Thatcherism* (London: UCL Press, 1993) also use the director as a key organizing principle.

[39] Christopher Williams, 'The Social Art Cinema: A Movement in the History of British Film and Television Culture', in Christopher Williams (ed.), *Cinema: The Beginnings and the Future* (London: University of Westminster Press, 1996), 194. In this respect, Williams is also arguing that the dominant tradition of British filmmaking should be regarded as 'social' rather than 'realist' and that 'realism' itself should be conceptualized in plural terms.

PLATE 2.   Generic hybridity: Bob Hoskins and Kathy Tyson in *Mona Lisa*

as *The Loneliness of the Long-Distance Runner* and *This Sporting Life.*[40] However, it is undoubtedly the case that this process gathered momentum in the
1980s and was given a particular impetus by Channel 4 as a result of its joint
commitment to the support of a 'national cinema' (which would win prestige
internationally by circulating as 'art') and to the fulfilment of a public-service
remit (which favoured a degree of engagement by cinema with matters of
contemporary social concern).

   This fusion of disparate artistic elements also characterized British cinema
in the 1980s more generally. On the one hand, popular genre conventions, such
as those of crime, horror, and science fiction, were mixed with art cinema
concerns in films such as *The Hit, Parker, Mona Lisa, Melancholia, The Company
of Wolves, The Magic Toyshop,* and *Hardware.* On the other hand, strategies
typically associated with the avant-garde also began to be converge with those
of the traditional art film. Bordwell's identification of 'art cinema' as a distinct
mode of film practice had, of course, rested upon a differentiation from not
only classical Hollywood but also the avant-garde. In this respect, art cinema
was to be distinguished from both a 'first avant-garde' devoted to non-narrative

---

   [40]   Erik Hedling pursues a similar argument in relation to the work of Lindsay Anderson in 'Lindsay
Anderson and The Development of British Art Cinema', in Robert Murphy (ed.), *The British Cinema
Book* (London: BFI, 1997).

formal experiment and a 'second avant-garde' in which formal and political radicalism were combined.[41] However, as Michael O'Pray suggests, it was much harder to draw such distinctions during the 1980s as these diverse strands began to come together.[42] Thus, in the case of filmmakers such as Peter Greenaway and Derek Jarman, there was a certain fusion of their earlier (first) avant-garde interests with those of the narrative art film. For David Bordwell, art cinema had represented a sort of 'domesticated modernism' in which modernist self-consciousness was combined with an interest in narrative and character. However, in the 'art cinema' of Jarman and Greenaway, there was much less interest in character (and often narrative) and an abandonment of many of the humanist themes that had been a feature of earlier art cinema. In this respect, their work represented less 'domesticated modernism' than an emergent post-modern art cinema in which eclecticism, the erosion of artistic boundaries, and significatory play were central features. A similar blending of elements was also apparent in the black film movement which carried on the political radicalism of 1970s 'independent' film (or the second avant-garde) but in a way which typically blurred the boundaries between avant-garde, art cinema, and documentary practices (see Chapter 11).

In both cases, television may also be seen to have contributed to this convergence of 'art cinema' and the 'avant-garde'. For as television, and Channel 4 in particular, emerged as a major patron of experimental work (both directly and, indirectly, via its support for the BFI and others) so it also exerted certain pressures on this work to accommodate to television (and television audience) expectations. The idea of 'independence', associated especially with the Independent Filmmakers Association in the 1970s and partly carried over into the work of the Department of Independent Film and Video, had placed an emphasis not simply on a particular kind of aesthetic practice (anti-illusionist and self-reflexive) but on new forms of engagement with an audience (involving, for example, discussion with filmmakers and accompanying documentation). The exhibition context for such work on television, however, was generally the same as that for more conventional television output and, inevitably, there were pressures to adapt to these new circumstances. As Sue Aspinall suggests, although Channel 4 opened up a space for the politically radical 'independent' sector and, to a lesser extent, the formally experimental avant-garde, the practices associated with them—such as non-standard running times, a formal interest in the medium, an emphasis upon ideas rather than production values—did not always sit easily with the requirements of television formats.[43] As a result, there was a growing pressure for films to adapt to television norms and to embrace more recognizable art cinema conventions, such as feature-length narratives and authorial signatures.

[41] For the key statement on the 'two avant-gardes', see Peter Wollen, *Readings and Writings: Semiotic Counter-Strategies* (London: Verso, 1982).

[42] Michael O'Pray, 'The British Avant-Garde and Art Cinema from the 1970s to the 1990s', in Andrew Higson (ed.), *Dissolving Views: Key Writings on British Cinema* (London: Cassell, 1996), 179.

[43] Sue Aspinall, 'The Space for Innovation and Experiment', *Screen*, vol. 25 no. 6 (1984), 74.

Conclusion: Television, Art Cinema, and Audience _____

If the involvement of television in British cinema may be seen to have encouraged a growing convergence around the practices of 'art cinema', then,
inevitably, this also had consequences for how the relations between film and
television in Britain were perceived. In particular, the growing involvement
of television in film was identified with a move away from 'popular' forms of
filmmaking and, as a result, the popular audience that British cinema is assumed
once to have possessed. Clearly, there is some justification for such a view. British
cinema during the 1980s did move away from straightforward genre filmmaking
towards often more difficult and demanding forms of cinema that were often
not shown widely in British cinemas. However, the question of the 'popularity'
of the British films that were then made is not entirely straightforward.

For, as has been seen, while films were no longer watched in the same numbers as they once were in the cinemas, they were watched in increasing numbers
on television and video (especially given the high level of TV and video penetration in the UK). Thus, in 1989, the viewing figures for the top seven films on
TV alone were greater than total cinema admissions for that year.[44] Hence, even
such apparently 'unpopular' British 'art' films as *Hidden City* (1987) and *Empire
State* were seen by over four and three million people respectively. Had these
figures been converted into cinema attendances, both films would have been in
the box-office top ten for that year. Thus, while television is often blamed for the
demise of cinema, it may in fact have encouraged many contemporary British
films, which are not regarded as especially 'popular', to be seen by as many, and
indeed more, people as 'popular' British films of the past.[45]

There are, of course, some qualifications. Although films can achieve very high
audience figures on television, it is, none the less, the case that other forms of
drama (especially serial drama) achieve even higher figures. Indeed, John Caughie
has reversed conventional arguments concerning television's supposedly detri-
mental effects on film by expressing an anxiety that the growth of television
investment in film production has led to a growth of drama on film aimed at the
international market at the expense of more local forms of television drama aimed
at the home market. In doing so, he contrasts the work of Ken Loach in the 1960s
and 1990s. '*Ladybird Ladybird*', he argues, 'circulates within an aesthetic and a
cultural sphere which is given cultural prestige (and an economic viability) by
international critics' awards, whereas *Cathy Come Home* circulated as a national
event and functioned as documentary evidence within the political sphere'.[46]

---

[44] 'Screen Finance Analysis: Top 20 Feature Films on TV in 1989', *Screen Finance*, 24 (January 1990), 11.

[45] For a fuller discussion of these issues, see Hill, 'British Cinema as National Cinema: Production,
Audience and Representation', in Robert Murphy (ed.), *The British Cinema Book* (London: BFI, 1997).

[46] John Caughie, 'The Logic of Convergence', in *Big Picture, Small Screen*, 219. Charles Barr has also
expressed the concern that television films were in danger of creating a 'TV/movie hybrid' that lacked
'the immediacy and urgency that TV drama used to have'. See 'A Conundrum for England', *Monthly
Film Bulletin* (Aug. 1984), 235.

However, if television drama circulates less as a 'national event' in the 1980s than it did in the 1960s, television involvement in cinema was not solely responsible. It is also a consequence of the transformations that broadcasting as a whole have undergone, especially the increase in channels (both terrestrial and non-terrestrial), the rise of video (and its opportunities for alternative viewing and time-shifting), and the fragmentation of the national audience which resulted. If the capacity of both television drama and film to function as a national event lessened, this was partly because the 'national' audience for either film or television did not exist in the same way as it did in the 1960s and because neither individual television programmes nor films were able to lay claim to the same cultural dominance within the entertainment sphere that they once could. In this regard, the audience for both film and television is more differentiated than it once was and the changing character of British cinema, and its movement towards 'art cinema', may be related to a certain reorientation towards a specific (but none the less substantial) section of the audience which is generally older and better educated than that for mainstream Hollywood (which is heavily skewed towards the 15–34 age group). Thus, while British cinema in the 1980s may, to some degree, have lost its earlier connection with a 'mass' audience at the cinemas, it is also worth noting that the 'mass audience' during this period did not represent, if it ever did, the 'mass' of people but only one—primarily youthful—section of it.

Representations of the Past _____

Part Two

Representations
Of The Past

chapter 4

The Heritage Film
Issues and Debates _____

Heritage Culture

During the 1980s there was a significant growth of interest in the past and in heritage. According to Robert Hewison, writing in 1987, the number of museums in Britain was double that of 1960 and, in 1990, visits to museums and galleries totalled 74 million.[1] Consumer spending on bodies such as the National Trust and English Heritage (established in 1984 and responsible for old buildings and monuments) also increased significantly during this period and heritage centres, involving recreations of the past, became increasingly popular.[2] Such developments have been linked to a number of factors. In general terms, they have been seen as one offshoot of the restructuring of the British economy which occurred during the Thatcher years, involving a decline in manufacturing and a growth in the services sector. Heritage, in this respect, emerged as an important economic activity and a significant part of the new 'enterprise' culture.[3] Thus, distinctive features of the 'new' heritage/museum industry were its private character and the involvement of small businesses. Such developments were, however, also encouraged by local authorities (particularly in those areas most seriously hit by de-industrialization and unemployment) and, as John Urry points out, the cultivation of the heritage industry has been a key part of local economic development strategies.[4] The appeal of the heritage industry, in this respect, has been not only that it creates jobs but also that it helps to provide

---

[1] Robert Hewison, *The Heritage Industry: Britain in a Climate of Decline* (London: Methuen, 1987), 88; Jeremy Eckstein and Andrew Feist (eds.), *Cultural Trends*, Issue 12: 1991 (London: Policy Studies Institute, 1992), 70.

[2] For figures on consumer spending on heritage, see Andrew Feist and Robert Hutchison (eds.), *Cultural Trends* Issue 1: 1989 (London: Policy Studies Institute, 1989), 30. Robert Hewison refers to forty-one heritage centres in Britain, most of recent origin. See *The Heritage Industry*, 24.

[3] John Urry notes that in a six-month period in 1988, £127.2 million was invested in heritage and museums. See *The Tourist Gaze: Leisure and Travel in Contemporary Society* (London: Sage, 1990), 105. It is also for this reason that Hewison complains that 'instead of manufacturing goods, we are manufacturing heritage', *The Heritage Industry*, 9.

[4] *The Tourist Gaze*, 107–8.

localities with distinctive identities that are attractive to investors and tourists alike. Tourism makes a substantial contribution to the British economy and, as John Urry argues, an emphasis on British heritage has been a significant way of marketing the country within 'the global division of tourism'.[5] In terms of domestic tourism, visits to museums and heritage centres have been greatest amongst white-collar groups and an interest in heritage has also been linked to the growth of a 'service class culture' which is largely based upon consumption.[6]

However, if the heritage industry has been seen to play a significant economic role, it has also been regarded as performing a number of cultural functions as well. Indeed, as Corner and Harvey suggest, while heritage, at an economic level, provides a model of enterprise, it may also be seen, at an ideological level, to be responding to the very upheavals for which a competitive 'enterprise culture' has been in part responsible. Hence, they suggest, that 'the remodelled versions of "identity" and "belonging" ' which the heritage industry has projected offer a form of compensation for 'the . . . destabilization and fragmentation' which the enterprise imperative has itself wrought.[7] From this perspective, the significance of heritage culture is located in its fascination with the past and the role which this plays in relation to the present. Thus, heritage culture is often regarded as a form of retreat from the present, providing satisfactions which the present does not provide or compensations for what it lacks. It is for this reason that the idea of heritage is commonly linked to that of nostalgia. As Fred Davis has argued, 'the nostalgic evocation of some past state of affairs' characteristically occurs in 'the context of present fears, discontents, anxieties, or uncertainties' and the growth of heritage culture in Britain has often been seen to have been a response to the anxieties and discontents created by social upheaval and tension, economic decline, and a loss of international standing.[8] As David Cannadine observes, a similar response also characterized previous periods of economic downturn at the end of the nineteenth century (when the National Trust was founded) and in the inter-war period (when the Council for the Protection of Rural England began).[9] Heritage culture, in this regard, is identified as not only seeking refuge in a past in which the problems of the present are presumed not to exist but also as offering images of stability at a time

[5] *The Tourist Gaze*, 108. On the importance of tourism to Britain, Nigel Thrift notes that, in 1987, 15.6 million foreign tourists spent more than £6 billion in the UK and that only the United States, Italy, Spain, and France make more money from tourism than Britain. See 'Images of Social Change', in Chris Hamnett, Linda McDowell, and Philip Sarre (eds.), *The Changing Social Structure* (London: Sage, 1990), 31.

[6] Nigel Thrift, 'Images of Social Change', 31–4. Thrift's use of the idea of the 'service class' is indebted to the work of Scott Lash and John Urry who define it in terms of 'those dominant positions or places within the social division of labour which do not principally involve the ownership of capital, land or buildings'. See *The End of Organized Capitalism* (Oxford: Basil Blackwell, 1987), 162. For a brief discussion of the term's origins and the debates surrounding it, see Philip Sarre, 'Recomposition of the Class Structure' in Hamnett *et al.* (eds.), *The Changing Social Structure*, esp. pp. 104–7.

[7] John Corner and Sylvia Harvey, 'Mediating Tradition and Modernity: The Heritage/Enterprise Couplet', in John Corner and Sylvia Harvey (eds.), *Enterprise and Heritage: Crosscurrents of National Culture* (London: Routledge, 1991), 46.

[8] Fred Davis, *Yearning for Yesterday: A Sociology of Nostalgia* (New York: Free Press, 1979), 34.

[9] David Cannadine, *The Pleasures of the Past* (London: Collins, 1989), 257–8.

of upheaval and a sense of continuity in a time of change. It is for these reasons that Hewison condemns heritage culture, and its accompanying nostalgia, as a 'social emollient' which offers a 'profoundly conservative' vision of the past and of national identity at a time of national decline.[10] However, although there is much that is apt in this view, it is also too simple. The heritage industry is not a unitary phenomenon and heritage culture is certainly more varied than Hewison suggests. As Adrian Mellor argues, the 'ideological significance' of heritage is not homogeneous and certainly cannot be reduced to a uniform set of meanings.[11] Moreover, as Mellor and others have also argued, the uses to which heritage culture is put by people are often more diverse, and reflexive, than critics of heritage allow and certainly involves more than a conservative nostalgia.[12] And, while heritage culture in Britain has a clear national dimension, it is also the case that the heritage industry is an international phenomenon as well and therefore cannot be explained solely in terms of national decline. The heritage industry, in this respect, may also be linked to more general developments within postmodern culture.

Indeed, according to Roland Robertson it is a feature of the late twentieth century that it is characterized by what he describes as a 'globally institutionalized kind of nostalgia'.[13] He distinguishes, in this respect, the synthetic 'wilful nostalgia' of the late nineteenth century which was associated with modernity, nation-building, and the 'invention of tradition' from a more economically driven and 'democratic' form of 'consumerist-simulational' nostalgia in the present. Nostalgia, in this regard, is both promoted by globalization and directed against it insofar as the break-up of bounded social systems and the deterritorialization of culture characteristic of globalization also encourages a longing for the 'security' of place and tradition.[14] What Robertson refers to as a new form of 'consumerist-simulational' nostalgia may also be linked to other general trends associated with the 'postmodern condition', such as an economy increasingly based upon the production and circulation of information and images and the proliferation of signs and meanings with a diminishing attachment to the 'real'. It is for these reasons that Fredric Jameson identifies postmodern culture with a 'crisis in historicity' in which 'real history' is replaced by nostalgic simulcra or pastiches of the past.[15] This line of argument has also been adopted by critics of

---

[10] *The Heritage Industry*, 47.

[11] Adrian Mellor, 'Whose Heritage?', *Journal of the North West Labour History Group*, Bulletin 14 (1989–90), 6.

[12] Ibid., also id. 'Enterprise and Heritage in the Dock', in Corner and Harvey (eds.), *Enterprise and Heritage*, 93–115. Stuart Tannock also argues that nostalgia should not be seen in unitary terms and that criticisms of nostalgia as sentimental and reactionary 'risk conflating nostalgia with its presence in, and use by, dominant and conservative groups'. See 'Nostalgia Critique', *Cultural Studies*, vol. 9, no. 3 (1995), 455.

[13] Roland Robertson, *Globalization: Social Theory and Global Culture* (London: Sage, 1992), 160.

[14] Writing in the context of Japan, Jennifer Robertson notes how the internationalizing impulse towards open markets and borders is opposed by a desire for 'native place-making', associated with 'parochialism, nostalgia, and protectionism'. See 'Empire of Nostalgia: Rethinking "Internationalization" in Japan', *Theory, Culture and Society*, vol. 14, no. 4 (1997), 97.

[15] Fredric Jameson, 'Postmodernism, or The Cultural Logic of Late Capitalism', *New Left Review*, no. 146 (July–Aug. 1984), 64–71.

heritage culture who have sought to distinguish its creations of simulations of the past from the cultivation of a more substantial historical understanding. Thus, for Stuart Cosgrove, the heritage industry is responsible for the construction of 'hyper-history' which he describes as 'a processed history rather than a history of social process'.[16] This construction of 'hyper-history' is linked to a postmodern aesthetic of display involving the invitation to look at artefacts, buildings, and historical reconstructions rather than necessarily understand them in a historical context.[17] Thus, for Patrick Wright, the heritage industry is guilty of substituting 'decoration and display' for 'active historicity' while for John Urry, if 'heritage history is distorted', it is primarily because of its 'emphasis on visualization'.[18] Given this criticism of heritage culture's dependence upon visual display, it is not surprising that the construction of the past in the heritage film should also have been the subject of a similar kind of scrutiny. It is, of course, the case that fiction films, unlike museums, do not have any particular mission to inform and educate about the past and therefore that the suspicion of display and visualization which is apparent in writing on heritage culture may, in the case of films, be misplaced. The heritage film, none the less, has been a significant source of meanings and attitudes towards the past in the 1980s and it remains important to examine what these have been and how they have been produced.

The Heritage Film

Although the term heritage has circulated quite widely within discourses of conservation and tourism, it is, of course, the case that the heritage film is not a term familiar to most cinemagoers. It is, in this respect, a critical term (like 'film noir') which has been applied retrospectively to a group of films which are identified as sharing a number of recognizable features. Although (again like film noir) both the status of the heritage film as a genre and the nature of its boundaries have been the subject of some dispute, there is, none the less, agreement about the general kind of film to which the term refers. Thus, in the 1980s and early 1990s, it would generally be seen to apply to films such as *Chariots of Fire* (1981), *Heat and Dust* (1982), *A Passage To India* (1984), *Another Country* (1984), *A Room with a View* (1985), *A Handful of Dust* (1987), *Maurice* (1987), *Little Dorrit* (1987), *A Month in the Country* (1987), *The Dawning* (1988), *The Bridge* (1990), *Fools of Fortune* (1990), *Where Angels Fear to Tread* (1991), and

---

[16] Stuart Cosgrove, in Paul Reas and Stuart Cosgrove, *Flogging A Dead Horse: Heritage Culture and its Role in Post-industrial Britain* (Manchester: Cornerhouse Publications, 1993).

[17] See Ludmilla Jordonova, 'Objects of Knowledge: A Historical Perspective on Museums' in Peter Vergo (ed.), *The New Museology* (London: Reaktion Books, 1989).

[18] Patrick Wright, *On Living in an Old Country: The National Past in Contemporary Britain* (London: Verso, 1985), 78 and John Urry, *The Tourist Gaze*, 112. In an interview, Wright does warn, however, against simply polemicizing against heritage culture as 'fake' and 'constructed' in favour of asking 'by whom, and for whom' heritage is constructed. See Patrick Wright in conversation with Tim Putnam, 'Sneering at the Theme Parks: An Encounter with the Heritage Industry', *Block*, no. 15 (Spring 1989), pp. 55 and 52.

Howards End (1991). These films, however, are not without precedent. As Charles Barr has argued, the British cinema has always sought to draw upon England's 'rich historical and cultural heritage' as a source of material for prestige drama and, in the case of the wartime 'heritage' film, was indeed 'almost a genre in itself'.[19] It is this idea which has been pursued by Andrew Higson in his discussions of the heritage film (which he suggests date back to at least the 1910s). For him, the heritage film demonstrates sufficient continuity to constitute a genre which he defines as one which 'reinvents and reproduces, and, in some cases simply invents, a national heritage for the screen'.[20] However, if it does so, the heritage (both historical and cultural) which the heritage film of the 1980s and 1990s reproduces is also of a particular kind.

For Raphael Samuel, the idea of 'heritage' is not a fixed one and may vary in relation to both social base and political source.[21] However, the weakness of his discussion is that he then proceeds to run together, almost indiscriminately, various versions of heritage while ignoring those which have become the most privileged or socially dominant. This is also relevant to a discussion of the heritage film. For although Corner and Harvey have identified three main emphases within heritage culture—the aristocratic, the rustic, and the industrial—it is clearly the aristocratic, or upper-middle-class, emphasis which the heritage film prefers.[22] The historical heritage which such films construct, therefore, tends to be a particular version of the national past: one which is associated with the privileged lifestyles of the English upper classes, élite institutions (such as Cambridge and Oxford universities), the country (and country house), the Home Counties, and ex-colonies. There is, in this respect, a certain similarity with the way in which the country house has assumed a significance within heritage culture more generally, a relationship which was cemented with the great success, in 1981, of Granada television's version of Evelyn Waugh's *Brideshead Revisited*, itself a part of a tradition of 'quality' television adaptations with links to the heritage film. For David Cannadine, 'the very idea of a "national" heritage . . . is often little more than a means of preserving the artefacts of an essentially élite culture, by claiming—in most cases quite implausibly—that it is really everybody's'.[23] This is a point pursued by Robert Hewison who claims that, in the case of the country house, 'the privilege of private ownership has become a question of national prestige'.[24] In the same

---

[19] Charles Barr, 'Introduction: Amnesia and Schizophrenia', in Charles Barr (ed.), *All Our Yesterdays: 90 Years of British Cinema* (London: BFI, 1986), 11.

[20] Andrew Higson, *Waving the Flag: Constructing a National Cinema in Britain* (Oxford: Clarendon Press, 1995), 26. See also his analysis of the 1980s heritage film in 'Re-presenting the National Past: Nostalgia and Pastiche in the Heritage Film', in Lester Friedman (ed.), *British Cinema and Thatcherism: Fires Were Started* (London: UCL Press, 1993) to which my own discussion is indebted.

[21] Raphael Samuel, *Theatres of Memory: vol. 1 Past and Present in Contemporary Culture* (London: Verso, 1994).

[22] John Corner and Sylvia Harvey (eds.), *Enterprise and Heritage*, 52–3.

[23] Cannadine, *The Pleasures of the Past*, 259.

[24] Hewison, *The Heritage Industry*, 72. For Mellor, however, there is still 'one element of our experience of the country house which radically upsets it (the formal presentation)—our simple presence'. See 'Whose Heritage?', 8.

one particular class's 'everyone' heritage

way, the heritage film may be seen, through the relatively 'democratic' mass media of film and television, to be presenting as 'national' the heritage of one particular class as the heritage of all. For, of course, if it is the property and lifestyle of a privileged upper class with which the heritage film is mainly concerned, it is not the social group to which the films primarily appeal. However, precisely because it is a 'heritage' which is now available to other social groups, its meaning is not only somewhat different but it is also a part of a new consumer culture offering cultural prestige to those groups (primarily the professional middle class) who constitute the main audience for it.

A SINGLE MAN

The heritage which these films construct, however, is not only historical but also cultural and it is a characteristic feature of the heritage film that it involves an adaptation from an English literary or theatrical source (*Chariots*, based on an original script is something of the exception here). During the 1980s it was E. M. Forster whose work proved the most popular and his books provided material for no less than five films (*A Passage to India, A Room with a View, Maurice, Where Angels Fear to Tread,* and *Howards End*). It is not, however, uncommon for films to involve adaptation and even such an 'unliterary' cinema as Hollywood has characteristically depended upon literary sources. What is significant in this regard is not only the cultural standing of the original work (Hollywood characteristically adapts popular sources which are therefore not regarded as adaptations as such) but the way in which it is adapted. Donald F. Larsson, for example, suggests adaptation may involve one of three main approaches to the original text: reproduction, alteration, and subversion.[25] Although the heritage film does, of necessity, alter its literary source, it avoids overt interference with the original and strives to suggest faithful reproduction. This may not always entail strict fidelity to the original text (as the controversial changes to *A Passage To India* demonstrate) but it does involve fidelity to the popular idea of 'great literature' or literary worthiness. The literary standing of the original is thus a part of the heritage which the heritage film displays and this in turn becomes a marker of the film's own claim to distinction, bestowing upon it a certain 'artistic' veneer.

A Room with a View chapter headings interrupt film

In this respect, the heritage film is a kind of 'art cinema' but one which derives its 'art' from extra-textual sources rather than its employment of the strategies of self-conscious narration and expressive visual style characteristic of art cinema in the 1950s and 1960s. Thus, even in the case of *A Room with a View* which interrupts its narrative with a series of titles, this is less informed by a modernist self-consciousness than a concern to imitate the original book's chapter headings and so display the film's literary credentials. The heritage film, in this regard, may be seen to occupy a kind of 'halfway house' between mainstream narrative cinema and earlier European art cinema. As such, its characteristic strategies are to modify rather than deviate significantly from the norms of

[25] Donald F. Larsson, 'Novel Into Film: Some Preliminary Reconsiderations', in Leon Golden (ed.), *Transformations in Literature and Film: Selected Papers from the 6th Annual Florida State University Conference on Literature and Film* (Tallahassee: University Presses of Florida, 1982), 74.

Hollywood's 'classicism'.[26] In doing so, such films may also be seen to be employing a familiar strategy available to national cinemas (as discussed in Chapter 3). Rather than attempting to compete with Hollywood directly by imitating its norms, this involves the adoption of aesthetic strategies and cultural referents which distinguish it from Hollywood and so foreground its 'national' credentials. Thus, just as heritage culture permits Britain to carve out a niche for itself within the global tourist economy so heritage films may be seen to provide the British cinema with a distinctive product in the international media market-place.[27] Heritage films, in this respect, have held a particular attraction for US audiences where they have often performed much better financially than in the UK. *A Room with a View*, for example, earned $23.7 million in the United States and Canada while *Howards End* took over three times as much in the United States (£12.2 million) as it did in the United Kingdom (where its gross was £3.7 million). This has also meant that heritage films have often opened in the United States rather than Britain (as was the case with *A Room with a View*), a strategy which has gained momentum in the 1990s with films such as *The Madness of King George* (1995) and *Sense and Sensibility* (1995).[28] However, although heritage filmmaking has provided the means for the construction of a specifically British (or, more properly, English) cinema, it is not a peculiarly British strategy of product differentiation and has been employed by other national cinemas as well. Pauline Kael, for example, described *Chariots of Fire* as the 'best Australian film made outside Australia'.[29] While this may seem, in the context of Britain's lengthy film history, an odd observation, it also reflects the international prominence of the Australian 'period film' in the late 1970s (especially in the wake of the international success of *Picnic at Hanging Rock* (1975)) and its occupation of a space within the market which the British, and more generally European, heritage films were destined to take over.[30]

[26] Ginette Vincendeau, in fact, argues that heritage films represent a 'classical European film style' in 'Issues in European Cinema', in John Hill and Pamela Church Gibson (eds.), *The Oxford Guide to Film Studies* (Oxford: Oxford University Press, 1997), 446.

[27] There is also a direct link between cinema and tourism in the way that film and televison locations encourage visitors. There was, for example, a sharp increase in the number of visitors to Castle Howard in Yorkshire in the wake of *Brideshead Revisited*. See Nichola Tooke and Michael Baker, 'Seeing is Believing: The Effect of Film on Visitor Numbers to Screened Locations', *Tourism Management*, vol. 17, no. 2 (1996), 89. This link between film locations and tourism is explicitly acknowledged in John Pym's *Merchant Ivory's English Landscape: Rooms, Views and Anglo-Saxon Attitudes* (London: Pavilion Books, 1995) which includes information about locations and relevant tourist advice.

[28] This option became especially popular after the runaway success of *Four Weddings and a Funeral* (1994) which earned over $52 million at the US box-office (see *Screen Finance* (22 Feb. 1995), 13). Although set in contemporary Britain, there is a sense in which *Four Weddings*, with its predominantly upper-class characters and use of stereotypically English and Scottish iconography (such as the country house, the rural church, and the castle), is itself a kind of modern 'heritage' film.

[29] Quoted in Graeme Turner, 'Art Directing History: The Period Film', in Albert Moran and Tom O'Regan (eds.), *The Australian Screen* (Ringwood: Penguin, 1989), 100.

[30] Richard Dyer and Ginette Vincendeau, for example, suggest that 'heritage' filmmaking emerged as a popular genre across Europe as a whole during the 1980s. The examples they provide—*Jean de Florette* (France, 1986), *Babette's Feast* (Denmark, 1987), and *Cinema Paradiso* (Italy, 1988)—do, however, suggest a more socially inclusive version of the national past than is provided in their British counterparts which are more typically fascinated with the upper classes. See their 'Introduction' in Dyer and Vincendeau (eds.), *Popular European Cinema* (London: Routledge, 1992), 6.

Thus, if the British heritage film is involved in the construction of a particular version of the national past and the national culture, it also does so in a way which distances itself from the mainstream conventions of Hollywood. In a manner typical of British cinema more generally, there is rarely one character who dominates the plot or provides it with its forward momentum. The emphasis, instead, tends to be upon a group of characters and the interaction and intrigues which take place between them. As a result of this, the films' plots tend to be much looser and episodic than those of 'classic' Hollywood and also to proceed at a much more leisurely pace (*Maurice*, for example, is heavily punctuated with fade-outs to black). There is also an avoidance of the physicality and action which is so often a feature of Hollywood films and a much greater emphasis upon characterization and conversational exchange. There is, in this respect, a certain premium placed upon 'good taste' and thus an aversion to the more melodramatic modes of expression employed by Hollywood. This is not to say that the plots do not contain melodramatic elements. Many of the characteristics of melodrama (impossible choices, renunciation, coincidence) are evident in the films. However, these characteristics are generally downplayed and do not involve the excess or extremes which more thoroughgoing melodramas involve. Thus, in *A Room with a View*, there is a sudden outburst of violence and murder in the scene in the Piazza della Signoria. Thematically, this signifies an encounter between English propriety and decorum (or 'bloodlessness') on the one hand and Italian passions on the other while, narratively, it helps to advance Lucy and George's relationship (investing it with a degree of vicarious excitement). However, it is a relatively fleeting moment which largely stands at odds with the rest of the film. As Peter Hutchings suggests, 'shock' isn't easily accommodated into the film's aesthetic and, as a result, there is a quick return to a 'romance mode'.[31]

The leisurely, episodic approach to narrative that is characteristic of the heritage film may be seen to link with what McFarlane and Mayer have described as a 'dawdling tendency' typical of British cinema more generally. This in turn, they suggest, is associated with a particular approach to visual style: a 'pictorial rather than dramatic' use of visual techniques.[32] It is this pictorial approach that the heritage film may also be seen to employ. Visual style is not only less narratively motivated (or harnessed to the purposes of the plot) than in classical Hollywood but is also less expressive of character and emotion than in the case of classical *mise-en-scène*. This is not to say that visual style does not perform a semantic function at all but that stylistic procedures characteristically exceed narrative or expressive requirements. This has two main consequences. Visual techniques are often employed in ways which are ostentatious (as in the use of one long take to shoot the freshers' gathering in *Chariots of Fire*) or just visually

[31] Peter J. Hutchings, 'A Disconnected View: Forster, Modernity and Film', in Jeremy Tambling (ed.), *E. M. Forster* (Basingstoke: Macmillan, 1995), 223.

[32] Brian McFarlane and Geoff Mayer, *New Australian Cinema: Sources and Parallels in American and British Film* (Cambridge: Cambridge University Press, 1992), 140. Andrew Higson specifically links the heritage film to a photographic tradition of 'pictorialism' in *Waving the Flag*, esp. pp. 51–8.

pleasing in themselves (as a result of the use of studied compositions or elegant camera movements). Such devices do not, however, indicate cinematic self-consciousness, or the director's signature, so much as a certain kind of 'artistry' and cultural worth which helps to distinguish such films from more popular genres. Visual techniques, however, are used not only to display some of their own artistry but also to display the iconography with which the genre is most associated: buildings, properties, costumes, and landscapes. As has already been suggested in the case of *Chariots*, compositions and camera movements are often motivated more by the desire to 'show off' settings than adhere to any strict dramatic logic and this may be related to a more general tension between narrative and spectacle or between the process of narration and the display of images which is often regarded as a characteristic of classic narrative cinema.[33] In the case of the heritage film, the balance between narrative and spectacle shifts in favour of 'spectacle' (albeit of a more discreet kind than in Hollywood) and the 'spectacle' or display of heritage assumes a particular prominence.[34] This is itself evident in the way that such films are advertised and promoted. John Ellis uses the term 'narrative image' to describe the idea of a film which is circulated by the industry in anticipation of the question, 'What is this film like?'.[35] In the case of the heritage film this 'narrative image' is often bound up with the promise of heritage spectacle as much as the prospective pleasures of the plot. Thus, in the case of the video cover of *Maurice*, the blurb has less to say about the film's actual content than the richness of its display of heritage elements. 'All the classic ingredients are here', the text reads, 'the exquisite period settings, breathtaking photography, and a superb cast.'[36]

As the last phrase suggests, the aesthetic of display also extends to the demonstration of a certain theatricality, involving 'quality' actors often more commonly associated with the stage or, if not, who demonstrate a more mannered style than that normally employed by Hollywood. Barry King, draws a distinction between 'impersonation', whereby an actor's own personality disappears into that of the character, and 'personification', whereby characterization is incorporated into a star's own persona.[37] However, in the heritage film (and much British cinema more generally) acting involves neither an immersion of the actor into a part nor a subordination of a role to their star image so much as

[margin handwritten note: actors associated with stage.]

---

[33] See, for example, Lea Jacobs and Richard de Cordova, 'Spectacle and Narrative Theory', *Quarterly Review of Film Studies*, vol. 7, no. 4 (1982).

[34] Andrew Higson discusses this aspect of the films in terms of the creation of what he calls 'heritage space' rather than 'narrative space' in 'Re-presenting the National Past', 117. This aspect of the heritage film would seem to be confirmed by the appearance of two large books devoted to the films of Merchant Ivory—Robert Emmet Long's *The Films of Merchant Ivory* (New York: Citadel Press, 1991) and John Pym's *Merchant Ivory's English Landscape*—which consist primarily of elegantly reproduced stills from the films.

[35] John Ellis, *Visible Fictions* (London: Routledge & Kegan Paul, 1982), 30. The idea derives from Stephen Heath, 'Film Performance', *Cinetracts*, no. 2 (Summer 1977), 12.

[36] This sense of the pleasures provided by the heritage film is also echoed in many of the reviews. As one critic put it of *A Room with a View*: 'Everything about this film is delightful: the sets, costumes, photography and James Ivory's subtle direction.' See Pat Anderson, *Films in Review* (June/July 1986), 362.

[37] Barry King, 'Articulating Stardom', *Screen*, vol. 26 no. 5 (Sept.–Oct. 1985), 27–50.

a 'performance' of the role, involving a clear display of 'actorliness'.[38] This, for example, is especially apparent in *A Room with a View* where a number of familiar actors and actresses with theatrical backgrounds (Maggie Smith, Judi Dench, Denholm Elliott, Daniel Day Lewis) give overtly theatrical performances which clearly announce their status as performances. Indeed, one of the most commented upon aspects of the film in the reviews was the extravagantly theatrical performance of Daniel Day-Lewis as Cecil Vyse which stood in such contrast to his earlier screen performance as Johnny in *My Beautiful Laundrette* and led Derek Malcolm to exclaim that the film as a whole succeeded in advertising 'English acting as about the best in the world'.[39] This appeal (and 'advertising') of theatrical performance may also be linked to the attraction of the use of spoken English, especially for US audiences. Charles Barr suggests that the attempt to construct a heritage cinema in the silent era was set back by the inability to make use of 'the prestige weapon of the educated English voice'.[40] In the 1980s heritage film, this is not, of course, the case and the display of refined English diction and the theatrical use of language is clearly a significant source of its appeal.

However, if the heritage film is concerned with the display of heritage properties (both historical and cultural), it is also a display of a particular kind. The presentation of the past by the heritage film not only involves a degree of 'spectacularization' of the past but also a certain concern with period detail and 'authenticity'. As Pam Cook suggests 'authenticity is a problem with all costume drama' and audiences generally accept, and indeed expect, a degree of historical licence in films which seek to recreate the past.[41] None the less, there is variation in the stress which is placed upon 'authenticity' by different costume dramas and it seems to be a feature of the heritage film that it attaches a greater importance to historical verisimilitude than more popular forms of costume drama or the historical film.[42] Heritage filmmaking, in this respect, may be seen as a

---

[38] It is, of course, the case that a number of actors and actresses (Helen Bonham Carter, Rupert Graves, James Wilby, Anthony Hopkins, Emma Thompson) reappear in different films and carry with them a certain association with the heritage genre. Martin A. Hipsky suggests how the Thompson–Hopkins match-up in *Remains of the Day* was crucial, following the success of *Howards End*, in drawing audiences back to the cinema. See 'Anglophil(m)ia: Why Does America Watch Merchant-Ivory Movies?', *Journal of Popular Film and Television*, vol. 22, no. 3 (Fall 1994), 101–2. Although this suggests a certain 'star' status, it is difficult to associate clear star personae with Hopkins and Thompson (other than a reputation for 'quality' acting).

[39] Derek Malcolm, *The Guardian* (10 Apr. 1986), 13. Peter J. Hutchings, referring, in particular, to Peggy Ashcroft in *A Passage to India* and Vanessa Redgrave in *Howards End*, suggests how the heritage film valorizes its actors and actresses as themselves 'national treasures'. See 'A Disconnected View', 221.

[40] Barr, 'Introduction: Amnesia and Schizophrenia', 12.

[41] Pam Cook, 'Neither Here nor There: National Identity in Gainsborough Costume Drama', in Higson (ed.), *Dissolving Views: Key Writings on British Cinema* (London: Cassell, 1996), 57.

[42] Marcia Landy draws a distinction between the historical film and costume drama. Historical films, she argues, draw upon real historical events and persons while the costume drama, although set in the past, uses fictional characters who are not so firmly tied to historical events. See Marcia Landy, *British Genres: Cinema and Society, 1930–1960* (Princeton: Princeton University Press, 1991), 53. Pam Cook, however, defines the historical film more generally as 'a hybrid genre which incorporates prestige literary adaptations, biopics, period musicals and comedies, Westerns, swashbuckling adventures, and romantic melodramas' and thus subsumes the costume drama under the category of the historical film.

subspecies of costume drama in which a greater premium is not only placed upon the artistic worthiness which is derived from literature or the theatre but also the degree of historical detail and 'accuracy' to which the film aspires.[43] This aspect of the heritage film is often recorded in the reviews which praise (and also, on occasion, deride) the films both for their fidelity to literary source and to historical period. This aspect of heritage filmmaking was at its most pronounced in the case of *Little Dorrit*, the publicity for which lay great stress on its concern with period 'authenticity' and the careful attention to detail which had gone into the costumes. These took twenty-five people over two years to cut, fit, and sew and also went on exhibition at the Museum of London.[44] Raphael Samuel, however, complains that this exaggerated 'concern for historical verisimilitude' merely results in a 'fetishization of period effects'. 'The sets, so lovingly reconstructed', he argues, 'take on a life of their own' while 'the period costume . . . turns the actors and actresses into clothes-hangers.'[45] For Samuel, this preoccupation with period 'authenticity' not only cuts across Dickens's own licence with history but also robs the novel of its gothic horrors. It may also be seen, ironically, to stand at odds with the very 'authenticity' for which it strives. The cult of 'authenticity' has been a feature of contemporary postmodern culture and has been in evidence not only in the conservationist concern for the built environment but also the return to 'authentic' instruments in 'early music' or the enthusiasm for 'original' editions of literary works or 'original' musical recordings. However, there is a sense in which this concern with 'authenticity' simply produces what is, in effect, 'inauthentic' simulation. As Crook *et al.* suggest, postmodern culture replaces the modern construction of traditions, containing an unfolding or 'inner' logic, with a postmodern 'archive' of varying styles in apparently contingent relationship. As a result, 'when the cult of authenticity takes popular hold', they argue, 'it encourages a postmodernizing depthlessness in which the "meaning" of the work is no more than the performance surface of colour and tempo'.[46] In the same way, the emphasis on period effects in the heritage film often leads to a similar preoccupation with 'surface' simulation of the past rather than the encouragement of a historical sensibility.

However, whether the 'genre' of the historical film then displays any shared conventions other than a setting in the past seems questionable. See Cook, 'Neither Here nor There: National Identity in Gainsborough Costume Drama', 58.

[43] Sue Harper records how Gainsborough costume dramas were often criticized for their lack of 'realism' and historical inaccuracy and how producer Sydney Box sought to win prestige for the films by increasing the historical fidelity of the costuming and décor. See *Picturing The Past: The Rise and Fall of the British Costume Film* (London: BFI, 1994).

[44] 'The Making of a Costume Drama', *Independent* (4 Dec. 1987), 28.

[45] 'Raphael Samuel, 'Docklands Dickens' in Samuel (ed.), *Patriotism vol. 3: National Fictions* (London: Routledge, 1989), 281–3. The visual display provided by *Little Dorrit* is, in some ways, distinct from other heritage films, however. The film has been completely shot in a studio with the result that the artifice of the sets (especially exteriors) is much more apparent than in other heritage films. The cinematographic style is also unusual. The camera tends to remain at fixed eye-level positions with the result that there are virtually none of the ostentatious camera movements and high angles which are often a feature of other heritage films.

[46] Stephen Crook, Jan Pakulski, and Malcolm Waters, *Postmodernization: Change in Advanced Society* (London: Routledge, 1992), 66.

Nostalgia

However, if the heritage film's approach to the past is linked with that of heritage culture more generally, what is the relationship between past and present implied in it and does it contain the nostalgia which has been commonly associated with heritage culture? The answer to this is probably more complicated than it at first appears. For Fred Davis, 'simple nostalgia' involves a straightforward belief in the superiority of the past over the present.[47] However, it would be hard to suggest that this was manifestly the case in the heritage film. As has been seen, *Chariots* was ready to acknowledge the shortcomings of the past: the anti-Semitism and snobbishness of the Cambridge Masters, for example. In the same way, other heritage films are prepared to identify the flaws of the periods with which they deal. *Maurice* and *Another Country* both deal with the intolerance shown to homosexuals and many of the films more generally are preoccupied with the social constraints imposed upon the expression of characters' desires (e.g. *Heat and Dust, Where Angels Fear to Tread, The Bridge*). Indeed, much of the comedy generated by *A Room with a View* derives from the spectator's amusement with characters (such as Helena Bonham Carter's Lucy) unable to give vent to their true feelings. In this respect, there is an implied superiority on the part of the spectator to those characters who remain trapped within social conventions and who only belatedly come to recognize what the audience already knows. In the same way, the pathos of *The Bridge* derives from the spectator's understanding of the inability of the main female character, Isobel Hetherington (Saskia Reeves) to achieve her desires in a society ruled by men and her coming to a realization of the deal struck between her husband and lover. As such the predicaments which the characters face are characteristically interpreted in terms of a contemporary sensibility which is assumed to be more humane and liberal than that prevailing in the past. This is also the case in the films' treatment of homosexuality where both audience understanding and enjoyment (as in Maurice's search for a 'cure' for his homosexuality) is predicated upon an attitude towards gayness which is not available to the characters themselves within the films.

So, if the heritage film implies a nostalgic relationship to the past, it is probably closer to what Davis calls 'reflexive nostalgia' than simple nostalgia. For Davis, this is a nostalgia which includes some recognition that the past it remembers is not entirely accurate or comprehensive. However, in the case of the heritage film, this reflexivity also resides in the acknowledgement that the past was not perfect and that, despite its many attractions, it also contained its faults. In this way, the limited reflexivity which the films provide may actually serve to ease access to the past: indulging the spectator in the pleasures of the past but also providing them with a kind of alibi to do so. There is, however, some further complication. For Davis, it is a characteristic of nostalgia in

---

[47] Davis, *Yearning For Yesterday*, 21.

individuals that it relates to lived experience and thus normally involves a yearning for childhood or adolescence. In the case of the heritage film, the past which is invoked is largely outside of the direct experience of the audiences to which it appeals. It thus provides a kind of 'secondhand' nostalgia for a past which was not lived through and is really only known through the cultural constructions of it. In this sense, the nostalgia of the heritage film is for images and imaginings of the past as much as any 'real' lived past and thus for a past which is dependent upon intertextual references to other representations of the past as much as it is to the referent of 'real' history.

A key intertextual reference in the heritage film is, of course, the original novel or play on which it is based. However, especially in the use of Forster, there is a significant element of transmutation involved. With the exception of *A Passage to India*, which is set in the 1920s, the bulk of the Forster adaptations are set in the Edwardian era prior to the First World War. In many respects, the watershed of the First World War has subsequently served to invest the Edwardian era with a pre-lapsarian sense of lost elegance and stability.[48] However, for Forster this period was not the past and an object of nostalgia but his contemporary reality. *Where Angels Fear to Tread*, *A Room with a View*, and *Howards End* had all been published by 1910 and *Maurice* was written during 1913 and 1914. His writings were therefore critical of the shortcomings of contemporary society and, if they contained nostalgia, it was for an earlier era that was now vanishing. This is perhaps clearest in *Howards End* in which the cultured world and 'inner life' of the Schlegels is contrasted with the business pursuits and 'outer life' of the Wilcoxes, and the settled way of life represented by Howards End is contrasted with the sense of 'continual flux' brought on by the onset of modernity, urbanization, and industrialism.[49] This world of change is typified by the motor-car. As Norman Page suggests, for Forster, the motor-car is not simply a new industrial product or mechanical invention but also a symbol of the way in which 'the very nature and quality of human perception' was being altered for the worse.[50] However, in the case of the film version, this concern with the quickening pace of life and the loss of connection which it brings loses most of its power and the symbolic force of the motor-car is fundamentally altered. Thus, in relation to the 1990s, the cars which appear in the film no

---

[48] For Stuart Tannock the 'rhetoric of nostalgia' involves a characteristic form of periodizing: 'first, that of a prelapsarian world (the Golden Age, the childhood Home, the Country); second, that of a 'lapse' (a cut, a Catastrophe, a separation or sundering, the Fall); and third, that of the present, post-lapsarian world (a world felt in some way to be lacking, deficient or oppressive)'. See 'Nostalgia Critique', 456.

[49] Cf. the novel's description of Margaret Schlegel's thoughts in the novel: 'The sense of flux which had haunted her all the year disappeared for a time. She forgot the luggage and the motor-cars, and the hurrying men who know so much and connect so litle. She recaptured the sense of space, which is the basis of all earthly beauty, and, starting from Howards End, she attempted to realize England' in E. M. Forster, *Howards End* (Harmondsworth: Penguin, 1979, orig. 1910), 204.

[50] Norman Page, *E. M. Forster* (Basingstoke: Macmillan, 1987), 82. Malcolm Bradbury describes the motor-car, in *Howards End* (the novel), as a symbol of the Wilcoxes 'practicality, their ceaseles urge to motion, their power to put things to use', in Malcolm Bradbury (ed.), *Forster: A Collection of Critical Essays* (Englewood Cliffs, N.J.: Prentice-Hall, 1966), 133.

longer signify the new but suggest instead a slowed-down pace and perception which involve much less of a divorce from natural rhythms. As a result, they themselves now become the object of nostalgia, captured in visually pleasing pictorialist compositions (such as when the Wilcoxes' 'vintage' car is seen crossing a bridge on the way to Howards End). In a sense, this is a difficulty for all of those heritage films (including *A Passage to India* written in the 1920s, and *A Handful of Dust* which was published in the 1930s) which translate novels of contemporary social criticism into period pieces. For what, in the originals, were the subject of attack can easily become, in the films, the object of nostalgic pleasure (albeit of a partly reflexive kind).[51]

Thus, as has been seen in the case of *Chariots of Fire*, while the plots of heritage films characteristically contain elements of social criticism, these are often undercut by the fascination of the films with the visually spectacular trappings of the past. Pam Cook has noted that, in the writings on Gainsborough costume drama, this tension between narrative and spectacle has often been read in a positive light.[52] The difference between Gainsborough melodrama and heritage filmmaking should, however, be evident. In the case of the former, the excess of spectacle may be seen to subvert what are characteristically conservative or moralistic narrative conclusions; in the case of the latter, the emphasis on visual display, by contrast, undermines plots characterized by liberal or 'progressive' sentiments. This may be seen, for example, in the first part of *Maurice*, which like *Chariots*, is set in Cambridge University where Maurice (James Wilby) and Clive Durham (Hugh Grant) first meet. However, despite the liberalism of the ideas concerning religion which Maurice encounters among his fellow students, the university itself is associated with intolerance. During his translation class, the Dean (Barry Foster) asks that the reference to the 'unspeakable vice of the Greeks' be omitted and subsequently sends Maurice down for missing classes and consorting with Clive. However, the Cambridge which the film presents is none the less visually seductive and appealing. In the very scene, not in the novel, in which Durham complains of the Dean's 'hypocrisy' and mocks religious belief, the men are shown punting in front of a picturesque university background. The scene which immediately follows also provides a visually splendid view of the chapel interior. In the same way, Maurice and Clive's first tentative embrace is preceded by no less than three 'establishing' shots of the university before there is a cut to a close-up of Clive's face. These shots not only provide the narratively surplus display of heritage properties which is a characteristic of the heritage film but also seem to celebrate the very culture which

---

[51] Richard Dyer has suggested that nostalgia may then have a value in the critique of the present which it provides. See 'Heritage Cinema in Europe', in Vincendeau (ed.), *Encyclopedia of European Cinema* (London: BFI/Cassell, 1995), 205. While it is possible to see the heritage films as canvassing certain liberal values of tolerance at a time when right-wing values were in the ascendant, it is none the less difficult to cast the nostalgia of the heritage film into too 'progressive' a mould given the narrow social base and sense of privilege upon which it rests.

[52] Cook, 'Neither Here nor There', 59.

... the full expression of their desires.[53] Indeed, the way in which the shots
...ked through overlapping sound (the choir) and visual style appears to
...ate their 'counter-love' (as homosexuality is described in the translation
... with the *mise-en-scène* of Cambridge and suppress the sense that they
might in any way be 'outlaws' (as Maurice subsequently puts it). And, given that
Maurice, as the representative of suburbia, is not automatically at ease with
Cambridge, there is a strong sense that his attraction to Clive and to the elegance
and values of Cambridge are interconnected.[54]

In the same way, the visual preoccupation with the decor, dress, and cere-
monies of the upper classes in *Another Country*, which also deals with the
repression of homosexuality, likewise transforms the ostensive object of criticism—the authoritarian public school—into a source of visual pleasure and
fascination. This process is aided by an opening out of the original play for purposes of filming and the use of a flashback structure (which is absent from the
original play). Thus, while Julian Mitchell's play is set almost totally inside—
in interiors (the library, the study, the dormitory) described by Bennett as
'dingy'—the film makes considerable use of picturesque exteriors (the school
courtyard, the playing fields, bridges, landscapes) and ceremonials (such as the
memorial service and military inspection which are only mentioned in the
play) which invest the past with a seductive allure.[55] Moreover, by adding a
flashback structure, in which Bennett is seen cramped inside his drab and com-
fortless Moscow apartment, it is the present which is now clearly seen as 'dingy'
and post-lapsarian (the narrative consequence, indeed, of Bennett's failure to
become a 'God').

This ambivalence in representing the past also has consequences for how the
films work through their central themes. As with *A Room with a View*, there
is, in *Maurice*, a romantic association between nature and the expression of
authentic desire. Thus, just as George in *A Room with a View* first kisses Lucy
amidst the cornfields and then runs home in the rain, so Maurice seeks to break
out of his confinement by opening windows and, in one scene, bathe in the rain
outside the Durhams' country house, Pendersleigh. This motif is returned to at

---

[53] Claire Monk has argued that criticisms of the heritage film have under-estimated the expressive use
of visual style and argues that, in *Maurice*, the '*mise-en-scène* is . . . schematically expressionistic, functioning in quite obvious ways to express the unconscious, sexuality, states of mind'. In line with work on
melodrama, she argues that the desire of the characters is sublimated into *mise-en-scène* and, therefore,
that these shots of the university contain clear phallic connotations. However, even if this is the case, the
significance of the symbolism retains a degree of ambivalence (also suggesting the university's patriarchal power) and certainly does not exhaust the 'pictorial' pleasures which the shots provide. See *Sex,
Politics and the Past: Merchant Ivory, The Heritage Film and its Critics in 1980s and 1990s Britain*, MA thesis, BFI/Birkbeck College (1994), pp. 28 and 35. Andrew Higson, responding to criticisms of his original
thesis, has also argued that while the images of the heritage film may be read in various ways, there is,
none the less, 'a massive encouragement in the culture at large to read the images as heritage images'. See
'The Heritage Film and British Cinema', in Higson (ed.), *Dissolving Views*, 246.

[54] In his 'Terminal note' on the novel, written in 1960, E. M. Forster suggests that 'Maurice is
Suburbia' and 'Clive is Cambridge'. See *Maurice* (Harmondsworth: Penguin, 1987, orig. 1971), 218.

[55] Julian Mitchell, *Another Country* (Oxford: Amber Lane Press, 1989, orig. 1982), 7.

PLATE 3. Shutting out passion: Hugh Grant and Phoebe Nicholls in *Maurice*

the film's end. Maurice has told Clive of his relationship with Alec Scudder (Rupert Graves). Clive then returns inside and the door is closed behind him by his butler Simcox (Patrick Godfrey). He joins the wife he has married for the sake of career and respectability and proceeds to close the shutters of his bedroom windows. We then see him from the outside, and a reverse point-of-view shot of Maurice at Cambridge follows. The implications of this are clear. In a scene replete with the connotations of sacrifice and repression familiar from melodrama, Maurice is shutting out the erotic passion represented by Maurice (now in the boathouse with Alec) and is, in effect, imprisoned within his own home. However, this sense of the repressiveness of the country house is also undercut by the way in which the setting has been presented. Despite Clive's complaint that his house is 'falling down', the film's heritage impulse has none the less shown it to be attractive and appealing. Thus, like the film's use of Cambridge, the setting is simultaneously condemned and enjoyed.

A similar tension between theme and style is apparent in *A Room with a View*. The film revolves, as does *Maurice*, around the theme of living honestly and without self-deception. This is made concrete through the experiences of Lucy whose encounter with direct and 'natural' passion in Italy contrasts with the stuffiness and propriety of life back in England. As a result the second part of the film concerns the eventual acknowledgement by Lucy of her desire for the proto-Lawrentian hero George Emerson (Julian Sands) rather then the self-conscious aesthete, Cecil. The film's criticism of Cecil, made initially via George, is that he only wants Lucy for 'a possession'—'something to look at like

a painting or an ivory box'. The problem for the film, however, is tha
preoccupied with looking at possessions and it is common for the film
its characters from the mid-distance in order to display the objects and
which surround them. Thus, when Lucy tells Cecil of her wish to break of
engagement, complaining that she does not wish to be seen as a pain
the scene is played—for little dramatic reason—across two separate room
which the furniture (the table, the bookcase) and objects (decanters, candle
paintings) assume a particular prominence. There is, of course, a semantic
dimension to this, insofar as these props are positioned in such a way as to
suggest both how they entrap and divide the characters concerned. However,
at the same time, they also implicate the film in the very 'aestheticism' from
which Lucy is attempting to escape (and it is therefore significant that while
she declares that she wants to be herself she is really only mouthing the words
which she has acquired from George).

This ambivalence is also true of the films' contrast of 'nature' and 'culture'
more generally. In *A Room with a View*, it is the representatives of 'culture' such
as Cecil, the English chaplain in Florence, Mr Eager (Patrick Godfrey), and, to
some extent, Eleanor Lavish (Judi Dench) who are criticized for their hypocrisy
and remoteness from genuine experience while George (the only character free
of deceit according to his father) is praised for his spontaneity and 'natural'
impulses. However, for all its mockery of pseudo-culture and good manners,
the film is itself heavily reliant upon a display of cultural reference points which
assume a certain amount of 'cultural capital' on the part of its audience. This is
manifestly the case in the scenes in Florence where the frescos by Giotti at the
church of Santa Croce, the statues in the Piazza della Signoria, and the use of
Puccini on the soundtrack clearly establish the film's cultural preoccupations. It
is also evident in scenes such as that between Cecil and the Emersons which
takes place in the National Gallery in front of Paolo Uccello's *Niccolo Da
Tolentino at the Battle of San Romano*. Although this painting, at a narrative
level, provides a link back to Florence and motivates the apparent coincidence
of Cecil's meeting with the Emersons, its use in the film is not only 'excessive' in
terms of the demands of plot and characterization but also assumes, on the part
of the spectator, a familiarity with the painting and the cultural universe which
the characters inhabit. As Pauline Kael suggests, it is a film which 'flaunts its culture' and, whatever its yearning for 'nature', it is none the less caught within the
cultural universe from which Lucy is apparently attempting to escape (and to
this extent wraps her up in the very 'art . . . books, and music' which Cecil is
accused of seeking to do).[56] So, while the film is critical of characters such as
Cecil whose experience of life and love is always mediated through art, its own
representations of romantic impulse and passion are themselves overlaid with

[56] Pauline Kael, *New Yorker* (24 Mar. 1986), 115. Noting the references to 'Dante, Giotto, Michelangelo,
R. W. Emerson, Beethoven, Greek myth, Goethe and Byron' in the film, Martin A. Hipsky describes *A
Room With A View* as 'a veritable survey course in the art of high cultural allusion'. He suggests this kind
of 'highbrow entertainment' holds a particular appeal to a US professional–managerial class' with a
liberal arts background. See 'Anglophil(m)ia: Why Does America Watch Merchant-Ivory Movies?', 103.

cultural references. George and Lucy's celebrated kiss in the barley field is accompanied by a Puccini aria (from 'La Rondine') while the romantic embrace which ends the film is lit and composed in such a way as to provide the spectator with a simultaneously pleasing 'view' of the Florence skyline.

As this suggests, the reliance upon a particular kind of cultural capital by heritage films inevitably compromises the degree to which they can give expression to, as the novel puts it, 'the 'holiness of direct desire'.[57] Both *A Room with a View* and *Maurice* exhort characters to break free of inhibition but as films are themselves inhibited due to the good taste and good manners that their approach to filmmaking involves. *Maurice* begins with a scene—complained of by some critics for its 'unnecessary' vulgarity—showing the schoolmaster Mr Ducie (Simon Callow) explaining the facts of life to the young Maurice. The scene ends with a young girl being ushered away from Ducie's drawings of genitalia on the sand with the words 'come, Victoria' and thus the promise of an assault on Victorian primness. However, the heritage style is itself characterized by a certain primness and, with its emphasis on tasteful cinematography and decorative *mise-en scène*, is much better suited to oblique suggestion than explicit portrayal of erotic desire. Thus, while homosexual desire is overt in *Maurice* (rather than latent as in *Chariots of Fire*), the film seems uneasy with how to show the physical desires of its characters and invests the earlier scenes of tentative physical contact with much greater charge than the scenes of actual lovemaking (which are themselves brief). Thus, for all of the urging of characters to honesty and frankness, the heritage film prefers decorum and restraint to the uninhibited expression of libidinal desires and, in a sense, upholds the very uptightness against which many of the characters are in protest.[58]

The mix of condemning and celebrating the past which is a feature of the heritage film's use of visual style also has implications for an assessment of the politics of the films. For Samuel, heritage belongs to neither the right nor the left but is available to both. However, as has been seen the mobilization of heritage by the heritage film is not generous in terms of social reach and is often characterized as socially conservative. However, it is also the case that many of the films' plots contain characters who seek to break out of the confines of one social group and forge relationships across social class (*Maurice, A Room with a View, Chariots of Fire, Howards End*) or other social divides (*Where Angels Fear to Tread, A Passage to India, Heat and Dust*). Indeed, in his discussion of film and television dramas dealing with the Edwardians, D. L. LeMahieu suggests that although these are concerned with the 'social preoccupations of a tiny élite' they none the less extend a democratic sympathy to 'outsiders' who generally possess virtues which the upper-class characters are seen to lack.[59] Thus, in many of the

[57] Forster, *A Room With a View* (Harmondsworth: Penguin, 1985, orig. 1908), 225.

[58] Gilbert Adair makes a similar point about *Another Country* in which he argues that the affair between Bennett and Harcourt (Cary Elwes) is shown with 'hypocritical chasteness'. See *Monthly Film Bulletin* (June 1984), 174.

[59] D. L. LeMahieu, 'Imagined Contemporaries: Cinematic and Televised Dramas About the Edwardians in Great Britain and the United States, 1967–1985', *Historical Journal of Film, Radio and Television*, vol. 10, no. 3 (1990), 249.

films above, it is characters who stand outside of or lack full integration with polite society (e.g. Alec in *Maurice*, Leonard Bast in *Howards End*, Gino in *Where Angels*, the Emersons in *A Room with a View*, Abrahams in *Chariots*) who possess the honesty or vitality which is missing in other characters. However, this social extension only goes so far. Abrahams and the Emersons, for example, may be 'outsiders' but they still enjoy comparative wealth and social standing (and, in the case of the Emersons, the social distinctions between them and the Honeychurchs are so fine that they barely register with a contemporary audience other than in terms of 'manners'). However, when characters are quite clearly of a different social background, as in the case of Alec and Leonard, then the films' capacities to forge genuine connections begin to falter.

It has often been noted that Forster himself had difficulty giving a satisfactory fictional embodiment to characters who lacked an unearned income and this is evident in the uncharitable way in which he deals with Leonard Bast and his cultural pretensions in *Howards End*. It was clearly unacceptable in the early 1990s simply to reproduce in the film the characterization of Bast contained in the novel and there is evidence of an attempt to invest him with enhanced dignity and psychological plausibility (making his relationship with Jacky less grotesque, providing him with a more extensive fantasy life, and rendering his relationship with Helen more explicable). Indeed, such are the changes wrought in relation to the Basts that Lizzie Francke goes so far as to suggest that they 'provide the moral and political standards for those around them'. She also argues that Leonard's recognition of the importance of money to a cultured life (embodied in his riposte to Helen that 'that's for rich people' when she claims that 'books are more real than anything') provides evidence of 'a more troubling and rigorous inquest' of the Edwardian past than is usual.[60] However, it is hard to accept that this is fully the case and the democratic sentiment that is extended to Bast only goes so far. The film is still most at home with the Schlegels and the Wilcoxes and cannot entirely escape the sense that Bast is less important in himself than the opportunities he provides to test the contrasting attitudes of humane concern and ruthless indifference associated with the Schlegels and Wilcoxes.[61] Thus, his death possesses little genuine tragedy and, indeed, has the air of a dramatically contrived situation to which Wilcox is required to respond. Moreover, the film's ending no more embraces modernity and the emergent social class of white-collar workers which Bast represents than the original novel (even if Helen does bear his child). Rather, the film's conclusion clearly involves an endorsement of the rural continuity which *Howards End* represents and, thus, a vision of community which stands outside of, and at odds with, contemporary urban realities.

[60] Lizzie Francke, Review, *Sight and Sound* (May 1992), 15.

[61] The scriptwriter, Ruth Jhabvala, has suggested that Leonard Bast was 'as much an embarrassment' to Merchant and Ivory as 'to E. M. Forster who didn't like to descend into that milieu'. Ivory disputes the charge but admits that it was 'more fun' doing the Schegels' home life than Leonard's and that he does 'best' with 'educated upper-middle-class people'. See John Pym, *Merchant Ivory's English Landscapes*, 86.

Similar difficulties of representation are also apparent in *Maurice*. Although, as in *A Room with a View*, a servant may occasionally intrude into a scene and momentarily remind us of the privilege upon which the lives of the main characters is based, *Maurice* accords a greater prominence to the servant class than is usual in heritage films. As Finch and Kwietniowski note, one of the significant changes to the novel is the enlarged role given to the servants as knowledgeable observers of the unfolding events.[62] Thus, the servants at Pendersleigh, and especially Simcox, are aware of the relationship between Maurice and Clive in a way that neither of their families are. There is clearly an irony in this and an implicit criticism of the divorce from reality which the better-off characters display. In the case of Alec Scudder, he not only recognizes the truth of Maurice's 'nature' which others miss ('I know, sir', he tells him) but is also prepared to act upon his desires (in a way that Clive is not). Thus, when Clive tells Maurice that he 'can't expect our standard of honesty in servants', the reverse is shown to be true. Alec, the gamekeeper, is 'honest' in a way that Clive isn't. However, if the film bestows upon the servants a degree of insight and honesty which may be set against the delusions and hypocrisy of the upper and middle classes, the film still inhabits the world of those it criticizes and develops little of an interior relationship with the characters whose 'honesty' it admires (this is also the case with the Italian lovers in *A Room with a View* and also, to some extent, Gino in *Where Angels Fear to Tread*). Alec, indeed, functions as something of a *deus ex machina* who belatedly arrives to introduce Maurice to sensual pleasure. Forster reports Lytton Strachey's response to a draft of the novel that the relationship of Maurice and Alec rested upon 'curiosity and lust' and would only last six weeks.[63] As a result, Forster laboured to give their relationship an after-life and to demonstrate the basis for its continuation. However, this is only partly successful and the film still has difficulty in rendering the relationship convincing.

Indeed, it partly acknowledges the fantasy element of Alec's role by having him appear in Maurice's bedroom after a dream sequence, almost as if he had been wished there by Maurice's unconscious. In this respect, Alec is less a working-class character whose experiences and values an audience are invited to understand than a middle-class fantasy of a working-class man who it is imagined holds out the prospect of an escape from a life of inhibition (similar questions concerning the representation of Italians in *A Room with a View* and *Where Angels Fear to Tread* could also be raised).

However, if the heritage film remains largely trapped within the boundaries of a particular social class, it does nevertheless seek to explore questions concerning gender and sexual orientation. According to Andrew Higson 'the national past' of the heritage film is characteristically 'male-centred'.[64] Although, as has been seen, this is true of *Chariots*, it is, however, less so of other

[62] Mark Finch and Richard Kwietniowski, 'Melodrama and "Maurice": Homo is Where the Het Is', *Screen*, vol. 29, no. 3 (1988), 77.

[63] Forster, 'Terminal note', *Maurice*, 219.   [64] Higson, 'Re-presenting the National Past', 114.

films which eschew its heroic historical drama in favour of the more intimate personal dramas associated with the comedy of manners. Indeed, it is often taken as a distinctive feature of the heritage film that it focuses on the small-scale and inter-personal rather than the 'big' moments of history. As such, it is actually women characters who figure the most prominently or, as in *Maurice*, gay men who deviate from the 'masculine norm'. As such, the heritage film may be seen to be much less centred upon heterosexual males than more mainstream popular cinema. Indeed, for D. L. LeMahieu, it is 'the struggles of Edwardian women for greater autonomy and social respect' which is a major source of appeal in such dramas.[65]

While this is certainly the case in a number of heritage films, it does not, of course, exhaust the range of representations of women contained in them. Brenda (Kristin Scott Thomas) in *A Handful of Dust*, for example, is less a liberal heroine than a *femme fatale* whose callousness and infidelity precipitates her husband Tony's (James Wilby) downfall (and puts the family home Hetton Hall in jeopardy). Women, moreover, can also be insidious agents of repression, working against the interests of other female characters and attempting to thwart their desires for personal fulfilment as in *Where Angels Fear to Tread* and *A Passage to India*. Moreover, in those films in which the 'struggles' of women are central, the representations of female autonomy which they provide can still be quite restricted. Thus, in *A Room with a View*, Lucy's struggle for 'autonomy' revolves around a choice between two different kinds of male suitor. Unlike certain earlier kinds of woman's film, she does not have to sacrifice love to duty or social obligation but is able—eventually—to choose George rather than Cecil. However, while this may be 'progressive' in terms of social class— George does not belong to 'proper society'—it is less so in terms of gender. Lucy's rebellion against social constraint is confined to the rejection of an unsuitable, if socially desirable, match and does not involve any querying of the institution of marriage itself (which is itself 'naturalized' as the appropriate outlet for the couple's 'natural' impulses).

Moreover, her 'coming-to-consciousness' is less the result of her own will and agency than a response to the pressure of circumstances and the chain of coincidences that have led George to be living close by. As has already been noted, the film employs a form of narration typical of melodrama in which the heroine belatedly recognizes what the spectator already knows (as is made evident in the film's use of titles which announce repeatedly that Lucy is 'lying' to various other characters).[66] The acknowledgement of the 'truth' of her situation (that she really loves George) is finally forced upon her by her encounter with Mr Emerson. Thus, whatever Mr Emerson's standing as a representative of liberal values, he also functions as a surrogate father-figure (Lucy's real father is dead) whose understanding of events is superior to that of Lucy (telling her that she

---

[65] LeMahieu, 'Imagined Contemporaries', 253.

[66] David Bordwell discusses the role, in melodrama, of both coincidence and omniscient narration in *Narration in the Fiction Film* (London: Routledge, 1985), 70–3.

has 'deceived everyone including yourself'). In this respect, Lucy's 'awakening' largely involves coming to accept what the men already know to be the case (and, thus, as has been noted, even when she breaks off with Cecil, she is largely repeating what George had previously told her).

The representation of women in the heritage film is also complicated by the treatment of the relations between men. For the heritage film not only deals explicitly with homosexuality (as in *Maurice* and *Another Country*) in a way that either marginalizes women or identifies them with the forces of constraint but it also invests many of its male relationships with a clear homo-erotic dimension. This is most evident in the adaptations of Forster (although it is also true of *A Month in the Country* (1987)). In the 1980s, the homosexuality of Forster was known about in a way that it was not at the time of the publication of the original novels and thus it becomes more visible within the films' textual operations.[67] Indeed, it is possible to detect a certain pattern in Forster's work, whereby the central heterosexual romance is blocked or thwarted in some way and the relations between men are invested with an added, characteristically homo-erotic, significance. This is particularly apparent, for example, in *A Passage to India* (discussed in the following chapter) and *Where Angels Fear to Tread*. In this respect, *Where Angels Fear to Tread* is unusual in terms both of its narrative organization and its treatment—in what might be regarded as a romantic comedy—of the main 'romantic couple'. The initial focus of the film is upon Lilia (Helen Mirren) who represents an archetypal Forsterian 'heroine' attempting to break out of the stultifying confines of English life, whose introduction in the film is associated with frenetic activity and sweeping camera movement. However, expected by her new Italian husband Gino (Giovanni Guidelli) to play the role of dutiful wife, her marriage fails to provide the release she desires and, in a striking narrative upset, she dies in childbirth. The thwarting of narrative expectations which the death of the heroine involves is matched by a similar refusal at the film's close to conform to conventional narrative expectations.

In the wake of Lilia's death, Philip Herriton (Rupert Graves) and Miss Abbott (Helena Bonham Carter) are thrown together as Philip and his sister, Harriet (Judy Davis) attempt to 'rescue' the child from Gino. Both undergo an experience which highlights the limitations of their lives in England (as Philip puts it 'here we see what asses we are') and there is a suggestion that they will come together as a couple. Back in England, they engage in conversation at the railway station ('I think you must know already') which suggests they may be on the verge of declaring love for each other. In fact, Miss Abbott declares her love for Gino and then Philip admits 'I love him too'. The prospect of a romantic

---

[67] Alexander Doty seeks to rescue the 'queerness' of texts from 'the twilight zone of connotation' by attaching it more firmly to an understanding of production and reception. See *Making Things Perfectly Queer: Interpreting Mass Culture* (Minneapolis: University of Minnesota Press, 1993), p. xii. However, although the known facts of Forster's life makes 'queer' readings of the heritage films more available, the 'queerness' of the films is still not always overt but remains (as in *A Room With A View* and *Where Angels Fear to Tread*) at the level of connotation.

conclusion is therefore undercut and the ending, with its associations with *Brief Encounter*, is redolent of lost opportunity and unfulfilled wants.

However, what this narrative of unexpected turns and failed resolutions also hints at is the homo-erotic romance which underlies much of the action. Philip is played by Rupert Graves (Scudder in *Maurice*) with a degree of camp suggestiveness that is absent from the novel and casts further doubt on his suitability as a romantic partner for Miss Abbott. Moreover, in contrast to his relationship with Miss Abbott, his fascination with Gino is much more overt and physical. When he returns to Italy to retrieve Lilia's child, he is reunited with Gino at the opera. Clutching a bouquet thrown back into the audience by the singer, he is pulled up to the balcony by a group of men and welcomed by Gino into his box ('Why haven't you written? . . . You can't escape me'). Elated by the experience, Philip subsequently embraces Gino in the street. The scene at the opera is, of course, central to the meanings of the film insofar as it sets up a clear contrast between the sterile propriety of the English—Harriet storms out of the theatre in disgust at its lack of respectability—with the warmth and openness of the Italians (whom Philip in effect 'joins'). However, it is also a theme worked out in terms of Philip's seduction by Gino's 'charm' and it this homo-erotic sub-text which also, in part, motivates the extended fight between the two men following the death of Gino's son. In strict narrative terms, Philip is not responsible for the death of the child (as it is Harriet who seized him). The struggle between the two men, therefore, works less in terms of dramatic necessity than as a kind of emotional catharsis. Although violent, it is also intense and intimate and hints at the kinds of passions for which Philip has been yearning. In this way, the conventional heterosexual romance that the film refuses seems to reappear, albeit in displaced form, in the form of the relationship between Philip and Gino (and, in doing so, to add another level to the film's critique of English repression and emotional dishonesty).

A similar disruption of the dominant discourse of heterosexual romance is also apparent in *A Room with a View* in which, as Claire Monk suggests, Freddy (Rupert Graves again) acts as a kind of 'double' for his sister Lucy, and acts out some of the impulses to which she cannot yet give free rein.[68] This can be seen, for example, in the pond (or 'sacred lake') scene in which George, Freddy, and Mr Beebe all bathe together. It is, of course, a scene which has clear links with the overriding themes of the film, signifying a certain freedom from restraint (Lucy poignantly tells Cecil that she herself bathed here until she was found out) and an opposition to the primness of Cecil and Mrs Honeychurch who, along with Lucy, unexpectedly come across them. However, the scene also goes well beyond these meanings, letting the scene run much longer than is dramatically necessary and, through lighting and composition, investing it with a clear erotic dimension (which is confirmed by the presence of Simon Callow whose cavorting with the younger men might otherwise seem odd behaviour for a vicar).

---

[68] Monk, 'Sexuality and the Heritage', 34.

PLATE 4. Opening up an ambivalence around sexuality: Rupert Graves, Simon Callow, and Julian Sands in *A Room With A View*

For Hutchings, while such connotations may be clearly 'readable', they don't seem 'to have any definite function' and seem to generate an 'awkwardness' about sexuality in such films.[69] In a sense, this is right. Judged in conventional terms, the bathing scene (like similar scenes in *Where Angels*) lacks adequate integration with the rest of the film and sets up a certain disjunction of tone and meaning. However, at the same time, it is precisely the resulting 'awkwardness' around sexuality that makes the scene so interesting. For while, at one level, the film may be seen simply to be reproducing a dominant notion of male hetero-sexuality in the way that it counterpoints the virile sexuality of George to the effeminacy of Cecil, the intimations of homo-erotic desires which run through the pond scene also disturb the film's predominantly heterosexual interests and complicate (as in *Where Angels*) the film's relationship to heterosexual romance. While this may not add up to an entirely coherent counter-discourse, it does at least open up a degree of ambivalence around sexuality, intimating a degree of fluidity (or perfomativity) around the ways in which sexual 'identities' are then occupied.[70]

[69]   Hutchings, 'A Disconnected View: Forster, Modernity and Film' , 224.

[70]   The idea of sex as 'a performatively enacted signification' has, of course, been influentially argued by Judith Butler, *Gender Trouble: Feminism and the Subversion of Identity* (New York: Routledge, 1990), 33.

Conclusion: The Heritage Film and Sexual Politics _____

For Claire Monk, the emphasis, in critical writing, upon the heritage film's relationship to national identity (which has partly been inherited from more general debates about heritage culture) has obscured 'the sexual politics and pleasures' which these films may be seen to provide.[71] There are, obviously, a number of interrelated issues at stake here. It has been suggested, for example, that dislike of the heritage film may be linked to a traditional suspicion of texts which primarily appeal to women (or gay men). In changing his mind about heritage culture, Raphael Samuel, for example, suggests that what he calls 'heritage-baiting' is 'an almost exclusively male sport' and that it may be the 'manifestation of femininity' in heritage culture which arouses most 'manly' ire.[72] In the same way, it has also been suggested that criticism of the heritage film may neglect the significance of the heritage film for women. Thus, just as feminism has found interest in traditional 'feminine' genres such as the 'woman's film', so the heritage film has been seen to possess a special appeal for women. The criticism of these films, it is suggested, has been too cognitive in orientation and has therefore neglected the sensuous appeal of these films and their appeal to a specifically 'feminine' reading competence. Thus Richard Dyer has argued that the 'sensuousness' of the films' attention to 'fixtures and fittings' may be seen to possess an 'iconographic expressivity' which typically requires 'the skilled reading of a female spectator'.[73] Claire Monk also argues that the de-centred narrative structures and spectatorial pleasures of the heritage film, in which it is men—rather than women—who are looked at, may be designated as 'feminine' in character.[74]

However, while it is probable (if not clearly established) that the heritage film holds a greater appeal for women than (straight) men, it is not always evident what follows from this.[75] There is a danger that a conventional (or essentialist) notion of the 'feminine' (an interest in clothes and appearance, for example) is simply validated (or claimed as 'subversive') without a critical inspection of how this 'feminine' appeal is ideologically mobilized. Stella Bruzzi, for example, argues that it is necessary to distinguish the different uses to which period costumes may be put and to recognize that these are not all equally 'progressive'. So

---

[71] Claire Monk, 'Sexuality and the Heritage', *Sight and Sound*, (Oct. 1995), 34. Monk develops a similar argument in 'The British "Heritage Film" and its Critics', *Critical Survey*, vol. 7, no. 2 (1995).

[72] Samuel, *Theatres of Memory*, 272.

[73] Dyer, *Encyclopedia of European Cinema*, 204.

[74] Monk, *Sex, Politics and the Past: Merchant Ivory, The Heritage Film and its Critics in 1980s and 1990s Britain*, chap. 4.

[75] It is interesting to note, for example, that research by Cinema and Video Industry Audience Research (CAVIAR) indicates that the audience for *Howards End* was fairly evenly split in terms of gender (49% male and 51% female). More striking is that while, in 1992, the over-35s accounted for only 19% of the cinemagoing audience they constituted 48% of the audience for *Howards End*. See *CAVIAR 10 vol. 1 Cinema, Report of Findings* (Feb. 1993), 12.

while the performative role of clothes may, in some films, challenge the fixities of social and sexual identities, this is not always the case, and, in heritage films such as *Howards End* and *Sense and Sensibility*, she argues clothes are simply subordinated to the demands of 'historical and literary authenticity'.[76] Similarly, the identification of the heritage film with a discursively constructed 'female' spectator or 'feminine' reading competence can lead to problematically unitary and ahistorical conceptualizations of *the* female spectator and 'subversive' feminine pleasures. In Monk's argument, for example, the theorization of the female spectator is linked to the heritage film's departure from the norms of male spectatorship as accounted for by 1970s film theory (and especially the work of Laura Mulvey). However, the 'transgressiveness' of the heritage film is then read against the spectatorial relations characteristic of certain kinds of 'classical' films of the past rather than in relation to the more plural forms of female spectatorship characteristic of contemporary media culture in which the 'taboos' against female and gay looking are much less apparent.[77]

A similar point may also be made in relation to the actual representations of women and sexuality that different films provide. Jeffrey Richards, for example, argues that criticisms of the 1980s heritage films as backward-looking and reactionary are misplaced. These films, he suggests, are 'profoundly subversive' insofar as they provide a 'comprehensive critique of the ethic of restraint, repression and the stiff upper lip'.[78] However, while this 'subversiveness' may be apparent in comparison to earlier British films from the 1940s and 1950s (*Brief Encounter* and *Woman in a Dressing Gown* are Richards's two examples), it is much less obviously so in the context of 1980s British filmmaking. In this respect, the British heritage film of the 1980s circulated within a culture in which much more open and questioning representations of gender and sexuality (including lesbianism which has generally been absent from the heritage film) were possible. As such, in comparison with many contemporary British films, the representations of gender and sexuality which the heritage film provided were often timid and restrained. So, while the emphasis upon the 'femininity', or potential 'queerness', of the heritage film may serve as a warning against too easy a dismissal of certain kinds of film, it still leaves open to question the extent to which different films may be seen to have opened up issues of gender and sexual identity. This is a particular issue for the way in which the heritage film deals with the representation of Empire and it is to this issue that I will now turn.

[76] *Undressing Cinema: Clothing and Identity in the Movies* (London: Routledge, 1997), 36.
[77] Monk, 'The British "Heritage Film" and its Critics', 120.
[78] Jeffrey Richards, *Films and British National Identity: From Dickens to Dad's Army* (Manchester: Manchester University Press, 1997), 169.

chapter 5

Films and Empire _____

The Raj Revival

If the heritage film more generally displayed an interest in issues of gender and sexuality, this was also so of the imperial heritage film, especially those concerned with India. What became labelled as a 'Raj revival' was a phenomenon of the early 1980s and coincided with the television transmission of *The Jewel in the Crown* and *The Far Pavilions* in 1984 and the arrival of *Heat and Dust* (1982) and *A Passage to India* (1984) in the cinemas. The appearance of such material also provoked a certain amount of debate concerning its ideological significance. The most influential contribution was that of Salman Rushdie who decried the 'refurbishment of the Empire's tarnished image' and 'recrudescence of imperialist ideology' which he argued such work displayed. 'The continuing decline, the growing poverty, and the meanness of spirit of much of Thatcherite Britain', he argued, 'encourages many Britons to turn their eyes nostalgically to the lost hour of their precedence . . . Britain is in danger of entering a condition of cultural psychosis, in which it begins once again to strut and to posture like a great power while, in fact, its power diminishes every year.' The 'rise of Raj revisionism' characteristic of this material, he concluded, was 'the artistic counterpart to the rise of conservative ideologies in modern Britain'.[1] However, if the Raj revival was encouraging nostalgia for a lost empire, it was also doing so, like the heritage film more generally, in an ambivalent way.

The Jewel in the Crown, *Heat and Dust*, and *A Passage to India* are all set at a time of imperial decline and, as Farrukh Dhondy suggests, allow 'the British to be self-obsessed and self-examining'.[2] As such, these films do not straightforwardly endorse the empire but reveal a liberal concern to show up its idiocies, injustices, and, to a limited extent, even its brutalities. However, as with other heritage films, there is also a sense in which the heritage conventions of seductive visual style and visually pleasing iconography undercut the criticism of empire contained within the plots. Thus, for Harlan Kennedy, the British films about

[1] Salman Rushdie, 'Outside the Whale', in *Imaginary Homelands: Essays and Criticism, 1981–1991* (London: Penguin, 1991), 91–2.
[2] Farrukh Dhondy, 'All the Raj', *New Socialist*, no. 16 (Mar./Apr. 1984), 46.

Empire represent 'double-standard moviemaking' at its best: offering 'severe reproaches to British history', on the one hand, but investing Empire with considerable visual 'glamour', on the other.[3]

This process may be seen at work in David Lean's version of *A Passage to India*. E. M. Forster's novel begins with a description of the city of Chandrapore which he describes as 'nothing extraordinary'.[4] As Norman Page suggests, there is a deliberate attempt in this opening chapter to avoid a suggestion of 'glamour and picturesqueness' which is, of course, typical of the novel's ironic attitude as a whole.[5] The film, however, begins differently and adds a number of scenes which pull in a different direction. Thus, unlike the novel, the film begins in England with the purchase of tickets for India by Adela Quested (Judy Davis). This scene not only places the focus of the film more firmly than in the novel on Adela (with whom the film also ends) but also helps to construct a strong sense of contrast between a drab and wet England and a bright and visually spectacular India (anticipated in Adela's look at the picture of the Marabar caves hanging in the sea company offices). The scene in England is then followed by the arrival of Adela and Mrs Moore (Peggy Ashcroft) in Bombay where they are greeted by the spectacle of the Bombay Gate, the 'Gateway of India', and a full-dress procession for the Indian Viceroy, who has also been on board their ship (the film also adds a further welcoming party, and accompanying ceremony, for the Turtons at Chandrapore). However, unlike the novel's concern to subvert romantic preconceptions of India, the film here gives them full rein and is even prepared to refashion the 'real' India to meet these requirements. Hence, carefully framed shots of the Gateway are edited together with footage shot elsewhere (New Delhi, the Malabar coast) in order to create the effect which the real location, surrounded by a harbour, failed to provide.[6] The point here is not that this licence with actual geography undermines any claims to 'realism' which the film may profess but that it lays bare the pictorialist impulse governing the film's staging of scenes and thus the investment of the Raj with the very glamour and picturesqueness which the novel had shunned. As Arthur Lindley suggests, 'virtually everything and everyone associated with the Raj is larger, handsomer, younger and/or more highly polished' than in the novel with the result that 'while we are invited to share in the novel's verbal criticism of the Raj, we are also implicitly encouraged to enjoy it as a show'.[7] Thus, even in the scene of the 'bridge party', which one critic describes as the film's 'satirical highpoint',

---

[3] Harlan Kennedy, 'The Brits Have Gone Nuts', *Film Comment* (July–Aug. 1985), 52.

[4] E. M. Forster, *A Passage to India* (Harmondsworth: Penguin, 1981, orig. 1924), 31.

[5] Norman Page, *E. M. Forster* (Basingstoke: Macmillan, 1987), 98.

[6] David Lean, 'Return Passage', Interview, *Stills* (March 1985), 30. In the same way, the Marabar Caves, described as quite commonplace in the novel, were dynamited by Lean to achieve a more spectacular effect just as a Bangalore mountain was chosen for the backdrop to the visually splendid journey to the caves.

[7] Arthur Lindley, 'Raj as Romance/Raj as Parody: Lean's and Forster's Passage to India', *Literature/Film Quarterly*, vol. 20 no. 1 (1992), 62. It is, therefore, unsurprising to learn that Lean deliberately sought to tone down some of Forster's complaints about the English. See Harlan Kennedy, 'I'm a Picture Chap' (Interview), *Film Comment* (Jan.–Feb. 1985), 32.

PLATE 5. The Raj as visual spectacle: *A Passage to India*

the absurdities of the occasion are staged with such an obvious relish and taste
for the pictorial that it is difficult to read the scene as one which is whole-
heartedly critical.[8]

A similar emphasis on visual display is also evident in *Heat and Dust*.
Although based on a novel by the film's scriptwriter, Ruth Prawer Jhabvala, the
film goes much further than the novel in making its story spectacular. Scenes
which are not in the novel (such as the Derva ceremony at the film's beginning)
are added for visual rather than primarily dramatic purpose. Other scenes—
such as when Olivia (Greta Scacchi) and Mrs Crawford (Susan Fleetwood) visit
the Begum (Madhur Jaffrey) or when the Nawab (Shashi Kapoor) hosts a banquet for the English—which are contained in the novel are greatly extended in
order to enhance their visual impact. And, just as *A Passage* lessens the more
unattractive aspects of Forster's portrait of India, so *Heat and Dust* softens the
original novel's treatment of characters and makes both Douglas (Christopher
Cazenove) and the Nawab more glamorous. The result is a film that was widely
praised for its visual richness. Philip Strick described the film as 'stunningly
photographed . . . beautifully costumed and set, with some tantalizing glimpses
of an extraordinary landscape' while Michael Wood went so far as to argue that
the film was actually '*about* its costumes and its setting': 'dusty plains, tombs,
shrines, palaces, reservoirs, bungalows. Ceiling fans, banquets, elaborate cere-
monies, the infinite wardrobe of the prince.'[9] However, while these remarks are
apt they do, of course, refer to only a part of the film.

For, unlike most of the heritage films, *Heat and Dust* is not set exclusively in
the past but intertwines two parallel stories: that of Olivia in the 1920s and that

[8] Michael Sragow, 'David Lean's Right of "Passage" ', *Film Comment* (Jan.–Feb. 1985), 26.
[9] Philip Strick, *Monthly Film Bulletin* (Jan. 1983), 15 and Michael Wood, *New Society* (10 Feb. 1983),
226.

of Anne (Julie Christie), her great-niece, in the 1980s who is partly retracing her forebear's steps.

However, if the plot of the film is concerned, almost laboriously, to suggest parallels between past and present it is also the case that, at the level of visual style and iconography, the film is concerned to indicate contrast. Thus, the bungalow where Olivia lived has become a government office while the Nawab's palace has been turned into a shabby museum. The grandeur which was associated with both the Nawab and the English colonialists has ended and been replaced by the noise, bustle, and turmoil of modern India. The visual techniques employed to show the old and the new reinforce this sense of difference. As Walter Lassally, the film's cameraman, reports, there was a deliberate effort to differentiate the two periods in terms of art direction, lighting, and camera movement. The modern sequences, he points out, were designed to be 'more strident in both colour and movement' than the scenes in the past which were intended to be 'gentle and pastel' (an effect achieved, in part, through a use of silk gauzes).[10] There is also a contrast in the use of the camera: many of the modern scenes have been shot with a handheld camera and a minimum of rehearsal (as when Anne is walking in the bazaar) whereas scenes in the past, in line with heritage conventions, have been shot using elaborate, and well-rehearsed, camera movements (such as the lengthy tracking shots which occur in the banquet scene). As a result, the film, as Andrew Robinson suggests, clearly demonstrates 'a nostalgic ambivalence towards the British period'.[11] Like *A Passage*, the past may be attacked for the failures of understanding and restrictions which it imposes, but it is also invested with a glamour which is apparently absent from modern-day independent India.

It is, of course, the case that the film more clearly draws attention to the dangers of nostalgia, or the romanticization of the past, than other heritage films. This is done by drawing attention to both the confessed nostalgia of characters such as Harry (Nickolas Grace) (who happily declares that it is 'not like it was' and tells Anne of her great-aunt's 'romantic' behaviour) and the foregrounding of Anne's efforts to reconstruct the past from her great-aunt's diaries and letters. However, the representation of the past which the film provides is not overtly marked as 'subjective' and, according to the conventions of 'classic realism', assumes an 'objective' status which is evidently independent of the recall of Olivia and Harry (who are not involved in some of the scenes shown) and the possible imaginings of Anne. In this respect, if the past is to be regarded as one which has been 'constructed', either through memory or fantasy, it is also a past which exceeds the consciousness of the characters who have been responsible for 'constructing' it. In this way, the film demonstrates a limited self-reflexivity which, like the heritage film more generally, permits enjoyment of the past while simultaneously encouraging a degree of knowingness towards it.

[10] Walter Lassally, *Itinerant Cameraman* (London: John Murray, 1987), 193.
[11] Andrew Robinson, *Films and Filming* (Jan. 1983), 21.

Orientalism

This element of nostalgia for the glamour of the colonial past which both *A Passage to India* and *Heat and Dust* contain may also be linked to a certain fascination with the 'other'. As with the heritage films previously discussed, both films display an interest in the clash of cultures and the possibility of overcoming social and cultural barriers. While, it has been suggested that this may encourage fantasies of the working class (*Maurice*) or stereotypes of other cultures (especially Italians as in *A Room with a View* or *Where Angels Fear to Tread*), the European encounter with India mobilizes particularly potent meanings. The history of empire and colonialism has not simply involved military and economic exploitation but also the cultural production of meanings and perceptions which have justified and supported the relations of domination characteristic of the imperial enterprise.[12] For Said, the colonial image of India has been inextricably bound up with what he calls 'orientalism' (which predates colonialism but was none the less mobilized in its service). The Orient, he argues, occupies 'a special place in European Western experience' and 'Orientalism' may be defined as 'a Western style for dominating, restructuring, and having authority over the Orient'.[13] For Said, Orientalism also provides the West with the source of 'one of its deepest and most recurring images of the Other'.[14] This 'otherness' may be figured in different and even inconsistent ways (such that the Oriental may be seen to be both a repository of violence and spirituality, for example) but what remains consistent is the 'flexible positional superiority' which it provides the European (or Westerner) who may enter 'a whole series of possible relationships with the Orient' without losing 'the relative upper hand'.[15] It is also this 'otherness' of the Orient which provides much of its fascination for the Westerner. If the Raj films indulge a taste for a glamorous imperial past, they also open up to the Western gaze the exotic 'otherness' of the Orient in which its characters are placed. Indeed, both *A Passage to India* and *Heat and Dust* display a further double-standard, in this respect. Both deal with characters who are caught up in romantic fantasies of

---

[12] Edward Said distinguishes 'imperialism'—'the practice, the theory, and the attitudes of a dominating metropolitan centre ruling a distant territory'—from 'colonialism' which involves the implanting of settlements on distant territories'. In this respect, 'direct colonialism has largely ended' while 'imperialism' continues 'in a kind of general cultural sphere as well as in specific political, ideological, economic, and social practices'. See *Culture and Imperialism* (London: Vintage, 1994), 8.

[13] Said, *Orientalism* (Harmondsworth: Penguin, 1985, orig. 1978), 1 and 3. It is, of course, precisely a feature of 'orientalism' that it homogenizes (and essentializes) the vast cultural diversity of those countries—from the Eastern Mediterranean to South-East Asia—which are regarded as 'oriental'. It is, none the less, important to recognize the historically specific forms through which orientalist discourse operates. For discussion of the extent to which Said's own analysis may relie upon a degree of ahistorical totalizing (of both East and West), see Dennis Porter, '*Orientalism* and its Problems', in Francis Barker *et al.* (eds.), *The Politics of Theory* (Colchester: University of Essex, 1983), and Aijaz Ahmad, '*Orientalism* and After: Ambivalence and Metropolitan Location in the Work of Edward Said', in *In Theory: Classes, Nations, Literatures* (London: Verso, 1992).

[14] Said, *Orientalism*, 1.   [15] Ibid. 7.

the 'other' which ultimately lead to disappointment. At the same time, the films themselves offer up exactly the same exoticism as a major source of voyeuristic pleasure for the audiences to whom they are addressed.

It is possible to elaborate further on the 'orientalist' dimensions of the East–West encounter which these films display. The first point is a relatively obvious one. In these films it is the Western response to the East which is deemed of most significance and, even when this may involve criticism of colonial relations, it is none the less a response mediated through a European consciousness. In this way, whatever the stance adopted towards colonialism, it is still assumed, as Said suggests, that 'the source of the world's significant action and life is in the West'.[16] Thus, while both *A Passage to India* and *Heat and Dust* include Indian characters of dramatic importance, they are rarely involved in scenes which don't include Europeans and there is little structuring of an inward relationship with them (indeed, it is precisely the 'unknowability' of the Nawab's true motivations in *Heat and Dust* which is established as a plot enigma). This can then lead to a discrepancy in the manner in which Eastern and Western characters are portrayed. In the case of the Raj films, psychological complexity and depth are much more likely to be bestowed upon the British characters than the Indian. This is most apparent in *A Passage to India* where there is a considerable simplification of the Indian characters in comparison to the original novel. Aziz (Victor Bannerjee) is shorn of many of his significant features (his Islamic religion, his subsequent conversion to Indian nationalism) and rendered partly comic (so eager to please his English guests that he is prepared to risk life by clambering along a train as it crosses an enormously high bridge). Similarly, the representation of Godbole, the Hindu professor (played by a white Alec Guinness) reduces his character to a banal stereotype of Oriental inscrutability. As Robyn Wiegman suggests, such 'role stratification' as this not only reproduces a racial hierarchy by denying non-white actors major film roles but also reproduces a form of ethnocentrism whereby white actors may 'occupy and signify the full range of humanity' in a way that non-white actors may not.[17]

If the narrative organization of the films around European characters encourages a privileging of a Eurocentric perspective, this is reinforced by an organization of the films' system of looks. For Higson, it is a characteristic of the heritage film that its gaze is often not identified with character point-of-view but with an anonymous 'public gaze'.[18] However, in the Raj films this notion of a shared 'public gaze' becomes problematic insofar as the spectacle which the film provides is offered for the benefit of a Western rather than Eastern public and is generally encoded in a language of the exotic which implies an observer

---

[16] Id., *Culture and Imperialism*, p. xxi.

[17] Robyn Wiegman, 'Race, Ethnicity and Film', in John Hill and Pamela Church Gibson (eds.), *The Oxford Guide to Film Studies* (Oxford: Oxford University Press, 1998), 164. She derives the term 'role stratification' from Eugene Franklin Wong, *On Visual Media Racism: Asians in the American Motion Pictures* (New York: Arno Press, 1978).

[18] Andrew Higson, 'Re-presenting the National Past', in Lester Friedman (ed.), *British Cinema and Thatcherism* (London: UCL Press, 1993), 117.

for whom the spectacle is assumed to be 'other'. Moreover, when we are invited to identify with characters' points-of-view it is characteristically European eyes with which we are asked to look. Higson suggests that 'the private gaze of the dramatis personae is reserved for romance: they almost never admire the quality of their surroundings'.[19] This is much less true, however, of the imperial films. In the case of *A Passage to India*, for example, the conventional romance between individuals is absent and, as will be argued, Adela's desiring gaze becomes focused upon an eroticized India instead. More generally, the view provided of India does tend to be shared with characters, very often with those who are new to the country and thus can perform the function of 'guide' (or substitute) for the spectator. Thus, in *A Passage to India*, there are a number of occasions in which we are invited to gaze with the English characters as they observe their new surroundings (e.g. when the women arrive at Bombay, when Ronny drives Adela and Mrs Moore through the market at Chandrapore, when Mrs Moore looks at the Ganges or Adela observes Chandrapore through binoculars). There is, however, a certain irony in evidence here. For, at the level of plot, there is an overt theme of the 'alien' character of India and the impossibility for the European of truly understanding or giving adequate representation to it. As Lindley points out of Forster's novel, 'India persistently defeats the impulse to reduce and tidy' and denies 'Western ideas of form, proportion, emphasis'.[20] In the film, however, whatever the characters' anxieties concerning what they see, the images themselves still demonstrate a pictorial control based upon conventional ideas of form and proportion. Thus, even in the scene prior to Adela's 'breakdown' in the cave, the final precipitating factor is a beautifully framed shot of Aziz, standing outside of the cave. It is, of course, by now a standard argument that the 'castration anxiety' aroused in the male spectator by the representation of woman in classic Hollywood cinema is characteristically resolved through fetishistic disavowal. In the same way, it is possible to argue that the anxiety which India provokes for the Western characters who struggle to make sense of it is also disavowed through the fetishistic pictorialism with which the Indian scenery is displayed (and which offers precisely the 'mastery' that is otherwise under threat).

Metaphors of Sexual Encounter

This issue of the ability of Europeans to make sense of India may also be related to another significant aspect of these films' treatment of the East–West encounter: the trope of sexual attraction which has been used to explore it. This is not, perhaps, surprising. As Jordan and Weedon indicate, the image of the East as 'a site of eroticism, decadence and sexual gratification' has had a lengthy history, stretching as far back as the Middle Ages, and this has formed a key

---

[19] Ibid.   [20] Lindley, 'Raj as Romance/Raj as Parody', 64.

element of the exoticism with which the East has been associated.[21] However, it is a trope that has also been subject to historical (and geographical) variation and the way in which the relationship between East and West has been imagined in sexual terms has not remained the same. In an unsigned discussion of 'sex and the Indian novel' in the journal *Cencrastus*, the author suggests three main ways in which this sexual metaphor has been employed in Anglo-Indian literature.[22] The first involves the figuration of the West as a man and the East as a woman, especially in the form of a bride who accepts the authority of a European husband. The second involves an attempt to reimagine the relationship between East and West in terms of male friendship while the third reverses the original version of the metaphor so that the East becomes represented by a man and the West by a woman.

These different inflections of the metaphor may be related to a changing relationship to the imperial or colonial project. The first of these—the West as a man and the East as a woman—is characteristically linked to a conquest, or civilizing, narrative involving an endorsement of imperial and patriarchal relations of power. The second two usually entail a more ironic or distanced attitude towards imperial relations. In the 1980s the first of these could only be mobilized with some difficulty. Thus, in the televization of M. M. Kaye's popular romance *The Far Pavilions*, Ash (Ben Cross), the white colonial hero of the original novel, is identified not simply as having been brought up amongst Indians but as actually being part-Indian himself. His relationship with the partly white Indian princess, Anjuli (Amy Irving), is therefore stripped of much of its former imperialist connotations. Indeed, rather than imposing order on the East, Ash's involvement with Anjuli leads him to resign from the British army and, in effect, 'go native' (or, more probably, go into exile given that both he and Anjuli are now effectively outcasts from their respective communities).[23] A similar threat to male, colonial order is also in evidence in *The Deceivers* (1988). In this case, however, the Eastern woman plays the role, not of the bride, but that of the dangerous seductress.

---

[21] Glenn Jordan and Chris Weedon, *Cultural Politics: Class, Gender and Race in the Postmodern World* (Oxford: Blackwell, 1995), 263. Marianna Torgovnick notes also, in relation to her discussion of the 'primitive', how readily 'global politics, the dance of colonizer and colonized, becomes sexual politics', in *Gone Primitive: Savage Intellects, Modern Lives* (Chicago: University of Chicago Press, 1990), 17.

[22] Anon., 'Sex and the Indian Novel', *Cencrastus*, no. 25 (Spring 1987), 34–40.

[23] The couple's romantic reunion at the end of the film (following Ash's rescue of Anjuli from death by suttee) is linked by the film to an uncovering of Ash's 'true self'—a 'third person' who is neither British nor Indian. However, this is undermined by the film's inability to find any—hybrid—space, other than apparent limbo, that Ash and Anjuli might then occupy as well as the visibly 'inauthentic' use it makes of white actors (not just Ben Cross and Amy Irving but also Christopher Lee and Rossano Brazzi). In her discussion of Rudyard Kipling's *Kim* (on which *The Far Pavilions* may be seen to have drawn), Anne McClintock argues that the ability of the main character to 'pass' as Indian does not destabilize colonial categories but signals the universalized 'privilege of whiteness'. See *Imperial Leather: Race, Gender and Sexuality in the Colonial Contest* (New York: Routledge, 1995), 70. In the same way, in *The Far Pavilions*, the ability of both the character of Ash and the actor performing the role to 'pass' as Indian not only prevents the film from being able to say anything significant about 'race relations' (or ethnic hybridity) but also reproduces, twice over, the 'racial' hierarchy that the drama wants to question.

Although produced by Ismail Merchant, this film deviates considerably from the norms of the heritage film. Its source is more popular than 'literary' (a John Masters novel), it has few recognized 'theatrical' actors and is unusually explicit in its portrait of action and violence (its use of a story involving the Thuggee cult had, in fact, been anticipated by the 1959 Hammer horror *The Stranglers of Bombay*). It is set in 1825 and concerns the encounter between the 'resident collector' for the British East India Company, William Savage (Pierce Brosnan) and the Thugs, or Deceivers, who strangle their victims in the name of the goddess Kali. It is, however, an encounter which leads to the collapse of Savage's certainties and initial moral uprightness. Following his decision to infiltrate the Thuggee cult, he is led into an 'exotic' world in which murder and sexual plea-sure are intertwined. According to Hussein (Saeed Jaffrey), a former member of the cult, 'Kali is beautiful . . . more beautiful than any woman' and 'to know her is to know ecstasy'. This then becomes explicit in a key scene in which Savage makes love to an Indian woman, whose image becomes confused with that of Savage's wife and Gopal's 'widow'. The three women then blend into one to cast a six-armed shadow representative of the Eastern goddess.

Two points are of note, in this respect. In the first case, it may be seen how the film deploys the imagery of a violent and eroticized East which the Westerner proves unable to resist. Although this conforms to orientalist preconceptions of Eastern indiscipline, it also suggests how this is also the projection of the Westerner's own repressed desires, and that the impulses to which Savage (note the name) gives way are within rather than without. It is, therefore, no accident that Savage, who is initially motivated by an apparently humane desire to pre-vent Gopal's 'widow' (Neena Gupta) from killing herself should end up fanta-sizing about her and murdering her husband.[24] Even though set in the early nineteenth century, the loss of self-control involved in Savage's immersion in the Thuggee cult also hints at a certain failure of the imperial enterprise. By the end of the film, Savage has returned to his own world but his former strength has deserted him. For Anne McClintock, the white man's ability to 'pass' as an Indian (in Kipling's *Kim*) signifies 'a reformed colonial control': 'the colonial . . . passes as Other the better to govern.'[25] In *The Deceivers*, however, Savage is enfeebled by his adoption of an Indian guise. At the film's end, he is seen sitting silently, his arm in a sling, and barely able to communicate to his wife. He then throws away the Christian cross, the symbol of the religion which he had ini-tially assured Hussein would protect him against the threat of Kali. In contrast to the colorial hero who is capable of imposing order upon the East, Savage has been rendered powerless by his encounter with India and the film itself begins to display a certain enquiring consciousness towards imperial rule, even though, in order to do so, it indulges in the very exoticism upon which the imperialist imagination has itself relied.

[24] The dramatic foregrounding of suttee in both *The Deceivers* and *The Far Pavilions* not only works to reproduce notions of the 'irrationalism' and 'barbarism' of the East but also permits another 'orien-talist' narrative trope of male colonial rescue.

[25] *Imperial Leather*, 70.

This more critical relationship to empire may be linked to the other permutations of the metaphor of sexual relations between East and West. As the author of 'Sex and the Indian Novel' suggests, it is Forster who is mainly responsible for the attempt to reimagine the relations between Britain and India in terms of 'a tender friendship between two men'.[26] This changing emphasis corresponds to a period of failing confidence in empire and an attempt to suggest a relationship based upon increased equality. Such a model is, of course, most evident in the relationship between Aziz and Fielding in Forster's *A Passage to India* but it is also found in the friendship between Ash and Wally (Benedict Taylor) in *The Far Pavilions* and in the (somewhat unclear) relationship between Harry and the Nawab in *Heat and Dust* Indeed, it has been suggested that the character of Harry was in part modelled on Forster, along with J. R. Ackerley, both of whom worked in India as private secretaries to Maharajahs. There is also a much darker echo of this relationship in *The Jewel in the Crown* in which the social 'upstart' Merrick expresses a perverse kinship with Indians through his sadistic homosexual encounters.

In many respects, it is the relationship between Aziz and Fielding (James Fox) that is central to *A Passage to India*. Unlike other representatives of the Raj, Fielding is alert to the absurdities of British rule and does not shun social contact with the Indians. Although his relationship with Aziz is not overtly sexual, it is one in which the noticeable intimacy of their relationship stands apart from all others in the film. Thus, just as Freddy had, on his first meeting with George, immediately invited him to bathe in *A Room with a View*, so Fielding's first meeting with Aziz in *A Passage* occurs when he is in the shower. Their conversation is immediately relaxed and informal and includes Aziz sitting on Fielding's bed. Fielding subsequently visits Aziz at his home. He too sits on the bed and engages in a discussion of love with Aziz. Fielding walks arm in arm with Aziz from the train following the incident at the Marabar caves ('I so wanted you', exclaims Aziz) and the camera lingers on Aziz applying make-up prior to Fielding's arrival after the trial. Richard Dyer suggests, however, that the film plays down 'the question of sexual feelings between men' and that it is difficult to tell whether such scenes as these are 'meant to have an erotic charge or not'.[27] While this may be so, it is also the case that it is the relationship between the two men that carries the greatest emotional weight within the film and which provides the final scenes with their most obvious justification.

Lean himself was not entirely happy with how he concluded the film and subsequently suggested that 'after the trial I should have just quickly tied up the loose ends and ended it'.[28] Given the film's much clearer focus on Adela than in the novel, this seems to make sense as once the trial is over she has little further dramatic role to play. Thus, most of what takes place following the trial concerns the relationship between the men. In a sense, this may be seen to follow

[26] 'Sex and the Indian Novel', 38.

[27] Richard Dyer, 'A Passage to India', *Marxism Today* (Apr. 1985), 43.

[28] Quoted in Stephen M. Silverman, *David Lean* (New York: Harry N. Abrams, 1989), 187.

classic romantic conventions: the two men are forced apart by the circumstances surrounding the trial but then are subsequently reunited ('he's come all
this way to find you', Godbole tells Aziz). By this time Fielding has, of course,
been provided with a wife, Stella, but the significance of this is downplayed (the
link with Mrs Moore notwithstanding). Stella is not permitted to speak and,
in an oblique acknowledgement of the film's subtext, is seen wearing a man's
hat, that Fielding has placed on her head, when the couple stop to observe the
Himalayas. It is also along these lines that the film's much-criticized ending may
be read. In the novel, the men are unable to regain their original relationship
and their horses symbolically swerve apart. In the film, the men do achieve
a degree of reconciliation and are seen to shake hands. While this has been
justified as a modern acknowledgement of India's independence, within the
terms of the film, it seems to have much more to do with the logic of personal
desire that has governed the two men's relationship and which therefore has
'required' what might otherwise have been a superfluous dramatic coda.

This does mean, of course, that there is then a minimization of the significance of the political divisions which continue to separate the men. In one
respect, this is the inevitable consequence of the film's more general adoption
of a more 'personalized' form of narration than the novel. However, it is also
connected to the choice of a relationship between men to symbolize the relationship between East and West. It has been suggested that one virtue of this
particular version of the sexual metaphor is that it does not depend upon 'a
perception of difference' but 'a recognition that they are both alike'.[29] However, against this, the weakness of this use of sexual metaphor is that the sense of
'likeness' which it suggests is only achieved by discounting, or rendering as less
important, the other signifiers of difference (of ethnicity, national allegiance,
religion, and so on) which necessarily cut across and complicate the idea of
comradeship amongst men. Thus, Edward Said complains of Forster's novel
that, for all its 'remarkable' qualities and ironies, it none the less 'founders on
the undodgeable facts of Indian nationalism' and inevitably plays down 'the
sense that India and Britain are opposed nations'.[30] If this is so of the novel, it
is even more clearly so of the film in which the personal drama may achieve a
certain resolution (in the form of displaced romance) but in which the larger
political one is necessarily left suspended.

The other aspect of this emphasis on the relationship between the men is
its implications for the representation of women. For Lindley, the relationship
between Aziz and Fielding, and the sense of connection which it involves, is
central to the novel insofar as it throws into relief not only the conceits of
colonialism but also the heterosexual assumptions (sexual fears of the threat
to white women from Indians) and practices (especially marriage) which collude with colonialism to restrict the ways in which the British and Indians
may relate. Thus, he suggests, 'heterosexual feeling . . . is presented throughout
the novel as a divisive force . . . that prevents men from connecting with other

---

[29] 'Sex and the Indian Novel', 36.   [30] Said, *Culture and Imperialism*, 245–6.

men'.[31] As a result, the novel throws up a number of unflattering portraits of women which carry over into the film. When Aziz and Mahmoud Ali (Art Malik) are knocked off their bicycles by the Turtons' car they decry the iniquities of the English, with Ali proclaiming that 'the women are worse'. Evidence of this is then provided by the snobbish and patronizing Mrs Turton (whom Adela describes as 'dreadful') and the equally unlikeable Mrs Callender (Ann Firbank) who first snubs Aziz and then goes off in his tonga. By the same token, Adela (who is described by Aziz as 'an awful old hag' in the novel) may also be seen to be an unsympathetic representative of colonial womanhood and is certainly the key character responsible for coming between Aziz and Fielding.[32] However, her representation is not entirely straightforward and the film does appear to show ambivalence towards her. This is the result of two factors: the association of Adela, along with Mrs Moore, with a certain scepticism towards colonialism and the investment of her relationship with India with a clear sexual dimension.

For if *A Passage to India* associates, in part, the excesses of colonial rule with the memsahib, it also allocates to women a more traditionally 'feminine' and enquiring consciousness which refuses to accept all the conventions of colonial behaviour.[33] This is most clearly exemplified in Mrs Moore who wishes to meet Indians 'as friends', counsels her son to be more Christian in his attitudes, strikes up an immediate rapport with Aziz despite his suspicions and is repelled by the treatment which he subsequently receives at the hands of the Raj. Adela shares with Mrs Moore this disdain for accepted conventions (worrying that Ronny (Nigel Havers) has become a sahib, 'ashamed' of the treatment of the Indians at the Bridge Party) and she too attempts to cross social and cultural barriers. She is keen to socialize with Aziz and Godbole (at Fielding's house) and to travel with Aziz to the Marabar caves despite Mrs Turton's warning, after Kipling, that 'East is East'. To this extent, she may be linked to other female characters in heritage films (such as Lucy in *Room with a View* or Lilia in *Where Angels Fear to Tread*) who wish to break out of their socially and culturally confined roles and establish new connections. However, in Adela's case, unlike Lucy's, the attempt at connection flounders. This failure is, in turn, linked to the desire for a cross-racial sexual encounter. Adela, in this respect, provides an embryonic embodiment of the third version of the sexual metaphor employed to signify relations between East and West: that of the East as a man and the West as a woman. A similar use of metaphor may also be found in *The Jewel in the Crown* (in which Daphne Manners falls for Hari Kumar) and *Heat and Dust* (in which both Olivia and

---

[31]   Lindley, 'Raj as Romance/Raj as Parody', 65. A part of the distance between the men at the novel's end, therefore, results from the fact that Fielding 'had thrown in his lot with Anglo-India by marrying a countrywoman and . . . was acquiring some of its limitations'. *A Passage to India*, 313.

[32]   *A Passage to India*, 252.

[33]   In his discussion of Paul Scott's *The Raj Quartet*, Bill Schwarz notes that 'the voices most deeply hostile to racial contempt and to the whole cultural apparatus of the Raj are generally female' in 'An Englishman Abroad . . . And At Home', *New Formations*, no. 17 (Summer 1992), 98. This point is developed by Richard Dyer in his discussion of the television adaptation of *The Raj Quartet*, *The Jewel in the Crown*. He argues that, while the women represent the 'conscience of empire', they are also 'impotent' and relegated to the status of 'doing nothing'. See 'There's Nothing I Can Do! Nothing!', in *White* (London: Routledge, 1997).

Anne pursue sexual encounters with Indian men). In *A Passage to India*, Adela does not actually have a sexual encounter with an Indian man but her enthusiasm for India none the less involves a sexual dimension and leads to her charge of rape against Aziz.[34] Indeed, it is the clear investment of Adela's desire to see the 'real India' with such a strong erotic charge which marks one of the most significant differences between the film and novel (and which, in a sense, 'straightens' out some of the novel's latent homo-eroticism).

It has been a commonplace to criticize the film for its removal of a number of political and religious elements which were in the novel and Lean himself has admitted his determination to streamline the plot and make it more 'personal'.[35] A key aspect of this process has been to interpret Adela's relationship to India in much more explicitly sexual terms. This is clearly signposted from an early stage when Adela and Mrs Moore share the train journey to Chandrapore with the Turtons. Mrs Turton informs Adela that Ronny has become a 'proper sahib' and the disappointment clearly registers on Adela's face. A throbbing sound is heard on the soundtrack before the film cuts to her view from the window and a shot of the river below. For Laura Donaldson, this sequence may be seen to involve a metonymic displacement of Adela's desires from Ronny onto 'India'.[36] However, given that Adela (who has not yet committed to marrying Ronny) has already been seen to gaze longingly at the pictures of India at the shipping company's offices, it may be more accurate to see the scene as giving notice of a growing sense that Ronnie is unable to satisfy the desires which Adela's yearning for 'adventure' in India involves. Thus, when she arrives in Chandrapore he kisses her chastely on the cheek. Later when he knocks at her bedroom door to wish her goodnight, he does not enter the room but simply leaves a disappointed Adela to study her own reflection in the mirror. Subsequently at dinner, Mrs Moore suggests that 'too much fuss is made about marriage' and that despite 'century after century of carnal embracement we're still no nearer understanding one another'. She then gets up to go, leaving a bemused Ronny and Adela sitting, firmly apart, divided by a candle placed centre frame on the table. This reference to 'carnal embracement' (which occurs much earlier than in the novel) then leads directly to the scene in which the link between Adela's unsatisfied sexual longings and their projection onto India becomes most explicit.

During a bicycle ride, she comes across a hidden temple containing explicitly erotic statuary. She gazes upon these with some fascination before fleeing from

---

[34] To some extent, the eroticization of the women's relationship with India may be linked to their marginalized relationship to the masculinist project of colonial rule and their resulting inability, as Dyer suggests, to do anything. In this respect, their role in India is less to 'act' than to 'experience' (the injustices of empire, the exoticism of place and its seductive allure). As Sara Mills observes of women's travel writing in the nineteenth century, travel involved less 'an adventure where things happened' than a 'mental journey', an encounter with places 'where physical sensations were noted' and 'certain thoughts were experienced'. See 'Discourses of Difference', *Cultural Studies*, vol. 4 no. 1 (1990), 132.

[35] Quoted in Rushdie, 'Outside the Whale', 91.

[36] Laura E. Donaldson, *Decolonizing Feminisms: Race, Gender and Empire-Building* (London: Routledge, 1992), 95. This interpretation rather too firmly anchors the meaning of the images in explicitly sexual terms—the imagery of light on water, for example, becomes a motif even more strongly associated with Mrs Moore (at the mosque and at her death) when it assumes spiritual connotations.

a group of monkeys who suddenly appear (like monsters from the id) at the top of the temple. This scene not only reinforces an image of India as 'exotic' and sexually dangerous but also gives expression to Adela's own unacknowledged sexual desires. She attempts to suppress these by changing her mind about marriage to Ronny (a decision in the novel associated with the unexplained accident in the Nawab's car and hence without a clear sexual connotation). However, at her own admission, 'nothing has really changed' and we see her gaze again at her image in the mirror as she had done on the night of her arrival at Chandrapore. Adela's sleep is then disturbed by memories of the statues while a cut from a shot of her in bed to a scene involving Aziz in his (looking at photographs of women in a magazine) sets up an association between them. This becomes even clearer in the scene at the Caves when Adela asks Aziz about love and marriage and apparently transposes her sexual longings onto him. In this way, her lack of sexual fulfilment and fascination with India finally merge in the scene in the cave which results in the charge of rape against Aziz. As a result of this careful plotting of events, what remains mysterious and, to some degree, uncertain in the novel becomes readily explicable in the film in terms of Adela's sexual hysteria.

For Laura Kipnis, this sexual hysteria represents a 'pathology' which the film deploys to lay the blame for colonialism upon women. The 'ideological project' of the film, she suggests, is 'to disavow the moral culpability for a tainted history and to sanitize that history by re-enacting colonialism as a female disease and thus confer responsibility onto the female'.[37] However, while it is clear that Adela's excessive sexual imaginings lead to the charade of colonial justice which follows her charge of rape, it is not so evident that colonialism should then be read as straightforwardly a female pathology. If a burden of blame falls upon the women in the Raj films it is less because they embody colonialism (although there are some who do) than fail to uphold it because of a failure to accept its conventions. This is a theme which becomes even more explicit in *Heat and Dust* in which Olivia is clearly transgressing what is acceptable to the English. In a sense, the women in the Raj films endanger British rule both because, as Mrs Moore, they have doubts about its moral basis and begin to question its legitimacy and because their attraction to Indians, or willingness to befriend them, upsets clear-cut divisions and weakens the British ability to rule. Women, in this respect, may be seen less to epitomize colonialism than to be putting it in jeopardy. As Lean himself so bluntly put it: 'It's a well-known saying that the women lost us the Empire. It's true.'[38]

The significance of the increased sexualization of Adela in *A Passage* may therefore be read somewhat differently. Hysteria is, of course, a common feature of the woman's film and there is a sense in which the organization of the film in terms of Adela's narrative trajectory has meant that the film is more clearly structured around female desire than in the novel. In this respect, the film centres upon a female protagonist who is the subject of desire but not its object

[37] Laura Kipnis, '"The Phantom Twitchings of an Amputated Limb": Sexual Spectacle in the Post-Colonial Epic', *Wide Angle*, vol. 11 no. 4 (Oct. 1989), 50.

[38] Quoted in Stephen M. Silverman, *David Lean*, 186.

(despite Lean's efforts to make Adela more attractive than in the novel). However, as in the woman's film, these desires are problematic and liable to frustration.[39] As with many heroines of the woman's film, Adela is confronted with a set of dilemmas with which she is unable to cope. This involves, not a choice between two kinds of men (or suitors), but between two kinds of experience. On the one hand, Ronny offers a dull and sexless existence as a memsahib; on the other, India, as a displaced object of desire, offers the excitement which the prospect of marriage to Ronny lacks. However, while Adela is unwilling to settle for Ronny she cannot find an alternative outlet for her desires with the result that they become, as in other woman's films, displaced into hysteria. From this point of view, *A Passage* reveals some of the ambivalence which the woman's film displays towards its heroines whose desires may be punished or lead to suffering but whose predicaments none the less engender sympathy or empathy.[40] In this case, Adela's initial actions may be seen to indicate a desire to rebel against the stuffiness and repression of the British Raj and the enclosure which it seems to require. Like Maurice in the film of the same name, Adela is seen to want to break out of enclosed spaces (looking out from Ronny's bungalow towards the Marabar Caves) and cross new thresholds (as the film's repeated use of passages and arches suggest). However, like Clive (in *Maurice*) she ends up a prisoner trapped inside her own home, seen in the film's final shot looking forlornly out of her rain-swept window. In the case of Clive, he has willed his own fate but Adela has not and, whatever her responsibility for falsely accusing Aziz, there is a degree of pathos involved in her situation and, at least implicitly, a degree of criticism of the society which has proved incapable of accommodating her desires.

There is something of a similar situation in *Heat and Dust*. Olivia has a husband with whom she enjoys a certain happiness and sexual fulfilment (the film makes no reference to the suggestion of impotence which is found in the novel) but she is none the less bored by Raj life and yearns, like Adela, for romantic excitement. She is, indeed, seen at one point looking out from behind the bars of her bungalow window in a familiar image of domestic entrapment. Her outlet is the Nawab who becomes the object of her romantic fantasy and appears to offer her access to a type of experience which her life with Douglas denies her.[41]

---

[39] In the woman's film, the woman who actively desires and looks is conventionally proven wrong or misguided. In *A Passage to India*, Adela's look is undermind not only because she is a woman (whose look is not reciprocated) but because her look is directed at an Asian man. In this respect, the imperial 'right to look' at the East is complicated by gender. For a discussion of the relations between 'the imperial gaze' and 'the male gaze', see E. Ann Kaplan, *Looking For the Other: Feminism, Film and the Imperial Gaze* (New York: Routledge, 1997).

[40] Richard Dyer notes the severe punishment meted out to Daphne, for her lovemaking with Hari in *The Jewel in the Crown*: 'she is raped and assaulted, never sees Hari again, causes him to be locked up and himself raped, and dies in childbirth'. See *White*, 198. In this respect, it can be seen to have affinities with a long tradition of what Mary Louise Pratt refers to as 'colonial love stories' in which 'the lovers are separated, the European is reabsorbed by Europe, and the non-European dies an early death'. See *Imperial Eyes: Travel Writing and Transculturation* (London: Routledge, 1992), 97.

[41] Olivia is, in this respect, rebelling against the 'norm' for imperial wives. As Jeffrey Richards comments on an earlier cycle of British films of Empire in the 1930s: 'The Imperial lady was required to devote herself to her husband and efface herself.' See *Visions of Yesterday* (London: Routledge & Kegan Paul, 1973), 93.

However, as in the woman's film, this active desire proves problematic and, ultimately, against her best interests. Although Olivia believes that she knows the Nawab better than the rest of the English, she fails to understand both his character (his involvement with the dacoits) and motivations (his engineering of the relationship to his political advantage and readiness to use her pregnancy to get back at the English). Indeed, her relationship with the Nawab is imbued with a clear masochistic connotation insofar as her seduction immediately follows the Nawab's encounter with the gang of dacoits and is intercut with Olivia's imaginings of a story, previously told by the Nawab, concerning the stabbing of Indians trapped in a tent.

In this way, Olivia is both rebel and victim. As Harry tells Anne she wasn't 'a proper memsahib' and outraged the 'conventions' of the English and Indians alike. As such she represents a sort of Achilles heel or, as the novel puts it, 'weak spot' of colonialism of which the Indians take advantage.[42] This is also true of Harry who has 'crossed over' and lives at the Nawab's palace and, in an echo of Olivia's situation, is fought over by the Nawab and Douglas who attempts to get him to go back to England. On the other hand, Olivia is also a victim. She is a pawn in a political battle which she does not understand and is effectively 'punished' for the transgressions which she commits. Thus, after her abortion she is forced to flee the Civil Lines and spends the rest of her days in effective exile, mostly alone in the Nawab's Himalayan house. In Kipnis' terms, this representation of Olivia may be read as a disavowal of colonial realities which displaces responsibility for colonialism onto the female figure (and, indeed, in doing so effectively reverses the actual power relations prevailing between East and West). On the other hand, Olivia is also a victim of colonial structures, brought down by her desire to defy colonial codes.

In this respect, the film also provides a comparison between the fate of the two English women who go to India before and after Indian independence. There is here an element of both contrast and similarity. Olivia, as Chid (Charles McCaughan) suggests, is something of a 'reincarnation' of Olivia. She traces Olivia's steps and visits the places with which she had a connection. Her story also develops along parallel lines to that of Olivia. She too becomes involved with an Indian, Inder Lal (Zakir Hussain), and becomes pregnant by him. However, there is also a contrast insofar as Anne now possesses the independence and control over her life which Olivia lacked. She is in a position not to tell Inder Lal about the pregnancy, choose not to have an abortion, and make the decision to have the child on her own. This contrast between Olivia's abortion and Anne's decision to have her child might suggest the possibility of a certain *rapprochement* between East and West which was not available to Olivia. However, as Philip French observes, 'Anne is as much an outsider as Olivia' at the film's end and this undercuts the optimism about Anglo-Indian

---

[42] In the novel Major Minnies (played by Barry Foster in the film) reflects that there 'are many ways of loving India . . . but all . . . are dangerous for the European who allows himself to love too much'. 'India', he warns, 'finds out the weak spot and presses on it.' Ruth Prawer Jhabvala, *Heat and Dust* (London: Futura, 1983, orig. 1975), 170.

relations which her pregnancy might suggest.[43] There seem to be a number of factors at work here.

It has already been suggested that the shift towards the imagining of the encounter between East and West in terms of a Western woman and Eastern man corresponds to a shift from a concern with how colonial India may be ruled, or have order imposed upon it (primarily by men), to a concern with how independent India may be experienced (primarily by women). However, it is also the case that the experience of India begins to defeat the Westerner's ability to define or understand it. Thus, in the case of *A Passage to India,* the experience of Mrs Moore of the caves involves a response to India which is profound but which is also incomprehensible and incommunicable.[44] *Heat and Dust* is likewise concerned with how the desire of the Westerner to connect with India proves elusive. Thus, while Olivia and Anne encounter very different Indias, neither succeed in forging a genuine connection. Hence, despite the contrast between the glamour of the Raj era and the hardships of modern India, the India experienced by Anne is less the 'real' India than the 'hard primitivist' India sought out by the 'alternative' European traveller in pursuit of 'authenticity' (a quest which is itself caught up in a Western desire for the 'other').[45] In this respect, Anne is partly linked with Chid, the American and loose counterpart to Harry, who is seeking his own form of connection with India by becoming a holy man. He is, however, temperamentally and physically unsuited to his adopted life and, following a bout of severe illness, opts to return to the US and, indeed, the 'cleanest city' in the country. Anne's attempts at involvement are not much more successful. She may, as Laurie Sucher suggests, seek 'a level of being . . . that might be deeper, more connected and less alienated' than before but, no more than Olivia, is she able to find this by her attempts to live with Indians or through sex with Inder Lal.[46] The result is that she too retreats to the mountains, away from the 'heat and dust' below.

The significance of this is not entirely clear. On the one hand, it seems to be associated with a certain degree of heightened consciousness and spiritual awakening. At one point in the novel, Anne reflects on Chid and wonders

---

[43] Philip French, *The Observer* (6 Feb. 1983), 31.

[44] The author of 'Sex and the Indian Novel' also argues how the inability of the Westerner to make sense of, or represent, the experience of India is also associated with hysteria, especially in the novels of Ruth Prawer Jhabvala (p. 40). So while Kipnis suggests that 'pathological female desire' (such as Adela's hysteria in *A Passage*) is linked to a colonial strategy of 'control', it may be equally argued that female hysteria derives precisely from a loss of control and a loss of the colonial ability to order and organize. See Laura Kipnis, ' "The Phantom Twitchings of an Amputated Limb" ', 50.

[45] Erwin Panofsky, after Lovejoy and Boas, draws a distinction between 'soft' and 'hard' primitivism. The first conceives of 'primitive life' in terms of happiness and plenty ('civilized life purged of its vices') whereas the second conceives of it in terms of hardship and suffering ('civilized life stripped of its virtues'). See 'Et In Arcadia Ego: Poussin and the Elegiac Tradition', in *Meaning in the Visual Arts: Papers in and on Art History* (New York: Doubleday Anchor Books, 1955), 297. In this respect, the contrast of imagery contained in *Heat and Dust* is less a contrast between a 'romantic' past and a 'realistic' present than between two forms of romanticism. For a discussion of travel in terms of a quest for imagined 'authenticity', see Jonathan Culler, 'The Semiotics of Tourism', in *Framing the Sign: Criticism and its Institutions* (Oxford: Blackwell, 1988).

[46] Laurie Sucher, *The Fiction of Ruth Prawer Jhabvala* (London: Macmillan, 1989), 10.

PLATES 6 (left) & 7 (below).
The English woman in India:
Greta Scacchi and Julie
Christie in *Heat and Dust*

whether the 'European soul', if not the European body, might survive in India.[47] In this sense, Anne's ability to stay on is predicated upon a divorce from the material realities of India and the adoption of the life of the 'soul'. However, given the film's general sense of the futility of the European search for spiritual or other values in India, it is difficult to tell whether Anne's decision to have her baby in the mountains is intended to be read as a genuine 'solution' to her predicament or simply a further 'false' avenue. Moreover, whatever the spiritual virtues that may be associated with her climb to the mountains, it also involves a strong sense of isolation and, given the parallels with Olivia, even banishment. In this respect, the emphasis upon the inability of the European genuinely to experience or, engage satisfactorily with, India leads to a deep pessimism about the possibility of genuine contact and connection between the two cultures. There is a certain irony here. The criticism of colonialism contained in these films characteristically assumes the form of characters who wish to break out of colonial straitjackets and reach out across cultural barriers. As Shohat and Stam suggest, 'the glimmerings of anticolonialist consciousness' are often provoked 'by transgression of the taboo on inter-racial desire'.[48] However, it is also the case that the transgression of this taboo fails to provide the fulfilment which characters wish for. As a result, the films seem to end up reinforcing the very barriers that they had previously appeared to want to bring down. In a sense, if the limited optimism represented by the men's handshake at the end of *A Passage to India* relies upon a suppression of difference, then the pessimism of *Heat and Dust* appears to rely upon a construction of irreconcilable difference. In this respect, they may also be seen to represent alternative sides of the same coin. For both conclusions in a sense issue from the Eurocentric position from which they begin. The films are characteristically organized around the problem of European experience, and the possibility of *its* fulfilment or frustration. The rather more difficult task of reimagining that experience in a more self-reflective and dialogistic form is, however, barely begun.

The Heritage Film and Ireland

Issues of gender, colonialism, and the crossing of social boundaries also emerge in those heritage films of the 1980s concerned with Ireland, especially *The Dawning* (1988) and *Fools of Fortune* (1990). Set in the past and focusing on the privileged lifestyles associated with the Anglo-Irish Ascendancy and the 'Big House', these were generally regarded by critics as being unexceptional examples of heritage filmmaking.[49] However, this is not as clear-cut as it might at first appear and the Irish subject-matter does seem to generate some special problems.

---

[47]   Ruth Prawer Jhabvala, *Heat and Dust*, 159.
[48]   Ella Shohat/Robert Stam, *Unthinking Eurocentrism* (London: Routledge, 1994), 123.
[49]   Although filmed in Ireland by an Irish director from an Irish novel, *Fools of Fortune*, for example, was still regarded by the critics as 'classically British film-making' and 'Illustrated Brit Lit'. See David Wilson, *Monthly Film Bulletin* (July 1990), 196 and Anne Billson, *Sunday Correspondent* (24 June 1990), 36.

There are two issues that might be raised in this regard. The first concerns the nature of the past which is represented. A part of the nostalgic appeal of the heritage film depends upon its presentation of a social world which is apparently more settled and stable than that of the present. However, Ireland in the 1920s, especially during the War of Independence, is much less readily available as an object of nostalgia than the comparable period in England (and even India). The past, in this respect, is so obviously characterized by violence and social tension that it is clearly difficult to project it as any kind of 'golden age'.

It is, of course, the case that heritage films, as has already been noted, do often chart the beginnings of the end of Empire, and thus the demise of the settled social order which British rule supposedly provided. However, the past which they represent does, it has been suggested, appear to be sealed off from the present. As Higson puts it, history is rendered 'as separate from the viewer in the present, as something over and done with, complete, achieved'.[50] In the case of Ireland, however, this separation from the past is much more problematic given the continuation of the 'troubles' into a much later era and, thus, the unresolved character of the conflicts with which they deal. Thus, while Higson suggests the heritage film holds the spectator at a distance and refuses 'the possibility of a dialogue or confrontation with the present', it is much more difficult, in the case of the Irish films, for the audience to avoid reading the presentation of the past in contemporary terms.[51] Thus, at least one critic felt able to claim of *Fools of Fortune* that its study of the effects of violence was, in fact, 'more relevant than ever'.[52]

It is, in fact, the interweaving of different time-scales and blurring of temporal boundaries that makes *Fools of Fortune*, in particular, such a distinctive example of heritage filmmaking. The film spans over twenty years and repeatedly jumps back and forwards in time (as well as between 'objective' and 'subjective' perceptions of events) in ways that are often quite confusing and which make it difficult to construct a temporally coherent 'story' out of the film's 'plot'. Thus, as the reviews reveal, at least some critics were misled as to when Willie (Iain Glen) left for the west of Ireland (in some cases, mistakenly assuming this to have occurred before, rather than after, Willie's killing of Rudkin (Neil Dudgeon)).[53] Inevitably, this loss of a clear temporal order within the film undermines the 'separateness' of the past and, insofar as the present is so clearly infused with the past's influence, prevents the past from functioning as a nostalgically desirable refuge from present conflicts. As Father Kilgarriff (Tom Hickey) explains to Willie, in lines eloquent of the film as a whole, 'We can't understand the present without knowing something about the past. The past is always there in the present.'

This confusion of temporal boundaries may also be linked to a further deviation from the norms of the heritage film which the film makes. As has been

---

[50] Higson, 'Re-presenting the National Past', 113.   [51] Ibid.
[52] Ronan Farren, *Sunday Independent* (24 June 1990), 30.
[53] Even the 'factual' plot summary provided by the *Monthly Film Bulletin* (July 1990, 196) is wrong on this score.

suggested, heritage cinema is characteristically associated with tastefulness and restraint and the offer of reassurance rather than shock. Indeed, director Pat O'Connor's earlier heritage film, *A Month in the Country* (1987), set in England in the aftermath of the First World War, was criticized by one critic precisely because of its 'too self-consciously English' reliance upon 'understatement and good taste'.[54] *Fools of Fortune*, however, is much less restrained and much more inclined to give rein to those melodramatic elements which are conventionally subdued within the heritage film. Thus, whereas William Trevor's original novel is characteristically taciturn and oblique, often relying on retrospective revelation, the film tends to be explicit and direct. It shows the burning of the Big House and subsequent killings which are only partly, and somewhat confusingly, described—from Willie's point of view—in the novel. Willie's repeated stabbing of Rudkin which is barely described at all in Trevor's original is also shown with a degree of gothic intensity. This sense of melodramatic excess is added to by the emotional pitch at which much of the action is played and the foreshortened and exaggerated sense of dramatic consequence that becomes particularly evident in the chain of events following the burning of the Big House at Kilneagh—the suicide of Willie's mother (Julie Christie), Josephine's (Niamh Cusack) failed romance and decline into mental instability, and Imelda's (Catherine McFadden) descent into hysteria and then silence (events that, in turn, conform to the characteristic emphasis of film melodrama on female masochism and suffering).

This wholehearted embrace of melodrama has further consequences for how the film treats the past. Peter Brooks has encouraged a view of melodrama as not simply a set of dramatic conventions but also as a mode of imagination: a mode which seeks to go beyond surface appearance and give voice to latent moral meanings ('the moral occult', in his terms).[55] The melodramatic excesses in evidence in *Fools of Fortune* thus suggest an attempt to go beyond the fetishistic surfaces and depthlessness of the heritage film in order to uncover a deeper pattern involving the destructive hold of the past over subsequent generations and the resulting repetition of history. The characters of the film, in this regard, become the 'fools of fortune' of the film's title: victims of a deadly 'heritage' of violence, hatred, and revenge. As such, the film locks into a well-established tradition of representing Ireland and Irish history in terms of fatalism and this necessarily disrupts the appeal which the past conventionally holds for the heritage film.[56]

While a structure of fatalism is characteristically associated with metaphysical meanings, it also plays a clear ideological role in the film, particularly

[54] Philip French, *The Observer* (22 Nov. 1987), 26.

[55] Peter Brooks, *The Melodramatic Imagination: Balzac, Henry James, Melodrama and the Mode of Excess* (New York: Columbia University Press, 1984, orig. 1976), 5.

[56] See John Hill, 'Images of Violence', in Kevin Rockett, Luke Gibbons, and John Hill, *Cinema and Ireland* (London: Routledge, 1988), 147–93. Although Brook (ibid. 15) links the 'moral occult' of melodrama to what he calls a 'post-sacred era', it is also apparent that the workings of fatalism in *Fools of Fortune*, as in other Irish-theme films such as *The Informer*, *Odd Man Out*, and *Cal*, is none the less connected to a religious sense of sin and possible redemption.

in relation to the representation of gender and national identities. For while the film displays a liberal concern to forge new social relations and identities, the movement of the film also works against this. As has been suggested, the past invoked by *Fools of Fortune* is partly resistant to nostalgia because it is so clearly flawed and unstable. However, while it is the external threat of the Black and Tans which destroys the security enjoyed by the Quintons at the film's beginning, the family's downfall is also seen to have its roots in its own internal instability. This is linked, in particular, with their confusion of identities and allegiances. As William Trevor has observed, the Quintons 'were people who were traitors to their class, and traitors to their background'.[57] So, although they are the Anglo-Irish occupants of the Big House they identify themselves as Irish; while they are Protestants they count themselves the 'friends' of the Catholics around them and permit the ex-priest Father Kilgarriff to live with them and educate the young Willie. They also identify with the cause of Irish Home Rule and lend their support to the IRA. Indeed, it is the visit to the house at Kilneagh by the IRA man, identified as Michael Collins in the original novel, which assumes a particular dramatic importance in triggering the film's fatal pattern. As he leaves the house he is watched by the informer Doyle (Sean McGinley) and is subsequently killed in a Black and Tan ambush; Doyle's body is then left hanging on the Quinton's land (where it is discovered by Josephine); the Black and Tans take their revenge by first burning Kilneagh and then, watched by his son Willie, killing Quinton (Michael Kitchen).

The significance of the Quintons' behaviour is, in this respect, complicated. At a surface level, the film may be read as offering sympathy to characters whose liberal sentiments and sense of justice encourage them to attempt to transcend the prejudices of their age and cut across conventional social barriers. It is significant, in this respect, that Trevor's work has been associated with that of E. M. Forster and, in particular, his dictum 'only connect'. However, as Gregory Schirmer argues, it is the tragedy of Trevor's stories that such attempts at connection invariably fail.[58] There is a comparison here with *The Dawning* and the work of Jennifer Johnston more generally. As Christine St Peter suggests, Johnston's stories revolve around characters 'who take risks to reach across class/age/sexual/religious divisions' and create new 'cross-caste relations'.[59] Thus, in the case of *The Dawning*, it is Nancy (Rebecca Pidgeon), the adolescent girl, who is prepared to strike up a relationship with the much older IRA man on the run, Angus Barry (Anthony Hopkins). However, such alliances are destined to be temporary and ultimately to fail. Hence, at the end of *The Dawning*, Angus is dead while Nancy is back 'home', less innocent than she was but socially in the same place as before. In the same way, the Quintons' desire to cut across

[57] Jacqueline Stahl Aronson, 'William Trevor: An Interview', *Irish Literary Supplement* (Spring 1986), 8. This idea is also expressed in the original novel: William Trevor, *Fools of Fortune* (Harmondsworth: Penguin, 1983), 28.

[58] Gregory A. Schirmer, *William Trevor: A Study of his Fiction* (London: Routledge, 1990), 1–2.

[59] Christine St Peter, 'Jennifer Johnston's Irish Troubles: A Materialist-Feminist Reading', in T. Johnson and D. Cairns (eds.), *Gender in Irish Writing* (Milton Keynes: Open University Press, 1992), 118.

traditional social divisions in *Fools of Fortune* also proves unsuccessful and is linked to a certain despair about the possibility of 'cross-caste' relations. Indeed, it is not only that the film is unable to envisage the success of such alliances but that, as a result of its employment of a fatalistic structure, appears to indicate that it is, in effect, the very confusion of identities and allegiances which the Quintons represent that has been responsible for setting the cycle of destruction in motion. In this respect, the film may be seen to be holding on to the very fixity of identities which, at a surface level, it appears to want to overcome. This is apparent in the film's treatment of both gender and national identities.

It has already been noted that a key factor in triggering the film's fatalistic plot is the apparent 'treachery' of the Quinton family. It is also noticeable, however, that, as in the Raj films, it is the Quinton women who most clearly represent liberal sentiments and are thus the most obvious 'traitors'. Three different generations of English women have come to live at Kilneagh and all have, in effect, 'crossed over'. The first of these was Willie's great grandmother, Anna Quinton, who was disowned by her parents, according to Father Kilgarriff, because 'during the Famine she begged everyone to do something about the terrible situation'. The second English woman was Willie's mother, Evie, who supports the Irish cause even more energetically than Willie's father. She tells the IRA man who visits their house that 'we want to do anything we can to be of help to you' and is prepared to let him drill in the grounds and store arms (even though her husband is not). Marianne arrives much later, after Irish independence has been achieved, but none the less rejects advice to go back to England and develops a strong sense of the injustices visited upon Ireland by the English. From one point of view, these women may be regarded as sympathetic characters who attempt to break out of their inherited identities and reach out to others. From another perspective, however, these women may also be seen to be blamed for the Quintons' (and the Anglo-Irish ascendancy's) downfall precisely because their 'love' of Ireland has involved a kind of 'treachery'. As such, they may be related to the women in *A Passage to India* and *Heat and Dust* who represent the 'weak link' of colonialism, cutting across traditional social divisions and undermining the masculine ability to rule successfully. The difference between *Fools of Fortune* and these films, however, is the fatalistic structure in which female 'weakness' is embedded (and the relative lack of sympathy extended to female characters, especially in the case of Evie). As a result, whatever admiration there is for the women's concern to achieve connection is tempered by an unusually dark sense of its consequence.

Seamus Deane has observed how rare it is to find a novel about the Big House in which a 'sinister element is absent' and identifies how, within a peculiarly Irish variant of gothic fiction, the Big House is 'transformed into a haunted mansion, beset by the ghosts of a guilty past'.[60] Significantly, Kilneagh also has its ghost: in this case that of Anna Quinton which, according to Father

---

[60] Seamus Deane, 'Jennifer Johnston', *Bulletin of the Department of Foreign Affairs*, no. 1015 (Feb. 1985), 4.

Kilgarriff, appeared shortly after her death. Her ghost is not seen but the film does repeatedly draw our attention to her portraits which may be seen to keep alive her spirit within the Quinton household. It is therefore significant that Father Kilgarriff's opening speech to Willie about the importance of the past should be introduced via a tracking shot across a sideboard on which Anna Quinton's picture is seen standing. A larger portrait is seen subsequently (when Father Kilgarriff explains her history) and then again when it is engulfed by flames during the burning of Kilneagh. The import of this shot is, however, ambivalent. In one respect, it may be taken to signify the failure, in the face of violence, of the 'love and mercy' which Father Kilgarriff suggests to Willie that Anna Quinton represents. On the other hand, within the structure of melo-dramatic fatalism which the film employs, it is also a somewhat melancholy reminder of the destabilizing role which the Quinton women have played his-torically and of the 'fatal flaw' which this may be taken to represent (a 'flaw' itself compounded, in the case of Evie and Marianne, by an 'unnatural' readiness to condone male violence). So although the portrait of Anna Quinton is a part of Imelda's vision at the end, it is perhaps symptomatic of the film's conservatism towards women that the youngest female Quinton has now fallen silent and lacks the 'voice' which her predecessors had possessed.[61]

There is a similar conservatism in the film's treatment of national identity. In the original novel, Willie, following the murder of Rudkin, becomes an itiner-ant, travelling from South America to Italy. In the film, however, he returns to Ireland where he travels to a remote island community on the western seaboard (Inis Oirr in Co. Galway). This is a significant change and brings a number of different associations into play. To some extent, it provides an element of the 'otherness' and exoticism which non-English landscapes characteristically provide for the heritage film. However, the imagery of the island is none the less distinct from that of other heritage films and possesses a specifically Irish dimension. As has often been noted, the west of Ireland and its association with bleakness and austerity has held a particular appeal for cultural nationalism for which it has provided a model of a distinctive and 'authentic' Irish identity. As Gibbons has argued, it was also this vision of the west which Robert Flaherty's *Man of Aran* (1934) so successfully embodied and which guaranteed it a sympa-thetic response in de Valera's Ireland of the 1930s.[62] The scenes set in the Aran islands in *Fools of Fortune* also occur in the 1930s and it is hard not to associate them with similar scenes in *Man of Aran* (especially such scenes as the landing of the fish). The imagery which the film employs, in this respect, is therefore

---

[61] Silence, in this respect, is linked to an ending of the perpetuation of the past through language and the stories which language permits. As such, the retreat of Imelda into silence may be seen to represent a 'positive' break with the past and even—as in a film such as *Ascendancy* (1983) where Connie (Julie Covington), the daughter of a Belfast shipyard owner, also ends up silent—a form of protest against the legacy of violence. However, if silence interrupts the continual retelling (and hence reliving) of the past, it is also achieved at a high price: the descent of Imelda into madness. In this respect, Imelda's silence is less an active resistance to the past than further evidence of its continuing destructiveness.

[62] Luke Gibbons, 'Romanticism, Realism and Irish Cinema', in Kevin Rockett, Luke Gibbons, and John Hill, *Cinema and Ireland*, 203.

hardly 'innocent' and carries with it a set of connotations that inevitably cut across the film's apparent intentions. So, while Willie's life in the west is, in dramatic terms, associated with a healing process, and a break with the legacy of the past, the imagery is, none the less, caught up in a backward-looking vision of its own: precisely that of a 'primitive' Irish society outside of the forces of modernity and change.

Moreover, while Willie, in the novel, is involved in an outward journey that, in a sense, offers him a reimagining of his Irish identity within an international frame, the film's use of the already ideologically laden imagery of the western seaboard associates Willie's return to health with the recovery of a sort of 'pure' Irishness, uncomplicated by external influence, and linked to the country, Catholicism, the Irish language, and traditional forms of masculinity. In a sense, Willie resolves the identity crisis of the Quintons by immersing himself in a clear-cut, exclusivist form of Irish identity which dispenses with the very in-betweenness of previous 'cross-caste' relations. In doing so, the film necessarily undermines its ostensive concern to imagine a break with the legacy of the past through the construction of new hybrid identities. For, unable to envisage the successful crossing of social boundaries and the emergence of the new identities to which these would lead, it ends up falling back on the very fixities of identity which its liberalism might, on the surface, be seen to striving to overcome. In a sense, this is true of all the films discussed in this chapter: they all offer scenarios of cross-cultural contact and connection that ultimately fail and, in doing so, end up leaving intact the very borders that characters had initially endeavoured to cross.

chapter 6

Remembering the 1950s
Dance with a Stranger

Versions on the 1950s

Although it was the first two decades of the twentieth century in which the British cinema of the 1980s was most interested, British films also showed some interest in other periods and especially the 1950s. For Fredric Jameson, writing in the context of the United States, contemporary perceptions of this period have less to do with 'facts or historical realities' than '*ideas* of facts and historical realities' (my italics).[1] From this perspective, ideas of the 1950s may have less to do with how it actually was than with how it is imagined to have been (the '1950s' rather than the 1950s). In terms of this active memorizing of the past, Jameson suggests that two versions have predominated: on the one hand, what he calls the 'conventional' 1950s and, on the other, what he refers to as the 'oppositional' 1950s. Although Jameson fleshes his observations out with references to the United States, these terms may also be applied to Britain.

Ironically, the idea of the 'conventional' 1950s is difficult to separate from the way in which the idea of the 1960s has been constructed. As was noted in Chapter 1, for the New Right in the 1980s, it was the 1960s which was characteristically identified as responsible for the onset of permissiveness and the breakdown of authority which they sought to reverse. As Mrs Thatcher declared in March 1982, '[we] are reaping what was sown in the sixties. The fashionable theories and permissive claptrap set the scene for a society in which the old virtues of discipline and self-restraint were denigrated'.[2] In this respect, the conventional 1950s may be seen to represent a settled and stable period prior to the upheavals of the next decade. As Peter Kellner puts it, in his account of nostalgia

---

[1] Fredric Jameson, 'Nostalgia for the Present', in *Postmodernism, or the Cultural Logic of Late Capitalism* (London: Verso, 1991), 279.

[2] Quoted in David Edgar, 'The Free or the Good' in Ruth Levitas (ed.), *The Ideology of the New Right* (Cambridge: Polity Press, 1988), 55. The Conservative party chairman, Norman Tebbit also complained, in 1985, of how 'the era of post-war funk which gave birth to the "Permissive Society" . . . in turn generated today's violent society.' Quoted in Peter Jenkins, *Mrs Thatcher's Revolution: The Ending of the Socialist Era* (London: Jonathan Cape, 1987), 326.

for the 1950s, images of this period evoke 'a mood of stability and optimism, when everyone . . . occupied their proper place in an ordered world'.[3] The '1950s', in this respect, may be seen to encourage a simple nostalgia for a time which was presumed to be simpler and, in many ways, better.

However, this is not the only way in which the 1950s have been remembered. There are two aspects to this. On the one hand, the 1950s may be conceived not as a period of stability and contentment but of repression and privation. As Kellner has argued, '[our] nostalgia for the supposed contentment of that era ignores a culture of suppression and censorship' and 'the impulse to glorify the fifties mistakes repression for happiness, complacency for stability'.[4] If this is so, it is this differing view of the 1950s which provides the backdrop to Jameson's 'oppositional' 1950s: the '1950s', as he puts it, as 'so many protests against the fifties themselves'.[5] This version of the 1950s invokes the constraints of the 1950s and the growing rebellion against them (by youth, women, gays, and ethnic minorities). The 1950s, in this respect, represent not so much a period of calm before the upheavals of the 1960s as the harbinger of things to come.

It is this version of the 1950s which the films of the 1980s primarily invoke. On the one hand, the constraints of the 1950s, and the growing tensions around class, gender, generation, 'race', and nationality are diagnosed and, retrospectively, read in ways which suggest the roots of future conflicts. *Absolute Beginners* (1986), for example, uses Colin MacInnes's 1959 novel to explore the beginnings of youth culture and the challenges to 'old' Britain represented by Americanized mass culture and Commonwealth immigration. It does so, moreover, in a way that blurs temporal boundaries by avoiding accurate period recreation and running together 'past' and 'present' (as in the scene when contemporary reggae singer Smiley Culture performs at an interracial street carnival in the wake of the clashes between whites and blacks). While *Absolute Beginners* simply evokes actual events, such as the Notting Hill riots of 1958, many of the films dealing with the 1950s, and closely related periods, draw directly on the lives of real people.

Wish You Were Here (1987) is loosely based upon the early life of Cynthia Payne, whose subsequent career as brothel-keeper also inspired the film *Personal Services* (1986); *Let Him Have It* (1991) is based on the case of Derek Bentley who was hanged in 1953 for alleged incitement to murder; *Chicago Joe and the Showgirl* (1989), set in the Second World War, takes the 'Cleft Chin Murder' as its inspiration; *The Krays* (1990) follows the career of the notorious Kray brothers; while *Scandal* (1988), set in the early 1960s, deals with the Profumo affair and the activities of two prostitutes, Christine Keeler and Mandy Rice-Davies. The treatment of these characters, however, is less governed by biographical or sociological accuracy than the symbolic value which they seem to possess. This mix of criminals, deviants, and social misfits seem to offer a set of characters who are in protest against the drabness and conformity of the society around them.

[3] Peter Kellner, 'It wasn't all right, Jack', *The Sunday Times* ('The Culture') (4 Apr. 1994), 12.
[4] Ibid. 13.   [5] 'Nostalgia for the Present', 279.

The central character Lynda (Emily Lloyd) in *Wish You Were Here*, for example, is seen as a proto-rebel against the restrictions and hypocrisies of small-town life (seen in a photograph at the film's beginning wearing a gas mask as if in danger of suffocation). In a key scene, she marches proudly through the town, dressed in a vivid yellow, pushing the pram containing her illegitimate baby. In *Let Him Have It*, Derek Bentley is associated with a desire to break out of austerity and suburban dullness through an identification with the glamour and fantasy of American popular culture (and gangster films such as *White Heat*). Thus, even in those cases where crimes were actually committed, these offences are often seen in metaphorical terms—as forms of social and sexual transgression as much as criminal acts.

Dance with a Stranger

Dance with a Stranger (1985) may be linked to this trend. Set in the 1950s, in what one critic describes as 'that strange limbo between austerity and affluence', it uses the character of Ruth Ellis (Miranda Richardson), the last woman to be hanged in Britain, to explore the class and sexual tensions of the period.[6] The interest of the film, however, is not in surface realism and, in common with the hybridity characteristic of so many films during this period, it brings together elements of the biopic, the film noir, and the woman's film. As a genre, the biopic may be identified with the telling of a story of a real historical figure, usually associated with some significant deed, discovery, or achievement.[7] However, although *Dance with a Stranger* is structured around the life of Ruth Ellis, it is really only concerned with a particular episode: her involvement with David Blakely. As such the film makes no attempt to trace the full life story of Ellis. There is virtually nothing about her life before meeting Blakely: her childhood and family background, her pregnancy by a Canadian soldier, her marriage to the alcoholic George Ellis. The film is also reticent about the events with which it deals, especially Desmond Cussen's role in the events leading up to the murder, and also the subsequent trial and campaign for her death sentence to be changed.[8] There is also little interest in why the case became so important and led to changes in the law (as with the Homicide Act of 1957 which introduced the plea of diminished responsibility). In a sense, this lack of interest in biographical and sociological detail underlines the film's real focus which is the social and sexual transgressions which Ellis is seen to embody. In this respect, the film may be seen to be as much a film noir as it is a biopic.

---

[6] Philip French, *The Observer* (3 Mar. 1985).

[7] For a discussion of the generic characteristics of the Hollywood biopic, see George F. Custen, *Bio/Pics: How Hollywood Constructed Public History* (New Brunswick, NJ: Rutgers University Press, 1992).

[8] For a discussion of Ruth Ellis's life, see Laurence Marks and Tony Van Den Bergh, *Ruth Ellis: A Case of Diminished Responsibility?* (London: Penguin, 1990, orig. 1977).

PLATE 8. Fatal passion: Miranda Richardson and Rupert Everett in *Dance with a Stranger*

A characteristic problem faced by the biopic in its telling of a life story is sustaining narrative suspense and momentum: the audience already know what a character is famous for and therefore can anticipate the film's ending. In the case of *Dance with a Stranger,* however, audience foreknowledge of Ellis's story is employed to create a mood of destructive passion and fatalism. Ellis, in this respect, is caught up in a fatal attraction from which she cannot extricate herself and which must ultimately lead to her doom. Early on in the film, Ellis reveals, in a conversation with her boss Morrie (Stratford Johns), her desire to improve herself and achieve respectability: in effect to stop being a whore and fulfil her role as a mother. As she talks to him, she turns up the radio in order to drown the noise of lovemaking elsewhere in the club. However, it is her inability to hold the disruptive forces of desire at bay which is to prove her downfall. The film makes play of her blindness without her glasses and, in a sense, this 'blindness' becomes a metaphor for the infatuation which she cannot contain and which is responsible for her demise. This is a theme reinforced by a striking scene in the fog, reminiscent of *The Informer,* when—despite Blakely's earlier maltreatment of her—she is unable to stop herself having sex with him, but more generally by the self-consciously noir techniques which the film employs: claustrophobic *mise-en-scène,* expressionistic colours, fatalistic angles, and the repeated use of shadows and mirror reflections.

But, if the style of the film is noir, and its mood is that of fatalism, Ellis is less a *femme fatale* than a victim. In this respect, the film employs its noir elements in the context of a plot more characteristic of the woman's film. Like the woman's film, *Dance with a Stranger* provides a woman-centred narrative in which the central character is caught up in a set of impossible choices: love versus duty, self versus family, passion versus domesticity. In effect, Ruth is caught between two kinds of male types: the *homme fatale* or playboy, Blakely (Rupert Everett), and the respectable Cussens (Ian Holm). Cussens is the 'proper' choice: the character who can financially support Ruth, provide her with a home and look after her and her son, Andy (Matthew Carroll). As is often the case with the woman's film, this division between male characters is also linked to social class: Blakely is clearly of a higher social class than Ruth and she is deemed unsuitable to meet his parents and is looked down upon by the snobby Findlaters. However, if Cussens is the 'right' choice, he is also, like 'the girl-next-door' in film noir, unable to provide the excitement and adventure which Ellis craves. It is therefore Blakely to whom Ellis is drawn, despite his irresponsibility and weakness. Pam Cook suggests of the woman's film that the woman's 'choice of the romantic hero as love object is usually masochistic, against her own best interests, and she suffers for her desire'.[9] This is clearly the case for Ellis who ultimately loses everything: her job, her pregnancy, her sanity, and, finally, her life.

However, if, in 'punishing' the woman for her choices or returning her to her 'proper' place, the woman's film may be seen to reinforce—albeit often ambiguously—an ideology of motherhood and familialism, *Dance with a Stranger* is clearly seeking to deploy these conventions in a way which shifts the blame from the woman herself to the society which she inhabits and which forbids her desires (and their combination with motherhood) or forces unnecessary choices upon her. As Graham Fuller suggests, 'it is the fifties themselves . . . that causes Ruth's downfall'.[10] In this respect, the film attempts to suggest how it is British society itself which is responsible for Ellis's demise, unable to countenance either her sexual desires (her wish to be both sexually active and a mother) or social transgressions (her attraction to a man of a higher social station). For the film's director, Mike Newell, the 1950s represents a 'pressure cooker society'.[11] Ellis, in this respect, may be read as a woman 'on the verge of revolt' whose embodiment of the social and sexual tensions of the period are indicative of a society about to explode.

However, although the film's intent is fairly clear, there are also complications in the way it is worked out. The pathos characteristically generated by the woman's film, for example, depends upon the empathy encouraged with the female lead. Despite the film's apparent desire to portray Ellis as a kind of proto-rebel, it is also reluctant to encourage too straightforward an identification with

---

[9] Pam Cook, 'Melodrama and the Women's Picture', in Sue Aspinall and Robert Murphy (eds.), *Gainsborough Melodrama* (London: BFI, 1983), 20.

[10] Graham Fuller, *Stills* (Mar. 1985), 61.

[11] Quoted in Chris Goodwin, 'Dance with a Stranger', *AIP & Co.* (Mar. 1985), 24.

her. Psychological motivations are often left opaque while her desires lack a compelling embodiment.[12] Her relationship with Blakely is not only seen to be clearly self-destructive but also relatively joyless, even at its start. An aspect of this is that Ellis's predicament is delineated in nowhere near as straightforward terms as those found in the conventional woman's film for Blakely is neither exciting enough, nor Cussens dull enough, to make her decisions entirely understandable. So, while Ellis suffers because of her choices, her suffering is seen to stem as much from her own inadequacies as the social forces which are arraigned against her. This movement away from social diagnosis is also reinforced by the film's use of noir techniques. Given the conventional association of these with metaphysical meanings such as fatalism, it is inevitable that the film also implies a pattern of causality which stands at odds with a more straightforwardly socio-cultural account of Ellis's downfall.

Moreover, despite the film's concern to indict the repressiveness of the era with which it deals, it is not entirely able to avoid an element of nostalgia. This is, in part, similar to the problems of the heritage film in which the attractiveness of the visual style and iconography may be seen to undercut the socially critical character of the plots. The 1950s films, however, are hardly heritage films in the same way. Most obviously, their focus is not upon the upper or upper-middle classes but working class, and often socially marginal characters. Indeed, *Dance with a Stranger* illustrates the 'alien' character of the conventional heritage milieu for its main character when it shows how out of place Ellis is in the traditional rural England where Blakely's parents live. As this would suggest, the 1950s films tends to be interested in the urban rather than the rural and with 'ordinary', rather than elite, social settings.

However, even this 'ordinariness' can assume the character of a visually engaging spectacle. Philip Strick, for example, has complained of the film's lack of 'feminist' or 'abolitionist' credentials, arguing that:

Its main objective seems to be nothing more than the immaculate reconstruction of an early Fifties setting: Pathé newsreels at the pictures, the Ted Heath Band at the dancehalls, the pogo-stick craze, the stuffy television interviews, the London fogs of unique density. As designed by Andrew Mollo it is a triumph of seedy nostalgia—there is not a fashion or furnishing out of place.[13]

This is both fair and unfair. It is undoubtedly the case that the *objets d'art* of the past do assume a certain fascination just as the media imagery of the period invokes a degree of nostalgic pleasure. Indeed, as Jameson notes, it is precisely the media output of the 1950s—the films, the TV, the music—rather than its actual events which so often are the source of nostalgic sentiment (as the various stylistic homages of *Absolute Beginners* would also indicate). None the less, the film's 'reconstruction' of the era does not fetishize period accuracy (or

---

[12] Significantly, Jacqueline Rose suggests that the threat which the real Ruth Ellis posed to the law was her absence of overt emotion and her display of 'supreme rationality'. See 'Margaret Thatcher and Ruth Ellis', *New Formations*, no. 6 (Winter 1988/89), 10.

[13] Philip Strick, *The Times* (1 Mar. 1985), 19.

'authenticity') in quite the way Strick suggests. The stylized way in which the past is evoked, for example, works against both 'realism' and nostalgic memory, as the fog scene, with its hallucinatory atmosphere and symbolic intent, suggests.

Moreover, the film also displays a degree of self-consciousness in the way it foregrounds the role of the media: not only, as Strick suggests, through the use of newsreel footage and TV imagery but in permitting Ellis at one stage to talk direct to camera when Cussen is taking a photograph. In a sense, the film is both inviting us into the conventional 1950s and offering some of the pleasures which it provides but also distancing us from them by acknowledging the tensions and conflicts which make the period much less attractive than nostalgia would admit. In this respect, the film is able to evoke the apparently nostalgic 1950s image of the family around the TV set but, in doing so, it also 'makes it strange', investing it with a much darker and troubled set of connotations than the view of the 'conventional' 1950s would have it.

part three

Contemporary Representations _____

chapter 7

The 'State-of-the-Nation' Film _____

Writing in the *Sunday Times* in January 1988, Norman Stone, Professor of History at Oxford and sometime adviser to Mrs Thatcher, took it upon himself to attack what he saw as an unappetizing trend in British film:

> They are all very depressing, and are no doubt meant to be. The rain pours down; skinheads beat people up; there are race riots; there are drug fixes in squalid corners; there is much explicit sex, a surprising amount of it homosexual and sadistic; greed and violence abound; there is grim concrete and much footage of 'urban decay'; on and off there are voice-overs by Mrs Thatcher, Hitler, etc.[1]

Fortunately for Stone, however, the 'tawdry, ragged, rancidly provincial films' which he decried (*Business As Usual* (1987), *Eat the Rich* (1987), *Empire State* (1987), *The Last of England* (1987), *My Beautiful Laundrette* (1985), *Sammy and Rosie Get Laid* (1987)) were not the only films which the British film industry was capable of producing and he identified 'some good . . . films of a traditional kind' such as *A Passage to India* (1984), *A Room with a View* (1985), and *Hope and Glory* (1987) which he was prepared to defend.[2] Whatever the merits of Stone's argument (and there are very few), he was none the less typical in characterizing British cinema in the 1980s as divided between two main types: on the one hand, a traditional (or 'heritage') cinema preoccupied with the past versus a more unorthodox, and socially aware, cinema concerned with the present. However, as Stone's indignant portrait suggests, the latter cinema is also a cinema which is itself predominantly critical of Thatcherism and indignant about the social tensions and hardships that resulted from the spread of Thatcherite policies and culture.

   Stone's polemic, however, is deeply problematic. He displays little awareness of the changed economic circumstances in which British filmmaking in the 1980s took place, nostalgically harking back to a bygone era of popular British

---

[1] Norman Stone, 'Through A Lens Darkly', the *Sunday Times* (10 Jan. 1988), reprinted in Kobena Mercer (ed.), *Black Film, British Cinema* (London: ICA, 1988), 22. Under the editorship of Andrew Neil, the *Sunday Times* during the 1980s abandoned its earlier liberalism in favour of a more strident and populist right-wing tone. Stone's article followed an earlier editorial in the same paper on 20 September 1987 complaining that 'most low-budget films these days have an agitprop purpose'. For a discussion of this campaign, see Julian Petley, 'The Price of Portraying a Less Than Perfect Britain', *The Listener* (21 Jan. 1988), 14.

[2] 'Through A Lens Darkly', 23.

cinema.[3] He is also insensitive to aesthetics and interprets the films he decries in crude political terms. It would be hard to guess from his descriptions how different the films he discusses actually are: ranging from the broad comedy of *Eat The Rich*, the politicized melodrama of *Business as Usual*, and the formal experimentalism of *The Last of England*. Although the films may share a—broadly anti-Thatcherite—political stance, the aesthetic forms which they adopt in order to address political issues are none the less quite distinct.

In some respects, what became known as the 'state-of-the nation' film during the 1980s may be linked to a longstanding tradition of socially critical cinema in Britain. However, while it has been common in writing on British cinema to identify this tradition with realism, this is not possible in the case of the 1980s. So while a number of the films of the period—such as *The Ploughman's Lunch* (1983) and *Rita, Sue and Bob Too* (1986)—quite self-consciously reworked some of the motifs of 1950s and 1960s working-class realism, for example, the 'state-of-the-nation' films of the 1980s did not consistently draw upon realist conventions. For, in a sense, what also becomes evident during this period is an implicit dissatisfaction with straightforward 'realism' and an accompanying concern to push back its boundaries (or to abandon it altogether).

Realism

The concept of realism is, of course, a complicated one. Although the term implies an aesthetic practice which assumes a privileged relationship to an external reality, critical writing on the subject has stressed the impossibility of any artistic work simply reflecting reality (however conceived) and the variability of the aesthetic means employed in showing the 'real'. Works of realism, in this respect, less reflect the real than construct versions of the real through the deployment of techniques and devices which are accepted by audiences as 'realistic'.[4] In the history of British cinema, the claim to realism has traditionally depended upon a number of elements: a focus on 'ordinary' lives, a refusal of both the classical and melodramatic conventions of mainstream Hollywood, a use of techniques associated with documentary such as the use of real locations, natural light, and unadorned camera movement. However, the meaning of such elements is dependent upon context and, thus, their capacity to signify 'realism' is always intertextual and relative to the cinematic norms prevailing. Realism, in this respect, is always in the process of change, refreshing its conventions when these seem in danger of becoming stale or conventional and, hence, of no longer appearing 'realistic' or 'true to life'.

---

[3] Derek Jarman, the director of *The Last of England*, the film which seems to have upset Stone the most, responded to Stone's attack the following week, claiming it was not possible 'to put the clock back, and the cinema is now split betwen specialist and commercial audiences'. See 'Freedom Fighter for a Vision of Truth', the *Sunday Times* (17 Jan. 1988).

[4] For a fuller discussion of these issues, see John Hill, *Sex, Class and Realism: British Cinema, 1956–63* (London: British Film Institute, 1986), esp. chap. 3 'Narrative and Realism'.

Raymond Williams has suggested that innovation within realism may be identified in terms of both content and form. In terms of content, he suggests this involves a process of 'social extension', or inclusion of hitherto 'invisible' social groups.[5] Traditionally, social realism within Britain has been associated with the making visible of the working class and, indeed, it is not uncommon for realism almost by definition to be associated with the representation of the industrial working class. However, what is striking about British 'realism' of the 1980s is just how little concern there is with the traditional working class and industrial activity. The context for this is clear. Chapter 1 indicates how the manufacturing sector went into decline during the 1980s, including the heavy industries conventionally associated with the traditional working class. The demise of the mining industry during this period provides one of the most salutary examples. This shift from manufacturing to services, along with the decreasing importance of the manual working class to the economy may be associated with reconceptualizations of the workings of contemporary society in which class is no longer seen to signify the main line of social division or provide the main source of social identity. The 1980s, in this respect, witnessed something of a shift from class politics to a 'new' politics of difference which sought to recognize the plurality of lines of social tension and social identities characteristic of modern societies: not just those of class but gender, ethnicity, and sexual orientation. Likewise, it is this sense of pluralism which characterizes many of the 'state-of-the-nation' films of the 1980s as they seek to do justice to the varying social constituencies and socio-cultural conflicts characteristic of the period. Thus, in the films of the 1980s, it becomes increasingly rare to find the working-class hero as the central protagonist, with his place increasingly being taken by working-class women, gays, blacks, and Asians.

The second part of Williams's formulation concerns innovation with respect to form. The inbuilt instability of the conventions of realism derives not just from the pressure upon them to be socially inclusive but also to do justice to the complexities of social reality. Two factors are relevant here. On the one hand, a common argument is that what is conventionally understood as realism is generally a realism of the surface, which by concentrating on surface realities necessarily misses out on other aspects of reality which are not immediately available for observation. An influence upon British realism of the 1980s, in this respect, was the BBC's television serial *Boys from the Blackstuff* (1982) which, while clearly within a tradition of British social realism, displayed a certain readiness to go beyond its conventions and make use of a degree of stylization and fantasy (as in 'Yosser's Story'). In a review of debates about realism, John Corner draws a distinction between what he describes as two kinds of 'realist project'. One, he suggests, is concerned with verisimilitude (being *like* the real); the other with reference (being *about* the real).[6] Making use of this distinction,

---

[5] Raymond Williams, 'A Lecture on Realism', *Screen*, vol. 18 no. 1 (Spring 1977), 63.

[6] John Corner, 'Presumption as Theory: 'Realism' in Television Studies', *Screen*, vol. 33, no. 1 (Spring 1992), 98.

it can be argued that while there was a continuing preoccupation with reference —with commenting upon contemporary social realities—in British cinema of the 1980s, there was also, in comparison with earlier periods of British film-making, a growing movement away from verisimilitude, or a concern simply to show the surfaces of contemporary life.

The other aspect is that the critique of realism's conventionality has itself led to a certain recognition of it as a style with no necessarily privileged purchase on reality. On the one hand, this has encouraged a growing self-consciousness about the medium of film and its role in the construction of reality (a light-hearted example of which is provided by the rioters in *Sammy and Rosie Get Laid* who obligingly pose for the cameras). In British films of the 1980s, it is therefore increasingly rare for realism to be delivered 'straight' without some indication of its status as a cinematic form or tradition. Moreover, in a culture characterized by postmodern eclecticism in which different forms and styles increasingly coexist and coalesce, realism also becomes perceived as just one set of conventions among others. In this respect, it also becomes less common for cinematic realism to remain 'pure' and, in British films of the 1980s, there is a growing tendency (as was suggested in Chapter 3) towards a mixing of realist devices with those of other aesthetic traditions such as the avant-garde, European 'art cinema', the thriller, the 'woman's film', and, in many cases, comedy. In this respect, the social consciousness tradition of earlier British cinema may be seen to have continued during the 1980s but through a use of film forms characterized by an increasing diversity and hybridity.

Thus, while many of the films which constituted the cycle of 'state-of-the-nation' films in the 1980s belonged to a longstanding tradition of realist British cinema, some also departed from it, reworking it in significant ways as well as mixing it with new kinds of cinematic concerns. As such the commonality of 'state-of-the-nation' films of the period tends to lie in an overlap of ideological concerns rather than a single shared set of aesthetic approaches. This may be seen in the discussion with follows. All the films discussed comment in some way on the 'state of the nation' but the ways in which they do so vary. By looking at *Britannia Hospital* (1982), *The Ploughman's Lunch* (1983), *Defence of the Realm* (1985), *The Last of England* (1987), and *The Cook, The Thief, His Wife and Her Lover* (1989) in turn, I will examine the different means employed by these films to address contemporary social realities and, in doing so, assess some of their strengths and weakness as forms of 'national allegory'.

As James Clifford indicates, the concept of allegory 'denotes a practice in which a narrative fiction continuously refers to another pattern of ideas or events' and, in doing so, offers a form of self-interpretation.[7] In this respect, the British 'state-of-the-nation' film characteristically 'interprets', or encourages readings of, narrative actions according to a more general pattern of political and 'national' events. For Fredric Jameson, the significance of allegory, in this

---

[7] James Clifford, 'On Ethnographic Allegory', in Steven Seidman (ed.), *The Postmodern Turn: New Perspectives on Social Theory* (Cambridge: Cambridge University Press, 1994), 207.

respect, is its potential to cross the divide between private and public worlds. He argues that 'one of the determinants of capitalist culture, that is, the culture of the Western realist and modernist novel, is a radical split between the private and the public, between the poetic and the political, between what we have come to think of as the domain of sexuality and the unconscious and that of the public worlds of classes, the economic, and of secular political power'.[8] He then goes on to draw a contrast between artistic practices which individualize and 'psychologize' political tensions and those which, he argues, allegorize private dilemmas in terms of public conflicts. Although Jameson identifies this latter strategy of 'national allegory' with 'third-world' texts, it does not appear to be confined, as he suggests, to 'third-world' countries.[9] Indeed, in the case of British cinema, there have been a number of significant movements (such as wartime cinema and Ealing comedies) that clearly invite the stories which they tell to be interpreted in precisely such 'national' terms.[10]

In the 1980s, this prediliction for allegory has been sustained but with a difference of emphasis. Thus, in contrast to wartime dramas which celebrated a nation pulling together to win the war, the bulk of 1980s films (*Chariots of Fire* is a notable exception) have used the tactics of allegory, not to project a world of unity and community, but rather to suggest a world of increasing social differences, divisions, and conflicts. This, in turn, may be seen to link with the fusion of art cinema and social realism (discussed in Chapter 3) insofar as the characteristic themes of traditional art cinema (such as anomie and alienation), along with the individualized impulses and desires typical of the art cinema protagonist, then become mapped onto a more public and social terrain. Although this mixture of individual alienation and social dysfunction is particularly evident in *The Ploughman's Lunch*, an influential 'anti-Thatcher' film of the period which is often credited with inaugurating the 'state-of-the-nation' cycle, the use of 'national allegory' to represent social breakdown was given one of its most forceful expressions in Lindsay Anderson's earlier film, *Britannia Hospital*.

Britannia Hospital

The film, in this respect, constitutes something of a companion piece to Anderson's earlier films *If . . .* (1968) and *O Lucky Man!* (1973) which had already explored, in loose allegorical form, the condition of Britain. All three films are scripted by David Sherwin and make use of a number of the same actors and, indeed,

[8] Fredric Jameson, 'Third-World Literature in the Era of Multinational Capitalism', *Social Text*, 15 (Fall 1986), 69.

[9] Aijaz Ahmad argues that Jameson both overstates the presence of 'national allegory' in third-world texts and underestimates its presence in the West in 'Jameson's Rhetoric of Otherness and the "National Allegory"', *Social Text*, 17 (Fall 1987).

[10] See, for example, Charles Barr's discussion in *Ealing Studios* (London: Cameron and Tayleur, 1977). Andrew Higson also identifies what he regards as a characteristic way of 'imagining the nation' as a 'knowable, organic community' in British films in *Waving the Flag: Constructing a National Cinema in Britain* (Oxford: Oxford University Press, 1995).

characters (Malcolm McDowell as Mick Travis and Graham Crowden as Dr Millar). As such, the film has echoes of the Boultings' institutional comedies of the 1950s (and *I'm All Right Jack* in particular) which also made use of a repertory of actors and characters and mounted similar, if somewhat more genial, assaults on the shortcomings of the age.

Like these earlier films, *Britannia Hospital* is loosely plotted, makes use of a number of central characters—who, in this case, are less psychologically rounded individuals than social types—from whom the film maintains a sardonic distance. It also provides a set of representations which clearly 'interpret', and are intended to be interpreted, as metaphors for the state of Britain. A short but telling scene, in this respect, occurs midway through the movie. It is the five hundredth anniversary of the hospital and the hospital management are identifying patients whom it would be suitable for a visiting member of the Royal Family (who turns out to be the Queen Mother) to meet. The representatives of the Palace, Sir Anthony Mount (Marcus Powell) and Lady Felicity Ramsden (John Bett) are introduced to a former government minister—'our most respected foreign minister since Palmerston'—played by the Anderson regular, Arthur Lowe. As the group gather round him, the character leans forward and begins to declaim an abbreviated version of John of Gaunt's speech from Shakespeare's *Richard II*: 'this sceptred isle . . . this other Eden, demi-paradise . . . this precious stone set in the silver sea . . . this blessed plot . . . this realm, this England'. He then falls back dead as a nurse declares that 'he's gone'. This is, of course, a famous speech which has given titles to at least four (three of them wartime) British films—*This England* (1941), *The Demi-Paradise* (1943), *This Happy Breed* (1944), and *This Other Eden* (1959)—and has traditionally served as a shorthand expression of national pride.

Its use in this context not only situates the film in relation to a tradition of representing 'Englishness' but also establishes the film's key themes of the disintegration of the national community and the 'death' of traditional English virtues. Anderson had employed Forster's phrase—'only connect'—to discuss Humphrey Jennings's wartime documentary *Listen to Britain* (1942) and his own documentary *Every Day Except Christmas* (1957) sought to give expression to the values of interconnection and community in the post-war period. In the Britain of *Britannia Hospital*, however, this sense of shared community values has disappeared and been supplanted by selfishness, inefficiency, and strife. At one point in the film, the hospital administrator Potter (Leonard Rossiter) makes a speech to the canteen workers, thanking them for 'showing once again that the British working man . . . and woman . . . will always put unity before anarchy, loyalty before self, commonsense before disruptive strike'. What, of course, the film shows is precisely the opposite as it proceeds to chart the virtual collapse of social order.

The film's opening is eloquent in this regard. Following shots of Big Ben and the Houses of Parliament (which immediately alert us to the scope of the film's satire and its allegorical ambitions), the film cuts to Britannia Hospital. Pickets march outside the hospital gates, protesting about the admission of a black dictator, Ngami (Val Pringle), to the hospital's private ward. An ambulance arrives but is only let through after the pickets have checked that the patient inside is on the verge of death. Once inside the hospital the patient is transferred to a trolley but is then left to die in a corridor by a nurse who is going off duty and card-playing portering staff who are taking a tea break. A slowed-down version of 'Rule Britannia' then plays over the opening credits.

This introduces a series of scenes which maintain a general sense of malaise and malfunctioning (even telephones and keys fail to work properly). Bombs are going off in the city but the admission of casualties is obstructed by the unions, who are also refusing to prepare special food for private patients. Violent protesters then gather outside the hospital gates and succeed in forcing the eviction of private patients. They also force their way into the hospital grounds once they discover that the Queen Mother (Gladys Crosbie) has been smuggled inside. A young female protester offers one of the policeman a flower but is met only with armed might. The TV crew, accompanying the investigative journalist Travis, are too stoned to notice that he has been discovered by Millar and then decapitated. Potter assaults an electrical worker, possibly killing him, to ensure that the royal visit will proceed while the royal party themselves display an archaic concern for social etiquette despite the mounting chaos around them. Although it is the workers and protesters who bear the brunt of the film's attack, the film is none the less relatively indiscriminate in its satirical sweep. There is, as Andrew Sarris suggests, 'no one to root for and not much hope'.[11]

This sense of all-embracing despair is given an additional emphasis by the introduction of a further area of narrative interest. Different levels of allegorical meanings may be evident in the same text and, in *Britannia Hospital*, it becomes clear that the film is intended both as a 'local' story of British social malaise and a more general, or 'universal', commentary on the state of humanity. This is most apparent in the story-line concerning Dr Millar, the scientist with a mission to create 'a new beginning for mankind'. This has two aspects. On the one hand, he carries on his interest, already evident in *O Lucky Man!*, with the transplantation of body parts to produce a new human being. On the other hand, he wishes to create 'a new intelligence' which 'can save mankind' in the form of an enlarged brain removed from the shackles of the body. Writing on the horror film, Andrew Tudor suggests how science-based horror movies traditionally 'postulate commitment to science as a central source of disorder' and how 'their key protagonists are devoted to the pursuit of knowledge at the expense of humane values'.[12] In this respect, *Britannia Hospital* mixes its social satire with the conventions of the horror film. Millar's 'mad scientist' is so committed to his vision that he is prepared to take one patient off a life-support system and murder the captured Travis. The resulting creation, however, is not the 'new man' which had been planned but a flawed 'monster' which attacks and strangles

[11] Andrew Sarris, 'The Gleeful Celebration of Chaos', *The Village Voice*, 15 (Mar. 1983), 41.
[12] Andrew Tudor, *Monsters and Mad Scientists: A Cultural History of the Horror Movie* (Oxford: Basil Blackwell, 1989), 137.

Millar's loyal assistant, Macmillan (Jill Bennett) and has to be immediately killed (amidst scenes of gothic flamboyance).

Millar's bodiless brain, 'Genesis', is no less flawed. In a key scene, the film's warring factions are temporarily united. Trade unionists, protesters, medical staff, and royalty sit together in the lecture hall as Millar explains both the short-comings of humanity ('We waste, we destroy and we cling like savages to our superstitions') and the 'era of infinite possibilities' which an age of science is now making possible. Genesis is then revealed and begins to speak by quoting from *Hamlet*: 'What a piece of work is a man! How noble in reason! How infinite in faculties! How like a god!' However, in the film's final squib, the brain almost immediately reveals its less than divine qualities by stalling and repeatedly intoning the phrase 'how like a god'. As Tudor suggests, by the 1970s, the 'decline in the efficacy of science' had become a key feature of science-based horror films.[13] In *Britannia Hospital* this declining confidence in the power of science is interlinked with a growing pessimism, characteristic of postmodernism, about the possibility of human progress or social improvement. If Millar offers science as the key to human perfectibility, the actuality of his experiments show him to be badly wrong.

The gloom and despair which is so apparent in this film was not well received on its release. The film was shown at Cannes in May 1982 and put on general release in June. Given that the war in the Falklands/Malvinas was still taking place, it was inevitable that it would seem at odds with the national mood. As one critic complained, 'in the thick of the Falklands conflict—and in the face of our nation's rekindled unity—he is marching into cinematic battle with a film that MOCKS us'.[14] Perhaps not surprisingly, the film fared badly at the box-office and enjoyed only a short run. However, while this might suggest how much at odds the film was with the resurgence of right-wing nationalism, it is also fair to note how much the film's dyspeptic vision had in common with the conservative agenda of this time.

Writing of the socially critical and satirical movies which were a feature of the 'new Hollywood' in the 1970s, Ryan and Kellner argue how such movies were in a sense complicit with the growth of the New Right. Not only did the diagnosis of the failings of institutions and those in power to be found in these films have much in common with right-wing criticisms but, by virtue of the 'sense of loss, pessimism, and despair' which they evoked, such films also contributed to the creation of an ideological vacuum which 'conservative values and ideals' proved best-placed to fill.[15] In the same way, it can be seen how the all-embracing negativism of *Britannia Hospital* overlaps with conservative criticisms of the social-democratic state in the 1970s and has the potential to fuel right-wing as much as left-wing 'remedies'. As Michael Wood observed at the time, by

---

[13] Andrew Tudor, *Monsters and Mad Scientists: A Cultural History of the Horror Movie*, 150.

[14] Victor Davis, 'What a Moment to Tear Britain Apart', *Daily Express* (25 May 1982).

[15] Michael Ryan and Douglas Kellner, *Camera Politica: The Politics and Ideology of Contemporary Film* (Bloomington and Indianapolis: Indiana University Press, 1988), 86–7.

treating everyone with equal cynicism, the film simply ends up voicing 'a sort of populist, conservative discontent'.[16] In this respect, the film, and its portrait of a social world more redolent of the 1970s than the 1980s, appears to give voice to a number of the discontents to which Thatcherism had already begun to offer its own solutions . Thus, the film's emphasis on union obduracy and industrial disruption clearly had echoes of the 'winter of discontent' of 1978/9 and added credence to Conservative demands to curb union power. In the same way, the film's portrait of managerial weakness in the face of union demands and willingness to make concessions (over the admission of bomb victims and the treatment of private patients) could be seen to reinforce a sense of the failings of 'consensus' management and the need for employers to reclaim the 'right to manage'. The mockery of the canteen workers' absurd demands for equality ('It's the same for everyone or nothing at all') locks into the anti-egalitarian thrust of New Right economic thinking while the breakdown of law and order, represented by riots in the streets, violent protest, and terrorist acts, reinforced Conservative demands for a strong state (and authoritarian solutions to social conflict). Even the film's attacks on the 'establishment', as represented by the Royal Family and their entourage, may be seen to link to renewed emphases upon enterprise and the need to push aside the *ancien régime* (or Tory grandees) in the interests of economic regeneration and efficiency.

Social Art Cinema: *The Ploughman's Lunch* and the Politics of History

A critique of the 'state of the nation' is carried on in *The Ploughman's Lunch* but, unlike *Britannia Hospital,* its targets are more explicitly linked to the 1980s and the rise of Thatcherism. As has already been suggested, the film may be seen as a kind of hybrid in which the interests and conventions of the realist tradition are combined with those of the European art film of the 1950s and 1960s. Thus, in common with conventional realism, the film distances itself from mainstream Hollywood conventions by downplaying plot incident and spectacle and focuses upon social issues of contemporary concern. In common with the art cinema tradition, it is also a film which is self-reflexive about its own status as a medium, drawing attention to the ways in which the media construct images of reality and 'quoting' from other cinematic and artistic styles. This mixing of elements is also apparent in the film's use of characterization. For David Bordwell, a key characteristic of the European art film, in addition to loosely structured plots and stylistic self-consciousness, is the use of confused or goal-bereft protagonists.[17] As befits its hybrid status, the central character in *The Ploughman's Lunch* is also something of a fusion: combining features of the working-class hero of the British new wave, on the one hand, with those of the alienated hero

[16] Michael Wood, 'Carry on Hamlet', *New Society* (3 June 1982), 393.
[17] David Bordwell, *Narration in the Fiction Film* (London: Methuen, 1985), esp. pp. 205–13.

of the traditional European art film, on the other. As such, the more existential alienation of the hero in the art film is overlaid on the more familiar social and sexual discontents of the working-class hero of social realism.

Indeed, as a number of critics have observed, *The Ploughman's Lunch* has clear links to the plot of upward mobility (and theme of 'escape') characteristic of British 'new wave' films and of *Room at the Top* (1959) in particular. *Room at the Top* tells the tale of Joe Lampton, the working-class lad determined to escape his working-class background and make it to the top despite the emotional and spiritual costs to be paid. His pursuit of upward mobility is made concrete in his pursuit of Susan, the woman from a higher social class whom he does not love but is none the less prepared to marry. *The Ploughman's Lunch* is organized around a similar tale of social climbing. Like Joe Lampton, James Penfield (Jonathan Pryce) wishes to be accepted into a higher social group. He is embarrassed about his background, reluctant to visit his parents despite the ill-health of his mother and is even prepared to lie about their existence. He is also involved in the pursuit of an upper middle-class woman, Susan Barrington (Charlie Dore), whom his friend Jeremy (Tim Curry) describes as 'way above his station'. Indeed, the published screenplay makes this theme explicit by suggesting that James's fascination with Susan 'owes as much to the certainties of her class as to her looks'.[18] Unlike *Room at the Top*, James does not ultimately get the girl but neither does he suffer the come-uppance experienced by Joe. He is, of course, 'betrayed' by Jeremy who succeeds with Susan where James has failed and this suggests an exclusion from the social world to which he has aspired. His book, none the less, is published and the final scene reveals his impatience to get on, even when at his mother's funeral. Tony Williams suggests, a little unconvincingly, that the final freeze frame image of James ('a petrified ahistorical frame') represents a symbolic form of 'punishment' for 'his complicity in the political distortions and cultural betrayals that characterize 80s England'.[19] However, there is also a sense in which the shot simply drives home how the character remains unchanged by his experiences and is destined to carry on in much the same way as before.

As with *Room at the Top*, the theme of upward mobility is used to query the value of the main character's ambition and make comment upon the quality of the society to which he aspires. For *The Ploughman's Lunch*, this is a world characterized by superficiality and self-interest, characteristic of the new Thatcherite era. Susan's mother, Ann (Rosemary Harris), describes her daughter's friends as 'rather empty people' and the film highlights Susan's ambition and desire for 'power' along with her readiness to put her own interests ahead of others (explaining to James, for example, her abandonment of the women's movement in favour of self-advancement). *The Ploughman's Lunch*, in this respect, picks up on the theme of spiritual 'emptiness' which had been a feature of the 'new wave' films but inflects it in the direction of a critique of the brash

---

[18] Ian McEwan, *A Move Abroad: or Shall We Die? and The Ploughman's Lunch* (London: Picador, 1989), 40.

[19] Tony Williams, '*The Ploughman's Lunch*: Remembering or Forgetting History', *Jump Cut*, no. 36 (1991), 17.

new world of the 'enterprise culture' and the 'yuppie' lifestyle associated with it. James and Jeremy are seen to enjoy ludicrously extravagant drinks at the Zanzibar cocktail bar, James's publisher Gold (David de Keyser) discusses James's book proposal over a substantial lunch at Langan's Brasserie while, in a half-knowing reworking of a famous scene from yet another social-climbing drama *Nothing but the Best* (1964), James and Jeremy talk facetiously about the Falklands war while engaging in a half-hearted game of squash. According to Susan's step-father, Matthew (Frank Finlay), Britain once led the world into the Industrial Revolution but now leads only in television commercials. In this respect, it is the commodified culture of a new service class, devoted to the production of signs rather than goods, that the film takes as a central symbol of the contemporary era's lack of substance.

In doing so, the film explicitly attacks the synthetic (and 'de-historicized') versions of the past which such a culture of appearance creates. Matthew himself works in advertising and, in one scene, we observe a comfortable pre-war middle class home and family before the camera pushes past to behind the set to reveal the artifice involved in the manufacture of such an image. In contrast to the nostalgic evocations of the past characteristic of the heritage film, *The Ploughman's Lunch* seeks to highlight the 'constructed' character of the past and the loss of historicity, in Jameson's terms, which accompanies it. Indeed, the film's very title—the ploughman's lunch—derives from an advertising invention which Matthew describes as 'a completely successful fabrication of the past'.

However, the film's criticism of these representations of the past is not simply that they lack depth and substance but that they are also mobilized according to the ideological demands of the present. In this respect, the film may be seen to offer a vivid illustration of Patrick Wright's argument that 'the national past is above all a *modern* past and . . . it is defined . . . around the leading tensions of the contemporary political situation'.[20] This process of constructing the past is explored by drawing a connection between the deception and evasion involved in James's desire for success and the more general deception and fabrication involved in the appropriation of the past by the political Right. The specific link is provided by James's activities as a historian. As McEwan himself suggests, James's personal life involves 'a sequence of betrayals and deceits' which then 'parallel the events he was distorting in history'.[21] James is writing a history of the Suez crisis in 1956 when the British were forced to back down from confrontation with the Egyptians, who had nationalized the Suez canal, when it became clear that the US did not support British actions. James wishes to rescue the history of Suez from its conventional associations with national humiliation and post-imperial adjustment (and, in doing so, also flatter the Americans who will be the book's primary market). In doing so, he may also be seen to be involved in 'correcting' the past in line with contemporary political exigencies.

---

[20] Patrick Wright, *On Living in an Old Country: The National Past in Contemporary Britain* (London: Verso, 1985), 2.
[21] 'Introduction' to *The Ploughman's Lunch*, 28.

At the very beginning of the film we hear a radio broadcast describe 'how the governments of Eastern Europe distort their recent past in history books to suit their present policies and allegiances'; the clear implication of the film is that James's own attempts to rewrite the history of the Suez affair amounts to something similar.

In this case, the contemporary political situation is provided by the consolidated power of the Conservative government in the wake of the Falklands victory (itself a rescue from 'national humiliation').[22] Although the initial draft of the script was completed prior to the war, the shooting of the film took place in its aftermath and provided the film's events with an immediate political context. As has already been noted, the Falklands victory rescued the Conservative government from a desperately low level of popularity and injected a new sense of self-confidence within the party. The film makes use of material shot at the 1982 Conservative party conference in Brighton, including Margaret Thatcher's famous 'spirit of the South Atlantic' speech in which she declared that British patriotism 'was never really lost'. In doing so, it invokes this new spirit of 'patriotism' as the context in which James's concern to rescue the disastrous events of Suez from their conventional association with imperial folly and failure may be located. As such, the restored sense of national pride for which the Tories claimed the Falklands war was responsible is linked to the 'patriotic' reworking of national history undertaken by James. The film concludes its use of Mrs Thatcher's speech with her claim that 'We will tell the people the truth, and the people will be our judge'. For the film, however, this is far from the case: it is 'truth' which has been the casualty as history is refashioned in accordance with contemporary political requirements.

This is also linked to the role played by the media in recording and representing public events. Ann suggests to James that, as a journalist, he constantly has to take decisions which depend upon his 'sense of history'. The film sees the modern media of public communication as involved in the construction of history and, accordingly, lays great stress upon the active *mediating* role which they perform. Hence, a majority of the key players in the film actually work in the media (James in radio, Susan in television, and Jeremy in newspapers) and the action of the film is constantly punctuated by the use of radio voice-overs and TV screens (as in the cocktail bar scene when a TV in the background announces the departure of the naval fleet for the Falklands). The role of the media in selecting and shaping the news is also stressed. Thus, there is a scene of a news conference involving James which not only highlights James's own 'bad faith' regarding the women at Greenham Common but also the editorial process whereby the reporting of opposition to the war is effectively marginalized. This possesses a particular irony given the involvement of Ann's former husband in the battle for the BBC's independence from government at the time of Suez; in this case, there may be formal independence but, the film suggests, it is not being exercised. In

---

[22] Following the Agentinian invasion of the islands, the then Foreign Secretary Lord Carrington resigned on 5 April 1982, declaring that 'what has happened in the Falkland Islands is a national humiliation'.

PLATE 9. Bad faith: Jonathan Pryce and Tim Curry in *The Ploughman's Lunch*

this respect, the complaint contained in the newspaper cutting read by the news editor that 'under cover of an authoritative news service' they are 'propagating a military definition of reality' is seen not to be so wide of the mark.

However, the film also wishes to suggest how reality may be defined differently and the past constructed in alternative ways. The relationship to history in Eastern Europe, introduced at the film's start, is returned to on a number of occasions. James and Susan, for example, go to see Wajda's *Man of Iron* (an example of a kind of political filmmaking which it has been suggested *The Ploughman's Lunch* seeks to emulate); Ann quotes Milan Kundera to the effect that 'the struggle of man against tyranny is the struggle of memory against forgetting'; while, most significantly of all, the Polish historian Jacek (Witold Schejbal), a dinner guest of Ann and Matthew, counterposes a conservative history characteristic of England, devoted to the memorizing of kings and queens, to a subversive history, to be found in Poland, concerned with moments of popular resistance.

Where the film is weak is in giving embodiment to the agents of popular resistance or the representatives of alternative values. This can be seen in the way in which the film portrays the three sets of characters who stand outside the dominant value-system which the film portrays: James's parents, Ann, and the women of Greenham Common. In the films of the 'new wave', it was the traditional working class who stood as representatives of an alternative set of values to those of commercialism and mass culture. Thus, in the case of *Room at the Top*, it is Joe Lampton's uncle and aunt who query his desire for 'brass'. In the case of *The Ploughman's Lunch*, however, James's parents cannot be seen to represent any particular countervailing set of values or cultural tradition. So, while the scenes between James and his parents are characterized by an acute sense of discomfort and unease, they do not suggest an alienation from a distinct set of cultural values so much as a simple embarrassment about, and impatience with, his relatively humble working-class or lower middle-class background. As such, the film confirms the general trend away from representations of the working class and any sense that they might function as a counter-balancing force to Thatcherism.

However, if the film is unable to locate positive values in its working-class characters, it has similar problems with the others as well. This is, for example, true of Ann, the older woman with whom James has an affair. Again, this may be compared with *Room at the Top* in which Joe also falls for an older woman, Alice Aisgill. However, it is the differences that are most significant. In *Room at the Top*, Joe is genuinely in love with Alice and his marriage to Susan thus exacts a real cost. James, however, is not really attracted to Ann at all and cynically makes use of her for the information about Suez which she can provide. And, while his relationship with Alice in *Room at the Top* allows Joe to 'be himself', James's relationship with Ann in *The Ploughman's Lunch* is permeated by deceit. The film, in this respect, also inverts the meanings which the 'new wave' characteristically attached to images of nature. In *Room at the Top*, for example, the 'naturalness' of Joe and Alice's relationship is underscored by the iconography of nature employed when the couple escape from the town. In the case of *The Ploughman's Lunch*, however, the fact that the affair between Ann and James is conducted in the country provides no defence against the duplicities characteristic of the city. As a result, the virtues which attached to Alice in *Room at the Top* are not inherited by Ann. She is constantly deluded about James's character and motives and, as a result, is made to appear highly gullible. She is also seen to be somewhat hypocritical, espousing radical political opinions but living extremely comfortably. Indeed, in a film characterized by a degree of visual dullness, some of the most ironic use of *mise-en-scène* occurs in scenes, shot in deep focus, showing Ann's domestic help working silently in the background.

And, although it is the Greenham women who have often been seen to be the most positive element within the film, a degree of scepticism about them is also evident. The first of the women whom James encounters is described in the script as 'almost childlike in her friendliness' and the women's openness to James, and confidence that he will help them, proves misplaced. As with Ann, there is a suggestion of gullibility and certainly a degree of naïvety with regard to the political forces with which they have to contend. McEwan has suggested that in *The Ploughman's Lunch*, he did not want to furnish 'good guys' and sought to avoid the conventional machinery of identification.[23] Characters, in this respect, tend to embody a degree of 'typical' traits rather than being fully psychologically rounded. The result is a film in which the spectator is distanced from virtually all of the characters irrespective of their political or ethical orientation. Although

---

[23] 'Introduction' to *The Ploughman's Lunch*, 30.

McEwan argues that, in this type of cinema, 'moral values' are then embodied in narrative structure rather than character, the use of such distancing strategies tends to encourage an ironic awareness, and even disenchantment, on the part of the spectator which vitiates against the delineation of a moral position other than a kind of generalized cynicism (to some extent, typical of the art film). As a result, the film is inevitably rather better at diagnosing contemporary ills than identifying a position from which opposition to these might be mounted.

The Political Thriller: *Defence of the Realm*

This is also the case with the cinematically rather different *Defence of the Realm* (1985). Like *The Ploughman's Lunch*, the film is concerned to reflect upon contemporary social ills and, in doing so, it also deviates from the traditions of social realism. In this case, however, it does so through an incorporation of elements from the criminal investigation or thriller. The film, in this respect, links to a body of material, appearing particularly on television, concerned with the exercise of power in contemporary Britain. *Edge of Darkness* (1985), for example, was concerned to explore the murky world of nuclear power while *A Very British Coup* (1988) examined the role of the security services in destabilizing a left-wing Labour government. Ken Loach's *Hidden Agenda* (1990) also pursued this theme but in the context of a cover-up of a 'shoot-to-kill policy' in Northern Ireland. In all cases, these television programmes and films reflect an anxiety about the growth of a state which has become increasingly powerful but also less accountable. They worry about just who is in charge and what relationship exists between democratically elected governments and the secret services. *Defence of the Realm* also has particular affinities with *Edge of Darkness* because both are concerned with the hidden world of nuclear power and the threat to democracy that inevitably accompanies the manufacture and ownership of nuclear weapons (the growth of 'a state-within-a-state').[24]

As such, the film draws on both a liberal Hollywood tradition of journalist movies in which a journalist hero exposes wrongdoing in high places and a more European tradition of political thrillers associated with filmmakers such as Costa-Gavras and Francesco Rosi. Indeed, *Defence of the Realm*'s co-producer, Linda Myles, explicitly acknowledged Rosi's *Illustrious Corpses* (1975) as an influence and screened the film for the crew before shooting.[25] The work of Costa-Gavras and Rosi exemplifies a model of political filmmaking which seeks to bend mainstream, 'entertainment' conventions (of narration, characterization, and style) to more overtly political ends. In the same way, *Defence of the Realm*

[24] The growth of a 'secret society' is also explored in *Hidden City* (1987) in which an academic researcher James Richards (Charles Dance) is drawn into a search for secret film footage, including material showing the effects of some kind of scientific testing—probably nuclear—in the 1950s.

[25] See Susan Barrowclough, 'In Britain Now: *Defence of the Realm*', *Sight and Sound* (Summer 1985), 191.

seeks to make use of the devices of the criminal investigation and thriller to raise questions about the state of contemporary Britain. Like *The Ploughman's Lunch*, the film is organized around a tabloid journalist, Nick Mullen (Gabriel Byrne), whose work is both relatively trivial (a colleague congratulates him on 'a nice wee piece on the bingo winner') and unscrupulous ('don't let the truth get in the way of a good story', scoffs his old-style journalist colleague, Vernon Bayliss (Denholm Elliott)). However, unlike Penfield in *The Ploughman's Lunch* who largely remains unchanged by events (and fails to uphold the conventional role of the journalist as a 'guardian of truth'), Mullen experiences a certain 'coming-to-consciousness', as he runs up against not only the sinister political forces at work in British society but also the political control exercised over his own newspaper. Thus, having broken the original Profumo-like 'call-girl and spy' story, that leads to the resignation of the MP Dennis Markham (Ian Bannen), he comes to realize that he has been fed false information by the security services and has helped to 'frame' Markham just as he was about to ask awkward questions, in the Houses of Parliament, about the death of a young man on the run from borstal. This, then turns out to be the 'real story': that the young man's death is linked to a near-nuclear accident at an American airbase, an event which the government has been attempting to cover up. However, Mullen's newspaper, which had enthusiastically run the original stories libelling Markham, now refuses to publish the results of his investigation. The newspaper's proprietor, Victor Kingsbrook (Fulton Mackay), it is revealed, is 'into the government for millions' and is more concerned about protecting his business interests than having his newspaper print the truth.

As Julian Petley observed at the time, the film provided a 'timely . . . representation of contemporary Britain' that was prepared 'to broach all sorts of directly political questions' including 'the politicization of the security services, the issues raised by the presence of American nuclear bases in Britain, and the reasons why Britain's press is so monolithically conservative'.[26] In this way, the film fed into public concerns regarding the government's obsession with 'official secrecy' as well as the anxieties surrounding the siting of Cruise missiles in Britain. As the narrowly averted nuclear crisis in the film results from a full-scale military alert in response to the bombing of the United States embassy in Ankara, there is even a degree of anticipation of the 'retaliatory' attacks on Libya by American airfighters only a few months after the film's release.

Nevertheless, although the film was undoubtedly successful in raising a number of pertinent questions about the state of British society, its use of the thriller format also had consequences for the kind of diagnosis it could offer. Traditionally, it has been the great strength of political thrillers to reach and maintain the interest of an audience who might normally be turned off by politics; however, the form of the thriller is not neutral and this inevitably has consequences for the way in which political questions are then handled.

[26] *Monthly Film Bulletin*, 338. In this respect, Petley much prefers the film to *The Ploughman's Lunch* which he argued simply offered 'the vague delineation of a generalized feeling of malaise (represented in terms of its central characters' moral paucity)'.

Three main issues are relevant in this respect: the use, by the political thriller, of mainstream narrative conventions, the adoption of the specific conventions of the crime film, and the relationship between text and spectator which these conventions encourage. It has, for example, been a common argument that mainstream narrative conventions (and the logic of character-based causality) typically encourage explanations of social realities in individual and psychological terms rather than economic and political ones while the conventions of 'classic realism', with their requirement of a convincing dramatic illusion, not only highlight observable, surface realities at the expense of, possibly more fundamental, underlying ones but also attach a greater significance to interpersonal relations than social, economic, and political structures.[27] Inevitably this has consequences for the key question which the political thriller raises: how is power exercised in society? The British political thriller of the 1980s is particularly concerned to uncover what is going on inside the 'secret state' and to make visible what the authorities would prefer to keep hidden. However, it is in the nature of the conventions employed that this process of investigation, and uncovering of 'hidden' realities, gravitates towards some kind of conspiracy theory insofar as it is possible to show—and dramatize—conspiratorial actions in a way that underlying social and economic forces cannot. As a result, it is the idea of a 'conspiracy' that typically becomes the preferred form of 'explanation' in accounting for how the 'secret state' works.

Thus, in *Edge of Darkness*, there is a conspiracy (involving the secret services, the government, and big business) to reprocess plutonium illicitly as part of an international military programme. In the case of *Hidden Agenda*, there are no less than two conspiracies—not only the conspiracy to pervert the course of justice by the security services in Northern Ireland in the early 1980s but also the conspiracy on the part of a small group of businessmen, security personnel, and politicians (led by a thinly disguised Airey Neave) to overthrow a Labour government and replace Edward Heath by Margaret Thatcher as leader of the Conservatives in Britain in the 1970s. In the case of *Defence of the Realm*, the conspiracy concerns, as has been seen, the attempt to conceal a near-nuclear accident. The film's key scene, in this respect, takes place when the journalist Mullen goes to confront Anthony Clegg (Oliver Ford Davies), the official who has been responsible for leaking false information about Markham. Mullen is seized by three men, taken from Clegg's club and then driven to an unidentified destination. Following a walk down a narrow corridor and a wait in an office, he is finally confronted with three unidentified men, seated behind a table, who proceed to question him about both his political beliefs and his intentions regarding his story. As in the scene in *Hidden Agenda*, when a Tory politician and senior member of MI5 are brought together to admit to the policeman Kerrigan (Brian Cox), what they have done, this is an episode which follows from the narrative's drive towards visibility (and the showing of power). However, it also highlights the weakness of the thriller's representation of political

---

[27] For a fuller discussion of these matters, see Hill, *Sex, Class and Realism*, chap. 3.

PLATE 10. Visualizing the secret state: *Defence of the Realm*

power, identifying the workings of the 'secret state' with a group of nameless conspirators whose identity still remains a mystery at the film's end. As Judith Williamson asks in relation to the film: 'Is "The State" really some kind of hidey-hole located, Narnia-like, behind a book-case and leading out onto back streets? Is it really a shadow-land filled with anonymous baddies who sit in triumvirate in salons full of statues and ask pointed questions?'[28]

Moreover, while such imagery may satisfy the desire to see the 'secret state' uncovered, it also has consequences for the kinds of 'politics' which the film can then provide. For conspiracy provides a problematic basis for political explanation and is largely unhelpful in accounting for the events—such as the rise of the New Right in the 1970s and 1980s—that constitute the backdrop to the film's actions. Conspiracy theory, in this respect, has the virtue of neatness—and, for film, the benefit of dramatic effectiveness—but its use is at the expense of genuine social and political complexity. As Michael Albert puts it, 'conspiracy theory has the appeal of mystery—it is dramatic, compelling, vivid and human'. But at the same time it is also flawed: it is, as he suggests, the 'sport fan's or voyeur's view of complex circumstances'.[29]

Furthermore, just as the political thriller tends to interpret state power in personal, conspiratorial terms, so it tends to conceive of opposition to the state as primarily an individual activity as well. This is encouraged not only by the

---

[28] Judith Williamson, 'The Lust For Truth and The Secret State', *New Socialist* (Feb. 1986), 41.
[29] Michael Albert, quoted in Jerry White, 'Conspiracy Thrillers: *Hidden Agenda* and *JFK*', *Jump Cut*, no. 38 (June 1993), pp. 15 and 18.

individualizing logic of mainstream narrative conventions but also by the specific conventions of the crime thriller, especially when structured around the investigation of an individual detective (or journalist) and his quest to reveal, or make visible, the truth behind a crime or enigma. Thus, in *Defence of the Realm*, the character of Mullen is cast in the archetypal mould of the loner. He lives on his own, has no apparent family ties, and, as his interrogators note, lacks any clear political allegiances. In this respect, he is even more 'cut off' from his roots than Penfield in *The Ploughman's Lunch*, whose family and class background are, at least sketchily, mapped out.

It is, of course, these qualities of the 'loner' that characteristically permit the individual investigator to stick to his task and uncover what others would prefer hidden. However, by sticking with the conventions of the investigation format in this way, it is inevitable that *Defence of the Realm* ends up downplaying more organized, or collective, forms of political protest and opposition.[30] It is the actions of the lone individual, Mullen, which are invested with significance while the role of the anti-nuclear movement in exposing or resisting the nuclear state is almost completely ignored. There is a brief scene in the film where Mullen is seen shaking hands with a retiring printer but, again, there is no suggestion of a link with organized labour. Indeed, the scene involves something of an elegy for a disappearing working-class culture and is associated, in the film, with the death of the decent, old-style, ex-CP journalist, Vernon, the news of which is reported to Mullen in the scene that immediately follows.[31] However, if the political thriller's emphasis upon the individual investigator leads to a downplaying of the role of collective action or protest, this also has consequences for how political change is then envisaged. This is particularly so when the thriller is also a conspiracy drama.

As has often been recognized, the conventional crime drama tends to rely upon a general confidence in the ability of the current social set-up to triumph over injustice and right wrongs (which are then characteristically identified as the responsibility of isolated or 'deviant' individuals rather than social institutions or political regimes). In the conspiracy thriller, however, it is those who are in power who are the source of wrongdoing and it is therefore much more difficult to identify the means whereby social ills may be remedied. Conspiracy thrillers, therefore, tend to blunt the affirmative (and socially conservative)

---

[30] Although the film's plot revolves around a character (Dyce) who gains unauthorized access to an American airbase, the script chooses not to link this with overtly political acts such as that of the women peace campaigners who successfully broke into the missile base at Greenham Common in December 1983.

[31] This sense of the waning relevance (and corruption) of old forms of organization to the politics of the nuclear age is indicated in virtually the opening scene of *Edge of Darkness* when the trade union official Godbolt (Jack Watson) pleads with the detective Craven (Bob Peck) to delay making his report on vote-rigging in the union's elections. It subsequently turns out that Godbolt is himself a part of the conspiracy against Craven, insofar as he has been working for the security services. The television series is more generally pessimistic about the value of protest, revealing the ecological movement Gaia to have been founded by a CIA agent and placing its faith in the assumed ability of the planet to 'protect itself' (as symbolized by the mysterious appearance of black flowers) rather than organized political opposition to the nuclear state.

impulses of the crime story by stressing the limitations of the individual detective hero and the difficulties of actually getting to the truth. Thus, the investigator may prove unable to solve the crime due to the complexity and deviousness of the forces confronting him or, if he does succeed in solving the mystery, he may then find himself powerless to do anything about it. The most memorable example of this is undoubtedly *The Parallax View* (1974) in which Warren Beatty's reporter uncovers the inevitable political conspiracy but is then himself assassinated. *Defence of the Realm* displays a number of similarities in this regard.

It is a film that has been associated with film noir and the ending of the investigation does, indeed, prove grimly fatalistic. As such, the film clearly departs from the standard plot-lines of liberal journalistic films. According to Matthew Ehrlich, the characteristic 'syntax' of the journalism movie involves a reporter grappling with an editor over a big story while simultaneously becoming involved 'romantically with a significant other'.[32] In both respects, *Defence of the Realm* inflects these conventions in a negative direction. As we have seen, Mullen's editor is at the mercy of his proprietor, Kingsbrook, who is himself a part of the 'conspiracy' that the film identifies and is thus able to ensure that Mullen's story is quashed. The film also provides Mullen with a 'significant other' but then thwarts the expectation of a romance. Mullen succeeds in enlisting the help of Markham's secretary, Nina Beckman (Greta Scacchi) but there is little sense of mutual attraction until the film's end when they meet in Mullen's flat. However, in a stark and startling conclusion, they are both blown up. In this respect, the anticipated coming together of the couple, along with their sense of triumph in uncovering the conspiracy, is effectively blocked.

Having worked out this bleak dramatic logic, the film does, of course, reinstate a degree of optimism: although Mullen and Nina have been killed they have succeeded in getting the information about the cover-up out of the country and published in foreign newspapers. However, there is a sense in which this ending is simply grafted on and, given what we have observed of the labyrinthine workings of the secret state, it is difficult to see just how newspaper revelations will lead to change. The film's final shot of the Houses of Parliament is ambivalent in this regard. The newspaper headlines that we see indicate a 'government cover-up'. However, the film's reluctance in identifying the conspirators, and its emphasis upon the shadowy role of the secret services, suggest that it is precisely the ability of a democratically elected government to impose its authority upon the secret services that is in doubt. Whether the faith in parliamentary democracy which the film's final image appears to suggest is warranted, therefore, remains open to question.

To this extent, the film may be seen to end up encouraging not only a sense of political powerlessness but also paranoia. For it is not just that conspiracy films characteristically associate the exercise of political power with conspiracy

---

[32] Matthew C. Ehrlich, 'Journalism in the Movies', *Critical Studies in Mass Communication*, vol. 14 (1997), 269.

but that the reliance upon conspiracy as a way of accounting for the workings of the 'secret state' inevitably encourages a sense of paranoia (rather than genuine political insight). And, while paranoia is an accompaniment of most conspiracy theories, it becomes especially acute with the rise of the nuclear state, and the anxieties concerning secrecy and lack of democratic accountability which arise from it. As Williason puts it: 'the nuclear state had become a bogey, a focus of half-formed fears and paranoias; and its representation as a sort of secret ministry keeps it conveniently vague, closer to psychical than political reality.'[33] Thus, when Mullen encounters his anonymous persecutors in an unidentified building, his sense of alienation is less political than existential as he struggles to make sense of the Kafkaesque world in which he has become embroiled. ('We are here to assess your case', he is told by the main spokesman for the group. 'What case?' is his incredulous reply).[34]

In a review of cultural trends during the 1980s, an edition of the BBC's *The Late Show* suggested that the cycle of 'conspiracy drama with its hero trying but failing to penetrate the heart of darkness' provided the 'perfect form' for the decade.[35] Given what I have argued, this is clearly a judgement which is problematic—for as a 'form' it is evident that conspiracy drama was quite limited in its ability to generate political insights. From another point of view, however, it was 'perfect': for the mix of conspiracy and paranoia, and the sense of helplessness which these thrillers characteristically created, was also a good expression of the strong sense of political impotence (and inability to effect change) that was felt by so many liberals and the left during this period. Something of a similar outlook is also apparent in *The Last of England*. Formally, however, it is a work that is radically different.

The Avant-Garde: *The Last Of England*

Underlying debates about the political thriller have been issues of form. Criticisms of the political thriller have focused not only on how form pushes content in particular directions but also how it encourages a particular mode of address to spectators. Thus, whatever the strengths and weaknesses of the actual message which the political thriller communicates, critics have suggested that it is still one that is, so to speak, 'pre-digested'. That is to say, by virtue of a reliance

---

[33] Judith Williamson, 'The Lust For Truth and The Secret State', 41. It is this 'psychic' reality of paranoia with which *Edge of Darkness* partly plays by having its detective hero, Craven (Bob Peck), teeter on the edge of breakdown in the wake of his daughter's murder. Craven's efforts to make known the nuclear conspiracy that he has uncovered are therefore undermined by the ability of others to label him as mentally unstable. For writer, Troy Kennedy Martin, the 'paranoia', or 'gloominess', of the series was warranted because of the 'paranoid times' in which it was written. See Troy Kennedy Martin, 'Introduction', *Edge of Darkness* (London: Faber and Faber, 1990), p. vii.

[34] In his classic essay on 'Z movies', Guy Henebelle follows Jean Fieschi and Emile Breton in identifying how political thrillers account for politics in terms of 'a clash between a solitary hero and a vast oppressive structure'. This is clearly the case with *Defence of the Realm* as well. See Guy Henebelle, 'Z Movies, or What Hath Costa-Gavras Wrought', *Cineaste*, vol. 6 no. 2 (1974), 29.

[35] *The Late Show* (BBC2) (11 Mar. 1991).

upon individual characters and stars with whom we identify, and upon the tightly structured patterns of narrative suspense which engage us emotionally, the political thriller is seen to 'make up our minds for us' rather than encourage us in critical reflection. It may question, as *Defence of the Realm* does, the prevailing ideologies of society but it does so by employing the same emotional patterns of involvement as films which offer the contrary view and hence fails to encourage audiences to engage critically with political ideas. To some extent, it could be argued that *Defence of the Realm* attempts to address these issues. The film's leading role is played by an actor—Gabriel Byrne—who, at least at that stage in his career, was relatively unknown. His character is also something of a 'type', rather than a fully fleshed-out character, with the result that the film tends to encourage identification with his situation rather than with his character. However, the film still only attenuates the logic of conventional narrativity and characterization rather than fully challenge it. In the case of Derek Jarman's vision of contemporary British decline and depression in *The Last of England*, however, the role of narrative and character is virtually abandoned altogether. But, in this respect, it is a film which is clearly informed by avant-garde practices, it does not straightforwardly slot into a tradition of the political avant-garde.

For, if Jarman's cinema is 'political', it is so in a broad sense and, in many ways, defies clear-cut categorization. Jarman began making 'personal' home movies and experimental shorts in the 1970s and, although he subsequently became involved in features, he maintained an interest in 'small' projects and often imported the aesthetics of his shorts into his features. His work displays the interest in the formal mechanisms and perceptual play which is a feature of the 'first avant-garde' but it is mixed with an 'underground' taste for the surreal and transgressive. Moreover, despite the aggressive avant-garde sensibility of much of his work, Jarman is by his own reckoning something of a 'traditionalist' whose work reveals a certain longing for a lost 'Englishness' and a relish for English landscape (with the motif of the 'garden' running through his work).[36] It is because of this strain in his work that Jarman's work is often located in relation to an English tradition of neo-romanticism and anti-industrialism.[37] This preoccupation with 'Englishness' (and 'tradition') is also manifest in Jarman's interest in reworking 'high cultural' works, such as those of Shakespeare (*The Tempest* (1979), *The Angelic Conversation* (1985)) and Marlowe (*Edward II* (1991)), but it is complemented by a fascination with 'popular culture'. Jarman made a number of pop videos, including for The Smiths and The Pet Shop Boys, and the sounds and imagery of popular culture are often incorporated into his

---

[36] In interviews, Jarman rejected 'marginalization', insisting that he was 'dead-centre' and 'upholding tradition'. See, for example, 'Doom! Doom! Doom!', *I-D Magazine*, no. 53 (Nov. 1987), 79. Jarman also cultivated his own garden of flowers, plants, stones, and sculptures (next to a nuclear power station) at Prospect Cottage, Dungeness and this became the inspiration for his film *The Garden* (1990).

[37] See Peter Wollen, 'The Last New Wave: Modernism in the British Films of the Thatcher Era', in Lester Friedman (ed.), *British Cinema and Thatcherism* (London: UCL Press, 1993) and Lawrence Driscoll, ' "The Rose Revived": Derek Jarman and the British Tradition', in Chris Lippard (ed.), *By Angels Driven: The Films of Derek Jarman* (Trowbridge: Flicks Books, 1996).

work (indeed, Jarman's *The Queen is Dead* videos partly anticipated the techniques employed in *The Last of England*). However, his interest in popular culture is by and large confined to what might be described as post-punk street culture rather than mass-produced culture of which he remains critical and which, once again, links him to a certain strand of traditional 'English' suspicion of mass culture and 'Americanization' (thus, there is a New York sequence in *The Last of England* that is intended to epitomize the emptiness of consumer culture).

Jarman's cinema, in this respect, may be seen to straddle a number of tensions: formalism versus political radicalism, modernity versus tradition, high culture versus low culture. It is a part of British art cinema but does not conform to traditional art cinema conventions, adopting a more extreme approach to narrative and displaying little interest in psychological complexity. It is a cinema indebted to a modernist avant-garde and its concerns to foreground the materiality of film and the signifying process but combines this with a set of personal and political obsessions more characteristic of 'underground' cinema (especially Kenneth Anger) and the second avant-garde. It is a cinema, moreover, that goes beyond the adversarial stances of modernist self-reflexivity to embrace a diversity of aesthetic means more characteristic of postmodernism. As such, it crosses a number of boundaries—between documentary and fiction, realism and expressionism, the personal and the political, 'high' and 'low' culture—to create a form of hybrid cinema in which a diversity of aesthetic means are employed to challenge, or 'make strange', our perceptions of both past and present.

This is particularly so given the determination of Jarman's films to give voice to gay experience and, in doing so, find new forms for its expression. In Jarman's work, there has been a recurring concern to retrieve gay cultural traditions or reread the past according to a gay, or 'queer', sensibility. This has included the reinterpretation of 'gay' artists as in *Caravaggio* (1986) in which the 'meaning' of Caravaggio's paintings are dramatized in terms of Caravaggio's sexuality or the 'rereading' of English literature from a gay perspective as in *The Angelic Conversation* (1985) (in which Shakespearian sonnets are read in homo-erotic terms) or *Edward II* (1991) (in which the king's sexuality is foregrounded).[38] Jarman's interest in a gay literary or artistic past, however, has never been antiquarian (or 'essentialist' insofar as it as much 'constructs' a gay history as reveals it) and has always been filtered through the concerns and sensibilities of the present. *Caravaggio*, for example, displays none of the fetishistic concern for period detail which characterizes the heritage film. The film is shot exclusively indoors and sets are spare and stylized. Costumes and props (including a pocket calculator, typewriter, and motorbike) are deliberately anachronistic and dialogue oscillates between stylized speech and contemporary vernacular. According to

---

[38] For a reading of Jarman's work, and *Edward II* in particular, in terms of a 'counter-hegominic' resistance to 'heterosexist oppression', see Martin Quinn-Meyler, 'Opposing "Heterosoc": Jarman's Counter-hegemonic Activism', in Chris Lippard (ed.), *By Angels Driven: The Films of Derek Jarman*.

Robert A. Rosenstone, the 'best historical films . . . interrogate the past for the sake of the present' and, in the process, don't just show 'what happened . . . but how what happened means to us'.[39] In this respect, Jarman's 'historical' films are as much about the present as the past and during the 1980s (a period in which, according to Jarman, 'all that was rotten bubbled to the surface') his work demonstrated a mounting sense of political outrage.[40] This was partly directed against the climate of homophobia which followed in the wake of the discovery of the HIV virus as well the growing intolerance towards non-straight sexualities exhibited by the New Right, and exemplified by Clause 28 (see Chapter 1).[41] More generally, Jarman's films hit out at the socially divisive and culturally damaging effects of Thatcherism and this is especially apparent in *The Last of England*, Jarman's most overt contribution to the 'state-of-the-nation' genre.

The film's title is taken from Ford Madox Brown's 1855 painting of the same name showing the departure of emigrants from England, an image which is echoed (though not directly quoted) in the scene involving the boat setting off at the film's end. The film is also something of a companion piece to Jarman's earlier film *Jubilee* (1978) in which Elizabeth I is transported from the sixteenth century to the present to discover the violent and bleak wasteland which Britain has become. For Jarman, in *Jubilee*, 'the past dreamed the future present' whereas in *The Last of England* 'the present dreams the past future'. It is in this respect the idea of a 'dream allegory'—in which 'the poet wakes up in a visionary landscape where he encounters personifications of psychic states'—which motivates the pattern of the film.[42] As such the film may be linked to a tradition of 'visionary film', or 'psychodrama', in which the authored status of the film is foregrounded and the film itself is 'subjectivized' in terms of a personal dream-like logic.[43] Thus, Jarman himself is seen at the film's beginning sitting at his desk writing; we subsequently see him pressing a flower, walking the streets with his camera, and as a child. In this way, the film also sets up a kind of dialectic between 'subjective' and 'objective' perspectives. Thus, while the film contains footage of real events (e.g. Jarman's childhood, inner-city riots) and real places (e.g. Docklands), these do not necessarily denote 'actuality' or 'realism' so much as a pattern of symbolism and significance that is anchored in the subjectivity of the director's vision. At the same time, however, unlike certain strands of psychodrama, the images and sounds are not simply private and personal but draw upon communal events (such as the Royal Wedding of 1981 or the Falklands/

---

[39] Robert A. Rosenstone, *Visions of the Past: The Challenge of Film to Our Idea of History* (Cambridge, Mass.: Harvard University Press, 1995), 238.

[40] Derek Jarman, *At Your Own Risk: A Saint's Testament* (London: Vintage, 1992), 95. Jarman is also writing in the context of the spread of the HIV virus and his own diagnosis, at the end of 1986, as HIV positive.

[41] Jarman dedicates the book of the script of *Edward II* 'to the repeal of all anti-gay laws, particularly Section 28', in *Queer Edward II* (London: BFI, 1991).

[42] Jarman, *The Last of England* (London: Constable, 1987), 188.

[43] P. Adams Sitney discusses the tradition of the 'trance film' in which the 'elements of dream, ritual, dance and sexual metaphor abound', in *Visionary Film: The American Avant-Garde, 1943–1978* (New York: Oxford University Press), 1979, 20–1.

Malvinas war) and an iconography of contemporary Britain that is also public. In this respect, the film may also be linked to a British tradition of 'poetic documentary', and to the work of Humphrey Jennings, with its mix of realism, surrealism, and national allegory, in particular. As Annette Kuhn suggests, *The Last of England* may, in this respect, be seen as a kind of 'negative', counter-mythic version of *Listen to Britain* (1941).[44]

The film itself is, more or less, organized into three parts. The first is concerned, as Jarman explains, with 'figures in a landscape', and combines images of decline and decay from Docklands, Liverpool, and New York; the second part is organized around scenes of people being rounded up by masked soldiers/terrorists who ambiguously represent state authority; the third section deals with institutions especially those of the royal family, and empire.[45] However, this is a very loose, and on occasion barely discernible, structure and the actual experience of the film is primarily in terms of its onslaught of images and sounds. A key part of the film's strategy, in this regard, is its rejection of the conventions of both classical narrativity and documentary. As Hacker and Price suggest, it is a film which is resolutely 'anti-naturalistic, abandoning narrative or psychological exploration, and replacing it with an unusual vocabulary of image, symbolism, colour and sound'.[46] So, while the film possesses a loose structure, it is the principles of juxtaposition and collage, the collision of images and sounds, which underpin the film's forward movement.

The film, in this respect, mixes together different types of footage (most of it shot on Super8), including already existing material which is invested with new meanings though a process of juxtaposition. This is especially true of the home movie material of Jarman's family and childhood which is intercut with newly shot material (as a way of exploring Jarman's own feelings about his childhood and relationship to family). However, much of the film's logic is also purely formal. Certain images, for example, are virtually drained of their referential content: Spencer Leigh's bloody hand shot in close-up from a peculiar angle, a figure at work welding, a floating wreath, the bottom of a bottle. These are, in turn, juxtaposed with other images to create unusual visual and kinetic patterns based on similarities and contrasts of colour, shape, and movement (as when a shot of a butterfly follows a shot of a silhouetted hand). Thus, shots of the bottom of a bottle, of a man drinking vodka, and the terrorists' burning bonfire are cut together in rapid succession while the floating wreath is both superimposed upon, and intercut with, images of fire and a semi-naked dancer. As with other images, the image of the wreath also occurs later in the film when it is effectively

---

[44] Annette Kuhn, *Family Secrets: Acts of Memory and Imagination* (London: Verso, 1995) chap. 7. Dick Hebdige also contrasts Jennings's *Spare Time* (1939) to Jarman's *The Queen is Dead* in 'Digging for Britain: An Excavation in Seven Parts', in Dominic Strinati and Stephen Wagg (eds.), *Come On Down? Popular Media Culture in Post-War Britain* (London: Routledge, 1992). Kuhn reads *The Last of England* primarily in terms of memory. However, it is not at all clear that the imagery of the film can simply be read as 'memory fragments'.

[45] Jarman, 'Home Movie Man' (Interview), *Marxism Today* (Oct. 1987), 41.

[46] Jonathan Hacker and David Price, *Take 10: Contemporary British Film Directors* (Oxford: Clarendon Press, 1991), 233.

'recontextualized' into new visual and symbolic patterns. The film's strategy in relation to sound is similar. There is no directly spoken dialogue in the film and the soundtrack consists of recorded speech (both pre-existing speech, such as Hitler declaiming about Czechoslovakia, and material especially recorded for the film), written voice-overs and various forms of music (including Bach, Marianne Faithfull, original music by Simon Turner, and industrial noise). Once again, the mixing of music follows both formal and symbolic patterns and these both work with, and against, the pattern of images.

The absence of dialogue also highlights the absence of conventional characterization and theatrical performance in the film. For Michael O'Pray, Jarman's cinema is a kind of 'gestural' cinema which does not rely upon narrative and character so much as gestic scenes which rely upon typification, outward behaviour, the physiognomy of actors, and the use of symbol.[47] The idea of the 'gestus' derives from Eisenstein and Brecht and involves scenes in which ideas or attitudes are expressed through stylization and much of *The Last of England* can be seen to work in this way as in the scenes of a man (Spring) masturbating over Caravaggio's *Profane Love*, the same man 'playing' pipes on a heap of a rubble while another man (Spencer Leigh) labours below him, the couple (one a soldier/terrorist) having sex on the Union Jack, Tilda Swinton's frenetic dance at the film's end.[48] Nevertheless, the meaning of such scenes is still not straightforward and, although clearly symbolic, cannot be reduced to unitary meanings.

This can be seen in the climactic scene involving Swinton. This comes at the end of a 'gestic' sequence parodying the Royal Wedding of Charles and Diana. While references to the Royal Wedding are heard over a discordant soundtrack, we see a wedding take place in a deserted and derelict warehouse. Swinton is attended by two bridesmaids (men in drag/pantomine dames/'queens') and a crippled boy chimney sweep ('Victorian values'). There is also a pram containing a baby wrapped in tabloid newspapers (noticeably *The Sun*), proclaiming the onset of the Falklands war ('War With The Argies Only Hours Away'), which has echoes of an earlier scene when a man had been seen pushing a pram through a darkened street while holding aloft a burning torch. This is immediately followed by a scene of Swinton ripping at her dress with large scissors, initially silently and then to the accompaniment of the haunting sounds of Diamanda Galas. During this, she tugs violently at the decorative flowers appliquéed to her dress (an 'English rose'?) and stuffs one into her mouth. The scene then bursts into colour as Swinton launches into a frenzied circular dance

---

[47] Michael O'Pray, 'Fierce Visions: Derek Jarman', *Art Monthly*, no. 117 (June 1988), 35. Even when Jarman does work with narrative, as in *Caravaggio*, the film consists primarily of a series of 'tableaux' which only loosely knit together.

[48] The sex scene on the Union Jack is characteristically read in homosexual terms and linked to the absence of 'positive' images of gay sex in Jarman's films and its association with violence and sado-masochism. See, for example, Martin Quinn-Meyler, 'Opposing "Heterosoc": Jarman's Counter-hegemonic Activism', 120. However, Jarman claims the scene is 'a trick' and the terrorist is actually a woman (*The Last of England*, 196). As the terrorist/soldier doesn't remove his/her balaclava, the film doesn't allow us to be sure of his/her sexual identity, although the uniform suggests (possibly misleadingly) a man.

PLATE 11. Tilda Swinton in *The Last of England*

to the rising volume of jarring electronic sounds. For O'Pray, Swinton's performance may be read as a kind of Brechtian commentary by the actress on the role of the bride.[49] It is, however, more than this as Swinton's performance is not attached exclusively to the 'character' of the bride but also to the wife/lover (her status is not made clear) of the 'character' played by Spencer Leigh, shots of whom—kissing Swinton, being executed by the soldiers/terrorists—are intercut with her dance (and to whose death the dance, in narrative terms, may be read as a response). A number of meanings are therefore condensed into the actress's performance.

It is, as Jarman himself suggests, a dance which involves the 'shredding' of 'illusions'.[50] It involves a rejection of the bogus 'nationalism' and jingoism which the Royal Wedding and the Falklands war inspired as well as the creeping authoritarianism of a state in which soldiers and terrorists are apparently indistinguishable. In this respect, the dance may be read as a powerful image of defiance, a release of what Jarman describes as 'elemental forces' in protest against the death, destruction, and absence of love that the film has portrayed.[51] Thus, as Jarman puts it, Swinton 'becomes a figure of strength who curses the world of the patriots' and 'projects and protects love's idyll'.[52] In this respect, the dance links to the film's final image of the group setting sail, with one of its members holding high a burning torch. The image of the burning torch recurs

---

[49] Michael O'Pray, *Derek Jarman: Dreams of England* (London: BFI, 1996), 163.
[50] Jarman, 'Home Movie Man', 41.   [51] Id., *The Last of England*, 207.   [52] Ibid. 203.

throughout the film (as, in line with Jarman's interests in alchemical symbolism, do images of fire more generally) and Jarman links this image with that of
the heretic in Goya's *The Disasters of War*.[53] As such, it may be seen, at the film's
end, to invoke the survival of the heretical spirit and a continuation of dissent
and resistance.

However, the images may also be read in terms of the despair of a 'character'
who is at the end of her tether (from the loss of her lover/husband) and 'out of
control'. In this respect, there is an elegiac undertow to the film's finale, a sense
of loss, closure, and, of course, the 'end' of England. The heretical spirit, in the
form of the lighted torch, may have survived but it is being carried away by a
boat that is leaving England for an unknown destination. This sense of elegy is
reinforced by the intercutting of images from the 'past'—Swinton in the country, a child in a pram—which celebrate a sense of innocence and connection
(with nature, with family) that is absent from the film's bleak post-industrial
'present' (or 'past future'). As Jarman admits, an element of 'nostalgia' runs
throughout the film and this is particularly evident in the home footage of his
childhood which is typically contrasted with the ugliness of the 'present' as
when a shot of Spring sprawled over *Profane Love* is followed by a shot of Jarman
as a child, grasping a tennis ball and running smiling towards the camera, or
when an image of Jarman and his sister picking flowers is followed by shots of
urban dereliction.[54]

This nostalgia is not, of course, without its ironies. Jarman's father was a RAF
pilot who was posted to Pakistan in the 1950s and the film includes, in addition to images of family life, home movie footage of Wellington bombers and
Pakistan. Thus, there is a sardonic sequence, cut to the sound of 'Land of Hope
and Glory', in which images of the 'past'—the Albert Memorial, scenes from
Pakistan (especially army ceremonial), and 1950s suburbia—are intercut with
those from the 'present'—shots of burning buildings, the riot police, and the
soldiers/terrorists. This sequence suggests how Britain's colonial past has paved
the way for the shabby imperial pretensions of the present (a scene of wreath-
laying with echoes of the Falklands war follows) and how the imperial realities
of the past were not 'innocent' but, in turn, relied upon violence and destruction. However, it also sets up a visual contrast between a dark, dreary, and
divided present (primarily shot in black and white) and a bright and ordered
past (shot predominantly in colour) that inevitably has echoes of imperial
discourses of 'loss' and 'decline'. In a sense, the sequence would appear to be
locked into the very discourse it is seeking to oppose: disputing the Thatcherite
claim to a resurgence of 'greatness' but still finding the past superior to (and
apparently more 'glorious' than) the ugliness and squalor of the present.

---

[53] Jarman, *The Last of England*, 207. Although Spencer Leigh is, at one point, explicitly dressed in the
costume of the heretic, the symbol of the burning torch, like all Jarman's symbols, is not used with strict
consistency. Thus, the actor Spring, who is associated with destructive forces in the film (stamping on
the Caravaggio, throwing bricks, injecting himself with heroin), is also seen to carry a torch at the film's
beginning as are the soldiers/terrorists when they circle their captives at the docks.

[54] Chris Lippard, 'Interview with Derek Jarman', in *By Angels Driven: The Films of Derek Jarman*, 162.

However, it is also the case that none of these readings can 'exhaust' the operations of the film's ending which remain open-ended and ambivalent. Jarman argues that traditional films 'manipulate' the audience whereas his own films permit the audience 'much greater freedom to interpret what they are seeing'.[55] For Bazin, montage cinema (especially as practised by expressive realists such as Eisenstein) was, of course, seen as an anti-democratic cinema, channelling spectators' responses in particular directions through the use of juxtaposition.[56] In Jarman's cinema, however, montage is used not so much to close down meanings as open them up to a process of play. This is particularly so given how a film such as *The Last of England* appeals primarily to the emotions and senses rather than to the critical faculties. Thus, the power of Swinton's final dance derives less from its symbolism—what it 'means'—than from its potent mix of cinematic elements: physical movement and expression, use of colour and black and white, grain of image, speeded-up and slowed-down images, disorienting camera movement and angles, quickfire editing, obtrusive use of sound and music. Given the aesthetic density of this scene, any interpretation of it is necessarily destined to be 'reductionist'.

This then has consequences for how the film is to be understood politically. Indeed, it has been common for the film to be criticized (and not just by Norman Stone) for its limited understanding of contemporary Britain and reliance upon conventional political signifiers.[57] Certainly, if read in straightforward political terms, the film is often crude in its effects. There is, for example, a sequence in which a naked and destitute man, chewing at a cauliflower, is intercut with a 'businessman' in a bowler hat and callipers stuffing himself with grain and then pouring it over his head. Interpreted in political-allegorical terms, this constitutes a relatively unsophisticated visualization of the suffering caused by Thatcherism and the growing divide between rich and poor. However, the strength of *The Last of England* is less its capacity to generate conventional political insights or analysis than its multivalent imagery and formal play. As such, the politics of *The Last Of England* depends less on the expression of clear-cut signifieds than the communication of various moods, attitudes, and feelings (including anger and despair) in response, at least in part, to Jarman's sense of, and anxiety about, the 'state-of-the-nation'. In this respect, it is also, like so many other 'national allegories' of the time, a pessimistic film but one in which the energy and intensity of the film's vision partly belies the lack of optimism (and sense of political agency) that it has to offer. As Jarman himself commented in response to criticisms that his films were 'negative': 'I didn't think negativity is negative' and the 'activity . . . [of filmmaking] . . . is the hope.'[58]

[55]   Jarman, *The Last of England*, 193.

[56]   See André Bazin, *What is Cinema?* (Berkeley: University of California Press, 1971).

[57]   Judith Williamson, for example, complained of the film's 'modish' images of 'urban decadence and decay' which she suggested were 'meaningless politically' in 'Pictures of Pictures', *New Statesman* (23 Oct. 1987), 26.

[58]   Jarman, *The Last of England*, 109.

The Cook, The Thief, His Wife and Her Lover

If, in a sense, the formalism of Jarman's film goes beyond its allegorizing tendencies, this is even more so of Peter Greenaway's use of political allegory in *The Cook, The Thief, His Wife and Her Lover* (1989). As Michael Walsh suggests, although Greenaway is 'not obviously or instinctively a political filmmaker', it is *The Cook*, of all Greenaway's films in the 1980s, that has most typically been discussed in political terms.[59] Indeed, for Gilbert Adair, the film 'succeeds in conveying the spirit of the gaudy, yobocratic Eighties more vividly than any number of paranoid thrillers and hectoring state-of-the nation disquisitions'.[60] This is, of course, a way of reading the film that Greenaway himself has encouraged. As he explained in an interview:

The film is a very angry one. The political situation that currently exists in Great Britain under Mrs Thatcher is one of incredible sense of self-interest and greed. Society is beginning to worry entirely about the price of everything and the value of nothing, and there is a way in which the *The Cook, the Thief* is an exemplum of a consumer society, personified in the Thief, Albert Spica. He is a man who is thoroughly despicable in every part of his character. He has no redeeming features and is consumed by self-interest and greed.[61]

In these terms, the film may be seen to portray a society in which money and consumption are the dominant forces. 'Money's my business, eating's my pleasure', Albert (Michael Gambon) tells the group at his table. Albert is a gangster, and although the precise nature of his 'business' is never made clear, his activities clearly emblematize the self-interested ruthlessness of 'business' in a period of unrestrained 'free enterprise'. As in the gangster film, 'business' interests go hand in hand with a capacity for violence and cruelty and Spica's resort to humiliation, torture, and murder is itself linked to the disciplinarian aspects of the Thatcherite 'strong state'. Thus, in what is surely a conscious homage to the Conservatives' remedy for juvenile crime, Spica knees a man in the gents' lavatory, telling him 'that's what people like you need—strong, sharp, shock treatment'.[62] As Greenaway indicates, Spica only understands the value of things in monetary terms and, as such, is counterposed to the film's other main characters. The lover, Michael (Alan Howard) is a bibliophile who reads while he eats and is taunted by Spica ('Does this stuff make money?', he demands); the

[59]   Michael Walsh, 'Allegories of Thatcherism: The Films of Peter Greenaway', in Lester Friedman (ed.), *British Cinema and Thatcherism*, 260.

[60]   Gilbert Adair, 'The Anatomy of a Film Director', *The Sunday Correspondent Magazine* (8 Oct. 1989), 41.

[61]   Peter Greenaway, Interviewed by Brian McFarlane, *Cinema Papers*, no. 78 (Mar. 1990), 38–9. In his discussion of the 'state of the nation', Peter Riddell notes how opponents of the Thatcher regime commonly lay stress on 'the selfishness, greed and lack of social responsibility of Mrs Thatcher's Britain'. See *The Thatcher Era And its Legacy* (Oxford: Blackwell, 1993), 173.

[62]   A system of 'short, sharp shock' was introduced by the Conservative government in the early 1980s. It was designed to deter persistent juvenile offenders by subjecting them to a harsh regime at special detention centres.

wife, Georgina (Helen Mirren), yearns for something other than 'the big house' and 'beautiful things' that her husband provides her with and is attracted to Michael (despite his age and appearance) by the sight of him reading; and the cook Richard (Richard Bohringer) is an 'artist' whose 'good food' is unappreciated by Spica (other than as a symbol of status) despite their business relationship. Indeed, Greenaway himself suggests how the 'perfectionist cook' is also 'the filmmaker' who 'invites the viewers to come into the cinema . . . provides the space for the actors to manipulate and organize . . . nudges the whole thing through and provides the dénouement'.[63]

However, it is also the case that this anti-Thatcherite allegory only stretches so far. As various commentators have noted, the condensation of the various forces at work in Thatcherism into the monstrous figure of Spica offers a relatively crude reduction of Thatcherism to naked appetite. Moreover, by contrasting Spica's materialism and vulgarity with the artistry, learning, and non-material yearnings of the other characters, the film also conducts much of its critique of Thatcherism (like Mike Leigh's *High Hopes*) in terms of the cultural tastes and values associated with it. As Richard Dyer suggests, 'one response to the emergence of "Thatcherism" was to identify it with the rise of a newly affluent working class, steeped in neither the middle-class sense of public service nor the older Tory noblesse oblige, a class type who had never before set the social agenda, ambitious, materialistic, insensitive, incipiently racist'.[64] In a sense, it is partly 'the rise of the C2s', or the skilled working class, who, gained economically under Thatcherism but lacked the 'cultural capital' associated with the traditional middle class and aristocracy, that the film embodies in the form of the *nouveau riche*, Albert Spica.[65] As such, it is the 'cultural barbarianism' of Thatcherism, rather than its economics and politics, that the film most heavily indicts.[66]

However, the strategies that the film employs also complicate a straightforward allegorical reading of the film. For allegory within a text, its process of 'self-interpretation', may be strong or weak, more or less clearly 'marked', more

[63] Peter Greenaway interviewed by Gavin Smith, *Film Comment*, vol. 26, no. 3 (May–June 1990), 56. This is not, of course, an entirely consistent metaphor insofar as the cook also represents the—voyeuristic—cinematic spectator. Georgina, for example, asks the cook how she could know whether her relationship with Michael was 'real' unless 'someone else was looking'. The cook then describes to Georgina 'what he saw', comparing their behaviour to 'lovers in the cinema'.

[64] Richard Dyer, *White* (London: Routledge, 1997), 196.

[65] There are, of course, echoes here of how Margaret Thatcher herself was perceived as a vulgar and philistine parvenu who had little understanding or appreciation of the arts. See Hugo Young's biography of Thatcher, *One of Us* (London: Pan Books, 1990), esp. chap. 18 'Treason of the Intellectuals'. However, it is probably Conservative chairman, Norman Tebbit, who epitomizes this trend the most. As Peter Jenkins notes, Tebbit was 'the archetypal Thatcherite, lower-middle class, unburdened by class guilt or social conscience, acquisitive in tooth and claw'. See *Mrs Thatcher's Revolution* (London: Jonathan Cape, 1987), 326.

[66] Michael Walsh complains that the film depicts 'politically questionable class relationships' by dramatizing 'imaginary contests between a cultured middle class and a brutish lumpenproletariat' in 'Allegories of Thatcherism: The Films of Peter Greenaway', in Lester Friedman (ed.), *British Cinema and Thatcherism*, pp. 275 and 271. While he is right to note how the film depends upon a sense of class superiority in the way that it indicts the vulgarity of Spica and his hangers-on, it makes little sense, in the context of Thatcherism, to identify Spica as 'lumpenproletariat'.

or less univocal. Moreover, the extent to which a text is 'readable' as allegory may be open to question. As Dana Polan has argued in relation to Jameson, the allegory may be 'something imputed to a text by the creative reader' rather than one which is clearly identifiable by others.[67] In a sense, the reading of *The Cook* as an allegory of Thatcherism has been strongly promoted by Greenaway himself in interviews but, *pace* Adair, is not as overtly marked by the text itself as some writers have suggested. Thus, one critic, analysing the film as an example of postmodernism, makes no reference to Thatcherism at all and notes how viewers of the film 'may well feel some annoyance with the film for failing to address 'our current experience' and for 'embodying beauty simply for its own sake and imparting "no knowledge about reality" '.[68] The 'failure' to detect allegory, in this case, is not, however, entirely surprising given the aesthetic devices that the film employs.

For, like Jarman's cinema, Greenaway's films are characterized by the cinematic self-consciousness and self-referentiality of modernism as well as the eclecticism and reworking of aesthetic traditions associated with postmodernism. *The Cook*, in this respect, is a film that self-consciously foregrounds its own status as a film and constantly reminds spectators of the 'artificiality' of what they are watching. As Greenaway explains, the film is 'not a slice of life, not a window on the world; it is . . . an artefact'.[69] Thus, the diegetic world which the film constructs is heavily stylized (shot entirely inside a studio) and also anachronistic insofar as costumes, objects, and settings suggest different historical periods.

The film begins and ends with the drawing of curtains which reminds the spectator of the film's status as performance and there are recurring references to the cinematic process (such as Michael's comment on the film he saw in which the main character—like himself—didn't speak for the first half hour) as well as 'quotations' from other films (particularly Alain Resnais's *Last Year in Marienbad*) and also paintings (especially Hals, Rembrandt, and Vermeer). Greenaway's interest in film as a medium, and indebtedness to structural filmmaking, is also apparent in the way that the film is patterned in terms of formal principles, especially the colour coding of scenes, the use of long takes and lateral camera movements, the avoidance of close-ups and 'classical' editing techniques, and a 'non-narrative' use of song and music.[70] In this respect, *The Cook's* subject-matter is pre-eminently film itself and the film's stylistic play effectively overwhelms its referential meanings. This is not, of course, to deny the film's undoubted force and power but it is to suggest that the film's 'allegorical dimension' may, in fact, be one of its less interesting (and worked-through) dimensions.

---

[67] Dana Polan, 'Brief Encounters: Mass Culture and the Evacuation of Sense', in Tania Modleski (ed.), *Studies in Entertainment: Critical Approaches to Mass Culture* (Bloomington and Indianapolis: Indiana University Press, 1986), 172.

[68] Nicholas O. Pagan, '*The Cook, the Thief, His Wife, & Her Lover*: Making Sense of Postmodernism', *South Atlantic Review*, vol. 60, no. 1 (1995), 46.

[69] Greenaway, *Cinema Papers*, no. 78, 38.

[70] For a more detailed analysis of the film's formal procedures, see William F. Van Wert, '*The Cook, The Thief, His Wife and Her Lover*' (Review), *Film Quarterly*, vol. 44, no. 2 (Winter, 1990–1).

Conclusion _____

In Chapter 1, it was argued that the Thatcherite project was only partially successful in the winning of 'hearts and minds' and benefited from the absence of convincing alternatives to it. In this respect, there may have been considerable discontent with Thatcherism during the 1980s but there was also no alternative social vision which appeared to be capable of either challenging it effectively or winning a place in the popular imagination. In the same way, the 'state-of-the-nation' films were characterized by a shared animosity towards Thatcherism, its attitudes and effects, but lacked an alternative, or more affirmative, vision of social being. Ironically, *The Cook* may be read as offering one of the more 'positive' endings in this respect: a 'popular alliance' of Spica's victims confront him and Georgina exacts her revenge. However, as been suggested, the vagueness of the film's allegory, and the self-conscious playfulness of this scene (involving a cooked corpse and exaggerated 'spider woman' imagery), vitiates against the attribution of a clear political significance to this. As such, the success of the 'state-of-the-nation' films was, like the heretic in *The Last of England*, to uphold the voice of dissent. However, in doing so, the films often remained locked within the very discourse they opposed, unable to give convincing voice to an alternative 'social imaginary'. Writing in the context of post-war literature, Alan Sinfield stresses the importance of creative work in offering 'a discourse of authority in the dispute about how to extend our sense of the possibilities of human lives'.[71] To this extent, one of the weaknesses of the 'state-of-the-nation' films was the relative absence of some kind of reimagining, and envisioning, of this extension of human possibilities.

[71] Alan Sinfield, *Literature, Politics and Culture in Postwar Britain* (Oxford: Basil Blackwell, 1989), 37.

chapter 8

Class, Gender, and Working–Class Realism _____

The Decline of the Traditional Working Class

In the previous chapter, it was argued that *The Ploughman's Lunch* both drew upon an earlier realist tradition of working-class realism and deviated from it. The view of the working class which was apparent in the social realism of the 1950s and 1960s grew out of a particular social moment of change. There was concern about the decline of the traditional working class and anxiety about the growing 'corruption' of the working class by consumerism and 'American-ization'; there was less emphasis upon collective class action than the trajectories of individuals, many of whom were seeking escape from the confinement of their class position; and there was characteristically an emphasis upon the working-class male hero who was often set in opposition to the constraint or superficiality which was identified with the women around him. In reworking the themes and motifs of *Room at the Top*, *The Ploughman's Lunch* may be seen to carry on the earlier film's critique of superficiality (and, indeed, its linking of this with femininity) but to have lost its concern with working-class culture. The film's central protagonist, James Penfield is effectively cut off from his roots at the film's start and there is virtually no attempt to sketch in working-class life, which is no longer seen as a source of either 'authentic' values or popular resis-tance. In this respect, it shares with many of the films that follow an increasing difficulty in representing the working class in terms other than decline.

In a sense, the erosion of the traditional working class which 1960s realism began to map reached a logical conclusion in films of the 1980s, where there is virtually no representation of 'community' as such and very few images of col-lective action. As in the earlier working-class films, it is the experience of the north which is privileged. In particular, the city of Liverpool—a leading seaport whose wealth was traditionally based on the export of textiles from Lancashire and Yorkshire—provided the setting for a number of working-class films of the period including *Educating Rita* (1983), *Letter to Brezhnev* (1985), *Business as*

Usual (1987), *No Surrender* (1986), *The Fruit Machine* (1988), and *Dancin' Thru the Dark* (1989).[1] What is novel about these films, however, is the emphasis that is placed upon urban and industrial decline. It is a north now blighted by unemployment and poverty and that stands testimony to the corrosive effects wrought by the 'two nations' policy of the Thatcher regime.

Inevitably, the imagery associated with the north has also altered. The iconography of rows of small terraced houses and cobbled streets characteristic of 1960s realism has given way to run-down housing estates with boarded-up windows (precisely the sort of estates just being built in films such as *Saturday Night and Sunday Morning* (1960)).[2] Factories (as in *Business as Usual*) have become wastelands and images of work, such as there are, are linked to the service sector (especially shops) rather than manufacturing. Scenes of actual work were, of course, rare enough in the working-class films of the 1960s. Inevitably, given the emphasis of the 1980s films on unemployment, they are even rarer in the later films where there is a concentration on the—often enforced—'leisure' activities of the characters: at home, on the streets, and in the pubs and clubs ('What's it like in here', asks one character of a club in *Letter to Brezhnev*. 'One table selling pot, one table selling knock-off').

As such, the 1980s films retain a concern, characteristic of the 1960s films, about the quality of working-class life. They also often focus on characters who wish to escape from the constrictions imposed upon them by their class position. However, unlike the earlier wave of films there is necessarily less concern with the supposedly stultifying effects of 'affluence' or the mass media. Rather it is the debilitating, and sometimes brutalizing, consequences of unemployment and poverty which are highlighted. In contrast, it is often the mass media or popular culture which provides a temporary respite from these, as the disco music in *Letter to Brezhnev* or the pop videos on TV in *Rita, Sue and Bob Too* might suggest.

---

[1] On television, both *Boys from the Blackstuff* (1982) and the popular Channel 4 soap opera, *Brookside* (1982–) were set in Liverpool as were Terence Davies's unsentimental films about working-class childhood, *Distant Voices, Still Lives* (1988) and *The Long Day Closes* (1992). Derek Jarman also filmed a number of the scenes of urban dereliction for *The Last of England* (1987) in Liverpool. Although representations of Liverpool provided the dominant images of the north, a number of films, especially those made by the Channel 4-funded workshop Amber Films, dealt with the north-east. Peter Hutchings suggests films such as *Seacoal* (1985) and *In Fading Light* (1989) provide an 'elegy for . . . working-class solidarity and communality', in ' "When The Going Gets Tough . . .": Representations of the North-East in Film and Television', in Tom Faulkner (ed.), *Northumbria Panorama* (Newcastle: Octavia Press, 1996), 284.

[2] The iconography of the housing estate employed in these films provides a clear commentary on the effects of Conservative housing policy. As Michael Ball explains: 'By the late 1980s, council housing faced severe problems. The sale of over a million dwellings in the 1980s and the virtual halt on new building at a time of acute housing crisis for low-income households are altering the social composition of council tenants. Increasingly commentators are suggesting that the tenure is becoming a ghetto for the dispossessed and poor.' See 'Housing : The State and the Market', in Michael Ball *et al.*, *The Transformation of Britain* (London: Fontana, 1989), 232.

Class and Masculinity

However, it is not simply that the traditions of the working class have been eroded by the decline of manufacturing and the traditional heavy industries. Insofar, as work (and industrial labour, in particular) has been central to the way in which the working class has been defined, these changes have also led to a weakening of the ideologies of masculinity which had traditionally underpinned work (pride in hard, physical labour) and also trade union power (a capacity for 'strong' industrial action). As Jonathan Rutherford argues, 'the changing nature of work . . . the introduction of new technologies and the subsequent deskilling of traditional male jobs' are all changes that have 'undermined traditional working-class masculinities'.[3] Thus, in focusing on unemployment and industrial decay in the north of England, the 1980s films often suggest the 'crisis' in traditional definitions of masculinity which followed the collapse of roles (such as wage-earner and head of the family) which historically reinforced a sense of male identity. This is, of course, a theme that is central to what might be regarded as the 'delayed' 1980s' film, *The Full Monty* (1997) which quite clearly links deindustrialization and unemployment to the loss of traditional male roles and identities (with men, it is suggested by one character, in danger of becoming 'obsolete').[4]

The theme, however, is already evident, in a film such as *Business as Usual* where Kieran Flynn (John Thaw) is an ex-union official who has been made redundant from the Tate and Lyle sugar refinery (now reduced to rubble). He has become, as the film informs us twice, a 'housewife', staying at home while the women in his family—his wife Babs (Glenda Jackson) and his son's partner Paula (Buki Armstrong)—go to work (significantly enough, in the service sector). He is responsible for the domestic chores, including child-minding, and has difficulty adjusting to this new role (complaining to Babs that he is not her 'poodle' and reminding her that 'I'm your husband'). He resents his wife's growing militancy, refusing to lend her his support, and, in a kind of compensation for his 'emasculation', retreats into an affair with the television journalist, Joan (Mel Martin), who had previously chronicled his public career as a trade union official. His sense of impotence in the film finds a parallel in Eddie (Craig Brown), the boyfriend of Josie (Cathy Tyson), the shop assistant whose claims of sexual harassment at the hands of the male boss lead to Babs' dismissal. Like Kieran, he too is unemployed, and feels strongly the sense of his own powerlessness, wanting to 'sort out' his girlfriend's harasser but unable to do so if she is to hold onto the job which she needs to support them both financially.

    [3] Jonathan Rutherford, 'Who's That Man?', in Rowena Chapman and Jonathan Rutherford (eds.), *Male Order: Unwrapping Masculinity* (London: Lawrence and Wishart, 1988), 23.
    [4] Another successful film of the 1990s, *Brassed Off* (1996) may also be regarded as a 'delayed' 1980s film. Although set in 1992, its story of a threat to a traditional mining community (and brass band) by pit closure is redolent of the early 1980s. As with *The Full Monty*, it is unlikely, however, that the film could have worked so effectively as *comedy* if it had actually been made during the early 1980s.

Indeed, images of failed, inadequate, or threatened masculinity are evident in many of the films of this period. In *Educating Rita*, Rita's husband, Denny (Malcolm Douglas), may be in work but he is crippled by his narrowness of vision and inability to accept his wife's desires to be independent and to 'find herself'. On discovering the birth control pills which she has been hiding, he burns her books (which include Chekhov) in a fit of impotent rage. In *Dancin' Thru the Dark*, also based on a Willy Russell play (*Stags and Hens*), Dave (Conrad Nelson) aspires to be 'a happy nomark'. At the end of the film he is unable to stand, virtually comatose with drink, and is abandoned by his fiancée, Linda (Claire Hackett) who decides to leave both him and Liverpool. Similarly, in *Letter to Brezhnev*, Tracy's (Tracy Lea) boyfriend, Mick (Ted Wood) is presented as typical of the Liverpool men from whom Elaine (Alexandra Pigg) wishes to escape. He is unemployed and primarily interested in Tracy's 'purse', ending his relationship with her once she is made redundant (and her redundancy money has been spent). In *Rita, Sue and Bob Too*, the combination of unemployment and alcoholism has turned Sue's father (Willie Ross) into a figure of impotence. 'You've done nowt and you've been nowt', as his wife derisively tells him. Even Sue's boyfriend Aslam (Kulvinder Ghir), who is initially gentle and gauche, turns jealous and physically violent. In doing so, he provides an ironic confirmation of a remark made by Sue earlier in the film. 'I've never been out with a Paki before', she tells him, 'but then again I don't suppose you'll be different from any other men.'

It is, perhaps, not surprising then that very few of the northern working-class films of the 1980s are centrally concerned with male characters. Those that are reveal some of the changes which the working-class hero has undergone. *Vroom* (1988), written by the playwright Jim Cartwright and directed by Beeban Kidron, is probably the film which quotes the conventions of 1950s and 1960s realism most directly, self-consciously reworking many of their themes and motifs. The film is set in a northern working-class town where Jake (Clive Owen) is a young working-class lad on the dole. He is not, however, ground down by his situation. He yearns for escape and, at the beginning of the film, is seen running up a hill with his friend, Ringe (David Thewlis). They reach the top and look back in a shot typical of working-class realism and emblematic of the desire to escape the confines of the city. Jake is also the typical male 'playboy', out for a good time ('he's out there in the night making the most of everything' exclaims one character) but 'punished' (albeit unjustly) by a beating-up. He falls for an older, and 'classier', woman, the divorcée, Susan (Diane Quick) whom he believes can provide the escape for which he yearns ('free, totally 100 per cent free and flying'). The two of them, accompanied by Ringe, set off on the road in their American car and, coming across a disused cottage, find a temporary rural idyll where they can hide away from the complications and constraints of their everyday lives.

At the same time, however, it is a film which can no longer invest these conventions with their original conviction. The dialogue and action is often stylized and there is a degree of knowingness in the way in which the story is told. This is particularly the case in the film's treatment of Jake's sexual prowess which is treated with overt comic exaggeration and excess. Thus, when Jake returns home in the morning, he is observed by his female neighbours, Lyn (Rosalind Bennett) and Tess (Moya Brady). Lyn is on the verge of hysteria ('someone's been inside his shirt, I know it') and has to be calmed by her sister Tess who proceeds to throw water over her. Jake receives a lift in his sister's car and girls wave from both a passing car and from the street. A supermarket checkout girl (Tricia Penrose) demands a kiss and feels his crotch while the rest of the shopgirls chorus 'goodbye Jake' in unison. In dealing with Jake in this way, the film is, in one sense, playing on the discrepancy between the perception of Jake as a super-stud and the actuality of his romantic infatuation with Susan. More significantly, however, the film appears to accept, and to want to show, that the myth of the sexually aggressive working-class male is, in effect, 'exhausted' and can now only be deployed when invested with a degree of self-conscious parody and playfulness.

The other notable departure from the earlier films lies in the film's use of the theme of escape.[5] It is a common feature of 1960s realism that, despite his yearnings to transcend the limitations of his environment, the male hero is forced to reconcile himself to reality and accommodate to social demands. This, in turn, often involves a rejection of unrealistic aspirations or fantasy. *Vroom* has a double take on this theme. On the one hand, both Ringe and Susan recognize that their flight from reality must come to an end. Ringe takes the job he is offered and Susan decides that she has to return home. Jake, however, refuses to compromise ('why do people always want to settle or go back', he demands). He returns to the top of the hill he had climbed at the film's beginning and literally 'takes off' in his car. Unlike so many earlier working-class films which end with the rejection of fantasy, *Vroom* concludes with a moment of explicit fantasy as Jake magically flies above the city. It is, however, hard to judge precisely the significance of such a scene. On the hand, it is a 'utopian' moment, celebrating the triumph of the human spirit over economic deprivation and social constraint (which is a theme more generally characteristic of the 1980s films as a whole). On the other, it is also, by virtue of its explicit reliance upon fantasy, an acknowledgement of the very 'impossibility' of escape, a 'magical' resolution to conflicts which remain unresolved, and an ironic recognition of the actual impotence which underlies this concluding image of 'phallic, narcissistic omnipotence'.[6] *Vroom*, in this respect, is a film which is happy to draw upon a working-class tradition of realism but which also questions its usefulness in relation to contemporary realities, a film which is conscious of the appeal of

---

[5] The theme of escape is explored with added intensity in screenplay writer Jim Cartwright's play, *Road* (which was subsequently filmed for television by Alan Clarke in 1987). The play (and film) end with four young people standing in a bare room together and chanting, repetitively and with rising volume, 'Somehow a somehow might escape'. See Jim Cartwright, *Road* (London: Methuen, 1986), 35.

[6] The phrase is from Laura Mulvey, 'Afterthoughts . . . Inspired by *Duel in the Sun*', *Framework*, nos. 15/16/17 (Summer 1981), 14. I have previously made use of it to describe the working-class hero in films such as *Sons and Lovers* (1960) and *Young Cassidy* (1965). See *Sex, Class and Realism* (London: BFI, 1986), 163.

PLATE 12. Existential angst: David Thewlis in *Naked*

the young, virile working-class hero but is, at the same time, suspicious and questioning of the model of 'resistance' which he is now able to provide.

In a sense, this problematization of the working-class hero becomes starkly evident, albeit in a different way, in Mike Leigh's *Naked* (1993) (which, although it follows shortly after the period with which this book is concerned, may usefully be seen in this context). In the previous chapter, it was argued that the central protagonist in *The Ploughman's Lunch* could be read as a fusion of two types of hero derived from working-class realism and the art film. This is also true of *Naked* except that the alienation of the male hero has become even more extensive and the anger, and misogyny, associated with the 'angry young man', has become even more pronounced. Accordingly, the parody and playfulness which is evident in *Vroom* is replaced in this film by the anguish and existential dread more characteristic of traditional art cinema.

Unlike previous Leigh films, *Naked* is dominated by one character in particular: that of Johnny played by David Thewlis. He is from the north—Manchester—and, at the film's start, flees south to London where he visits his former girlfriend, Louise (Lesley Sharp), and her flatmate, Sophie (Katrin Cartlidge), before embarking upon a mini-odyssey of the city (Homer is actually referred to at one point in the film). Johnny, in this respect, represents a working-class rebel whose refusal to 'settle' now assumes expanded dimensions. Thus, while the film has been seen by some to be about homelessness or the legacy of Thatcherism, the film's adoption of arthouse conventions—the goal-bereft protagonist, weakly motivated narrative causality, emphasis upon psychological states rather than social conditions—encourages a reading of the film less in social and political terms than in terms of the more general 'existential' themes of alienation, communication breakdown, uncertainty, and emotional discontent characteristic of the traditional art film. Thus, the sequence in which Johnny encounters the homeless couple, Archie (Ewen Bremner) and Maggie (Susan Vidler), is shot in, for Leigh, an untypically stylized fashion which plays down the specificities of place in favour of a more expressive, or metaphorical, use of *mise-en-scène* (as when Johnny and Maggie walk across a barren piece of waste ground). In this sense, the film is about 'homelessness' in the more 'existential' sense of characters (most of whom are living in 'homes' which are not their own) who are detached from their traditional moorings and have no settled place in the world. This is also true of Johnny whose discontent (and lashing out at others) assumes less of a social and political character than a more generalized form of angst. It has been suggested, for example, that Jimmy Porter in *Look Back in Anger* may be seen as one of Johnny's precursors.[7] Johnny's 'anger', however, has little of the social content of the earlier play and film, with their attacks on the class-ridden character of post-war British society. He may share Jimmy's vituperative outbursts of language, but his protest is less 'political' than apocalyptic, incorporating a demented mix of references to Nostradamus, the Book of Revelations (claiming that the 'mark of the beast' is, in fact, the bar code), and James Gleick's *Chaos*. A key scene, in this respect, is that between Johnny and Brian (Peter Wight), the guard of an empty office block, in which they are shot in silhouette while they discuss the 'end of the world'.

However, if Johnny is less 'angry young man' than nihilistic prophet of impending doom, his alienation from the world around him, like that of Jimmy Porter, still finds an outlet in the form of aggressive masculinity. The film begins in semi-darkness as the camera pushes forward to reveal Johnny having violent, and painful, sex with a woman against a wall. Her subsequent threat that he's 'dead' then leads him to flee Manchester for London. His subsequent journey through the city results in similar encounters: rough sex with Sophie and a violent response to her declaration of love; cruelty towards the lonely woman (Deborah MacLaren) in the flat whom he initially spies from the office block; verbal abuse of Louise and the woman from the café (Gina McKee) once she asks him to leave the house where she is staying. In this respect, *Naked* pushes the sexual aggression which characterized the male working-class hero of the 'new wave' films to new extremes. Leigh has suggested that Johnny should, in social terms at least, be seen as a 'victim'.[8] Accordingly, as in the earlier 'new

---

[7]   Mike Leigh refers to *Look Back in Anger* as one of the films to which *Naked* has been compared in his interview with Graham Fuller in *Naked and Other Screenplays* (London: Faber and Faber, 1995), p. xxxv.

[8]   Lee Ellickson and Richard Porton, 'I Find the Tragicomic Things in Life: An Interview with Mike Leigh', *Cineaste*, vol. xx, no. 3 (Apr. 1994), 13. Johnny's disdain for women is, of course, paralleled by the brutalizing treatment of women meted out by the odious yuppie, Jeremy (Greg Cruttwell) to the waitress Giselle (Elizabeth Berrington) and Sophie. Jeremy's sexual violence, in this respect, is more straightforwardly an exercise of his economic position and selfishness than is the case with Johnny, whom, it could be argued, is made more sympathetic by virtue of this implicit comparison.

wave' films, the exercise of the working-class hero's—verbal and physical—power over women may be read as a compensation for his actual social and political impotence. In this way, the excessive violence of Johnny's character represents yet another form of response to the 'crisis' of masculinity brought on by changing economic and social roles.

However, the film also identifies the inadequacy of this model of masculine 'resistance'. As with the kitchen-sink films, Johnny experiences a serious beating (which although executed by an anonymous gang is linked to the 'beating' he was due to receive for his sexual violence at the film's start). Louise offers him the possibility of some kind of redemption and suggests that they return to Manchester. The north, in this respect, functions slightly differently from some of the other films of the period (and traditional working-class realism) in which characters wish to escape the confines of their northern city settings. In *Naked*, a return to the north appears to hold out the possibility of a certain form of identity and inter-connection which is absent from the film's portrait of London as a city of lonely and alienated people. However, the option of a return 'home' is rejected by Johnny as he hobbles off down the road on his own as the film ends. In these circumstances, however, the male hero's desire for escape now seems to assume the status of a pathology. Traditionally, the male hero's fear of domesticity, or settling down, is associated with a fear of emasculation or symbolic 'castration'. The image of an enfeebled Johnny as he sets off on his aimless journey once more suggests, however, that it may be the drive to escape from intimacy and co-dependence which is itself crippling.

While the film, in this respect, does not endorse the misogyny of the film's character, it is, none the less, weak in giving a satisfactory expression to an alternative ethos of interdependence. There is a quietly effective scene between Sophie and Louise in the pub—when Sophie complains how men 'Don't like you if you're strong, don't like you if you're weak; hate you if you're clever, hate you if you're stupid'—but this is a relatively isolated moment in a film largely devoted to Johnny's relentless outbursts. In this respect, for all its apparent critique of Johnny's actions, the film is unduly in thrall to him and continually forces the spectator to see the world from his viewpoint. As a result, the film is much more successful in giving voice to Johnny's rage than embodying the experiences of the women characters. A symptomatic scene comes at the very end when Louise and Sophie's flatmate, Sandra (Claire Skinner), returns from Zimbabwe. In the film's final encounter, Sandra asks Johnny why he insists on 'takin' the piss' and asking 'silly questions'. However, whatever validity her remarks may have are undermined by Claire Skinner's clever but heavily mannered performance, characterized by high-pitched vocals, an inability to complete a sentence, and excessive movements of the hands (which, as the following chapter indicates, corresponds to a pattern of acting in Leigh's films). In this way, her response to Johnny is seen simply as silly and suggests a reluctance on the part of the film to make use of the women characters to interrogate more fully the behaviour of its central male character. It is, nevertheless, the role of women that becomes particularly important in other films of the period.

Class and Femininity

For, while a number of films of the 1980s and after, responding to the changing economic and social circumstances of the period as well as to the challenges of feminism, began to render the male working-class hero problematic other films simply pushed him to the margins. Thus, while it was the young working-class male who provided the narrative with its momentum in the working-class dramas of the 1950s and 1960s, in films such as *Educating Rita*, *Letter to Brezhnev*, *Rita, Sue and Bob Too*, *Business as Usual*, it is the working-class woman who is the film's main driving force. Like *Vroom*, however, these films are rarely straightforwardly works of social realism (and demonstrate the 'hybridity' that was a feature of 'state-of-the-nation' films of this period). Thus, *Educating Rita*, *Letter to Brezhnev*, and *Rita, Sue and Bob Too* are also comedies of social manners that deliberately play with class and gender roles for comic effect. The films are also, in some respects, 'woman's films' that focus upon the conditions of women's lives and foreground questions of female desire. However, just as these films both use and subvert the traditions of 1960s working-class realism, so they also both adopt and adapt the conventions of the woman's film.

As noted in previous chapters, the term, 'the woman's film', has conventionally been employed to refer to films involving women-centred narratives and dealing with what is traditionally taken to be the central spheres of women's experience (love, motherhood, family life).[9] Historically, the plots of women's films may be seen to have been schematic, even didactic, confronting characters with stark, and often impossible, choices which result in either sacrifice or punishment (and a corresponding sense of pathos for the spectator). However, if the women-centred narratives of these films of the 1980s make use of this tradition, they also deviate from it as well. The role of women is not necessarily confined to domestic interiors but is also associated with public spaces (and sometimes work). Nor are the characters necessarily faced with the same kind of 'impossible' choices as their predecessors, and they often evade the punitive or constricting solutions which earlier films imposed upon them. As a result, endings are characteristically more optimistic, and tend to avoid giving full rein to the pathos that is typical of their precursors.

In the woman's film, for example, it is often the home which is the central setting for the films' actions and the locus of the films' conflicts as female characters seek to escape, or adjust to, marriage and domesticity. In the 1980s films, however, the home is no longer the main realm of female activity and the women characters have become much more 'public' figures. In her discussion of 1960s British realism, Terry Lovell suggests how these films typically follow 'the young male hero . . . into the more actively masculine spaces of the street,

---

[9] For a useful introduction to debates about melodrama and the woman's film, see Pam Cook, 'Melodrama and the Women's Picture', in Sue Aspinall and Robert Murphy (eds.), *Gainsborough Melodrama*, BFI Dossier 18 (London: BFI, 1983).

the workplace, the pub, where he negotiates potential sexual encounters'.[10] This is also true of *Vroom* and *Naked* where it is the men, and especially Jake and Johnny, who enjoy a free sense of movement through the town and city. In these women-centred films, however, women begin to appropriate these traditionally 'masculine spaces' and make them their own.

Thus, in *Rita, Sue and Bob Too*, the film's stylistic trademark—fast, lateral-moving long takes—is particularly associated with the energy of Rita and Sue and their movement through the public spaces of the estate and elsewhere. The opening of the film begins with a sweeping aerial shot over a working-class estate in Bradford. As the camera moves down onto a pub exterior, it picks up a drunk (who subsequently turns out to be Sue's father) with a takeaway. The camera then follows his drunken stagger across the estate (as he walks home, not from work as in films such as *A Kind of Loving* (1962) but, from enforced 'leisure'). As he comes towards the entrance to the block of flats in which he lives, a young woman, Sue (Michelle Holmes), comes out. He demands to know where she is going and tells her not to be out all night. She, in turn, tells him to mind his own business and that she'll be back when she wants. The camera then follows her across the estate, as she appropriates the public space from him (the impotent patriarch). A subsequent shot sees her entering the back door of a run-down house, with motorbikes and a wheel-less car (itself a sort of symbol of declining industrialism) littering the front garden, before she emerges through the front door with Rita (Siobhan Finneran) with whom she con-fidently marches off. After a cut, they are seen striding through a more well-to-do middle-class estate where they are due to baby-sit for Bob and Michelle. These are highly stylized shots and, by conventional standards, exceed the requirements of narrative exposition. Their role is partly to establish a sense of place and lay out the new geography of the 'haves' and 'have-nots' in con-temporary Britain. However, they are also shots in which the women are the dominant presence and which challenge the conventional association of such places, in the realist tradition, with the young working-class male.

Similarly, it is Rita who is seen at work, on the street, on the bus, at the railway station, and at summer school in *Educating Rita*. In contrast, it is her husband Denny who is associated with domestic space and, it is only at the film's end, after he and Rita have split up, that he is finally seen on the street (significantly enough, with his new, and pregnant, wife). In *Letter to Brezhnev*, Teresa (Margi Clarke) is never actually seen at home at all. Her character is a female inver-sion of the working-class 'playboy': like Arthur in *Saturday Night and Sunday Morning*, she has a boring (if relatively less well-paid) job which she hates and dedicates her leisure time to the pursuit of enjoyment and pleasure. As Elaine explains to Peter, 'she works long hours in the chicken factory . . . so when she finishes work she likes to go out and have a good time'. Accordingly, it is Teresa and her friend Elaine whom we follow through the public spaces of Liverpool's

---

[10] Terry Lovell, 'Landscape and Stories in 1960s British Realism', *Screen*, vol. 31, no. 4 (Winter 1990), 365.

streets and clubs. It is also the two women who take an active role in 'negotiating sexual encounters'. It is Elaine who actively looks around the club and turns the Russian sailor, Peter (Peter Firth), into the object of her romantic gaze and it is Teresa (with her 'degree in men') who takes the initiative in going over to him and his friend, Sergei (Alfred Molina) and encouraging their interest. They also take the initiative in stopping the bus which, as a result of a misunderstanding, Peter and Sergei have boarded and then in taking them to a hotel (for which, with some misgivings, they are even prepared to pay).

However, if the novelty of these films is a narrative organization which is centred upon female characters, there is still a degree of continuity with earlier working-class realism in the emphasis upon the theme of escape from the constrictions of working-class life. The focus upon female characters (and the use of elements from the woman's film) does, however, alter how the motif of escape is worked through. For escape is not simply a matter of class but may also be overlaid with the desire for escape from the demands of a traditional female role as well.[11] So, while in earlier realist films it is often domesticity that the men fear, in these films women themselves are querying, in part, the traditional expectation that they assume domestic roles. This does not amount to an explicitly feminist form of questioning but does, none the less, grow out of a changed social landscape in which the 'normality' of conventional male and female roles is no longer taken for granted. Thus, in *Educating Rita*, Rita is in rebellion against both the cultural limitations and philistinism which the film associates with her class background as well as the domestic subordination which her role as wife and prospective mother involves. The transplantation to film of Willy Russell's original play involves a degree of opening out of the film's action to include scenes (such as those involving her husband and father who both wish to see her pregnant) which stress the extra pressures upon her as a woman. Thus, whereas in traditional working-class realism, domestic space is associated with women and the entrapment of men, in *Educating Rita* the home becomes a form of imprisonment for her, a theme visually suggested by the

---

[11] Justine King identifies five films of this period—*She'll Be Wearing Pink Pyjamas* (1985), *Letter to Brezhnev*, *Wish You Were Here*, *Educating Rita*, and *Shirley Valentine* (1989)—as constituting a 'coherent cycle' of films unified by the 'recurring motif of escape'. See 'Crossing Thresholds: The Contemporary British Woman's Film', in Andrew Higson (ed.), *Dissolving Views: Key Writings on British Cinema* (London: Cassell, 1996), 219. This is probably overstated. More than just these five films make use of this motif and not all are restricted to women-centred films (cf. *Vroom*, *The Fruit Machine*). In terms of my own interests, although these films share conventions derived from the woman's film, they do not all fall clearly within a tradition of working-class realism. *Wish You Were Here*, for example, is set in the 1950s and more obviously belongs, as Chapter 6 indicated, to a cycle of retro movies (such as *Dance With a Stranger* and *Let Him Have It*) dealing with the tensions of that period. *She'll Be Wearing Pink Pyjamas* is set in the present but the women who attend the outward bound course are predominantly middle class and social class is not emphasized as an issue. *Shirley Valentine* (which, like *Educating Rita*, is based upon a play by Willy Russell) is, perhaps, closer to a tradition of working-class realism. However, Shirley (Pauline Collins) lives comfortably in suburbia with a husband who appears to run his own business. Her desire for escape is, therefore, primarily from the roles of wife, mother, and housewife rather than from the limitations of her class position (although, like *Educating Rita*, there is a distinct sense that she also seeks a form of cultural self-improvement that inevitably sets her apart from the parochialism of her fellow holiday-makers in Greece).

claustrophobia of the high-angle shot used to record her initial entrance into the house (and given an added resonance by her subsequent assault on the sitting-room wall with a hammer).

However, it is also the case that the desire for escape in working-class realism has traditionally been individual in emphasis. As Higson puts it, 'the "kitchen sink" films are less about the conditions of the industrial working class and their collective class consciousness, than they are about the attempts of individuals to escape from those conditions and that consciousness'.[12] This is also true of a film such as *Educating Rita* where Rita's desire for self-discovery places her in conflict with her class background. She is, thus, a kind of female version of the 1950s 'scholarship boy' whose involvement in education and middle-class culture inevitably takes her away from her social origins.[13] In this respect, the film follows the older school of working-class films in placing particular emphasis upon cultural rather than economic divisions. Unlike many of the working-class films that follow it, there is little evidence of unemployment or poverty. What Rita (who is herself employed) aspires to escape is not so much economic hardship as 'cultural deprivation'. This is most in evidence in the scene in the pub where her husband and parents are part of a group seen singing along to a jukebox ('we're so happy together, and that's okay'). However, as Rita subsequently explains to Frank (Michael Caine), her lecturer, 'we're not all okay' and, in the words of her mother, 'there must be better songs to sing than this'. In this way, like earlier kitchen-sink films, it is mass culture, rather than economic disadvantage, which is identified as the main source of impoverishment, and lack of 'spiritual' nourishment. As Rita herself puts it, while the group in the pub may seem to be happy, they are not 'surviving with the spirit intact'.

However, unlike earlier realist films, there is no evidence of looking back to an 'authentic' traditional working-class culture (the evidence of which is largely absent from these films). The clash of culture in *Educating Rita* is straightforwardly between the mass culture of the working class (records on the jukebox, popular novels, men's magazines) and the literary-based culture of the educated middle classes. The novelty of the film, in this respect, is that the film does not see Rita's emulation of the middle classes as unproblematically a gain. As she acquires the tools of literary criticism she is seen to be in danger of losing the directness and originality of response which had characterized her earlier reading; her flatmate Trish (Maureen Lipman), whom Rita admires for her apparent sophistication and cultural capital (as well as her independence), despairingly attempts suicide; her tutor Frank is not only an alcoholic but inhabits a middle-class world of sexual infidelities and hypocrisy that appears no less shallow than the one she is leaving. This refusal to offer a simple endorsement of the assimilation of middle-class values by the working class does, however, place Rita in an

---

[12] Higson, 'Space, Place, Spectacle: Landscape and Townscape in the "Kitchen Sink" Film', *Screen*, vol. 25, nos. 4–5 (July–Oct., 1984), 14.

[13] Richard Hoggart famously discusses the position of 'scholarship boys' who 'under the stimulus of a stronger critical intelligence or imagination' are 'uprooted from their class' in *The Uses of Literacy* (orig. 1957) (Harmondsworth: Penguin, 1959), 242.

ambivalent position at the film's end. On the one hand, she is cut off from her family and class but, on the other, is detached from the middle-class culture to which she has been aspiring. In the same way, while she has left her husband behind, she rejects the possibility of a relationship with Frank, who had wanted her to accompany him to Australia. In a number of respects, this is, of course, a positive ending. Rita, now Susan, is no longer dependent (upon Frank) and is able to make the choices she wants. In a reversal of roles (related both to class and gender), she sees Frank off at the airport just as he had once seen her onto the train to summer school. However, her independence is also a kind of isolation and the film's final shot is of her on her own, walking off down the airport corridor and away from the camera. It is, of course, a shot which is intended to leave open the choices ahead of Rita. However, insofar as the film has proved reluctant to map out just what Rita is escaping *to* rather than *from*, so it is a shot which also accentuates the individualism (and lack of connectedness) which is at the heart of the film's theme of escape.

A similar theme of escape is also to be found in *Letter to Brezhnev*. As the shot of her through a wire fence would suggest, life for Elaine in Liverpool is a kind or prison. She is on the dole with few prospects and yearns for something more. The political irony of the film is that it is the Soviet Union which seems to offer the possibility of escape. Although warned of the country's reputation for 'food shortages' and 'lack of freedom', Elaine's experiences at home suggest she has nothing to lose ('just take a walk into any back kitchen round here and you'll soon see food shortages' she tells a sceptical journalist). It is in this sense that the film won its reputation as an anti-Thatcherite piece, suggesting how the debilitating effects of unemployment and poverty in the north were such that it made living in the Soviet Union attractive by comparison. As Elaine herself puts it to the Foreign Office official (Neil Cunningham) who attempts to stop her leaving: 'Going to live in Russia can't be any worse than living here—so why are you trying to discourage me escaping?' Elaine's desire for escape, however, is not only motivated by a dissatisfaction with her economic circumstances but also her frustration with the inadequacies of the local men.

She is, as she tells her friend Tracy, 'sick of the men' in Kirkby who've got 'no romance in them' and yearns to be elsewhere (in 'Casablanca or somewhere'). Her subsequent meeting with the Russian sailor Peter (who is on a 'public relations' visit to the city) therefore represents a kind of wish-fulfilment and provides her with the opportunity for the 'romance and adventure' for which she'd earlier craved (a phrase employed tellingly by Teresa as the two women are squeezed into the starkly unromantic setting of a lavatory cubicle). Later, she and Peter walk through the city at night, filmed in expressionist red and gold, and stop to look at the stars. As they do so, the camera moves off them onto a 'typical' Liverpool couple snarling at each other as they go by. In linking the two couples in this way, the film sets up the choice (typical of melodrama) now facing Elaine: of accepting her lot ('That's what happens, when you have to give up', Elaine says of the couple) or of giving rein to her romantic desires and 'following her star'. She opts for the latter course and, with the help of her letter to Brezhnev, secures the ticket that will take her to the Soviet Union and Peter. The film then ends with her at the airport, preparing to leave the country. As has already been noted, it is common, in working-class realism (and the woman's film), for the desire for escape to prove 'impossible', or to demand too high a cost, and, as a result, for characters to accommodate themselves to compromise and an eschewal of fantasy. This is not, however, the case with *Letter to Brezhnev*. As with *Vroom*, there seems to be a conscious attempt to challenge this convention and celebrate the triumph of fantasy and desire over everyday constraints and the routine (a theme which is also implicit in the way that Teresa transforms herself from factory worker to Marilyn Monroe 'lookalike' early on in the film).

However, as with *Educating Rita*, there is also a degree of ambivalence about the film's ending. As with other films of the period, the form of the film is not straightforwardly 'realist' but a mix of various aesthetic ingredients. Thus, along- side the familiar realist elements (of location shooting, casual camerawork, ordinary urban settings and characters), there is a self-conscious appropriation of the conventions of Hollywood romance and cinematic fantasy. Indeed, the film may be read as a kind of homage to *On the Town* (1949), with the film attempting (as the final graphic of the Liverpool skyline might suggest) to invest Liverpool with the kind of 'mythic' cinematic identity characteristically associ- ated with New York. As a result, the stylistic straightforwardness of the film's 'realism' is mixed with a heavily stylized, and at times expressionistic, use of cin- ematic techniques. Thus, the romance between Elaine and Peter is deliberately associated with a degree of cliché, cinematic quotation, and other-worldliness. This is particularly evident in their opening encounter at the club when the repetition of extended shots of the couple's softly lit faces and use of 'subjective', extra-diegetic music sets them apart from the scene around. Inevitably, this self- consciousness in the film's style (and overt acknowledgement of the 'fairytale' character of its romance) has reverberations for the ending.[14] As with *Vroom*, Elaine's escape may, at one level, be seen to involve the victory of fantasy over constraint. At the same time, however, the clear inscription of fantasy into the style of the film also undercuts some of the optimism associated with her escape by laying bare some of its fundamental 'unreality'. Thus, we do not actually see Elaine's eventual reunion with Peter, who, given the stylized and semi-subjective treatment of the couple's first encounter, retains a certain air of exoticism and fantasy (as in the film's initially deceptive scene of Elaine apparently boarding his ship).

This is a point which is reinforced by the way in which the film, like *Vroom*, also offsets the 'escape' of its central character with the experiences of others (in a way that *Educating Rita* does not). Thus, in *Letter to Brezhnev*, Elaine is seen off by Teresa who indicates that she wishes she was going as well. Encouraged by Elaine to do more with her life, Teresa explains that it is she, rather than Elaine,

---

[14] Frank Clarke, the writer of the film, in fact, described the film as a 'romantic fairytale' which reflected his own love for Hollywood movies. See Quentin Falk, 'How the Reds Scored Twice in a Fairytale Finish', *Guardian* (26 Oct. 1985), 11.

who is 'the straight girl from Kirkby' and that 'drinking vodka, getting fucked and stuffing chickens' is all that her 'dream' consists of. The film then ends with a shot of Teresa, facing the camera as it pulls away from her. She stands and then rushes forward, coming into close-up as she whispers, 'Tell Igor I love him'. In this way, the emphasis of the film is thrown back from Elaine onto Teresa, the character who, for all her wit and energy, remains at home, trapped in a life which, unlike Elaine, she is unable to escape. As we have seen, it was a recurring feature of 1960s working-class realism that the emphasis upon the theme of escape led to an emphasis upon the exceptional individual set apart from the rest of his class. The ending of *Letter to Brezhnev* partly plays with this idea. In a film characterized by comic ironies and reversals, it is the apparently 'outrageous' woman, Teresa, who is revealed as 'conventional' while it is the 'straight girl' who turns out to be the one who is 'different'. However, despite this play with type, the film appears to recognize that Elaine's trajectory *is*, none the less, 'exceptional' and that it is the experience of Teresa, the woman who stays behind, that is more typical of Kirkby women. It is, therefore, on a close-up of Teresa that the film ends. In this way, the pathos (characteristic of the woman's film) which is generated by the film's ending derives not only from an identification with the predicament of Teresa but also from a recognition that the escape route which her friend Elaine has taken is not one that is generally available.[15]

A further question-mark also hangs over the film's ending. As has been noted, the women-centred films characteristically use the motif of escape to raise questions of both class and gender. However, the articulation of these concerns is not necessarily evenly balanced. Thus, in the case of *Letter to Brezhnev*, Elaine's flight from Liverpool may be away from a life on the dole but it is not, it appears, an escape from domesticity. As she confirms to the Foreign Office official, she simply wants 'to settle down . . . to marry and have children'. Her escape, in this regard, involves, as Justine King suggests, more of a flight from her class position than it does from 'the traditional expectations of her gender'.[16] However, while this seems to be the case, it is also a reading that underestimates the impact of what has gone before. The film has successfully played with gender roles, allocating to the women the strength and resourcefulness that most of the men around them lack. As a consequence, there is a sense in which the images of the women's energy and high-spiritedness which dominate the first part of the film threaten to subvert the film's ending—putting into question

[15] The theme of the impossibility of escape is even more pronounced in *The Fruit Machine* (1988), also written by Frank Clarke. This film focuses on two young gays, Eddie (Emile Charles) and Michael (Tony Forsyth), who flee from Liverpool to Brighton after witnessing a murder. Eddie is a dreamer who lives in a fantasy world of old movies and opera and is unable to act like the 'real man' his father wants him to be. In Brighton, his predicament is linked with that of Sooty the dolphin who is 'trapped' in a dolphinarium. However, while Michael succeeds in freeing Sooty, 'reality' catches up with Eddie who is fatally wounded by the killer Echo (Bruce Payne) and, in a scene of self-conscious pathos, dies in Michael's arms as his lover sings the Marilyn Monroe song 'Running Wild' from Billy Wilder's *Some Like It Hot* (1959).

[16] Justine King, 'Crossing Thresholds', 226.

whether Elaine will simply 'settle down' once she gets to Russia or whether Teresa's fear of 'what's round the corner' will really prevent her from getting on. Indeed, Elaine is still not completely sure that Peter is unmarried while Teresa's line, 'Tell Igor I love him', involves such an unexpectedly sentimental narrative twist that it seems to run counter to what we have previously observed. More-over, as King herself suggests, the film's refusal to show the reunion of Elaine and Peter and the concentration, at the end, on the relationship between the two women reinforces the sense that it is 'their strong, mutually supportive friend-ship which is the privileged pairing of the text' rather than Elaine's romance with Peter.[17] In this respect, an additional element of pathos is added to the film's ending by the separation of the two women that is involved in Elaine's departure and the way that this is registered as a significant loss for both characters.[18]

There are more than a few echoes of *Letter to Brezhnev* in *Rita, Sue and Bob Too*. Rita and Sue are like young cousins of Teresa, desperate for something to lift them out of an everyday reality characterized by poverty, violence, and lim-ited life-chances. Their 'escape', such as it is, takes the form of the man for whom they baby-sit, Bob (George Costigan), who offers them rough and ready sex in his car. There is, however, little of the romantic yearnings or aspirations to be found in *Letter*. The girls have few illusions about Bob. They accept his infidel-ities to his wife as normal ('can't expect owt else', comments Sue) and expect little from him, seemingly content with his graceless sexual performances ('he certainly knows how to give lass a good time', says a grateful Rita after their initial 'jump' on the car front seat).[19] The girls are also quite content to share Bob until the departure of Bob's wife, Michelle (Lesley Sharp), and Rita's preg-nancy, lead Bob to invite Rita to move in with him. This leads to a temporary rift between the girls ('you dirty cow—just leaving me like that', complains Sue) but, as with *Letter*, it is the bond between the women which proves the strongest relationship in the film. After her miscarriage, Rita goes to reprimand Sue for 'doing the dirty' on her while she was in hospital. However, faced with Aslam's violence against Sue, she comes to Sue's rescue and takes her into her new home as a 'lodger' where they cheerfully return to sharing Bob. This ending, however, like that of *Letter to Brezhnev*, is hardly free of unresolved tensions.

In one sense, the women have achieved some kind of escape from their previous existence. Their 'taking over' of Bob's home (temporary though it

---

[17] Ibid.

[18] Linda Williams indicates, in relation to the key woman's film *Stella Dallas* (1937), how the optimism of the film's ending (the marriage of Stella's daughter) is undercut by the sense of the 'loss' of mother to daughter and vice versa. See ' "Something Else Besides a Mother": *Stella Dallas* and the Maternal Melodrama', in Christine Gledhill (ed.), *Home is Where the Heart Is: Studies in Melodrama and the Woman's Film* (London: BFI, 1987), 316. In a sense, it is possible to argue that there is a similar under-cutting of the optimism surrounding Elaine's romance with Peter by the sense of loss that the splitting up of the two women invokes.

[19] Although this line of dialogue is similar to one spoken by Sue in Andrea Dunbar's original play, the girls' approval of Bob's performance is also accompanied by a degree of criticism of him in the play. Hence, Rita complains that Bob 'hurt me a bit at the first' while Sue observes that Bob 'seemed to enjoy it a lot more than we did'. See Andrea Dunbar, *Rita, Sue and Bob Too with The Arbor and Shirley* (London: Methuen, 1988), pp. 49 and 50.

is likely to be) has freed them from the oppressiveness of their own domestic backgrounds and from Sue's 'imprisonment' at Aslam's sister's. In class terms, the film appears to see in this a certain triumph of working-class bawdiness and vitality over middle-class frigidity and sterility (a sort of reversal of the 'embourgeoisification' process undergone by Rita's namesake in *Educating Rita*). As baby-sitters, the girls have brought a frenetic activity to the middle-class house, converting it into the 'house of fun' of the Madness video seen on TV. Michelle, in comparison, is relatively joyless (turning off the TV as soon as she comes in), has been sterilized, and confesses that she no longer enjoys sex. In terms of gender, however, the women's position is less clear. Initially, it appears as if Bob may receive his come-uppance. Rita has discovered his betrayal of her and has arrived at a new *rapprochement* with Sue (suggesting, as in *Letter to Brezhnev*, that it is the bond between the women that is most important). When Bob returns home, he finds that they have ignored the domestic duties formerly carried out by his wife and have failed to make his tea ('What about my tea?' 'What about it?'). Moreover, it also looks as though he is to be evicted from his own bed as Rita and Sue inform him that they will be sleeping together. However, as he disconsolately goes upstairs for a bath, he finds the two women waiting for him under the duvet. Although the girls may be seen to be there on their terms (and in a situation that preserves the relationship between them), they are also in a position of apparently accepting Bob's shortcomings and his desire to have them both. As such, they may have taken over his house but they have also done so on terms which appear to favour Bob the most (and reward him for his illegal seduction of under-age schoolgirls).[20]

In his review of the film, Philip French argues that it 'mocks the high-minded morality, sexuality, and politics of "Saturday Night and Sunday Morning" and similar British realist movies of 30 years ago'.[21] He is clearly right to draw this contrast. Unlike the working-class films, the main characters avoid any 'punishment' for their sexual transgressions. Michelle discovers Bob's relationship with Rita and Sue and there is a noisy confrontation, involving Rita and Sue's family, in front of Sue's house but there is no real price to be paid by the three main protagonists. Bob does, of course, lose his wife and family but there is no evidence that this involves any emotional or psychological cost to him. Thus, in contrast to the earlier realist films, where there is a tendency towards morally conservative endings which channel the characters' sexuality towards marriage and reproduction, *Rita, Sue and Bob Too* finishes with a replacement of the conventional family by an unconventional *ménage-á-trois*. Indeed, insofar as Bob is less middle-class than a working-class lad made good (as his earthy manner, tattoo, and dubious taste in interior decoration would seem to suggest), he may be read as a kind of latterday Arthur Seaton *after* he has been married but once more in conflict with social constraints.

---

[20] Significantly, the original play places much more emphasis upon the fact that the girls are only 15 and that Bob could be sent to prison. See Andrea Dunbar, *Rita, Sue and Bob Too*, pp. 56 and 63.

[21] Philip French, *The Observer* (6 Sept. 1987), 21.

However, as this suggests, while the film may avoid the conservatism of a more traditional ending (and challenge the ideology of 'familialism' associated with the Thatcherite politics of the period), the prospects which it holds out for its female characters are limited. The problem which the film faces, in this regard, is that, in rejecting the moralism of its precursors and seeking to avoid judging its characters from the position of moral or cultural superiority that was a feature of working-class realism in the 1950s and 1960s, the film also undermines its own capacity to engage critically with the characters and their predicament. This is partly to be seen in the film's approach to style. In the 'kitchen sink' films of the British 'new wave', the position of superiority *vis-à-vis* characters was often inscribed into the style of the films themselves which, through a use of stylistically overt techniques, made manifest the split between observer and observed. A similar disjunction is also in evidence in *Rita, Sue and Bob Too*, especially as a result of the film's use of the stylistically obtrusive travelling shots that characterize much of the film.

As has been noted, these shots perform a certain expressive and semantic function (signifying the energy of the girls as well as their resistance to confinement). However, they also render visible the presence of the camera and, in doing so, the presence of a directorial consciousness beyond that of the characters themselves.[22] The effect of this self-conscious use of film technique, however, is less the aestheticization of poverty (or industrial cityscapes) characteristic of earlier films than a sort of detached comic gaze. In a manner typical of the director Alan Clarke, the film draws upon an observational (or 'documentary realist') style based upon long takes and the avoidance of point-of-view shots and reverse-field cutting. In this way, the film stands back from the characters and discourages the strong sense of involvement and identification which is typical of the 'woman's film'. At the same time, the use of this style is also highly elaborated and is deployed in such a way that the techniques themselves become overt. They do not, however, go so far as to rupture the narrative illusion and thus there is a stepping back from the sort of critical 'dialogue' with characters that a more radical, or 'Brechtian', cinema might provoke.

In this way the film imposes a formalized distance from its characters which prevents it from either fully engaging emotionally with their predicaments or commenting effectively upon them. The problems to which this then leads may be observed in the way in which certain Asian characters are treated. After Aslam has offered to take Sue to his sister's, there is a shot of his sister pushing a child in a buggy while Aslam and Sue walk alongside, discussing whether Sue would like to go to Pakistan. The shot itself is one continuous take, a lateral tracking shot of the kind which by then has become familiar. As such, it is also a shot which seems primarily to follow an aesthetic logic (of formal pattern and rhythm) rather than one with a clear narratively motivated purpose. While such

---

[22]   David Thomson notes this tension when he describes director Alan Clarke's 'great formal interest in film as a way of seeing or presenting'. 'He seemed', Thomson continues, 'always on the urgent beat of news stories, yet he was forever testing out his own savage stylistics'. See 'Walkers in the World: Alan Clarke', *Film Comment* (May–June 1993), 80.

PLATE 13. An unconventional *ménage-à-trois*: George Costigan, Michelle Holmes, and Siobhan Finneran in *Rita, Sue and Bob Too*

formal inventiveness is one of the undoubted pleasures of the film, it is also the case that this foregrounding of technique is also symptomatic of a certain refusal by the film to engage seriously with the Asian characters (this is the only shot in which Aslam's sister appears) or to tackle the questions to which the relationships between the Asian and white characters (many of whom indulge in racist remarks) give rise. In a sense, while it is a strength of the film that it refuses the moralizing around sexually active female characters that is typical of both earlier working-class realism and the woman's film, it is at the expense of virtually abandoning perspective altogether, particularly in relation to a male character such as Bob. In this respect, the apparent amoralism of the film's detached comic gaze is, in fact, an endorsement of a certain kind of male irresponsibility. This is particularly clear in the way in which the film departs from Andrea Dunbar's original play. In this, Bob marries Rita but Sue does not move in with them. Moreover, the play ends with a conversation between Sue's mother (who complains that 'all men are no good') and Michelle (significantly, treated with a much greater degree of sympathy than in the film) who begin to forge a certain bond (born out of shared female experience).[23] In this way, the play offers a—feminine—perspective on events, as well as a distance from Bob's actions, that the ending of the film entirely removes.

Women and Political Action

For all the play with gender roles and upsetting of expectations surrounding 'feminine' behaviour in films such as *Letter to Brezhnev* and *Rita, Sue and Bob Too*, the response of the female characters to their situation remains largely 'apolitical', in terms of both class and gender. A more politicized kind of female resistance, however, is found in *Business as Usual*. In contrast to most of the other films, the central protagonist of this film is middle-aged, married, and a mother rather than a young single woman; the focus of the action is on work and industrial action rather than on leisure and 'play'; and the female lead is involved in a collective struggle to improve the lot of herself and others rather than an individual form of escape or flight from her class.[24] In this respect, the film's emphasis is upon the 'respectable' working class rather than the 'rough' working class of *Rita, Sue and Bob Too*. As the film's writer and director Lezli-An Barrett explains, she wanted to counter what she describes as 'crude kitchen-sink stereotypes' and to show Babs Flynn (Glenda Jackson), the film's main character, as a woman 'who is conservative with a small "c", a little bit moralistic, and who tries hard to get on in the world'.[25]

Partly based on the real-life case of Audrey White, Babs is the manageress of a clothes shop who loses her job for complaining to her boss about his sexual harassment of one of her staff. As a result, she is destined to join the ranks of the unemployed in a city beset by industrial decline and hardship. The question which the film addresses is the one which Babs herself puts to a packed meeting towards the end of the film 'What do you do when you get the sack? Do you go on the dole like all those millions of others or do you stand up and fight?' The film's answer is, of course, the latter and the film traces the growing conflict between Aelita, the company which owns the shop, and Babs and her supporters. In doing so, the film pits different versions of contemporary Britain against each other. Aelita is based in London and is associated with a new 'enterprise' culture based on display and 'designer' values which stands at odds with the

---

[23] See Dunbar, *Rita, Sue and Bob Too*, 72–3.

[24] Although households were often seen to be dominated by strong mother figures in 'new wave' films of the 1950s and 1960s such as *Saturday Night and Sunday Morning* and *A Taste of Honey*, this is not generally the case in the working-class films of the 1980s in which mothers are either absent or marginal. While some films of the 1980s do provide images of dominant mothers, these tend to be set in the past. See Mary Desjardins, 'Free from the Apron Strings: Representations of Mothers in the Maternal British State', in Lester Friedman (ed.), *British Cinema and Thatcherism* (London: UCL Press, 1993).

[25] 'The Knack and How to Get It', Interview with Pam Cook, *Monthly Film Bulletin* (Sept. 1987), 263.

economic realities of the north of England. One of the new Aelita boutiques in Liverpool is actually seen to be located next to the job centre. The name Aelita, moreover, is derived from the 1924 Russian science-fiction film of the same name. The company's commodification of the imagery of revolutionary Russia is contrasted with the continuing commitment to revolutionary politics of the Militant supporters in Liverpool while its idealization of an image of woman-hood (derived from Princess Aelita) is set against the very different model of femininity provided by Babs and the other women in the film (and the treat-ment to which they are subjected).

In counterposing the new enterprise culture of the south with a tradition of working-class radicalism in the north, the film explores two different kinds of possible action. The first is associated with Babs's husband, Kieran, the ex-union official who counsels restraint and 'talking to the bosses'. His politics are associated with an earlier era of union–management collaboration which, none the less, failed to prevent, after years of discussion, the closure of the Tate and Lyle refinery. 'Talking did you a lot of good, didn't it?', taunts his Militant-supporting son, Stevie (Mark McGann). Babs is initially persuaded to try this route but is ignored by a remote and uncaring managing director who, in the film's opening scene, had announced his belief in the 'manager's right to man-age'. This leads her to seek the aid of the union which, following a further refusal by management to negotiate, organizes a picket (headed by unemployed Mil-itant supporters) outside the shop which has now re-opened as a glittering new boutique ('a new enterprising concept in boutique marketing' as the television news bulletin puts it). Despite the use of the police against the pickets (in line with anti-picketing laws introduced by the Conservative government), their actions (including the extension of the picket to other branches) succeed in bringing the business to a virtual halt. Finally, the company is forced to capit-ulate and Babs is restored to her old post.

Lezli-An Barrett had already made a short experimental film, *Epic Poem* (1982) focusing on the suffragette Mary Richardson and her smashing of Velazquez's *Rokeby Venus*. Although there are clear areas of common concern (the position of working women, the images of women constructed by men, the imprisonment and violation of women's bodies), *Business as Usual* abandons the earlier film's formal self-consciousness and use of montage techniques in favour of a more conventional approach to filmmaking which makes use of mainstream conventions of narrative and characterization but inflects them in a more political direction.

As Barrett has argued, she wanted the film not only to 'reflect ordinary people's lives' but also to contain 'the normal narrative threads of a Hollywood picture —a downtrodden woman who rises up and wins'.[26] As such, the film is organized around the central character's trajectory from political passivity to engaged political action. Babs begins as a relatively apolitical figure, sceptical of her son's approach to politics, but coming to appreciate not only the benefits of collective

[26] Quoted in Elaine Paterson, 'Doing the Business', *Time Out*, no. 890 (9–16 Sept. 1987), 33.

action but also her own strength (taking over from the union representative in the final negotiations and forcing through her own demands). Although this approach encourages spectators to identify with a strong 'positive' heroine, it is also the case that the emphasis upon the individual which results from the use of 'the normal threads of a Hollywood picture' may undermine the more political aspects of the plot by laying stress on the 'exceptional' attributes of the central character rather than the shared character of her political predicament.[27]

The film, however, is careful to emphasize the 'ordinariness' of Babs (even if the casting of Glenda Jackson partly works against this) and to locate her politicization in a context of collective involvement. Thus, while Babs displays a number of significant qualities (determination, a sense of right and wrong), her growing political consciousness is, none the less, dependent upon the encouragement, advice, and support which she receives from those around her (and who convince her of the need to 'fight'). The film, moreover, is concerned to stress the multi-dimensional character of the conflicts in which Babs is immersed. By interlinking Babs' dismissal with the issue of sexual harassment, the film seeks to raise not just concerns of class, and economic power, but also issues of gender both at the workplace and in the home. In this respect, the film counterposes the growing self-confidence of Babs in the public sphere with the strain her growing politicization places upon her marriage.

However, while it is characteristic of the 'woman's film' to counterpose a woman's involvement with work to her responsibilities at home, *Business as Usual* does not force a choice upon Babs but, by ending with the tentative reconciliaton of herself and Kieran, holds out the possibility of Kieran coming to terms with their changed social and economic roles. These issues of class and gender are, in turn, connected with the politics of race when Paula, who is arrested as a part of the picket outside Aelita, is subject to racist questioning and subsequently strip-searched by the police.

There is, of course, a certain schematization to all of this and a rather too easy alignment of different kinds of politics (which, in other films of this period often sit uneasily together). The film, in this respect, offers its own kind of fantasy, not of escape but of political optimism at a time when, in reality, both the unions and Militant were in retreat.[28] In the film, Kieran tells his son, Terry (Stephen McGann) that the pickets don't have 'a hope in Hell'. The union official, Brian Lewis (Jack Carr), who is prepared to compromise with management, also

---

[27] Annette Kuhn, for example, argues that while the Hollywood 'working-class' film, *Norma Rae* (1979) is unusual in portraying 'a strong woman who is not only working class but is also victorious in a class-related struggle', the explanation of *Norma Rae*'s success in unionizing the textile factory where she works is primarily in individual, rather than social and political, terms. See *Women's Pictures: Feminism and Cinema* (London: Routledge and Kegan Paul, 1982), 136.

[28] The Militant Tendency was a Trotskyist grouping operating within the Labour Party. Following the local elections of 1983, Militants controlled the Labour majority of the Liverpool City Council which it led into a confrontation with national government over 'rate-capping'. The then Labour leader, Neil Kinnock, famously denounced Militant at the 1985 Labour Party Conference and, following a report on Liverpool Militant to the Labour National Executive in 1986, a number of leading Liverpool Militants were expelled from the party.

warns that 'we can't win with all the odds stacked against us'. Although both men are proved wrong in the film, they are, none the less, right in terms of the broader political and economic battles which were being fought during the 1980s (with their history of anti-trade union legislation and political defeat). The novelty of the film, however, is precisely its concern to offer an 'optimism of the will' at a time when 'pessimism of the intellect' might have been expected. As has been noted, the bulk of the anti-Thatcherite films of the period were characteristically better at lamenting the effects of Thatcherite policies (materialism and greed, on the one hand, poverty and unemployment, on the other) than identifying a viable source of opposition or imagining a better way of being. For all of its possible naïvety, *Business as Usual* is nevertheless one of the few films to attempt to imagine things differently (and in a way which emphasizes shared, and not just individual, experience).

The interweaving of individual and collective actions that is found in *Business as Usual* is also in evidence in David Hare's *Strapless* (1988). Unlike the films just discussed, this is not a northern realist film but it is centred on a female protagonist and does attempt to address socio-political concerns. The film is, in fact, a good example of the kind of hybrid 'social art' cinema to which the 1980s gave rise. It's loose plotting, emphasis upon character and ideas rather than action, and degree of narrative ambiguity and open-endedness situate it within an arthouse tradition. However, its central story-line—an American doctor working in the NHS who meets a mysterious stranger in Italy and falls in love— falls firmly within the tradition of the 'woman's film' and its conventions of romantic melodrama. In addition, the film's concern with deteriorating conditions in the National Health Service (NHS), and the possibility of political opposition to government health policies, link it to a tradition of socially conscious filmmaking. Like *Business as Usual*, the story concerns a 'coming-to-consciousness' of the central female character and, in doing so, a certain contrast between public and private life is drawn.[29] However, it is how this tension is then worked out that makes the film of particular interest (and invests the film with a certain allegorical dimension).

At one level, the events of the melodrama and those of the social drama seem to be set in opposition to each other and pivot, like so many of the realist films, around the idea of escape. Lillian Hempel (Blair Brown) is a hardworking doctor, dealing daily with pain and death (as represented in the film by the suffering of the terminal cancer patient Mr Clark). The appearance of Raymond Forbes (Bruno Ganz), at the film's start, therefore opens up romantic possibilities which will permit some kind of escape from the demands and constraints of everyday life and work. As she explains to her colleague Harold Sabola (Cyril Ni), 'I've done nothing but give . . . just give . . . but when do I get something

---

[29] This tension (and contradiction) between public and private is also in evidence in Hare's treatment of a female Tory politician, Clara Paige (Charlotte Rampling) in *Paris By Night* (1989). However, in highlighting Conservative 'double standards', the film also, in effect, 'punishes' the career woman for her social and sexual transgressions and, thus, for all of its anti-Thatcherism, reproduces a fairly conventional perspective on gender.

back?' Raymond himself plays upon this. Following his proposal of marriage to Lillian, he pursues her to her office where he asks her knowingly 'what life do you have?' As he does so, the camera follows his look to reveal a plate of congealed, half-eaten food and a copy of the *Journal of Radiology* sitting untidily upon her desk. It is at this point that Lillian decides to skip work and go with Raymond in a taxi (and then on to the registry office).

However, like Peter in *Letter to Brezhnev*, Raymond is also a character whom the film constructs in an ambivalent manner. *Strapless*, like so many other films of the period, is a film which is self-conscious about its own status as cinema and which knowingly draws upon traditional cinematic codes. By associating Raymond with dramatic exaggeration and romantic cliché, the film draws attention to his status as a figure of romantic fantasy and, hence, as a kind of wish-fulfilment for Lillian. Thus, at the film's start, Lillian is seen, in a church in Italy, looking at the suffering Christ on the cross in front of her. A head-and-shoulders shot of her is held rather longer than is normal and her face and feelings become the focus of attention. Her gaze, however, is not followed by the expected point-of-view shot but a somewhat jarring cut to her left foot where we see a white handkerchief (which we have not seen her drop) on a bright red carpet and an unidentified hand in the process of picking it up. As a result of this play with shot length and editing, Raymond's initial appearance is invested with a certain ethereal and semi-subjective quality upon which the rest of the film then builds by making him a larger than life romantic figure.

In this respect, the film may be seen to be following in the footsteps of the woman's film. For, as has already been noted, it is a common characteristic of the woman's film to mark the desires of the heroine as 'fantasy' and, in doing so, to reconcile her to the 'realities' of her normal life. At first glance this might also seem to be the case in *Strapless*: Lillian is abandoned by Raymond and she comes to learn not only that he has a history of womanizing but that he also remains married. However, the strategy of the film is more complex than this and, while it makes use of traditional romantic conventions, it also inflects them in an unexpected direction.

For unlike romantic melodrama, in which the heroine may learn too late that she has been deceived or cheated (a discovery which may itself be a punishment for the giving of free rein to her desires), Lillian is conscious of the extent of her collusion in a romantic fantasy. As she explains to her sister Amy (Bridget Fonda), 'I went along with it. But I knew he was running on empty'. Moreover, Lillian is not 'punished' (except financially) for her fantasy or forced back into an unsatisfying existence. Instead, her relationship with Raymond, for all its disappointments, becomes a source of release and empowerment, permitting her to break out of her isolation and reconnect with others. 'They shouldn't stand up . . . but they do', Amy says of the strapless dresses she has designed and, whatever the merits of this as a metaphor, it is also true, the film suggests, of Lillian. In this respect, the contrast between work and romantic fantasy which the film has employed is not invoked to counsel acceptance of the status quo but rather to reinvigorate Lillian's sense of self and her commitment to others.

This is, perhaps, clearest in her relationship with her colleagues at the hospital. The hospital is experiencing cuts and beds and jobs are being lost. During the course of the film, Lillian is asked to help lead the fight against the cutbacks. However, she is reluctant to do so and tells Romaine (Suzanne Burden), a young radiotherapist, that, because she's an American, it isn't really her fight. By the end of the film, however, she has changed her mind and is prepared to fight back. 'If we do nothing—don't protest, don't organize', she tells a group of assembled hospital workers, 'then we collude in the system's decline.' In this way, the central female character, like Babs in *Business as Usual*, has moved from passive acceptance of decline towards active political involvement. In doing so, she has also moved from isolation towards community in a way which reverses the motif of individual escape.

As with *Britannia Hospital*, it is also clear that the film wishes to be read in national-allegorical terms. In mounting her call to action, Lillian makes an appeal to the strengths of 'English values' which she reflects that, as a foreigner, she may 'care more about . . . than the English themselves'. The scene, in this respect, has loose echoes of wartime movies such as *In Which We Serve* (1942) or *Henry V* (1944) in which morale-boosting speeches which uphold traditional English virtues are delivered to an assembled group (of sailors and soldiers). The film makes use of the associations which these references bring but also distances itself from them. On the one hand, it seeks to wrest the idea of the 'nation' away from the conservative nationalism associated with Thatcherism and push it in a more social-democratic, or 'national-popular', direction (more typical of the Second World War). In doing so, it also seeks to reinstate the importance of the values of community and public service which the National Health Service embodies and which are under threat from the Thatcher government.

A telling scene, in this regard, involves Lillian and the hospital administrator, Mr Cooper (Alan Howard). Following Raymond's disappearance, Lillian breaks down and hides in a hospital cupboard. Cooper follows her in and offers her a cup of tea, quietly telling her, 'You have to go back to work . . . It's good work. You bring comfort.' This is a scene which clearly locks into a British cinema tradition of getting on with things, a tradition of emotional self-restraint and 'British understatement' famously lampooned by Lindsay Anderson in his attack on *The Blue Lamp*.[30] As such, there is little doubt that this scene in *Strapless* is partly a knowing one, initially generating humour in the way in which a cup of tea is tendered as an all-purpose panacea for emotional distress. None the less, it is also a scene which is invested with considerable dignity and a quiet awareness of the strengths of 'British understatement' and, indeed, 'British values' of 'good work' and public duty. In this respect, the film links the decline of the NHS less with the erosion of 'national' values, as in *Britannia Hospital*, than with their abandonment by those in power, particularly the Thatcher regime.[31]

---

[30] Lindsay Anderson, 'Get Out and Push!', in Tom Maschler (ed.), *Declaration* (London: MacGibbon & Kee, 1957).

[31] As Hare has observed, 'Thatcherism . . . made conservatives of us all . . . we found ourselves defending institutions which previously we would have no time for, because those institutions were better than barbarism.' See David Hare, *Asking Around* (London: Faber and Faber, 1993), 228.

On the other hand, unlike the earlier films which it partly quotes, there is no automatic assumption of who represents the 'nation' or of what constitutes 'Englishness'. When she addresses the hospital workers, the group to whom she speaks is not the homogeneous white male group of the earlier films but one which is visibly differentiated by gender and ethnicity. The vision of the 'national' community which the film provides, in this respect, is remarkably plural and diverse and there is clearly an effort in this scene to 'make strange' traditional conceptions of 'Englishness' and reimagine a more inclusive version of national identity (and identities within the nation). As such, *Strapless* not only seeks to counter the sense of despair which is evident in a film such as *Britannia Hospital* but also to link its political concerns to a reworked understanding of the 'nation' and the 'national' community. These are themes that are also relevant to the films discussed in Chapters 10 and 11.

chapter 9

Class, Politics, and Gender
High Hopes and *Riff-Raff*

Mike Leigh and Ken Loach

Issues of class, gender, and politics were also central to two films which appeared towards the end of the 1980s and the beginning of the 1990s: Mike Leigh's *High Hopes* (1988) and Ken Loach's *Riff-Raff* (1991). *High Hopes* was Mike Leigh's first film for theatrical release since he made *Bleak Moments* in 1972. In the intervening period he had worked in both the theatre and for television and his television film *Meantime* (1983)—made by Central for 'Film on Four' but not shown in cinemas—was a significant work in laying bare some of the hardship and desolation that characterized lives at the bottom of the heap in Thatcher's Britain. Loach, too, was responsible for making one of the first films of the 1980s to deal with the destructive effects of Thatcherism with *Looks and Smiles* (1981), a melancholy reflection upon the plight of young people on the dole. For Loach, however, the film was insufficiently hard-hitting and, for the next few years, he moved into documentary filmmaking as a way of dealing more directly with the politics of the time.[1] He returned to feature filmmaking with *Fatherland* (1986) and *Hidden Agenda* (1990) but it was with *Riff-Raff* that he returned to the kind of filmmaking, and class themes, with which he is most associated.[2]

Both *High Hopes* and *Riff-Raff* were intended as explicit commentaries on the Thatcher years. For Leigh, *High Hopes* sought to express the 'frustration and confusion' wrought by eight years of Thatcherism, while Loach wanted to show, in *Riff-Raff*, 'the effects of the early Eighties and Thatcherism ... but ... without a political lecture'.[3] The strategies which the two films adopt also overlap. Unlike

---

[1] For the details, see Paul Kerr, 'The Complete Ken Loach', *Stills*, no. 27 (May–June 1986).

[2] For a discussion of *Fatherland* and *Hidden Agenda*, see Hill, 'Finding a Form: Politics and Aesthetics in *Fatherland, Hidden Agenda* and *Riff-Raff*', in George McKnight (ed.), *Agent of Challenge and Defiance: The Films of Ken Loach* (Trowbridge: Flicks Books, 1997).

[3] Mike Leigh, *Naked and Other Screenplays* (London: Faber and Faber, 1995), p. xx; Gavin Smith, 'Sympathetic Images', Interview with Ken Loach, *Film Comment*, vol. 30 no. 2 (Mar.–Apr. 1994), 60. In *High Hopes*, Cyril and Shirley's largest cactus is called 'Thatcher' because, as Cyril explains, it's 'a pain in the arse'.

many of the working-class films of the 1980s, both films are set in London (although, in the case of *Riff-Raff*, a number of the characters are originally from the north of England and Scotland) and they both focus on an extended range of characters. Their plots are leisurely paced and episodic and concentrate much more on character and situation than action and event (balancing, as Loach puts it, 'forward movement' and the 'little asides or looks . . . that help to describe people').[4] Both films, in this respect, are relatively 'undramatic' and the emphasis is on the significance of 'ordinary', as opposed to 'exceptional' or unusual, experience and behaviour. However, while the two men's work is often regarded as stylistically and politically similar, significant formal and thematic differences are also apparent in these two films.

High Hopes

Thus, while *High Hopes* shares *Riff-Raff*'s interest in the apparently 'ordinary' and everyday—it's key narrative moments revolve around a character locking herself out of her house and a failed birthday party—it does not (and this is typical of Leigh's films) place the same emphasis upon work or the group (that is shaped by work). The film is much more concerned with the lives that people lead in the home and it is by interweaving the 'stories' of three very different kinds of couples—Laetitia and Rupert Boothe-Braine (David Bamber and Lesley Manville), Martin and Valerie Burke (Philip Jackson and Heather Tobias), and Cyril and Shirley (Philip Davis and Ruth Sheen)—that the film attempts to map out the contours of 'Thatcher's Britain'. These three couples represent very different 'lifestyles' (to use a term which became increasingly popular during the 1980s) which, in line with Leigh's emphasis upon the domestic, are seen to be the most revealing aspect of class distinctions. By setting these lifestyles alongside each other, the film then offers less an attack on the economic hardship suffered by the losers in Thatcher's Britain (as in *Riff-Raff*) than a critique of the cultural 'barbarianism' associated with its economic beneficiaries.

Thus, it is the Boothe-Braines and the Burkes who most starkly epitomize the cultural values of the Thatcher age. Rupert and Laetitia are an unappealing pair of 'yuppies', who live next door to Cyril and Valerie's mother, Mrs Bender (Edna Doré), the last council tenant in a newly gentrified street. Rupert works 'in wine'; Laetitia is a rather brainless socialite. They have a town house with 'original features', weekend in the country, and go to the opera (despite Rupert's lack of understanding of it). They are also snobby and selfish and treat Mrs Bender with both insensitivity and condescension when she locks herself out of her house. The Burkes, on the other hand, are a vulgar *nouveau riche* couple who epitomize the new 'enterprise culture'. Martin is a self-made man who owns 'a second-hand car emporium' and 'Burger Bar'. He is scornful of Cyril's 'principles' and advises him to form 'a little company' so that 'all the other wallies do the dirty

[4] Smith, 'Sympathetic Images', 59.

work'. His wife Valerie meanwhile displays the brashness and vulgarity asso-ciated with the newly well-off and her clothes, house, and car all testify to her lack of 'good taste' and refinement.

Valerie, in this respect, follows in the footsteps of Beverly (Alison Steadman) in Leigh's *Abigail's Party* (1977) who had already given vivid expression to the social pretensions and suburban tastes of the upwardly mobile working class. Her character also harks back to the tradition of British working-class realism of the 1960s (and a film such as *A Kind of Loving* in 1962) which not only criticized the 'corruption' of the working class by consumerism but characteristically associated superficiality and an 'excessive' interest in acquisitions with women characters—who were then often symbolically 'punished' for their apparent threat to 'authentic' working-class masculinity and male virility. Although Leigh's work does not associate superficiality and pretentiousness exclusively with female characters, it is generally the women who display these attributes most clearly. Indeed, such is the degree of Valerie's grotesquerie in *High Hopes* that the film extends her virtually no sympathy at all and, as in earlier working-class realism, effectively 'punishes' her by making her suffer in a way that none of the other characters have to and by reducing her to a state of hysterical collapse. In doing so, there is a certain parallel with how the film itself treats the character and how she is treated by her husband Martin, who not only regards her with contempt but is also physically violent towards her (as well as his mistress). Although it is often argued that the representation of misogyny in Leigh's films is not the same as its endorsement, the problem, in the case of *High Hopes*, is that Martin's disdain for Valerie is shared by the film and, thus, runs perilously close to colluding with his behaviour towards her.[5]

Characterizations such as Valerie's are also indicative of the kind of 'realism' in which Leigh's films are involved. While this demonstrates a concern with social comment and reference, it is only partly concerned with observational accuracy. As Richard Combs suggests, Leigh's films go beyond normal social realist conventions to produce something which is 'riven and contradictory'.[6] The distinctive aspect of Leigh's work, in this respect, is its combination of unobtrusive visual techniques with a performance style that is much more overt and excessive. His films are characteristically shot on location, employing techniques that are austere and precise. Shots are often static and can be quite lengthy, permitting situations or conversations to evolve (as in the case of that between Cyril and Shirley at the film's end). In the case of exteriors or interior full-shots, the camera may also be held for a period before or after an action occurs in a way that reveals a non-narrative interest in the spaces that surround characters (the most striking example of which, in *High Hopes*, is when there is a lengthily held shot from inside the Gore-Booths' house involving a pan into

[5] Michal Coveney, Mike Leigh's biographer, draws attention to the repeated 'eruption of sadistic sex-ual violence' in Leigh's films but, in his enthusiasm to defend Leigh against all criticism, fails to weigh up how this impacts on the films themselves (irrespective of Leigh's own personal attitudes). See Michael Coveney, *The World According to Mike Leigh* (London: HarperCollins, 1997), 118.

[6] Richard Combs, 'Cross-sectioning Society', *The Times Literary Supplement* (20 Jan. 1989), 62.

an empty room). However, if Leigh's visual style, based on a paring down of camera movement and cutting, is then 'quiet' and undemonstrative (in a way that is often compared to that of Ozu), it is also crossed with styles of performance that are conspicuously 'loud'.

Thus, for David Thomson, the central aspect of Leigh's work is less 'social realism' than the observation of 'the process of acting'.[7] Leigh himself suggests how he is concerned with 'behavioural study' and his films exhibit a fascination with physical idiosyncrasies, bodily mannerisms, and patterns of speech and accent.[8] The lengthy process of improvisation which he undergoes with his cast therefore tends to produce performances in which such 'behavioural' traits are magnified and the 'actorliness' of the performance is apparent.[9] In this respect, the acting in Leigh's films is characteristically based upon an isolation, and exaggeration, of external mannerisms which result in performances which are histrionic and 'gestural' (signifying social types) rather than ones which are psychologically accurate or 'naturalistic' (and in which the 'acting' aspires to invisibility).[10] This approach to acting is, in turn, linked to the ways in which characters are represented and responses to them are encouraged.

Thus, the overt 'performativity' of the acting tends not only to inhibit the spectator's emotional identification with characters but also to encourage a degree of critical distance from, and superiority to, them. Moreover, insofar as so many of Leigh's films deal with the social attitudes and cultural tastes of the upwardly mobile working class and lower middle class (while being primarily addressed to an educated middle class), it is inevitable that this superiority is linked to a sense of 'superior' taste and 'cultural capital' that the spectator is presumed to possess but not the characters themselves.[11] Thus, in the case of Valerie in *High Hopes,* her character is precisely 'comic' because she lacks 'good' dress sense, has suburban tastes (e.g. an imitation log-fire, ornamental brass fruit, a two-tier tea trolley) and is generally pretentious (proudly displaying a glass chess set in which the pieces are laid out wrongly). In this respect, there is also

---

[7] David Thomson, *A Biographical Dictionary of Film* (London: Andre Deutsch, 1994), 432.

[8] Lee Ellickson and Richard Porton, 'I Find the Tragicomic Things in Life: An Interview with Mike Leigh', *Cineaste,* vol. xx, no. 3 (Apr. 1994), 12. Michael Coveney also indicates how the 'external aspects' of character, such as 'costume, hairstyle, accent, physical mannerism and movement' are given special weight by the acting in Leigh's films. See Michael Coveney, *The World According to Mike Leigh,* 122.

[9] A discussion of Leigh's methods of improvisation may be found in Paul Clements, *The Improvised Play: The Work of Mike Leigh* (London: Methuen, 1983).

[10] In her discussion of performance style in D. W. Griffith's Biograph films, Roberta E. Pearson distinguishes 'histrionic' and 'verisimilar' codes of acting. Although it would be against the spirit of her historically contextualizing approach to film study to apply these concepts directly to contemporary films, there is, none the less, a sense in which the acting in Leigh's films may be seen to display an oscillation between what might be referred to as 'histrionic' and 'verisimilar' styles of acting. See Roberta E. Pearson, *Eloquent Gestures: The Transformation of Performance Style in the Griffith Biograph Films* (Berkeley and Los Angeles: University of California Press, 1992).

[11] It is for this reason that Leigh is often criticized for 'patronizing' his characters. Andy Medhurst attempts to rescue Leigh's work from such complaints by arguing that its representations of the working class are, in fact, 'accurate'. However, this seems to ignore how so much of the comedy—or, indeed, satire—of Leigh's work rests upon an implicit distance from the behaviour and tastes of the characters whom we see. See Andy Medhurst, 'Mike Leigh: Beyond Embarrassment' in *Sight and Sound* (Nov. 1993), 10–11.

a degree of gradation (or moral hierarchy) in the performances in Leigh's films. For the degree of acting which is 'displayed' by actors varies and it is characteristically the least likeable characters who are associated with the most 'excessive' performances (and, hence, criticism). Similarly, a less mannered form of acting can signify a certain change of emotional register in the same character (as in the 'climactic' scene between mother and daughter in *Life is Sweet* (1990) when Alison Steadman sheds some of the more histrionic features that had characterized her performance earlier in the film).

This correlation between characterization and style of acting is clearly in evidence in *High Hopes* where the most sympathetic characters, Mrs Bender, Cyril, and Shirley, are largely played without the exaggerated mannerisms that typify the playing of the Burkes and Gore-Booths. This downplaying of 'performance' not only permits a degree of involvement with these characters which is denied to the others but also takes on a certain 'moral' character. For, if the Burkes and Gore-Booths embody the shortcomings (and spiritual emptiness) of the age, Cyril and Shirley, an unmarried working-class couple with left-wing sympathies, are taken to stand for a more decent set of caring and socially responsible values. Thus, in stark contrast to the way that Mrs Bender is treated by the Gore-Booths, they selflessly help out the hapless Wayne (Jason Watkins) at the film's beginning and are happy to give Suzi (Judith Scott) a bed for the night. Unlike Valerie, whose beneficence towards her mother seems to have more to do with her own wants than those of Mrs Bender, Cyril and Shirley show genuine concern towards her and resolve, at the film's end, to offer her more help in the future. As Medhurst suggests, it is a preoccupation with 'mutuality . . . communality . . . (and) connectedness' which is the 'basic emotional and political wellspring' of Leigh's films and, in *High Hopes*, it is Cyril and Shirley's ordinary sense of goodness and concern which stand in opposition to the selfish temper of the times.[12] In this respect, the film is one of the few films of the period to attempt to give a positive embodiment to traditional socialist values. However, it is a portrait of 'practical socialism' that only goes so far.

Leigh's universe is primarily that of families and his films generally deal with the successes and failures of communication and connection within them. At one point, Cyril argues that families 'fuck you up' and are 'no use any more' and, as if to bear out his thesis, his own family is riven with conflicts and misunderstandings. Thus, in a telling scene, the camera holds on the face of a forlorn Mrs Bender as Cyril and Valerie bicker off-screen, accusing each other of having 'breakdowns'. However, if families are flawed, they seem, none the less, to be all that the characters have to hold on to, given that other forms of communality, extending beyond the family, are either inadequate or non-existent. Thus, while Cyril hopes for a world in which everyone has 'enough to eat' and, on his visit to Highgate cemetery, praises Marx ('Without Marx there wouldn't have been nothing . . . There'd be no unions, no welfare state, no nationalized industries'), it turns out that he isn't actually a member of a trade union himself

----

[12] Andy Medhurst, 'Mike Leigh: Beyond Embarrassment' 11.

PLATE 14. The vicissitudes of socialism: Ruth Sheen and Philip Davis in *High Hopes*

and is dismissive of Suzi's revolutionary politics (and her confidence in people 'fighting' back against unemployment and poverty).[13] And while the film chides the lack of neighbourliness shown by the Booth-Braines towards Mrs Bender, there is no evidence of any 'community' in the block of flats in which Cyril and Shirley live (where no neighbours are seen, or identified, at all). Indeed, the film's final scene, in which Cyril and Shirley take Mrs Bender up on the roof and look down on the railway station where Cyril's father used to work, has a strong sense of the passing of a traditional working-class culture, rooted in manual labour and a sense of place (such that a view of the gasworks can be seen, by Mrs Bender, as representing 'the top of the world'). In this respect, for all of their intuitive humanism, Cyril and Shirley would appear to lack any clear sense of connection or involvement with a more broadly based social or political community and tradition.

Cyril, indeed, admits as much when he explains to Shirley how he feels 'cut off' and that he 'don't do nothing' except 'moaning'. The way out of this for him seems to be an acceptance of fatherhood. For most of the film, he is against having a child, not only because 'families fuck you up' but because 'no one gives a shit what sort of world . . . kids are . . . born into'. However, by the end of the film he is prepared to try, with Shirley, for a baby. It is, of course, significant that all of the couples are childless in the film and, in the case of the Gore-Booths

---

[13] There is a general suspicion of political ideologies in Leigh's work which is manifest in the way that it is characteristically inadequate characters, lacking in human warmth and commonsense (such as Suzi), who are most drawn to them. Thus, in *Life is Sweet* (1990), it is the lonely and bulimic Nicola (Jane Horrocks) who mouths political clichés as a defence against genuine human contact.

and Burkes, this is associated with the 'sterility' of the values they represent. In the same way, Suzi's revelation that she has had an abortion seems, for the film, to underscore the fruitlessness (and lack of 'humanity') of her politics. The decision of Cyril and Shirley to have a child, therefore, invests the end of the film with a degree of optimism (or 'high hopes') about the future. However, while the film may, in this way, succeed in expressing values of care and responsibility which cut across the prevailing ethos of Thatcherism, it only does so by partly reproducing conservative (and, indeed, Thatcherite) values regarding the family and women.

Indeed, while it is a theme that is not made explicit in *High Hopes*, the film clearly links Valerie's hysteria and unhappiness (as well as her sexual grotesquerie) with her apparent failure to become a mother (and, significantly, her pet dog is called 'Baby'). Childless women recur in Leigh's films and the inability to have a child is associated with an obsessive interest in home decoration and furnishings in both *Meantime* and *Secrets and Lies* (1996). Valerie's drunken collapse at the end of *High Hopes* also has clear echoes of a similar scene in *Meantime* when Barbara (Marion Bailey), who also cannot have a child, sits huddled and drunk in the corner of the room she had been planning to redecorate.[14] In this respect, it is not just that consumerism and social climbing are associated with femininity, as noted earlier, but that this is an apparently 'flawed' femininity, characterized by the failure to fulfil the 'proper' or, given the way that mother-to-be Shirley is associated with plants and cultivation, 'natural' female role of motherhood (and it is notable that none of the childless women in these films are offered any alternative kind of fulfilment in the form of work or activity outside of the home). As such, a film like *High Hopes* ends up conforming to a conservative ideology of 'familialism' that is little different from that associated with Thatcherism. Moreover, in celebrating the virtues of the privatized family as a kind of escape route from political impotence and passivity, the film, for all its apparent 'socialism', appears to end up reinforcing the very scepticism about more collective (or 'socialist') forms of political action that was already such a feature of this era.

Riff-Raff

This issue of political agency, and opposition to Thatcherism, however, is central to *Riff-Raff*. The film, in this respect, maintains Loach's traditional interest in the working class and is centred upon the experiences of a ragtag group of labourers who have been forced to travel the country in pursuit of casual employment. Some of the men are themselves homeless—such as Stevie (Robert Carlyle) who is initially seen sleeping in a shop doorway—and, in a kind

---

[14] Beverly in *Abigail's Party* is also childless and confesses to a lack of 'mothering instinct'. Michael Coveney argues that 'the whole point about Beverly is that she is childless' but fails to consider the implications of this observation. See *The World According to Mike Leigh*, 120.

of metaphor for the time, they are involved in converting a disused hospital (symbolic of the demise of the welfare state) into private luxury apartments for the rich (London Heritage Homes no less). In doing so, the film is also concerned to lay stress upon the 'reality' of the experiences with which it deals. The film's script was written by Bill Jesse and is based on his own experiences on building sites. The film was shot on an actual building site and the cast (some of whom were not professional actors) were expected to have had some experience of working as labourers. They were also encouraged, through improvisation, to bring their own experiences to bear upon their performances. Loach's use of improvisation, however, is very different in purpose from Leigh's. Unlike Leigh, Loach seeks to minimize the sense of an actor's 'performance' and he commonly surprises an actor in order to achieve an unrehearsed and, for Loach, more 'authentic' form of 'acting'. In this respect, whereas Leigh's cinema announces its 'performativity' through an exaggeration of external traits, Loach's films enunciate a kind of anti-theatricalism in which the 'performances' of the actors lay claim to 'reality' by virtue of their departure from, and signalling of a distance from, conventional 'actorly' modes of gesture and dialogue (which may be 'poorly' delivered by conventional standards or difficult to hear).

This concern to signal distance from conventional dramatic forms is also reflected in the film's approach to style. For while this has some similarities with Leigh's (such as a liking for unbroken takes), what is particularly distinctive about Loach's style is his adoption of techniques that have an affinity with documentary. Although Loach's films only rarely dramatize actual events (as in _Ladybird Ladybird_ in 1994), they do, none the less, aim to provide something of the appearance of a documentary (even though the methods used to achieve this involve careful planning and rehearsal). The 'documentariness' of Loach's films, in this respect, derives less from their use of real people or real events than an approach to style and technique which approximates to that of the documentary film (and thus draws on some of the associations with real people and real events that the traditional documentary carries). This involves the avoidance of 'dramatic' lighting and compositional effects and a use of longer-than-average shots which generally maintain a distance from the actors. It also involves, as John Caughie suggests, a playing down many of the editing techniques associated with classical narration—or 'classic realism'—such as reverse-field cutting, eye-line matches, and point-of-view shots which draw the spectator into a fictional world.[15] 'Documentary realism', in this respect, maintains a more distanced and observational stance than 'classic realism' and invites the spectator to look upon, as much as to look with, the characters in front of the

---

[15] John Caughie, 'Progressive Television and Documentary Drama', _Screen_, vol. 21 no. 3 (1980), 27. The idea of 'classic realism' is discussed by Colin MacCabe in 'Realism and the Cinema: Notes on some Brechtian Theses', _Screen_, vol. 15 no. 2 (Summer 1974). Insofar as MacCabe's definition of 'classic realism' is fundamentally a formalist one (resting upon the privileged role of visual narration in classical film), it actually refers to the 'illusionist' conventions of 'mainstream Hollywood and, therefore, to films that are often not regarded as 'realistic' at all (such as _The Wizard of Oz_). For MacCabe, Loach's television play _Cathy Come Home_ (1966) only represents a 'progressive' form of 'classic realism' whereas Caughie seeks to differentiate Loach's work from classic realism on the basis of its use of naturalist and documentary techniques.

camera. Thus, in the emotional confrontation between Stevie (Robert Carlyle) and Susie at the building site near the film's end, the camera maintains its distance from the couple rather than employ the reverse angles and close-ups that would normally accompany such a dramatic climax.

The strength of this form, as Caughie suggests, is simply its ability to *show*, and give testimony to, experiences which are not traditionally dignified with cinematic representation. Thus, for Loach, the primary purposes of his film were to give expression to the lives of 'people who get by on the margins' (forced, because of the lack of opportunities to work legitimately, into 'ducking and diving') and to give recognition to both their plight and to their fortitude in the face of hostile economic circumstances.[16] In doing so, the film may also be seen to represent something of a break with earlier working-class films of the 1980s. For Loach, 'the heart of the struggle' remained that of class and, thus, unlike many of the earlier films, the emphasis of the film is firmly upon the world of work (rather than leisure) and the experiences of the male working class (rather than the female working class). The emphasis is also upon the shared character of experience and the sense of solidarity which emerges from this. One of the film's most powerful scenes occurs when Larry (Ricky Tomlinson) reproaches the audience at the club for jeering, and forcing off the stage, the would-be singer Susan (Emer McCourt). When Susan returns to the stage she launches into 'With a Little Help From My Friends' and the audience cheerfully join in. It is a scene which not only provides a rebuke to the individualism (and appeal to selfishness) characteristic of the Thatcher era but also reinstates a sense of community (however contingent) missing from many of the films of the period. Terry Lovell suggests how a central appeal of 'realism' may be its ability to provide 'pleasures of common experiences . . . solidarity . . . and . . . a sense of identity and community'.[17] In this scene and others (when the men help Stevie obtain a squat or when they exchange banter in the kitchen), it can be seen how the film seeks to give acknowledgement to the virtues of 'society' (and sociality) in the face of economic hardship, the decline of traditional forms of working-class community and allegiance, and the growth of self-interested individualism.

In this respect, the film is also reluctant (unlike some of the earlier films of the 1980s) to see individual escape as a solution to the problems it identifies. Stevie aspires (in a downmarket version of the 'enterprise culture') to sell boxer shorts and set up his own market stall but is no nearer his goal at the end of the film than at the beginning. One of the black workers Desmonde (Derek Young) aspires to go to Africa but is chided by Kojo (Richard Belgrave) for his unrealistic expectations and, at the film's end, is nearly killed by a fall from the unsafe scaffolding. However, if the prospects for individual improvement are limited, so, despite the evidence of camaraderie, are those for organized collective action. In the film, the men are not unionized and Larry, the Liverpudlian activist who

---

[16] Quoted in *The Evening Standard* (20 June 1991), 35.
[17] Terry Lovell, *Pictures of Reality: Aesthetics, Politics and Pleasure* (London: BFI, 1980), 95.

PLATE 15. 'With a Little Help From My Friends': Emer McCourt in *Riff-Raff*

rails against the Thatcher government and urges the men to organize, is quickly sacked following his complaints about work and safety conditions (just as two other men are also summarily dismissed by their heartless foreman (Willie Ross)). However, what the film shows is not just the ruthless, cost-cutting tactics of the employers but also how the workers themselves, who have virtually no employment rights, generally lack the means and the will to fight back. The film does, of course, end with an arson attack on the building site by Stevie and Mo (George Moss) following the dismissal of Shem (Jimmy Coleman) and the hospitalization of Desmonde. Mo had previously remonstrated with Larry for his political sermonizing and had, in turn, been criticized by Larry for his lack of political consciousness (claiming that Marx had him in mind when he invented the term 'lumpenproletariat'). To this extent, both Stevie and Mo move away from apathy towards active resistance against the employers. However, as Loach himself acknowledges, this act does not constitute a 'formed political response' but rather a 'classic case of alienation' which may be a form of hitting out against the system but will actually leave them worse off.[18] Moreover, while the men's action may indicate their refusal to accept their situation, it also, to a certain extent, goes against the grain of what has preceded, representing a sort of grafted-on defiance which has not emerged 'naturally' from the drama itself. As Quart suggests, it is a somewhat 'apocalyptic' conclusion, deriving more from Loach's political vision than from the consciousness of the characters themselves.[19]

Thus, while the film draws attention to the widening of economic divisions characteristic of the Thatcher years, it is also circumspect about the possibilities for self-confident forms of working-class action. Moreover, in giving pre-eminence to class issues the film also reveals a degree of awkwardness in dealing with other matters. As with *High Hopes*, this is particularly the case with the representation of women. For Loach, one of the attractions of combining fictional drama with documentary techniques is that it enables a movement between private and public worlds: 'to get', as he puts it, 'the insights into personal relationships and experiences that you can get through fiction, and yet to set them in a firm, concrete context'.[20] In *Riff-Raff*, this double focus is particularly evident in the way that the film combines the scenes of the men at the building site (working, arguing, resting) with those charting the evolving relationship between the young Glaswegian, Stevie, and his would-be singer girlfriend, Susie, who temporarily move in together. As befits the loose structure of the film, the relationship develops in a relatively haphazard way and the film deliberately avoids investing it with excessive significance, either as a 'refuge' from the stresses of work or as a particularly significant form of personal and romantic fulfilment. However, for John Caughie, this mix of documentary and drama—and public and private—in documentary realism is an uneasy one and there is always a 'risk' that the films end up being about 'privileged, centred individuals' rather than 'the community and the social environment'.[21] In the case of *Riff-Raff*, however, it is not so much that the private, personal drama of the young couple is privileged as that the 'political' world of work and the 'private' sphere of relationships and romance are, by and large, kept separate from each other and, ultimately, end up counterposed.

[18] Quoted in Hill, 'Interview with Ken Loach', in McKnight (ed.) *Agent of Challenge and Defiance*, 166.

[19] Leonard Quart, '*Riff-Raff*' (Review), *Cineaste*, vol. xx no. 2 (1993), 55. To some extent, the scene represents the 'realism plus hypothesis' that Raymond Williams identified in relation to Loach's *The Big Flame* (1969). See 'A Lecture on Realism', *Screen*, vol. 18 no. 1 (Spring 1977) 71. However, it can also be seen as a sort of debased 'hypothesis' given *Riff-Raff*'s shrunken sense of the possibilities of organized working-class action in comparison to that of *The Big Flame*.

[20] Kerr, 'The Complete Ken Loach', 146.

[21] Caughie, 'Progressive Television and Documentary Drama', 30.

Thus, while in Leigh's films, it is domestic realities that are of most significance (and work barely impinges on characters' lives), it is virtually the reverse in *Riff-Raff*. The relationship between Stevie and Susie ultimately fails and Susie herself is revealed as a dreamer (living in a 'bubble' according to Stevie) who is associated with half-formed 'new age' ideas (such as avoiding dairy products and caffeine, reading her stars, and practising the I Ching) and the use of heroin. As Leonard Quart suggests, 'romantic affairs are never of prime interest' for Loach and the emphasis of the film is on 'the world of laborers, whose repartee, warmth, and supportiveness help them survive on the job'.[22] However, it is not simply that Stevie's experiences with Susan are then seen as simply less interesting than those involving the male group but that they are virtually set in opposition to them as well. Thus, while the camaraderie amongst the men is shown as 'supportive' and encouraging, Susie is generally revealed as wearisome, demanding, and dependent. In the same way, her ideas and attitudes are associated with private forms of escape and a divorce from 'reality' that stand at odds with the harsh economic circumstances confronting the men (and the forms of political resistance to them advocated by Larry). As such, there is a degree of internal 'logic' in the way that Stevie's break-up with Susie near the film's end is followed soon after by his move towards direct 'political' action. Thus, it can be argued that, by reinstating the primacy of class experience (and associating this with male work), *Riff-Raff* also ends up marginalizing the experience of women which other films had brought into focus.

For similar reasons, Peter Ansorge has also suggested that Loach has never tackled the subject of racism.[23] This is not entirely true: a number of workers in *Riff-Raff* are black and issues of race are raised. In some respects, the film acknowledges that the social composition of the working class has undergone change and that class solidarity must depend upon an alliance of workers from diverse ethnic and regional backgrounds (in a kind of 'unity-in-diversity'). In this respect, the film may be seen to offer a certain riposte to the potentially fragmenting character of the 'new' social movements. However, it is also fair to say that the film's emphasis upon class solidarity, irrespective of racial differences, also downplays the specificity of racial, as opposed to class, disadvantage (as when Fiaman (Ade Sapara) complains to his white co-worker 'they treat us all like blacks on this site'). This tendency is also in evidence in the way that the film identifies the rich when, in one scene, Larry is unexpectedly interrupted in the bath of a show flat by three veiled women. For all its humour, this scene betrays a problematic response to the changing ethnic composition of Britain by not only reproducing relatively crude stereotypes of rich Arabs (and Arab women) but also rendering them as completely 'other' to the white British working class (with whose eyes we are invited to look).

---

[22] Quart, '*Riff-Raff*', 55.
[23] Peter Ansorge, *From Liverpool to Los Angeles: On Writing for Theatre, Film and Television* (London: Faber and Faber, 1997), 111.

In contrast to Loach, Ansorge goes on to suggest that Leigh's *Secrets and Lies* (1996) is a 'breakthrough' film in being prepared to explore the issue of 'a working-class family coming to terms with black Britain'.[24] This, however, is a problematic description of the film. For while the black character, Hortense (Marianne Jean-Baptiste) provides the catalyst for the self-examination of the white characters, there is little interest shown by the film itself in either black life or culture (or the effects of white Britain on black families). To this extent, Leigh and Loach's work is broadly similar insofar as the provenance of their films has largely remained white, just as it has been largely heterosexual. Questions of race and ethnicity have, of course, figured much more prominently in other films of this period and it is to these films that I will now turn in the two chapters that follow.

[24] Peter Ansorge, *From Liverpool to Los Angeles: On Writing for Theatre, Film and Television* (London: Faber and Faber, 1997), 111. There are, of course, hints of this theme in Leigh's earlier work such as *Abigail's Party* (in which Laurence complains of the changes to the neighbourhood) and *Meantime* (which attends briefly to the tribulations of a young black couple) but these are not central to the films' concerns.

chapter 10

'Race' and Cultural Hybridity
My Beautiful Laundrette and
Sammy and Rosie Get Laid

Hanif Kureishi and Stephen Frears

Writing in the diary accompanying the script of *Sammy and Rosie Get Laid*, the writer Hanif Kureishi suggests that what he regards as the 'freshness' of many British films of the 1980s was 'due partly to the . . . exploration of areas of British life not touched on before'. 'Just as one of the excitements of British culture in the sixties', he continues, 'was the discovery of the lower middle class and working class as a subject, one plus of the repressive eighties has been cultural interest in marginalized and excluded groups.'[1] He is, of course, identifying his own work with this trend and it is apparent how his films with Stephen Frears—*My Beautiful Laundrette* (1985) and *Sammy and Rosie Get Laid* (1987)—both carry on a tradition of 1960s social realism and deviate from it. It has already been noted how the social context of the 1980s made the representation of working-class experience more problematic and it is striking how absent the working class are from Kureishi and Frears's work. Although there are rhetorical asides about the working class in *Sammy and Rosie Get Laid*, the social network that the film explores is largely that of the professional classes and an urban 'underclass'. This is also true of *My Beautiful Laundrette* where the declining confidence in the agency of the working class is manifest in the portrait of Omar's father, Papa (Roshan Seth), a former socialist journalist who lies in bed drinking and, at one point, tells his son how 'the working class are such a great disappointment' to him (his decline is also an index of the relative lack of value which is attached to education and culture in Thatcher's Britain). Geoff Eley argues that the difficulty 'of imagining forms of self-confident and attractive working-class agency' which was evident in British cinema of the 1980s led to a

[1] Hanif Kureishi, *Sammy and Rosie Get Laid: The Script and the Diary* (London: Faber and Faber, 1988), 63.

shift of interest away from the industrial north (the privileged site of working-class realism) towards metropolitan London.[2] Although this underestimates the importance of Liverpool in defining the experience of the 1980s, it is certainly the case that a number of the films of the period, such as *Empire State* (1987) and *Close My Eyes* (1991), make self-conscious use of the new London to explore the changing contours of British society.[3] The 'inner city' also becomes a key index of economic and social life in both *Sammy and Rosie Get Laid* and *My Beautiful Laundrette*.

Sammy and Rosie, for example, begins with a shot of urban wasteland over which is heard the voice of Margaret Thatcher declaiming, 'we've got a big job to do in some of those inner cities'.[4] The scenes which follow in the course of the film invest this with an ominous tone: a middle-aged black woman (loosely based on Cynthia Jarrett) is shot in her own home by the police, rioting and looting takes place in the streets, and property developers evict the commune of caravaners from the land first seen in the opening shot. For Colin McArthur, the two films may be seen, in this regard, to offer a 'dystopian view of the city as urban battleground' more characteristic of American films.[5] However, while for Kureishi, the city is, indeed, characterized by 'uprising and deterioration' it is also a place of 'fluidity and possibilities' in which characters may establish new forms of relationships and identities.[6] The city, in this respect, may be seen to offer a kind of 'interstitial' space in which new forms of social connection are rendered possible. The idea of an 'interstitial area' was used by the Chicago school of urban sociology to describe the changing 'social ecology' of the inner city and, for Frederic Thrasher in his study of gangs, was characterized by social dysfunction.[7] In the Kureishi films, however, such 'interstitial' areas are also seen to be a source of creative energy in which new forms of social and cultural identifications may be realized. It is these connections and 'interstitial' subjectivities, characteristic of contemporary urban life, that a film such as *Sammy and Rosie* attempts to map. This ranges from the film's self-conscious homage

[2] Geoff Eley, '*Distant Voices, Still Lives*, The Family is a Dangerous Place: Memory, Gender, and the Image of the Working Class', in Robert A. Rosenstone (ed.), *Revisioning History: Film and the Construction of a New Past* (Princeton, NJ: Princeton University Press, 1995), 24.

[3] *Close My Eyes* was written and directed by Stephen Poliakoff. Along with *Runners* (1983), which Poliakoff wrote, and *Hidden City* (1987), which he wrote and directed, the three films constitute a loose trilogy of 'London films' which work hard to avoid conventional London imagery and to invest the city with an unfamiliar dramatic life.

[4] Kureishi indicates in his diary that the use of the Thatcher material (Mrs Thatcher is also heard near the end of the film) was a late addition by Frears following the June election of 1987 and gave the film 'a hard political edge'. See Hanif Kureishi, *Sammy and Rosie Get Laid*, 126.

[5] Colin McArthur, 'Chinese Boxes and Russian Dolls: Tracking the Elusive Cinematic City', in David B. Clarke (ed.), *The Cinematic City* (London: Routledge, 1997), 35.

[6] Kureishi, *Sammy and Rosie Get Laid*, pp. 88 and 101. As David Mason indicates, ethnic minorities in Britain have been concentrated in the most highly urbanized areas. See *Race and Ethnicity in Modern Britain* (Oxford: Oxford University Press, 1995), 38. However, while, amongst ethnic minority groups, there has been a trend towards spatial concentration, the level of ghettoization has been low (and considerably less than in the US). See Robin Cohen, *Global Diasporas: An Introduction* (London: UCL Press, 1997), 141.

[7] See Fredric Thrasher, *The Gang* (Chicago: University of Chicago Press, 1967, orig. 1927), esp. pp. 20–2.

to London (in which Sammy explains to his father the attractions of the city) to the apparent hotchpotch of characters and events that constitute the film.

In attempting to give expression to this sense of the shifting and contingent character of urban living, both *My Beautiful Laundrette* and *Sammy and Rosie Get Laid* reject the individualism and forward-moving dynamics of classic narration in favour of narratives that are loosely structured and episodic and in which narrative attention is shared amongst a variety of characters. Spivak describes this as a concern to shift from narratives which involve a personal positioning in relation to politics towards a form of 'more collective representation'.[8] Thus, while the stories of Johnny and Omar in *My Beautiful Laundrette* and Sammy and Rosie in *Sammy and Rosie Get Laid* are central to these films, they are none the less interwoven with a series of other characters and stories to convey a network of social relations and diverse social identities. In relation to the tradition of British social realism, the films therefore may be seen not simply to be substituting one form of protagonist—the heterosexual working-class male—with another—black, female, or gay—but attempting to explore a range of identities and differences across a particular social space (which are, in turn, rather different from the traditional 'communities' characteristic of earlier realism).

In this respect, the films exhibit a concern to problematize the very notion of social identity in the contemporary—postmodern—world and, in Paul Gilroy's phrase, do justice to 'the decentred and inescapably plural nature of modern subjectivity and identity'.[9] Thus, in common with postmodern thinking, there is a strong sense of the constructedness and fluidity of social identities, and a rejection of any sense of fixed identities or 'essences'. As Stuart Hall argues, 'the postmodern subject' is conceived not as having a 'fixed, essential or permanent identity' but rather as assuming 'different identities at different times'.[10] Moreover, the multiple and overlapping forms of identification—of 'race', nationality, gender, sexuality, class—which constitute identity do not necessarily coexist in an easy alignment but set up, in Hall's terms, a 'series of different positionalities' which are 'often dislocating in relation to one another'.[11] Such

---

[8]   Gayatri Chakravorty Spivak, 'In Praise of *Sammy and Rosie Get Laid*', *Critical Quarterly*, vol. 31 no. 2 (Summer 1989), 80.

[9]   Paul Gilroy, *The Black Atlantic: Modernity and Double Consciousness* (London: Verso, 1993), 46.

[10]   Stuart Hall, 'The Question of Cultural Identity', in Stuart Hall and Tony McGrew (eds.), *Modernity and its Futures* (Cambridge: Polity Press, 1992), 277.

[11]   Hall, 'What is This "Black" in Popular Culture?', in Gina Dent (ed.), *Black Popular Culture*, A Project by Michele Wallace (Seattle: Bay Press, 1992), 31. As the inverted commas indicate, the term 'race' is here used to indicate a discursive construction that relies upon the selective identification and classification of some physical characteristics rather than others. As Robert Miles and Annie Phizacklea explain, ' "Race" is not an objective, biological feature: it is an idea . . . Hence, "races" only exist insofar as people think, and behave as if, they exist.' See *White Man's Country* (London: Pluto, 1984), 13–14. The term 'ethnicity' is conventionally distinguished from that of 'race' by being defined in terms of cultural distinctiveness rather than physical appearance. In this respect, 'ethnic identity' is neither fixed nor unchanging but is, as David Mason suggests, 'situational' (though not then simply 'voluntaristic'): 'The implication is that people have different ethnic identities in different situations. . . . Thus it is possible to be simultaneously English, British, and European . . . Similarly, the same person might identify as Gujerati, Indian, Hindu, East African Asian, or British depending on situation, immediate objectives, and the responses and behaviour of others.' See *Race and Ethnicity in Modern Britain*, 13.

formulations are helpful in accounting for the strong sense of the criss-crossed nature of identities which are a feature of the Kureishi/Frears films. Characters' identities are constructed across different axes—black/white, male/female, gay/straight—which also place them in 'different' and complicated 'positionalities' to others. Thus, in the case of the Asian lesbian, Rani (Meera Syal) in *Sammy and Rosie Get Laid*, her 'identity' is not simply Asian, female, or lesbian but one which is 'overdetermined' and shifting (both constituting her as a part of the Asian community in Britain, for example, but problematizing her relationship to it as well, as her ferocious row with Rafi after he has found her in bed with Vivia would suggest). Moreover, identities in these films are not then simply overlaid, or added on top of each other, but are themselves 'interstitial', formed, as Bhabha puts it, ' "in-between", or in excess of, the sum of the "parts" of difference' (of race, class, gender, sexual orientation, and generation).[12]

Living with Difference

The approach of the films to these themes is therefore complex. This complexity may be linked with what Stuart Hall argues represents something of a shift in 'black' cultural politics in the post-war period.[13] The first 'moment' he associates with a cultural politics which seeks to contest 'the marginality, the stereotypical quality and fetishized nature of images of blacks, by the counter-position of a "positive" black imagery'.[14] In some respects, *My Beautiful Laundrette* and *Sammy and Rosie Get Laid* may be seen to share these concerns. For, these are films which not only wish to give voice to the black and Asian experiences in Britain but also to challenge traditional images and representations of these ethnic groups as well. *My Beautiful Laundrette*, in particular, may be read as something of a riposte to the Raj films of the early 1980s and self-consciously makes use of actors—such as Saeed Jaffrey and Roshan Seth—who appeared in both *A Passage to India* and *Gandhi*. As Hanif Kureishi explains, in his introduction to the script, he 'was tired of seeing lavish films set in exotic locations': it seemed to him 'that anyone could make such films, providing they had an old book, a hot country, new technology, and were capable of aiming the

---

[12] Homi K. Bhabha, 'Frontlines/Borderposts', in Angelika Bammer (ed.), *Displacements: Cultural Identities in Question* (Bloomington and Indianapolis: Indiana University Press, 1994), 269.

[13] Just as the term 'ethnicity' involves a 'situational' aspect, so the concept of 'blackness' has been identified as a shifting rather than a fixed term. As David A. Bailey and Stuart Hall put it, 'black is a cultural term, a political term . . . a choice of identity' rather than a given category or 'innate' ethnic attribute. See 'The Vertigo of Displacement', *Ten 8*, vol. 2 no. 3 (Spring 1992), 20. In relation to the political and cultural context of Britain, therefore, it may be seen how the term 'black' has been used both to refer to all those of African, Afro-Caribbean, and Asian origins as well as a more narrowly defined group that does not include Asians. It is also worth noting that, in the British context, the term 'Asian' has been typically employed to refer to those of Indian, Pakistani, and Bangladeshi descent. Although there is a significant Chinese population in Britain, this group has been less visible in the films of this period. *Ping Pong* (Po Chih Leong, 1986) and *Soursweet* (Mike Newell, 1988) are two exceptions.

[14] Hall, 'New Ethnicities', in Kobena Mercer (ed.), *Black Film, British Cinema* (London: ICA, 1988), 27.

camera at an attractive landscape in the hot country in front of which stood a star in a perfectly clean costume delivering lines from the old book'.[15] Thus, in *My Beautiful Laundrette* the encounter between East and West found in the Raj film is revisited but the context (or 'contact zone') is upturned: it is not the past experience of whites in India with which the film is concerned but rather the experiences of Asians in contemporary Britain.

However, if the two films reveal a concern to contest the dominant images of 'blacks' and 'Asians', they do not do so through a straightforward provision of 'positive' imagery. In this respect, the films are more accurately located in relation to Hall's second 'moment' of black cultural practice in which there is a recognition of 'the extraordinary diversity of subjective positions, social experiences and cultural identities which compose the category "black"' and, thus, which signify 'the end of the essential black subject'.[16] This is a position echoed by Kobena Mercer who argues that 'if there has been one salient feature in black visual art in Britain in the '80s it has been the recognition of difference within and between our "communities"'.[17] He argues, moreover, that this is itself a way of challenging stereotypes and popular misconceptions. For the 'myth' of 'a homogeneous, monolithic, self-identical and undifferentiated entity essentially defined by race (and nothing but race)', he argues, is itself one of the assumptions underpinning 'ideologies of racism'.[18] It is this insistence upon difference that is central to *My Beautiful Laundrette* and *Sammy and Rosie Get Laid*. These films do not attempt to give expression to one 'authentic' or 'essential' 'black' or 'Asian' experience, or offer straightforwardly 'positive' images, but rather place the stress upon heterogeneity and, what Hall has referred to, as the 'living' of 'identity through difference'.[19]

---

[15] 'Introduction to *My Beautiful Laundrette*', in Hanif Kureishi, *My Beautiful Laundrette and The Rainbow Sign* (London: Faber and Faber, 1986), 43.

[16] 'New Ethnicities', 28. Despite their challenge to white stereotypes, Cornel West argues that the cultural production of 'Black "positive" images' remained within the terms set by 'non-Black paradigms' insofar as they 'proceeded in an assimilationist manner that set out to show that Black people were really like White people—thereby eliding differences (in history, culture) between Whites and Blacks' and also depended upon a 'homogenizing' assumption that 'all Black people were really alike—hence obliterating differences (class, gender, region, sexual orientation) between Black peoples'. See 'The New Cultural Politics of Difference', in Russell Ferguson *et al.* (eds.), *Out There: Marginalization and Contemporary Cultures* (Cambridge, Mass.: The MIT Press, 1990), 27.

[17] Kobena Mercer, 'Black Art and the Burden of Representation', *Third Text*, no. 10 (Spring 1990), 71.

[18] Ibid.

[19] Hall, 'Old and New Identities, Old and New Ethnicities', in Anthony D. King (ed.), *Culture, Globalization and the World-System: Contemporary Conditions for the Representation of Identity* (Basingstoke: Macmillan, 1991), 57. Jim Pines, however, has argued that such formulations as this should not lead to the denial of 'any coherent sense of (ethnic) identity' at all for the 'black subject' in 'British Cinema and Black Representation' in Robert Murphy (ed.), *The British Cinema Book* (London: BFI, 1997), 214. This point is reiterated by bell hooks who notes a concern that postmodern critiques of the 'subject' have come at a time when 'many subjugated people feel themselves coming to voice for the first time'. She goes on to argue, however, that there is 'a radical difference between a repudiation of the idea that there is a black "essence" and recognition of the way black identity has been specifically constituted in the experience of exile and struggle'. See 'Postmodern Blackness' in *Yearning: Race, Gender and Cultural Politics* (London: Turnaround, 1991), pp. 28 and 29. Gayatri Chakravorty Spivak has also suggested the political possibilities of a self-consciously 'strategic essentialism' for subaltern groups. See *The Post-Colonial Critic: Interviews, Strategies, Dialogues* (New York: Routledge, 1990), esp. chap. 8.

This emphasis upon heterogeneity and difference may in turn be related to what Mercer has described as a 'displacing' of 'the burden of representation' in black and Asian cultural work.[20] Mercer notes how the idea of 'representation' carries with it not only a sense of signifying practice but also of 'delegation', or representativeness, such that 'the black artist is expected to *speak for* the black communities as if she or he were its political "representative"'.[21] For Mercer, however, the expectation of 'speaking for' the black and Asian community relies upon the very same—essentializing—assumption of homogeneity as racist ideologies. He, therefore, places the emphasis upon ' "speaking to" each other', rather than 'speaking for' the socially and culturally diverse groups which constitute the black and Asian 'communities'.[22] In the same way, the work of Hanif Kureishi can be seen to stand opposed to this 'burden of representation' (or what he refers to, in his novel *The Black Album*, as 'the brown man's burden').[23] Thus, while he acknowledges that his representation of Asians as 'drug dealers, sodomites and mad landlords' in *My Beautiful Laundrette* does not flatter Asians in Britain, he argues that he does not pretend 'to be a spokesman for the Asian community' and therefore should not be expected 'to do PR for them'.[24]

As a consequence, the Asian characters in both *Laundrette* and *Sammy and Rosie* engender complex responses as they are neither 'positive' in terms of behaviour and attitudes nor especially sympathetic (to either left-wing or right-wing audiences). As Kureishi points out, none of his Asian characters may be regarded as 'victims' and, in *My Beautiful Laundrette*, the main Asian characters are successful businessmen, seemingly at ease with the Thatcherite culture of enterprise, and devoted to making money by both legitimate and illegitimate means (Salim, played by Derrick Branche, deals in drugs).[25] In this respect, a part of the film's strategy is to use the business success of the Asian characters to invert old imperial power relations. In this way, as Boyd Tonkin suggests, the

[20] Kobena Mercer, 'Recoding Narratives of Race and Nation', in Kobena Mercer (ed.), *Black Film, British Cinema* (London: ICA, 1988), 8.

[21] 'Black Art and the Burden of Representation', 65.   [22] Ibid. 73.

[23] Kureishi, *The Black Album* (London: Faber and Faber, 1995), 6. Kureishi's refusal to accept the 'burden of representation' is taken further in *London Kills Me* (1991), which he wrote and directed. In this, the main characters—such as Clint (Justin Chadwick) and Muffdiver (Steven Mackintosh) are white and the young Indian member of the 'posse', Bike (Naveen Andrews), remains largly—and, perhaps, somewhat problematically—silent.

[24] Kureishi, 'Scenes from a Marriage', Interview with Jane Root, *Monthly Film Bulletin* (Nov. 1985), 333. In an essay for *Time Out*, Kureishi also argued that 'if there is to be a serious attempt to understand present day Britain, with its mix of races and colours . . . it has to be complex. It can't apologise or idealise. It can't . . . attempt to represent any one group as having a monopoly on virtue'. 'Dirty Washing', *Time Out* (14–20 Nov. 1985), 26. This is a point reinforced by Salman Rushdie's defence of *My Beautiful Laundrette*. While he acknowledges how the film's satire of certain Asian characters may feed into the 'divide-and-rule' perspective of the dominant culture, he goes on to claim that 'the real gift which we can offer our communities is not the creation of stereotyped positive images to counteract the stereotyped negative ones, but simply the gift of treating black and Asian characters . . . as complex creatures, good, bad, bad, good'. See 'Minority Literatures in a Multi-Cultural Society', in Kirsten Holst Petersen and Anna Rutherford (eds.), *Displaced Persons* (Sydney: Dangaroo Press, 1988), pp. 40 and 41.

[25] Kureishi, 'Scenes from a Marriage', 333. For a discussion of 'Asian enterprise' in Britain, see Philip Sarre, 'Race and the Class Structure', in Chris Hamnett *et al.* (eds.), *The Changing Social Structure* (London: Sage, 1990), 149–53.

film may be viewed as a kind of 'revenge film' in which a contrast is set up between an unemployed white 'lumpenproletariat', or 'underclass' (the victims of deindustrialization), who aimlessly wander the streets and an Asian business class who have succeeded in becoming the new 'masters'.[26]

As Uncle Nasser (Saeed Jeffrey), the owner of a garage for well-heeled clients, observes: 'We're professional businessmen. Not professional Pakistanis. There's no race question in the new enterprise culture.' Thus, the film begins with Salim, aided by black (Afro-Caribbean) heavies, evicting Johnny and Genghis (Richard Graham) from their room, in a sort of symbolic 'taking over' of the white characters' 'home'. A similar inversion of roles is also evident in the relationship between Omar (Gordon Warnecke) and Johnny (Daniel Day Lewis). Omar, according to his cousin Tania (Rita Wolf), treats Johnny 'like a servant' and he relishes the way in which he can get his own back for being kicked around at school by making Johnny wash the laundrette floor. Johnny's erstwhile friends also complain that he is 'grovelling to Pakis'. In this respect, the ways in which the film mobilizes sympathies are quite complex. The film is critical of Thatcherism and the materialism and selfishness which it generates; however, it also identifies how, for sections of the Asian community, the enterprise culture provides opportunities which cut across traditional relations of power and furnishes them with status ('we're nothing in England without money' Salim sadly declaims). At the same time, it is also aware of how even the possession of money is not necessarily a defence against racism (in a society in which racism remains rampant). Thus, just as Nasser declares England to be 'a little heaven' because 'unlike Pakistan' it 'has not allowed religion to interfere with making money' so the film cuts to a savage attack on Salim at the hands of violent white youths.

Similar tactics may also be seen to be at work in *Sammy and Rosie*. Like Nasser and Salim in *Laundrette*, Sammy enjoys material comfort and business success. As Raymond Durgnat suggests, 'Sammy and Rosie's marriage is practically The State of England; a love–hate stalemate between two halves of the middle class.'[27] However, it is the British Asian, Sammy (Samir) (Ayub Khan Din) who represents 'the capitalist half': a well-off accountant and symbol of consumerist excess (who is seen, at one point, looking at a porn magazine while snorting cocaine, eating a take-way burger, and listening to headphones). Rafi (Shashi Kapoor), his father, is even better off, and keen that his son should use his money to buy a new house away from the inner city and begin a family. He was also a politician in Pakistan with a responsibility for the use of torture. However, although Sammy is offset against Rosie (Frances Barber), the radical social worker, and Rafi against the feminist lesbian Rani, who investigates his past crimes, the film does not simply endorse or condemn individual characters. Thus, just as Nasser's materialism and domination of his family coexist with his generosity and appetite for living in *My Beautiful Laundrette*, so Rafi is invested with a degree of complexity despite the hideousness of his crimes.

---

[26] Boyd Tonkin, 'Jewel in the Laundrette', *New Socialist* (Jan. 1986), 23.
[27] Raymond Durgnat, 'Sammy and Rosie Get Laid', *The Virgin Film Yearbook* (London: Virgin, 1988), 89.

As Leonard Quart suggests, despite the films' left-wing sympathies, one of their key strategies is irony and, as a result, 'no social group has a monopoly of virtue or wisdom'.[28] This also explains, in part, why the film was disliked by so many within the Asian community. For the film's sense of the complexity of identities necessarily makes clear-cut identifications on the part of the audience difficult. Hence, *My Beautiful Laundrette* was criticized from within the Asian community both for its presentation of homosexuality and representation of Asians as 'money grabbing'.[29] It is, however, a deliberate strategy of the film to eschew positive images and, in doing so, emphasize the plural, complex, and criss-crossed character of identities, including 'black' and 'Asian' identities, in the contemporary world.[30]

If the ironies of characterization, and avoidance of 'positive' images, make straightforward identification with the Asian characters difficult, this is added to by the way in which the films self-consciously avoid 'speaking for' a unified Asian community. The films are acutely sensitive to the specificities of social life and explore, in particular, how the black and Asian communities are themselves differentiated by class, gender, generation, and sexual orientation. Thus, *My Beautiful Laundrette* is careful to delineate the different generational experiences of Omar and Tania (Rita Wolf) in relation to those of their parents and the film concludes with Tania's decision to leave the parental home. In the case of Tania, her situation is also related to gender and her desire to break out of a traditional female role. In this, she is contrasted with the women of an earlier generation, not just her mother, Bilquis (Charu Bala Chokshi), who is illiterate and forced to endure her husband's infidelities but also her father's white mistress, Rachel (Shirley Anne Field), whom she berates for living off her father. In defending herself to Tania, Rachel asks her to understand how 'we are of different generations, and different classes' and this is a theme which is echoed in *Sammy and Rosie Get Laid*. Generational tensions are manifest not only in the father–son relationship of Rafi and Sammy but also through the figure of Alice (Claire Bloom), the lover whom Rafi left behind in England (and who functions as a kind of older generation counterpart to Rosie). Through her encounters with younger women such as Vivia (Suzette Llewellyn), she comes to resent the 'denial' that was expected of her class and generation and, at the end of the film, comes to discover a certain commonality with the group of women (of differing ethnic backgrounds) in Sammy and Rosie's flat. In both films, these issues of ethnicity, class, and gender are also allied to questions of sexual orientation.

[28] Leonard Quart, 'The Politics of Irony: The Frears-Kureishi Films', *Film Criticism*, vol. xvi, nos. 1–2 (Fall/Winter 1991–2), 41.

[29] Mahmood Jamal, for example, complains that the film reinforces stereotypes of Asians as 'money grabbing, scheming, sex-crazed people' in 'Dirty Linen' in Kobena Mercer (ed.), *Black Film, British Cinema*, 21.

[30] Michele Wallace does, however, complain that the Frears/Kureishi films contain an implicit hierarchy of 'literate and prosperous' Indians and 'illiterate and impoverished' blacks. See *Invisibility Blues: From Pop to Theory* (London: Verso, 1990), 190. To some extent, this perception results from the film's primary emphasis upon Asian, rather than Afro-Caribbean, characters. However, it is also the case that the films tend not to invest their black characters with the same degree of complexity as their Asian ones (even if it is the black character Danny who provides *Sammy and Rosie* with its moral centre).

Sexuality

Kureishi has suggested how he wanted *My Beautiful Laundrette* to be 'a bit like *Butch Cassidy and the Sundance Kid* with kissing'.[31] However, in making a gay relationship central to the plot he also chooses, as with his treatment of Asians, not to portray this as a 'problem' or to show his main characters as 'victims' (in this case, of homophobia). As Kureishi has again observed, in dealing with gayness he wanted it to be 'taken for granted' rather than foregrounded as an issue.[32] The film, in this respect, uses traditional romantic conventions to 'normalize' gay sexuality; while, at the same time, using its gay relationship to subvert those very same conventions. For Philip French, the film celebrates 'a gay love affair' that 'transcends race, class, upbringing and social chaos'.[33] However, the film may in fact be seen to be doing the reverse: suggesting how the most intimate of acts are none the less implicated in a complex set of social determinations. As Kureishi has himself argued, he is interested in 'sex as a focus of social, psychological, emotional, political energy'.[34] As such, far from Omar and Johnny's relationship transcending time and place, it is actually structured in terms of the ethnic and class relationships in which it is embedded. In this respect, the film may be seen to be self-consciously reworking the old colonial habit of interpreting East–West relations in terms of a sexual metaphor, recalling the Forsterian interest in the bonds between men in particular. In doing so, it is not only able to make the homo-erotic subtext of the colonial narratives explicit but also upturn the relations of power involved.

This is an argument that is reinforced by *Sammy and Rosie*. Sammy informs his father that Rosie is writing a book: 'The Intelligent Woman's Guide to Kissing in History'. Rosie herself explains that it is concerned with 'snogging as a socio-economic, political-psychological event sunk in a profound complex of determinations' and proceeds to illustrate her thesis by first kissing Sammy and then, much more passionately, Danny (Roland Gift) ('a different kind of kiss, with a different social and political meaning') before finishing with a light peck for her father-in-law, Rafi. Clearly, 'The Intelligent Woman's Guide to Kissing' also applies to the film itself which stages scenes of kissing, as when Rani and Vivia kiss in a deliberately provocative fashion in front of Rafi, in order to bring out the socio-political context of sexual desire. As with *My Beautiful Laundrette*, the film, almost didactically, explores a variety of sexual permutations, both straight and gay. This reaches its fullest expression in the scene in which three couples— Rosie and Danny, Rafi and Alice, Sammy and his American lover, Anna (Wendy Gazelle)—are intercut making love, culminating in a split screen shot in which all three couples are seen together (a moment described by Kureishi as 'the fuck

[31] Hanif Kureishi, 'Disposing of the Raj', *Marxism Today* (Jan. 1987), 43.
[32] 'Scenes from a Marriage', 333.   [33] Philip French, *The Observer* (17 Nov. 1985), 29.
[34] Kureishi, 'My Beautiful Britain', Interview with David Nicholson, *Films and Filming* (Jan. 1988), 10.

PLATE 16. Shirley Anne Field and Saeed Jeffrey in *My Beautiful Laundrette*

sandwich').[35] This has echoes of the famous scene in *My Beautiful Laundrette* when we see, through a one-way mirror, Nasser and Rachel waltzing in the background while Johnny and Omar make love in the foreground. In both scenes, couples are interlinked by shared passions but also differentiated by the age, ethnicity, or sexual orientation of those involved (although, in the case of *Sammy and Rosie*, all three couplings are heterosexual).

As in the Raj films, the Frears/Kureishi films use interracial sexual encounters as one of their central tropes (indeed, all of the five liaisons described above are interracial).[36] However, unlike the Raj films, these liaisons are not presented as floundering on the rocks of irreconcilable difference. At one point in *My Beautiful Laundrette*, Omar announces to Salim that, in his opinion, 'much good can come from fucking'. This is a view which the films appear to share, suggesting how sexual desires may permit the crossing of borders and provide forms of connection which subvert conventional social divisions or pieties. There is, to an extent, a degree of old-fashioned sexual utopianism here which is deliberately mobilized against the conservative moralism of Thatcherism. For the New Right of the 1980s, as has been noted, it was the 'permissiveness' of the

---

[35] Kureishi, 'Requiem for a Rave', Interview with Philip Dodd, *Sight and Sound* (Sept. 1991), 11.

[36] bell hooks complains, however, that the 'fuck sandwich' scene in *Sammy and Rosie* consists only of sex between non-white men and white women and that this is symptomatic of a more general absence of black women in the film in 'Stylish Nihilism', in *Yearning: Race, Gender and Cultural Politics*, 161. While this is an important point, there is also a sense in which the scene is playing with old colonial fears of the 'threat' to white women represented by non-white men. See, for example, Paul Hoch's discussion of the 'defence of the White Goddess' in *White Hero, Black Beast* (London: Pluto, 1979), 43–50.

1960s which was commonly held responsible for the social and moral decline of the nation. In *My Beautiful Laundrette* and *Sammy and Rosie Get Laid,* on the other hand, there is an effort to restate the merits of 1960s-type sexual liberation by celebrating the possibilities, in Kureishi's words, of sexual 'openness and choice'.[37] However, in doing so the films also maintain an awareness of the social and cultural context in which relationships are enacted. In this respect, the films celebrate sex less as a humanist triumph over social obstacles than as themselves significant forms of social encounter in which various identifications (male/female, gay/straight, black/white) are implicated.

'In-Betweenness'

However, if Kureishi's films upturn conventional ways of representing East–West relations, they also seek to subvert the very binarism which has traditionally structured the East–West divide in films of empire. When Omar visits Nasser's house in *My Beautiful Laundrette*, Salim's wife Cherry (Souad Faress) complains she is fed up with 'in-betweens' such as Omar. However, it is precisely the fixities of identity which such a character is presumed to fall between which the film disputes. For *My Beautiful Laundrette* and *Sammy and Rosie Get Laid,* social and cultural identity is nearly always 'impure' (or 'in-between') and it is the very condition of 'in-betweenness', of identities created out of the intersection of various influences and allegiances, which the film maps out (indeed, there is a striking shot in *My Beautiful Laundrette* when Omar and Johnny look at each other through a one-way mirror and their faces are temporarily superimposed). For Corrigan, this 'in-betweenness' may be linked to a new postmodern era in which identities are no longer grounded in an identification with place. The characters in the films, he argues, are 'without homes or traditional historical places' and involved in 'shifting' and 'contingent' 'social alliances and subjectivities'.[38] More specifically, however, the films may be seen to articulate the 'in-betweenness' of the black and Asian experience in Britain, conceived not as a 'problem' or pathology (or a 'falling between' two cultures) but rather as a site of mutually productive cultural intersection.

In doing so, the films may also be seen to be questioning not only the homogeneity of the black and Asian identities but the homogeneity of national identities as well. For Stuart Hall, it was a feature of black cultural work in the 1980s that it also sought to contest conventional notions of 'Englishness' by insisting that 'Englishness is black'.[39] As Paul Gilroy argues in his influential work, *There Ain't No Black in the Union Jack,* the 'populist nationalism' of the Thatcher

---

[37] In his diary, Kureishi openly acknowledges how his attitudes were formed by the 1960s and that these include the beliefs that 'openness and choice in sexual behaviour is liberating . . . (and) . . . that there should be a fluid non-hierarchical society'. See *Sammy and Rosie Get Laid: The Script and the Diary,* 77.

[38] Timothy Corrigan, *A Cinema Without Walls: Movies and Culture after Vietnam* (London: Routledge, 1991), pp. 220 and 227.

[39] Hall, 'Old and New Identities, Old and New Ethnicities', 59.

regime characteristically rested upon an 'ethnic absolutism' which identified the 'nation' with 'whiteness'.[40] It is, however, precisely this 'ethnic absolutism' which films such as *My Beautiful Laundrette* and *Sammy and Rosie Get Laid* challenge. Thus, just as the Asian business class are shown to identify with Thatcherite economic precepts in *Laundrette* so they are also seen to have a strong identification with England. As Nassar explains to his mistress Rachel, in one of those speeches which seems to have been inserted primarily in order to make a point about the complexities of national identity: 'In this damn country which we hate and love, you can get anything you want . . . That's why I believe in England.' However, it is in Nasser's nephew, Omar, that these issues are most pronounced. He is a second-generation Pakistani in England who appears never to have been to Pakistan. His father is Asian and his mother is white and he has grown up identifying with England as his home. In the same way, Sammy, who was abandoned by his father as a child, has spent all of his life in England.

In a sense the problematic of Englishness, identified by Hall, is predicated upon the experiences of this second generation who are no longer from elsewhere (or 'immigrants') but born and brought up in England.[41] At one point in *Sammy and Rosie Get Laid*, Rafi suggests to Sammy that he should leave London and 'come home'. However, as Sammy points out, 'I am home, Pop. This is the bosom.' In this respect, by paying particular attention to such characters as Omar and Sammy, the films are necessarily involved in a dialogue with inherited notions of 'Englishness' and an expansion of them to include black and Asian experiences. When Johnny begins working for Omar in *My Beautiful Laundrette*, Genghis implores him not to 'cut yourself from your own people . . . Everyone has to belong.' In *Sammy and Rosie*, Alice likewise declares that 'being British has to mean an identification with other, similar people'. It is, of course, the opposite of these propositions which is the implicit argument of the two films. 'British' (or 'English') identity can no longer (if it ever could) be conceived in exclusivist, white terms (as in the narrow purview of the National Front of which Johnny was once a supporter) but must also incorporate heterogeneity and difference. As Kureishi has himself observed, 'British people need to recognize that Pakistani and Indian people are living here as part of the life of England. The definition of what it is to be British has to change.'[42]

Formal Hybridity

In this respect, the idea of 'in-betweenness' may be extended to the films' formal strategies, which themselves involve a degree of mixing of different

---

[40] Paul Gilroy, *There Ain't No Black in the Union Jack: The Cultural Politics of Race and Nation* (London: Hutchinson, 1987), esp. chap. 2.

[41] By the beginning of the 1990s, over half of the population regarded as 'members of New Commonwealth descended ethnic minorities' had been born in Britain. There was also a rapidly growing group who had been born to parents of different ethnic origins. See David Mason, *Race and Ethnicity in Modern Britain*, pp. 40–1 and 131.

[42] 'Scenes from a Marriage', 333.

aesthetic conventions. This is a point missed by many of the criticisms of the film (such as those of Labour MP, Keith Vaz, who complained that the film failed to show any poor Asians) which have tended to rely upon assumptions that the film could be read simply in terms of sociological accuracy or fidelity to the real. As Henriques observes, many critics refused 'to look at the film in any other way than as a piece of realism' and, in doing so, missed out on how the film broke with the realist tradition and employed non-realist techniques to express an 'imaginative contradictory world'.[43] Thus, while the films share many of the features of social realism—a concern with current social issues, a loose plot structure, 'ordinary' characters, location shooting—they also deviate from realist norms. As the director, Stephen Frears himself suggests of *My Beautiful Laundrette*, the 'realistic material' which the film contains 'gets treated in a rather odd way'.[44]

A number of strategies may be identified here: a combination of the conventions of realism with those of other genres, the employment of stylization and heightened *mise-en-scène*, the use of pastiche, and a resort to overt symbolism. It has been something of a feature of Frears's work, for example, to combine elements of popular American cinema with British material. This can be seen in *My Beautiful Laundrette* which is something of a generic hybrid, combining elements of realism with romance, comedy, and the thriller. Kureishi originally envisaged the film as a kind of Asian *Godfather* and the gangster element survives in the plot-line concerning the drug-dealing of Salim (and the iconography of his house). The interest in American cinema is also evident in the way in which the film makes use of cinematic quotation, including, for example, homages not only to Butch Cassidy (in the bicycling scene) but also to Nicholas Ray and Vincente Minnelli.[45] More generally, the film shifts between realism and stylization, staging certain scenes with self-conscious artifice as in some of the action outside the laundrette (such as when Johnny is fixing up the 'laundrette' sign or Rachel and Nasser argue after their confrontation with Tania). In some cases, the film embraces full-blooded expressionism as is the case when Salim is confronted by a menacing gang of white youths.

Similar tactics are also in evidence in *Sammy and Rosie* which Kureishi describes as 'continuation of the work' begun in *Laundrette*: a 'mixture of realism and surrealism, seriousness and comedy, art and gratuitous sex'.[46] As with *Laundrette*, the film combines elements of social realism with scenes of physical comedy (such as Rafi sliding down a drainpipe to escape Rani and Vivia), genre pastiche (the 'western' ride-out of the 'wagon-train' of caravans at the film's end), and even the musical (the straggly band of musicians who thread their

[43] Julian Henriques, 'Realism and the New Language', in Kobena Mercer (ed.), *Black Film, British Cinema*, 19.

[44] Quoted in 'Sheer Frears', *Stills* (Nov. 1985), 13.

[45] For a fuller discussion of Frears's mixing of British and American elements, see Hill, ' "Enmeshed in British Society but with a Yen for American Movies": Film, Television and Stephen Frears' in John Hill and Martin McLoone (eds.), *Big Picture, Small Screen: The Relations Between Film and Television* (Luton: John Libbey Media/University of Luton Press, 1996).

[46] *Sammy and Rosie Get Laid: The Script and the Diary*, 64.

way through the movie in a loose homage to Cliff Richard films). There is also a heavily stylized use of *mise-en-scène* at various junctures, including the scenes of rioting which assume a staged and hallucinatory quality, and a move towards overt symbolism in the form of the ghost, the representative of Rafi's tortured victims and his ultimate nemesis.

This use of symbolism is also in evidence in *My Beautiful Laundrette*. The laundrette itself is less a 'real' laundrette than a sort of imagined space in which personal desires and social tensions are worked out. It is, however, as with so much in these films, an ambivalent symbol. On the one hand, it stands in testimony to the enterprise culture and the power of self-help. It is also a symbol of the importance of 'spectacle' in the post-industrial economy and the rise of the service sector (and it is significant that none of the economic activities in the film involve manufacturing). On the other hand, it is a space which opens up the possibility for new forms of social connection and provides an outlet for socially transgressive desires. In wishing to maintain this ambivalence and give expression to the complex, plural, and shifting identities characteristic of contemporary British society, the film may therefore be seen to be pushing the boundaries of realism outwards in order to give expression to those 'realities' which a realism 'of the surface' might not otherwise be equipped to provide. This 'pressure' on the conventions of realism is even greater in the films of the black film workshops and it is to these films that I now turn.

chapter 11

'Race' and the Politics of Form
The Black Workshops and
the Films of Isaac Julien _____

The exploration of 'black' experience in Britain, and the fashioning of novel aesthetic forms to give it expression that is evident in the Kureishi/Frears films, may also be found in the films of the black workshops. The development of the black workshops occurred in the wake of the 1981 riots and the stimulus which this gave to the funding of black cultural work. The Greater London Council (GLC), in particular, was responsible for support for this work and provided, for example, initial funding for the Sankofa workshop, the makers of *The Passion of Remembrance* (1986).[1] The other key agency was Channel 4's Department of Independent Film and Video which, under the Workshop Declaration, franchised black workshops such as Sankofa Film and Video, the Black Audio Film Collective, and Ceddo Film/Video Workshop (see Chapter 3). For Kobena Mercer, the significance of these workshops was their creation of 'a kind of counter-practice' which contested the dominant representations of blacks in Britain and also the forms in which these representations were conventionally produced.[2]

In this respect, the films may be seen to share certain ambitions with the Frears/Kureishi films: to challenge conventional stereotypes of black people (as threats, problems, or victims) and to articulate the diversity of the black experience in Britain. Where they begin to diverge, however, is the extent to which they are concerned to challenge conventional cinematic forms in order to give

---

[1] A new Labour administration, under Ken Livingstone, came to power in London in May 1981 and adopted a more 'populist' approach to arts funding, redirecting funds towards 'community' and 'ethnic' arts. Between 1982/3 and 1985/6 the budget of the Ethnic Arts sub-committee of the GLC Arts and Recreation Committee increased from £30,000 to over £2 million. See Kwesi Owusu, *The Struggle For Black Arts in Britain* (London: Comedia, 1986), 84. For a more general assessment of the GLC's record of arts funding in this period, see Franco Bianchini, 'GLC R.I.P. Cultural Policies in London 1981–1986', *New Formations*, no. 1 (Summer 1987).

[2] Kobena Mercer, 'Recoding Narratives of Race and Nation', in Kobena Mercer (ed.), *Black Film, British Cinema* (London: ICA, 1988), 8.

expression to this diversity. Thus, while the Frears/Kureishi films attempt to push back the boundaries of social realism, they still remain within the ambit of traditional 'art cinema' and its fusion of narrative and expressive concerns. The black workshop films, by contrast, have tended to depart much more decisively from the conventions of both classical narrativity and realism.

The films, in this respect, may be seen to have elements in common with a political avant-garde that historically has sought to combine political with aesthetic radicalism.[3] It may also be seen to share a common impulse with the feminist avant-garde which has sought not only to challenge the dominant stereotypes of women but also to subvert the cinematic conventions (and 'language') through which women have been traditionally represented.[4] In doing so, a number of shared features are evident: a self-consciousness about the filmmaking process and an emphasis upon film as a medium; a refusal of the conventional mechanics of identification and an encouragement to the spectator to maintain a critical relationship to what is shown on the film screen; an eclecticism of aesthetic means and a readiness to mix fiction and documentary.

As Jim Pines has argued, the relationship of these films to the documentary tradition is particularly significant.[5] This tradition, he argues, has a particular historical importance not only because it has provided the main vehicle for the dominant white tradition of representing blacks in Britain but also for black filmmakers seeking to counter dominant (or racialist) images of blacks. It is, therefore, unsurprising that this is a tradition which the workshop movement has partly carried on. Ceddo, for example, was involved in relatively conventional documentary filmmaking which tended to challenge the content of dominant representations but not their form. Thus, in a film such as *A People's Account* (1986), the story of the riots—or 'uprisings'—in Brixton and Tottenham is told from a black perspective, giving the other side of the story which is normally missing from mainstream media accounts, but within a form which mirrors that of the conventional documentary.[6] However, what is probably most striking about the workshop films (especially those from Black Audio Film Collective and Sankofa) is that while they recognize the importance of the historical legacy of the documentary film (and the meanings around 'race' which it has constructed), this is accompanied by a concern to enter into a dialogue with this tradition and to forge a new cinematic language which will do justice to the complexity of black experiences. Thus, in the case of *The Passion of Remembrance*, the film was initially conceived of as a documentary project which would explore the history of black people and policing in Britain. However, in

---

[3] See Peter Wollen, *Readings and Writings: Semiotic Counter-Strategies* (London: Verso, 1982).

[4] See E. Ann Kaplan, *Women and Film* (London: Methuen, 1983) for a discussion of the feminist avant-garde.

[5] Jim Pines, 'The Cultural Context of Black British Cinema', in Mbye B. Cham and Claire Andrade-Watkins (eds.), *Blackframes: Critical Perspectives on Black Independent Cinema* (Cambridge, Mass.: MIT Press, 1988), 29.

[6] Ceddo was, however, responsible for the more experimental *Time and Judgement* (1988), directed by Menelik Shabazz, which combined documentary material with dramatic sketches in order to trace the recent history of Africa, and the African diaspora.

the course of their research, the filmmakers decided that 'a documentary would be too limited . . . for all the things we wanted to say'.[7]

The suspicion of documentary which characterizes many of the workshop films is premised upon two factors. On the one hand, this work is critical of the assumption that documentary and realism can simply show things 'as they really are', that a realism 'of the surface' can capture the complexities of social and historical process. On the other hand, it is critical of the assumption that film is simply a transparent medium or 'window on the world'. It is work which is very conscious of the mediating role which film itself performs in the production of the meanings of actions and events. As Mercer explains, the black films are premised upon a conception of representation: 'not as mimetic correspondence with the "real", but as a process of selection, combination and articulation of signifying elements in sound and image.'[8] As such, representation is conceived of as an active process of signification rather than any simple 'reflection' of the 'real'. Moreover, by making use of pre-existing documentary materials and re-employing them in novel contexts, the films seek to challenge or subvert the meanings which attach to these and suggest, or bring out, new ones.

Black Audio Film Collective's *Handsworth Songs* (1987), for example, is about the 1985 Handsworth riots, their historical context and representation in the media. By making use of pre-existing news and archive footage, found sound, and quotations, along with original material, the film seeks to rework their significance and reveal 'the ghosts of other stories'. Thus, for example, Mrs Thatcher's notorious comments (made on television in 1978) regarding the 'swamping' of Britain by 'people of a different culture' are intercut into a complex 'sequence' involving archive footage concerning immigration (and the break-up of traditional working-class communities), silent documentary material on the making of chains, tableaux of objects related to British colonial history, slow-motion news footage of a black youth being beaten by policemen to the accompaniment of a new musical soundtrack, interviews with Handsworth community representatives, and a shot of a mural dealing with black history and culture.[9] The 'effect' of this sequence is not only to subject Mrs Thatcher's remarks to a critical interrogation but also to open them up to, and 'recode' them in terms of, a whole series of different meanings around the history and experiences of blacks and Asians in Britain.

The films, in this regard, may be seen to have links with a postmodern cultural practice of 'resistance'.[10] While the aesthetic characteristics of postmodernism

[7] Sylvia Paskin, 'Without Heroes or Victims', *Monthly Film Bulletin* (Dec. 1986), 363.

[8] Mercer, 'Recoding Narratives', 11.

[9] For a more extended discussion of the 'transformative work' performed by the film, see John Corner, *The Art of Record: A Critical Introduction to Documentary* (Manchester: Manchester University Press, 1996), chap. 10.

[10] Hal Foster draws a distinction between a conservative 'postmodernism of reaction' and a more radical 'postmodernism of resistance' which challenges the status quo. See 'Postmodernism: A Preface', in Foster (ed.), *The Anti-Aesthetic: Essays on Postmodern Culture* (Port Townshend: Bay Press, 1983), p. xii. For a general discussion of the application of ideas concerning postmodernism to film, see Hill. 'Film and Postmodernism', in Hill and Church Gibson (eds.), *The Oxford Guide to Film Studies* (Oxford: Oxford University Press, 1998).

(such as eclecticism, the erosion of boundaries, and a declining emphasis upon originality) are often associated with surface play or 'depthlessness', an alternative—resistant—tradition of postmodernism may be seen to involve a critical project to 'deconstruct' or 'denaturalize' old meanings through the repositioning or 're-functioning' of artistic and cultural discourses.[11] This form of critical engagement with prior representations may be seen to be especially attractive to filmmakers who wish to challenge the traditional ways in which particular (especially minority or subaltern) social groups have been represented. Thus, in the case of women, Janet Wolff argues how postmodern tactics of 'quotation and juxtaposition' permit feminist artists to engage directly with 'current images, forms and ideas', subvert their intent and (re)appropriate their meanings.[12] Likewise, films, from the black workshops, such as *Territories* (1984) and *Handsworth Songs* are involved in a similar process of reappropriation of pre-existing imagery of blacks. In doing so, however, the films clearly distinguish themselves from the stylistic plunder, or significatory play, which is a feature of mainstream postmodernism. Thus, while Fredric Jameson associates the dominant 'cultural logic' of postmodernism with 'depthlessness', a 'weakening of historicity', and 'a waning of affect', Paul Gilroy argues that the black cultural politics, which the workshop films embody, is 'not about depthlessness but about depth, not about the waning of affect but about its preservation and reproduction, not about the suppression of temporal patterns but about history itself'.[13] As such, these films are not simply engaged in 'deconstruction' (of pre-existing imagery) but also a 'reconstruction' of meanings and identities appropriate to the 'in-betweenness', or 'interstitial', character (already noted), of the cultural space occupied by blacks in Britain.

The eclecticism characteristic of the black workshop films is therefore of a particular kind and corresponds to the new cultures of hybridity that have emerged in the wake of post-colonial migration. As Paul Gilroy puts it:

Black Britain defines itself crucially as part of a diaspora. Its unique cultures draw inspiration from those developed by black populations elsewhere. In particular, the culture and politics of black America and the Caribbean have become raw materials for creative processes which redefine what it means to be black, adapting it to distinctively British experiences and meanings. Black culture is actively made and re-made.[14]

[11] See, for example, Laura Kipnis, ' "Refunctioning" Reconsidered: Towards a Left Popular Culture', in Colin MacCabe (ed.), *High Theory/Low Culture: Analysing Popular Film and Television* (Manchester: Manchester University Press, 1986).

[12] Janet Wolff, *Feminine Sentences: Essays on Women and Culture* (Cambridge: Polity Press, 1990), 88.

[13] Fredric Jameson, 'Postmodernism, or The Cultural Logic of Late Capitalism', *New Left Review*, no. 146 (1984), 58–61. Paul Gilroy, 'Nothing But Sweat Inside my Hand: Diaspora Aesthetics and Black Arts in Britain', in Mercer (ed.), *Black Film, British Cinema*, 46. John Akomfrah of Black Audio Film Collective links the work of the group with a 'postmodernist reappropriation of the past' but without the 'play' that is often associated with (consumerist) postmodernism. See Coco Fusco, 'An Interview with Black Audio Film Collective: John Akomfrah, Reece Auguiste, Lina Gopaul and Avril Johnson', in Fusco, *Young British and Black: The Work of Sankofa and Black Audio Film Collective* (Buffalo, N.Y.: Hallwalls/ Contemporary Arts Center, 1988), 48.

[14] *'There Ain't No Black in the Union Jack': The Cultural Politics of Race and Nation* (London: Hutchinson, 1987), 154. To some extent, arguments concerning diasporic cultures (and hybridity) are

The strategies of 'syncretism' and 'hybridity' which the black British films display, in this regard, do not simply correspond to a generalized condition of (postmodern) decentred subjectivity but rather give articulation to the 'diasporean', and 'post-colonial', conditions in which the black communities in Britain are located (and to which they are responding). As Stuart Hall puts it, '[since] migration has turned out to be *the* world-historical event of late modernity, the classic postmodern experience turns out to be the diasporic experience'.[15]

This emphasis on the diasporic experience may also be linked to a certain revival of interest in the idea of 'third cinema'. The concept of 'third cinema' was initially employed by the Argentinian filmmakers Fernando Solanas and Octavio Getino to identify an emergent revolutionary cinema which was distinct from both mainstream Hollywood (first cinema) and European 'art' cinema (second cinema).[16] While this concept was initially associated with a particular type of cinema in the Third World (and Latin America in particular), it has, more recently, been applied to films in the 'First World' as well. Globalizing economic forces and increased geographic mobility have created increasing economic and cultural interdependence (if not equality) between the 'First' and 'Third' worlds while mass migration has brought the 'Third World' into the very heartlands of the 'First'.[17] In this respect, the project of third cinema may be seen to extend to the diaspora culture of ethnic and cultural groups dispersed across the globe, including the Asian and Afro-Caribbean communities in Britain. Thus, for Paul Willemen, it is precisely the 'in-between position' of black British filmmakers in particular—the sense of being both inside and outside the dominant culture—that has encouraged a critical cultural practice that is based on a recognition of the 'the many-layeredness' of the 'cultural–historical formation' of British society.[18]

a mixture of observation and advocacy. Hence, Jonathan Friedman attacks Gilroy's celebration of hybridity, somewhat unfairly, as no more than the cultural expression of a cosmopolitan intellectual elite with little connection to 'the everyday problems of identity in the street' in 'Global Crises, The Struggle for Cultural Identity and Intellectual Porkbarrelling: Cosmopolitans Versus Locals, Ethnics and Nationals in an Era of De-hegemonisation', in Pnina Werbner and Tariq Modood (eds.), *Debating Cultural Hybridity: Multi-Cultural Identities and the Politics of Anti-Racism* (London: Zed Books, 1997), 74. What this suggests, as Robin Cohen argues, is that more empirical investigation of the idea of a 'cultural diaspora' has to be undertaken. See *Global Diasporas: An Introduction* (London: UCL Press, 1997), chap. 6.

[15] Stuart Hall, 'The Formation of a Diasporic Intellectual' (Interview with Kuan-Hsing Chen), in David Morley and Kuan-Hsing Chen (eds.), *Stuart Hall: Critical Dialogues in Cultural Studies* (London: Routledge, 1996), 490.

[16] 'Towards a Third Cinema' (orig. 1969) in Michael Chanan (ed.), *Twenty-five Years of the New Latin American Cinema* (London: BFI/Channel 4, 1983).

[17] Thus, for Aijaz Ahmad it makes more sense to conceive the world in terms of 'a hierarchically structured whole' rather than as 'three worlds'. See 'Three Worlds Theory: End of a Debate', in *In Theory: Classes, Nations, Literatures* (London: Verso, 1992), 316.

[18] Paul Willemen, 'The Third Cinema Question', in Jim Pines and Paul Willemen (eds.), *Questions of Third Cinema* (London: British Film Institute, 1989), pp. 28 and 4. This development of the concept of 'third cinema' may also be linked to Homi Bhabha's notion of a 'Third Space', i.e. an 'in-between space' that is not based on 'the *diversity* of cultures' but on 'the inscription and articulation of culture's hybridity'. See Bhabha, 'The Commitment to Theory' in *Questions of Third Cinema*, 131.

This reconceptualization of the idea of 'third cinema' has, in turn, involved a move away from the 'universalism' of earlier models of political filmmaking ('counter cinema' and the 'second avant-garde') towards an increasing emphasis upon the local and the specific. As Ella Shohat argues, while the idea of post-colonial hybridity has developed as a response to 'the mutual imbrication of "central" and "peripheral" cultures' in both the 'First' and 'Third Worlds', it is not a unitary phenomenon and assumes diverse and ideologically varied forms.[19] As a result, 'third cinema', and the characteristics it develops, vary as well. Teresa De Lauretis draws on both feminist and third cinema debates in order to indicate how a 'universal' model of (feminist) counter-cinema, addressed to an undifferentiated (female) spectator is no longer viable (if it ever was). Making use of Solanas and Getino's idea of a 'guerrilla' cinema, she argues that, while both 'third cinema' and an 'alternative women's cinema' are 'informed by a global perspective', they, none the less, carry on the project of a politically questioning cinema by engaging 'current problems . . . on a local scale' and addressing a particular audience 'in its specific history of struggles'.[20] In doing so, the aesthetic strategies that these cinemas adopt also vary. Thus, while the black workshops have inherited the tradition of the European avant-garde, they have also, in response to the specific 'post-colonial' circumstances of blacks in Britain in the 1980s, moved beyond it, pushing it in new directions and mixing it with novel elements.

The Passion of Remembrance

It is in the light of these arguments that the strategies of *The Passion of Remembrance* (written and directed by Maureen Blackwood and Isaac Julien) may be understood. In terms of traditional representations of blacks in British cinema, Jim Pines suggests the film is significant because it seeks to avoid the 'race relations' discourse that has dominated so many previous films.[21] As members of the Sankofa collective, Robert Crusz and Maureen Blackwood, put it themselves, they 'were more interested in gender, the ideology of the image, etc.' than in 'race relations' and were not trying to 'explain' themselves to white people in the manner of previous race relations documentaries.[22] As a result, the film is not primarily concerned with relations between black and white

[19] Ella Shohat, 'Notes on the "Post-Colonial"', in Padmini Monga (ed.), *Contemporary Postcolonial Theory* (London: Arnold, 1996), 329. Ruth Frankenberg and Lata Mani also argue that 'the notion of the "postcolonial" is best understood in context of a rigorous politics of location, of a rigorous conjuncturalism' which is alert to questions of power. See 'Crosscurrents, Crosstalk: Race, "Postcoloniality" and the Politics of Location', *Cultural Studies*, vol. 7 no. 2 (May 1993), 307.

[20] Teresa De Lauretis, 'Guerrilla in the Midst: Women's Cinema in the 80s', *Screen*, vol. 31 no. 1 (Spring 1990), 17. Paul Willemen also discusses the parallels between third cinema and feminist cinema, based on their break with 'the dominant, habitual patterns of a society', in 'Is Your Filmmaking "Revolutionary"?' (Interview), *Filmwaves*, no. 1 (Aug. 1997), 12.

[21] Pines, 'The Cultural Context of Black British Cinema', 27. Pines also identifies Menelik Shabazz's *Burning an Illusion* (1981) as an important precursor in this regard.

[22] See 'Sankofa Film and Video', *The Business of Film* (June/July 1991), 42.

(the only white 'characters' as such being some racist thugs and ineffectual neighbourhood policemen) but rather with experiences *within* the black communities. However, in shifting the focus of attention to intra-black issues, the film is also concerned to resist the expectation that, in focusing upon black characters, it can then represent the totality of black experiences (even if it does want to tackle an exceptionally wide range of issues including racism, sexism, homophobia, post-industrial decline, the 'break-up' of Britain, and the possibilities for different forms of political and cultural resistance).[23]

A significant scene, in this respect, involves the Baptiste family watching a black couple on a TV quiz show. Maggie (Antonia Thomas) observes the difficulty to which their appearance gives rise: it is as if, she says, that 'every time a black face appears we think it has to represent the whole race'.[24] Like the Kureishi films, *The Passion of Remembrance* is reluctant to accept this 'burden of representation', seeking to challenge the notion of a singular and homogeneous 'black community' and to emphasize the differences and diversity amongst blacks in Britain (as well as the complexity of current-day 'Britishness'). In particular, it is concerned to distance itself from a unitary (or 'nationalist') black politics derived from 1960s black radicalism. For Cornel West, 'the decisive push of postmodern Black intellectuals toward a new cultural politics of difference has been made by the powerful critiques and constructive explorations of Black diaspora women' and it is through Maggie, in particular, that the film criticizes the aggressive male activism of the past which is seen as having inhibited a proper recognition of both feminist and gay issues.[25] Thus, in one scene, Maggie attacks her brother Tony's (Jim Findley) male-centred version of black politics. 'You can't even talk about communities', she complains as the camera moves in on his face. 'It's always homogeneous. At the end of the day, it's about how you define things because you've got the power.' To this extent, a primary concern of the film is to give voice to different black—gay and female—perspectives and, in doing so, give prominence to scenes involving only women or gay men.

An important scene, in this regard, occurs when we see Maggie and her friend Louise (Janet Palmer) preparing to go out. They are seen dressing, putting on make-up, and dancing to a cassette (Aleem's 'Get Loose'). In part, this scene reflects a concern, similar to that of *My Beautiful Laundrette*, to lay stress on the range (and complexity) of black experiences and identities. Thus, images of the women dancing are intercut with shots of the older men below—Maggie's father Benjy (Ram John Holder) and her brother Tony dancing to a calypso record—in order to suggest differences (and, to some extent, divisions) related

---

[23] As the film's producer, Martina Attille, explained, 'there was a sense of urgency to say it all, or at least signal as much as we could in one film. Sometimes one can't afford to hold anything back for another time.' '*The Passion of Remembrance*', *Framework*, nos. 32/3 (1986), 101.

[24] Ironically, the same expectation seemed to meet the film when it was transmitted on Channel 4 in 1988. Following the film's transmission, a black (male) viewer appeared on the channel's 'talk back' show, *Right to Reply*, to complain that the film 'wasn't a true representation of typical black family life' and that 'black people were degraded' (*Right to Reply*, Channel 4 (5 Nov. 1988)).

[25] Cornel West, 'The New Cultural Politics of Difference', in Russell Ferguson *et al.* (eds.), *Out There: Marginalization and Contemporary Cultures* (Cambridge, Mass.: The MIT Press, 1990), 29.

to age, gender, cultural traditions, and imaginative identifications. It is also a scene that challenges conventional stereotypes of the political activist and refuses a simple dichotomy between the 'personal' and the 'political' (of which we are reminded by the posters of striking workers on the wall). As Martina Attille explains, the filmmakers wanted 'to make a statement about pleasure and women's culture' and challenge the 'myth that feminism and lipstick are incompatible'.[26] Moreover, it complements the film's images of more direct political struggle by celebrating, in the 'private sphere', the women's self-confidence, their intimacy and their pleasure in their own bodies. As bell hooks argues, the scene works against 'conventional racist and sexist stereotypical representations of black female bodies' by displaying them, not for (male/white) voyeuristic spectacle, but in order to encourage 'that look of recognition that affirms their subjectivity'.[27] The looks of the women in the bedroom mirror, in this respect, parallel the recurring images of mirrors used in the archival material and seem to suggest the sense of power that derives from such a process of self-recognition (and it is, therefore, significant that the bedroom scene ends with a shot of the mirror and the photograph of a black woman that is attached to it).

However, like the Kureishi films, such affirmations of subjectivity are also complex and positional. For Teresa De Lauretis, a key aspect of 'alternative women's cinema' is that it addresses 'a female social subject engendered, constructed and defined by *multiple* social relations (of class, race, sexuality, age, etc.)'.[28] In the case of *The Passion of Remembrance*, it is equally important for it to recognize and address a 'black' social subject who is similarly defined by a multiplicity of social relations. Maggie's images of 'protest and celebration of solidarity' involve not just black women but also white men and women, both gay and straight, and suggest the different alignments to which different kinds of politics give rise. As she says to one of the discussion group, her tape consists of images from different occasions and places 'where black people, gay black people, white gay people, old people and young people all marched—so what's your problem?' This 'overlapping' of identities is particularly evident in the case of Gary (Carlton Chance) and Michael (Gary McDonald) whose sexuality positions them in a complex way to the other black men in the film. Thus, while Gary and Michael share, as blacks, a common situation (such as unemployment and the possibility of racial attack) with characters like Tony and Benjy, they are also separated from them by virtue of their homosexuality. Thus, they are not fully accepted by either Tony or Benjy (who criticizes Maggie for going to a gay club with Gary) and encounter prejudice at the black discussion group (where Gary, as a result, declares that he's glad that he was 'barred from the straight race'). At the same time, they are seen to belong to a 'gay culture', observed in the clubbing sequence, that includes both black and white (and male and female). As such, they are seen not simply to belong to one community (or to possess one

---

[26] '*The Passion of Remembrance*', 103.
[27] bell hooks, 'The Oppositional Gaze', in *Black Looks: Race and Representation* (Boston, MA: South End Press, 1992), 130.
[28] 'Guerrilla in the Midst: Women's Cinema in the 80s', 14.

PLATE 17. The 'speakers' drama': Anni Domingo in *The Passion of Remembrance*

'identity') but to have affinities, and affiliations, which cut across, and undermine, clear-cut lines of identification and 'community'.

However, if the film is, in this way, concerned both to contest dominant representations of blacks and to query the homogeneity of black experience, it is
also concerned to do so in a formally innovative fashion. There are a number
of ways in which this is achieved, particularly through the film's approach to
narrative, the mixing of fiction and documentary, and its self-conscious use
of the film medium. In the case of the film's use of narrative, the film refuses to
offer a unified diegesis, or fictional world, but consists of a series of scenes and
dramatic moments organized into two stories, or dramas, which interrupt each
other and provide a degree of commentary upon each other. These may be divided
into what the film's credits identify as the 'speakers' drama' and 'Maggie's drama'.
Although interlinked, both are radically different in treatment. The speakers'
drama involves a black woman (Anni Domingo) speaking first against a red
backdrop and then in argument with a black man (Joseph Charles) in a deserted
quarry. This drama is deliberately stylized and abstract. The characters are
nameless and are less 'realistic' characters than representatives of particular intellectual, and political, positions (partly based on Malcolm X and June Jordan).
Their argument is set in a dream-like 'no man's land' devoid of realistic reference
and is filmed in sweeping semi-circular camera movements. Cutting is erratic
and obtrusive and knowingly defies the procedures of reverse-field cutting conventionally associated with the filming of conversations. This stylization, and

rejection of realism, derives from a wish to present a dialogue between differing political perspectives rather than individual characters. The woman offers a feminist critique of male-dominated black politics, criticizing its subordination of women in the struggles of the past (licking stamps, making tea), and demanding her 'satisfaction'. At the end of the last scene located in this setting, the question of 'who should cross to who' is raised but not resolved: the male speaker turns his back on the woman and walks away, almost literally disappearing into dust.

This abstract political drama is set against the more conventionally realized drama of the Baptiste family in which the issues raised in the speakers' drama become specific and concrete. In this, Maggie is counterpointed to her brother Tony, a 'brother' of 1960s vintage, who is resistant to seeing his black politics challenged by what he regards as 'white-informed' issues of gender and sexuality. In this way, the issues raised in the speakers' drama become individual, personal issues as well, particularly as mediated through the experiences of Maggie (seen in one scene having her space 'invaded' by Tony when he interrupts Maggie and Louise watching the video). However, because the two stories are interwoven, the individualizing logic of conventional narrative realism is also avoided and the issues raised around gender and sexual orientation are seen not only to be personally felt but also collectively shared.

The narrative organization of Maggie's drama is, however, complex. The 'story' is loose and episodic and consists of a number of relatively self-contained scenes that follow a thematic rather than strictly narrative order (as in the montage of shots of London in which images of City affluence are contrasted with the urban dereliction through which Benjy and Tony are seen walking). The drama is also told in a way that is temporally complicated and, even, confusing. The first scene involving the Baptiste family, for example, takes place following the discussion group which Maggie, Tony, and Gary had been attending. The actual discussion (and its significance), however, is not revealed until much later. Moreover, when it is shown, it is in the form of a flashback as Maggie, watching her video compilation on her own, remembers the discussion that took place after she had screened it earlier. In the same way, there is a shot of a grieving mother (Mrs Campbell) at the end of the first Baptiste family scene, following a comment by Mrs Baptiste about the death of Mrs Campbell's son. However, it is not entirely clear what status this image has (dissolves suggest it could even be Maggie's imagination) and it is only near the film's end that the details (based on the case of Colin Roach) of the death of a young black man in police custody are provided.[29] In blurring temporal relations in this way, the film makes it clear that its interest is less in telling a linear story, involving characters with whom we become emotionally involved, than exploring (in the

[29] Colin Roach, a young unemployed black man not long out of prison, was found dead, in unexplained circumstances, at Stoke Newington police station in January 1983. The film's co-director, Isaac Julien, had previously produced a video, *Who Killed Colin Roach?* and the initial idea behind *Passion* had been to put his death in a political and cultural context. For a discussion of the Colin Roach case, see Keith Thompson, *Under Siege: Racial Violence in Britain Today* (London: Penguin, 1988), 23–4.

form of a visual and aural montage) ideas, meanings, and connections (both cognitive and affective) which critically engage and stimulate us (and which, in part, correspond to Maggie's own response to, and thinking through of, her experiences and the issues they have raised).

The flow of Maggie's drama is also broken by the use of archive and documentary footage. These are narratively motivated by the montage tape which Maggie has made of past moments of struggle—marches, rallies, picket-lines— but they also punctuate the film according to a logic which is not confined to her dramatic situation (thus when we first see the historical footage at the film's beginning it has yet to be placed in relation to Maggie's drama). The uses which the film makes of this material are multiple. First, by interweaving actuality footage with the two fictional dramas, an additional public and political dimension is added to the issues which the dramas raise. It also provides a commentary on the current 'state of England', charting the conflicts and divisions that have been a feature of recent history and the common experiences of white strikers (especially the miners) and black protesters at the hands of the police (with cameras characteristically placed in front of, rather than behind, police lines). Thus, after one sequence, Louise observes how 'a lot of people's eyes must be open now' and declaims in mock-Shakespearian tones, 'England, oh England. This nation that is my lifeblood. What is to be done?' Secondly, the footage provides a record of the past which the characters within the film both wish to remember (and draw strength from) and also resist. Like the characters in Jean-Luc Godard's *Tout va bien* (1972), who are looking back at the events of 1969 in order to take stock of their political situation in 1972, so the characters in *The Passion of Remembrance* refer back to the images of the past in order to assess their relevance for the present. Indeed, the name—Sankofa—used by the group refers to a bird with its head turned backwards, suggesting how the past is to be reclaimed from a perspective that is grounded in the present.

However, for the film there is no one 'past' out there simply to be remembered and the film raises the question of whose past and whose images are to be recalled. A seminal image for the film is the black fist salute of the US athletes, Tommy Smith and John Carlos, at the Mexico Olympics in 1968 and its association with the black power movement of the 1960s. However, while this is an important image, the film, via Maggie, is at pains to recall other, less 'masculine' images. Hence, Maggie's tape foregrounds different images of struggle, of women (as in the material of the Grunwick workers where East African Asian women were involved in a long-running dispute over unionization) and of lesbians and gays that highlight their contribution to the politics of the past.[30] However, if the past has to be actively engaged and reactivated for the present,

[30] Ellis Cashmore discusses how the dispute at the Grunwick Processing Laboratories in 1976 succeeded in 'undermining the stereotype of black and Asian workers, especially women' in *United Kingdom? Class, Race and Gender since the War* (London: Unwin Hyman, 1989), 134. Avtar Brah also recalls how disputes such as Grunwick's provided images of Asian women workers as 'striking icons of this "post-colonial" moment' in *Cartographies of Desire: Contesting Identities* (London: Routledge, 1996), 8.

the film is also aware that the past, in a sense, only exists as representation and, thus, in problematizing the notion of the 'past' it is also problematizing its representation, the means whereby the past is mediated to us.

Thus, Maggie's footage does not simply present images from the past but refashions and reworks them to create new meanings and significances, sometimes against the grain of their original use. This involves re-editing the material to make it function in novel ways but also a reworking of the materiality of the medium itself (as in structural filmmaking). Hence, the film alters the colour and changes the speed of its footage, uses techniques such as freeze-frame, and fashions novel combinations of image and sound in order to foreground the materiality of the representational process and to question its claims to photographic 'authenticity'. For the film, then, the past is not just a question of *who* gets represented but also of *how* it gets represented. This process of meditating upon the process of mediation is at the film's heart and it is a recurring situation within the film to have groups discuss the images they are watching— the family watching the quiz programme, the discussion group reflecting upon Maggie's compilation, Maggie, Louise, and Tony discussing the Olympics footage —in a way that is paradigmatic for how the film itself invites its own images to be reflected upon.

Looking for Langston

The concern to interrogate the past that is evident in *The Passion of Remembrance* is carried on in Sankofa's later film, directed by Isaac Julien, *Looking for Langston* (1989). This is described by the opening titles as a 'meditation' upon the black poet Langston Hughes and the Harlem Renaissance of the 1920s. The term is appropriate as the film is neither a straightforward documentary nor a conventional fictionalization of the poet's life but rather a dream-like montage, incorporating archival material (film, radio, photographic stills), dramatized segments, poems, readings, and music. According to Isaac Julien, he was attempting to achieve three main objectives:

> to illuminate the necessary contestation which takes place over the memory, the legacy and the representation of an important cultural icon like Langston Hughes . . . to explore the possibility of having a sexual identity that many blacks would identify as a betrayal of their racial authenticity . . . and . . . to popularize . . . interesting debates . . . around the history of black literature and cultural expression.[31]

The resulting 'meditation' provided by the film is concerned, in particular, with the homosexuality of many of those, including Hughes, involved in the Harlem Renaissance and in black culture more generally (the film, for example, is dedicated to James Baldwin). As Mercer explains:

[31] Paul Gilroy, 'Climbing the Racial Mountain: A Conversation with Isaac Julien', *Small Acts* (London: Serpent's Tail, 1993), 169–70.

Langston Hughes is remembered as the key poet of the Harlem Renaissance and has come to be revered as a father figure of black literature, yet in the process of becoming such an icon, the complexity of his life and the complexity of the Harlem Renaissance itself has been subject to selective erasure and repression by the gatekeepers and custodians of the 'colored museum'. Hughes is remembered as a populist, public figure, but the enigma of his private life—his sexuality—is seen as something better left unaddressed in most biographies, an implicit gesture of denial which buries and represses the fact that the Harlem Renaissance was as gay as it was black, and that many of its key figures—Claude McKay, Alain Locke, Countee Cullen, Wallace Thurman, and Bruce Nugent—were known to be queer, one way or another.[32]

Looking for Langston is therefore in part an act of historical recovery, a bringing to the surface of what had been previously 'hidden from history'. However, because the sexuality of Hughes remains contested, it is also a film which is not so much about the 'real' Hughes as 'Langston Hughes'—'Hughes', as Scott Bravmann puts it, as 'a rich sign in popular memory and cultural practice'.[33] As a result, *Looking for Langston* is not so much a conventional historical film as a meditation upon the process of constructing 'history'. The opening sequences make this clear.

The film begins with images of old Harlem while Toni Morrison is heard reading an eulogy on the soundtrack. A cut to a head-and-shoulders shot of a black man, a mourner, follows. The camera temporarily holds on his face before moving down onto the casket to reveal the dead 'Hughes' (a part taken by the director of the film, Isaac Julien), whose head is seen gently to 'revolve'. The camera then moves across the faces of the mourners (shot in a striking *chiaroscuro* style) before cutting to a full shot of the group around the casket. From there, the camera moves elegantly downwards from what is now seen to be the upper storey of a 1920s club to reveal a number of dancers in a frozen tableau below. As Hughes is heard on the soundtrack declaiming, 'Why should it be my loneliness? why should it be my song? why should it be my dream deferred overlong', the film's title appears.

A complex montage of sound and image then follows. Parts of a radio tribute to Hughes following his death in 1967 is heard over an archive shot taken from a train arriving at 125th Street. We then see footage of Hughes reciting his own work ('I feel the blues a comin', wonder what the blues will bring') to the accompaniment of a jazz band before there is a cut to a shot of a record on an old gramophone being listened to by the fictional Alex (Ben Ellison) (who may also be interpreted as the young 'Hughes'). Hughes's words overlap with those of the contemporary black gay singer Blackberri ('Blues for Langston') which are, in turn, intercut with a short extract of the blues singer Bessie Smith. As

[32] Kobena Mercer, 'Black Gay Men In Independent Film', *Cineaction*, no. 32 (Fall 1993), 59.

[33] Scott Bravmann, 'Isaac Julien's *Looking for Langston*: Hughes, Biography and Queer(ed) History', *Cultural Studies*, vol. 7, no. 2 (May 1993), 318. Bravman also highlights how postmodern arguments concerning the contingency of 'gay identity' may be in tension with the project of uncovering a 'hidden' gay identity in history.

Blackberri's song continues ('things haven't changed much, we still find power in our words'), various still photographs of Hughes and others are seen.

The film, in this respect, shares many of the features of the 'postmodern history film' as identified by Robert A. Rosenstone: the abandonment of conventional temporal order, the interrogation of the past from the perspective of the present, self-reflexivity, the mixing of 'contradictory elements', alteration or invention of incident, the use of 'fragmentary or poetic knowledge', and an open-ended rather than totalizing approach to the meaning of past events.[34] Thus, in *Looking for Langston* the 'contradictory elements' of 'factual' and fictional material are combined; past, present, and imagined events are run together; the past is imaginatively invented rather than accurately recreated; images are edited together according to a 'poetic' rather than a narrative or clearly 'rational' logic; and the meanings which the film generates are plural and ambiguous (and affective as much as cognitive). Montage is the film's key strategy and, through a complex and shifting articulation of sound and image, various boundaries—between 'fact' and fiction, 'real' and imaginary, past and present—become blurred and new and unexpected meanings are fashioned through the juxtaposition of images and sounds from different sources, periods, and places.

The 'history' which the film produces is therefore complicated and multivalent. Archival material of various kinds is intercut with dramatized material and these provide different regimes of 'knowledge' of the past which are played off against each other (partly reflecting a division between the 'official' history of the Harlem Renaissance manifest in the documentary material and the repressed, 'unofficial' history of gay sexuality evident in the drama). The fictional material is, however, heavily stylized and does not attempt to reproduce period surfaces accurately. In this respect, settings such as the club are less reconstructions of actual places than imaginative spaces in which the themes of the film may be played out. Accordingly, the film presents less a 'real' past, which could be judged by standards of historical evidence, than an imagined (or 'projected') past which follows the logic of dream and the unconscious (as the repeated reference to 'the deferred dream'—a phrase from Hughes's poetry—might suggest).

For the film, however, the past is not simply 'out there' anyway and not straightforwardly separate from the present. Temporal boundaries are unclear and one period merges into another. Thus, the wake at the film's beginning is occurring at the time of Hughes' death in 1967 but the clothes of the actors and the settings, along with the archive material, indicate the 1920s. The recitation of the older Hughes is listened to by Alex (or the younger 'Hughes') in the 1920s. The songs and words of the present (Blackberri) are mixed with, and overlaid upon, the sounds and images of the past. As with *The Passion of Remembrance*, *Looking for Langston* is, in this respect, a film which is self-consciously interrogating and imagining the past from the perspective of the present. As Henry Louis Gates, Jr. argues, 'the film's evocations of the historical Harlem Renaissance is,

---

[34] Robert A. Rosenstone, *Visions of the Past: The Challenge of Film to Our Idea of History* (Cambridge, Mass.: Harvard University Press, 1995), 206–7.

among other things, a self-reflexive gesture' establishing an 'analogy between contemporary . . . black creativity and an historical precursor'. 'We look for Langston', he goes on, 'but we discover Isaac', an association which is explicitly suggested by the director's assumption of the role of Hughes's corpse.[35] What this analogy suggests, however, is less that the film's director, Isaac Julien, is seeking to take the place of Hughes but that the film is entering into a dialogue with the past from the point-of-view of its own contemporary artistic and (sexual-)political concerns and meditating upon the imaginative relationships between the two periods.

This dialogue, moreover, extends not simply across time but also across place. At the end of the film, there is a scene of frenetic partying at the club, accompanied by contemporary dance music ('Can You Party' by Royal House). A group of 'thugs and police', as the credits put it, break into the club but only to find its inhabitants gone. The sequence illustrates both the 'poetic' logic by which so much of the film works as well as the by now familiar collapse of temporal distinctions and diegetic consistency. The characters in the 1920s dance to 1980s music while the thugs and police are in contemporary dress. Moreover, the uniforms of the police indicate that they are British even though the club is apparently in Harlem (and the scene itself has echoes of the attack on the club which ends the pioneering black British feature, *Babylon* (1980)). Just as *Passion* looked back to the 1960s politics of Black Power in America and reflected upon its relevance for a 'politics of difference' in 1980s Britain, so *Looking for Langston* looks back to the experience of blacks in the USA in the 1920s and explores some of the connections with the experience of blacks in Britain in the 1980s. Black Britons, as Mercer suggests, have often identified politically and culturally with black America and it is the 'the imaginary and symbolic conduits' through which these connections are forged with which the film is partly concerned.[36]

In particular, the film finds in the Harlem Renaissance a certain anticipation of its own 'hybrid' aesthetic practices and appropriation of modernist technique. At one point in the film, the narration (a reading by Stuart Hall) comments over archive footage: 'It was a time when the Negro was in vogue. White patrons of the Harlem Renaissance wanted their black artists to know and feel the intuitions of the primitive. They didn't want modernism.' At this point, we see an image of a black artist at work on a cubist canvas. In this sense, the film seeks not only to reclaim the gay contribution to the Harlem Renaissance but also its contribution to the development of, what Henry Louis Gates, Jr. refers to as, '*sui generis* African-American modernist forms'.[37] The relationship of the Harlem Renaissance to modernism has been the subject of some debate and Houston A. Baker Jr. has argued how the refusal to include the Harlem Renaissance within the

---

[35] Henry Louis Gates, Jr., 'The Black Man's Burden', in Gina Dent (ed.), *Black Popular Culture* (Seattle: Bay Press, 1992), 77. This point is confirmed by Julien himself who has argued how the film comes out of 'a very genuine search for desire, for my own desire'. Quoted in Bravmann, 'Isaac Julien's *Looking for Langston*', 321.

[36] Mercer, 'Black Gay Men In Independent Film', 58–9.

[37] Henry Louis Gates, Jr., 'Harlem on our Minds', in *Rhapsodies in Black: Art of the Harlem Renaissance* (University of California Press: Berkeley, 1997), 166.

history of modernism (or to see it as other than 'failed' modernism) is simply to accept a definition of modernism in terms of 'British, Anglo-American, and Irish creative endeavors'.[38] By way of contrast, Baker wishes to argue that the Harlem Renaissance belongs to an Afro-American tradition, or 'black sounding', of modernism, characterized by the dual strategies of 'mastery' and 'deformation' of 'form'.[39] In this regard, the poetry of Hughes may be read in terms of its 'mastery' and then 'deformation' (or 'blackening') of poetic form through an appropriation of black cultural traditions such as jazz and blues.[40] In a similar manner, Manthia Diawara has argued that the black British workshops may be seen to occupy an analogous place in relation to postmodernism, taking a 'black sounding' on postmodern aesthetic practices and investing the white Euro-American tradition of the avant-garde with a black idiom.[41] Thus, while the film generally follows in the footsteps of a formally self-conscious avant-garde cinema, and more specifically draws on the gay cinema of Jean Cocteau, Jean Genet, and Kenneth Anger, it also inflects this tradition with textual resources derived from black American literature and popular music. In this way, Paul Gilroy's idea of 'the Black Atlantic'—of a connected black culture, spanning the Atlantic, and dialogically transmitting ideas, influences, and cultural forms —may also be seen to inform the film's practice and underpin its hybridized form (and sense of hybridized identities outside of the ambit of the 'national').[42] Thus, for Gilroy, a key element of 'the black Atlantic world' is that it represents 'a fluid and dynamic cultural system that escapes the grasp of nation-states and national conceptions of . . . development'.[43]

The central aspect of the film's imaginative engagement with black America, however, is its exploration of the 'hidden history' of gay men's contribution to the Harlem Renaissance. By bringing to the surface the previously repressed voice of the black gay man, the film carries on from *The Passion of Remembrance*

---

[38]   Houston A. Baker, Jr., *Modernism and the Harlem Renaissance* (Chicago: University of Chicago Press, 1987), p. xiii. It is, of course, the case that Irish modernism, emerging out a colonial context, does itself represent a distinct 'sounding' of modernist concerns. See, for example, Fredric Jameson's arguments concerning 'the special case' of Irish literature, and Joyce's *Ulysses* in particular, in *Nationalism, Colonialism and Literature: Modernism and Imperialism*, Field Day Pamphlet No. 14 (Derry: Field Day, 1988).

[39]   *Modernism and the Harlem Renaissance*, p. xvi. Baker argues that the relationship between 'mastery and deformation' is 'fluid and . . . interdependent' and creates a field of 'expressive possibilities' for black spokespersons, writers, and artists (68).

[40]   For Baker, '*poetic* mastery discovered as a function of deformative *folk* sound' constitutes 'the essence of black discursive modernism' (93).

[41]   Manthia Diawara, 'The Absent One: The Avant-Garde and the Black Imaginary, in *Looking for Langston*', *Wide Angle*, vol. 13, nos. 3 & 4 (July–Oct. 1991), 106. This argument may be linked with Isaac Julien's own response to Alan Lovell's suggestion that the films of the black workshops failed to escape from 'the dead ends of 1970s aesthetics' (see Alan Lovell, 'That Was the Workshops That Was', *Screen*, vol. 31 no. 1 (Spring 1990), 105). For Julien, however, it is precisely 'the unfinished business of . . . the politics of race and representation' that 'demand a reconceptualisation of the debates around aesthetics and politics' and that is manifest in the workshop films. See 'Diaries' in Isaac Julien and Colin MacCabe, *Diary of a Young Soul Rebel* (London: BFI, 1991), 65.

[42]   Paul Gilroy, *The Black Atlantic* (London: Verso, 1993). It is, of course, the case that films such as *Looking for Langston* have themselves fed back into US black culture in terms of the debates which they have generated amongst black American theorists.

[43]   'Nationalism, History and Ethnic Absolutism', in *Small Acts*, 71.

in seeking to 'de-essentialize' black identities and to query the dominance of a particular (heterosexual) version of masculinity in black cultural politics. In doing so, the film is also marked by what Hall refers to as the 'return of desire' into black politics.[44] There is a scene in *Passion* in which we first see Michael swimming and then, later, he and Gary in the water together. The shots have little narrative motivation and the images of the graceful motion of black bodies are offered as a source of pleasure in their own right. The scene is relatively short but begins to open up a number of issues which are explored much more fully in *Langston*: the visualization of the black male body and the dynamics of (homo-erotic) looking. In this regard, *Looking for Langston* is not only engaged in the activity of looking but is also *about* the activity of looking.

Acts of looking are, of course, implicated in relations of domination and subordination and it is the act of looking at the black male body which becomes a central concern of the film. In this respect, the film is, according to Mercer, working both 'in and against' a logic of objectification and fetishism in the depiction of black male bodies.[45] It is a film which is clearly conscious not only of the use made of the black male body in mainstream popular culture (and its common association with either violence, threat, or exoticism) but also by the white, gay image-maker (such as Robert Mapplethorpe, a book of whose images a white character is seen to flick through near the film's end).[46] Thus, in one particularly striking scene, a white actor is seen wandering through sheets on which are projected images of black men, some naked, which he moves around and caresses. The light from the projector draws attention to the 'mediated'—and voyeuristic—status of the images and, on the soundtrack, the poetry of the contemporary black gay writer Essex Hemphill is used to query the relationship of the white, gay man to his black object of desire ('You wanted pleasure without guilt or capture . . . you don't notice many things about him. He doesn't always wear a red ski hat, eat fried chicken, fuck like a jungle'.) The sequence then ends with the white man lying on a bed giving a black man money.

However, the film also seeks to hold on to the visual pleasure of looking at the black male but divesting it of some of the relations of power implied in this scene. In another scene in the film, the character called 'Beauty', who is seated at a white man's table, becomes the object of the erotic gaze of Alex/Hughes who is seated at the bar. His face is lit with a kick light and surrounded by shadow. There follows a 'fantasy' scene in which the camera travels along Beauty's naked body and Alex is seen walking through a field where he finds Beauty, again naked. Bruce Nugent's short story 'Lillies and Jade' is heard on the soundtrack as the men stand facing each other. Shots of Alex and Beauty in bed together then

[44] Hall, 'New Ethnicities', 29.
[45] Mercer, 'Dark and Lovely: Notes on Black Gay Image-Making', *Ten 8*, vol. 2 no. 1 (Spring 1991), 81. A similar argument is also developed in José Arroyo, 'Look Back and Talk Black: The Films of Isaac Julien', *Jump Cut*, no. 36 (1991).
[46] For a discussion of the ambivalent responses which Mapplethorpe's photographs of naked black men can inspire, see Mercer, 'Just Looking for Trouble: Robert Mapplethorpe and Fantasies of Race', in Lynne Segal and Mary McIntosh (eds.), *Sex Exposed: Sexuality and the Pornography Debate* (London: Virago Press, 1992).

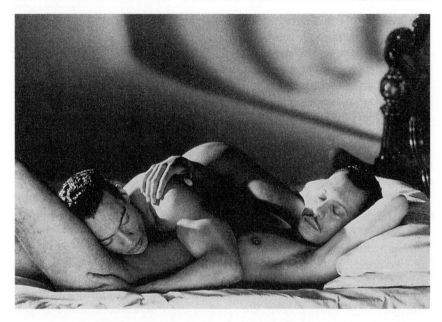

PLATE 18. Intimacy and softness: Matthew Biadoo and Ben Ellison in *Looking for Langston*

follow, including a shot of the two men kissing and an elegant travelling shot along their entwined bodies. A subsequent scene finds Alex in a similar position at the bar. Blackberri's song 'Beautiful Black Men' ('You're such a beautiful black man who somehow has been made to feel that your beauty's not real') is heard on the soundtrack. Another black man sits alongside Alex and becomes the focus of his, and the camera's, admiring gaze as we watch him turn his head. Archive footage is intercut with the characters in the bar, suggesting some of the impulses underlying the creative work of the Renaissance. In scenes such as these there is an effort to furnish images of black sexuality which are inscribed in the relations between black men and which possess an unfamiliar intimacy and softness (as the camera holds on the still bodies of the two men in Alex's fantasy the words of Bruce Nugent are heard—'he could feel Beauty's body close against his . . . hot, tense and soft . . . soft'). Mercer singles out in particular the sensuous close-up shot of Beauty's mouth in the scene in the field (when Beauty, in an English accent, says 'I'll wait'). The film, argues Mercer, 'takes the artistic risk of replicating the racial stereotype of the "thick lipped Negro" ' in order 'to re-position the Black subject as subject, and not object, of the look . . . and to represent the Black man who wants (to look at) another Black man'.[47]

---

[47] Mercer, 'Dark and Lovely', 81. bell hooks also argues that one of the key elements in the film is its disruption of how black men are looked at. 'The image of the black male body as vulnerable and soft', she argues, is 'antithetical' to the way 'black maleness' is conventionally represented. See 'States of Desire: Isaac Julien in Conversation with bell hooks', in Isaac Julien and Colin MacCabe, *Diary of a Young Soul Rebel*, 131.

Young Soul Rebels

Isaac Julien's next film after *Looking for Langston, Young Soul Rebels* (1991) is a much more conventional film than either *The Passion of Remembrance* or *Langston* as Julien wanted to make a film that would be seen 'by a wider audience' than his earlier films.[48] *Young Soul Rebels*, therefore, adopts a largely linear and diegetically coherent narrative, makes use of the genre conventions of the thriller (by incorporating an element of murder mystery), and relies heavily upon a popular music soundtrack. The film does, however, maintain many of the interests of the earlier films, both by questioning conventional ideas of black 'identity' (and black masculinity in particular) and exploring the 'transgressive' dynamics of sexual desire (in the context of 'race'). In this respect, the film partly returns to an interest in 'race relations' but from a very different perspective from British films prior to the 1960s. Whereas British films of the 1950s and 1960s were organized around white characters, and their experience of blacks, *Young Soul Rebels* is primarily focused upon black characters, and deals with *their* encounters with whites (as well as relations amongst blacks). This has two main aspects. On the one hand, the film deals with the realities of racism: the menacing presence of skinheads on the streets and of National Front graffiti on the walls, the unsympathetic treatment of blacks by the police, and the mixture of fear of and desire towards blacks which leads Ken (Dorian Healy), a white man, to kill TJ (Shyro Chung) in the park.

On the other hand, the film also traces the role of desire in unsettling ethnic divisions and reimagining new forms of community (in a way that has significant echoes of *My Beautiful Laundrette*). The film is set in 1977 at the time of Queen Elizabeth II's Silver Jubilee. As with *Looking for Langston*, the film is concerned to retrieve a particular moment of black history that complicates the more familiar accounts of the period. On the one hand, the film seeks to counter the resurgent patriotism and white chauvinism (or 'ethnic absolutism') that was associated with the Jubilee. On the other hand, it is also concerned to complicate the alternative narrative of the period provided by punk, of its opposition to the Jubilee and protest against 'England's dreaming'.[49] In particular, the film wishes to reinstate the importance of soul music and the role that it played in relation to the politics of race and gender in this period.

For Julien, soul music may be seen to have permitted a distance from both conventional structures of black masculinity and the 'tough masculine left politics' of 'black nationalism'.[50] He argues that the soul clubs of this period

[48] 'Soul to Soul', Interview with Amy Taubin, *Sight and Sound* (Aug. 1991), 16.

[49] 'There is no future in England's dreaming' is a line from The Sex Pistols' *God Save the Queen* (1977). For a discussion, see Jon Savage, *England's Dreaming: Sex Pistols and Punk Rock* (London: Faber and Faber, 1991).

[50] Julien, 'Introduction', in *Diary of a Young Soul Rebel*, 2. It is also significant that soul and funk were primarily American forms and thus permitted, as in Gilroy's idea of the 'black Atlantic', another mode of non-national identification for young British blacks (and, indeed, whites).

opened up a 'wonderfully hybrid space' that was simultaneously 'black/white' and 'gay/straight'.[51] It is this 'utopian space' that the film seeks to explore through its reconstruction of the 'Crypt', a soul club where black and white, gays and straights, punks and soul boys all mix (and dance to music such as Funkadelic's 'One Nation Under A Groove'). This vision also underpins the relationship that develops between the black DJ, Caz (Mo Sesay) and the white punk, Billibud (Jason Durr) whose lovemaking is accompanied by (the black and gay) Sylvester's 'You Make Me Feel (Mighty Real)', a song that 'magically' bursts onto the soundtrack after Billibud has failed to impress Caz with either punk (X-Ray Spex's 'Identity') or reggae (Junior Murvin's 'Police and Thieves'). As Julien argues, although soul and disco were often regarded as 'apolitical', especially when set against the more 'militant' sounds of punk and reggae, it none the less opened up a different kind of 'politics' around sexuality and put into question some of the certainties that a 'politics of identity' conventionally provided.[52] In a sense, the 'utopian space' that the film then celebrates is given its most vivid evocation at the film's end when the film's main characters (black and white, male and female, gay and straight) at first tentatively, and then more confidently, begin to dance in step to El Coco's 'Let's Get It Together'. While this scene may be seen as 'sentimental', it also represents, as Gilroy has suggested, a genuine attempt to find a 'symbol' for precisely 'the anti-racist, polysexual, democratic aspirations' that the film has been advocating (and which soul and funk may be seen to have been facilitating).[53]

Conclusion

In a somewhat controversial discussion, Judith Williamson has counterpointed what she regards as the accessibility and enjoyability of *My Beautiful Laundrette* to the relative difficulty and cognitive orientation of a film such as *The Passion of Remembrance*.[54] Paul Gilroy has raised similar questions in querying whether there is a 'base or context' for the types of films to emerge from the black workshops, such as Black Audio, 'within the black communities within this country'.[55]

[51] Julien, 'Introduction', in *Diary of a Young Soul Rebel*, 6.

[52] Ibid. 2. In the film Billibud is also a political activist associated with the Socialist Workers Party (SWP). The complication of his politics is dramatized in the scene at the tube station where he encounters Caz and tries to encourage him to attend the 'Fuck the Jubilee' concert. A SWP colleague, however, tells him off for not having 'more important things' to talk about than music and for having 'cock on the brain'.

[53] Paul Gilroy, Stuart Hall, and Homi Bhabha (in discussion), 'Threatening Pleasures', *Sight and Sound* (Aug. 1991), 19.

[54] 'Two Kinds of Otherness: Black Film and the Avant-Garde', in *Black Film, British Cinema*, 35–6.

[55] Gilroy, 'Cruciality and the Frog's Perspective: An Agenda of Difficulties for the Black Arts Movement in Britain', in *Small Acts*, 114. In doing so, Gilroy also asks whether black British film culture has been too dependent upon an 'agenda' set by 'international film festival circuits'. One problem with this criticism, however, is that it ignores how the 'base and context' for all British filmmaking changed during this period and how, as a result, the film festival circuit increased in importance for the whole of British film culture (see Chapter 3).

In doing so, Gilroy goes on to call for a 'populist modernism' which is more clearly 'aligned to vernacular forms and modes of expression' and rearticulates 'the positive core of aesthetic modernism into resolutely populist formats'.[56] To some extent, *Young Soul Rebels* may be seen as a kind of response to this type of criticism. However, despite the relative accessibility of *Young Soul Rebels* compared with *The Passion of Remembrance* or *Looking for Langston*, it would be a mistake to set the two kinds of aesthetic strategy which they represent in opposition to each other.

For *Young Soul Rebels* itself can be seen as a 'difficult' film which, in foregrounding issues of masculinity and homosexuality, may challenge and upset the audiences to whom it is addressed. The film, in this respect, is not so much an overtly 'popular' film as a different take on, and aesthetic approach to, shared concerns. In the process, there are both benefits (such as increased accessibility) and costs (such as the loss of a certain degree of complexity and aesthetic richness). In his introduction to the published script, Colin MacCabe (one of the film's executive producers) reflects upon his own contribution to '*Screen* theory' of the 1970s by returning to Brecht's 'A Short Organum for the Theatre'. In doing so, he points to a 'subterranean discourse' which argues for the production of 'new forms of knowledge' which are not 'scientific' (or based upon the insights of historical materialism) but are 'intimately related to pleasure'.[57] However, while MacCabe is right to argue against the reduction of art to the political, he rather too quickly links the issue of pleasure and film with the adoption—as in *Young Soul Rebels*—of a more 'popular' cinematic format, and thus underplays the significance of the different kinds of pleasure (including aesthetic pleasures) which films such as *The Passion of Remembrance* and *Looking for Langston* provide. As Julian Henriques pointed out, in his review of the film, the sensuality of *Young Soul Rebels* is actually rather 'tepid' when compared with 'the sexual tenderness and ravishing style' of *Looking for Langston*.[58]

Accordingly, a call such as Gilroy's for the adoption of 'popular' or 'vernacular' forms by black cultural producers should be seen as a demand for extending the compass of black filmmaking rather than restricting it to one cultural space (which would simply reproduce the very manœuvres of 'exclusion' that writers such as Houston Baker have complained of in relation to the contribution of black artists to 'high modernism'). As John Akomfrah of Black Audio has argued, the project of black British filmmakers has been to expand the 'range and variety' of work that is associated with the black and Asian communities rather than to limit it to one type of practice (or, indeed, to assume that it is directed towards a unitary 'black'—or 'white'—audience).[59] Unlike earlier debates within Anglo-American theory concerning the relative merits of 'realism' and 'political modernism' (or 'counter-cinema'), it is unhelpful, as

---

[56] Ibid. 110 and 103.   [57] *Diary of a Young Soul Rebel*, 12–13.
[58] Julian Henriques, *Sight and Sound* (Sept. 1991), 55.
[59] Interview with John Akomfrah, *Black and White in Colour* (d. Isaac Julien, BBC, 1992).

debates concerning third cinema suggest, to cast different types of cinema into a stark 'either/or' opposition. In this respect, black British cinema of the 1980s did not correspond to one model of filmmaking, or to one conception of a 'black aesthetic', so much as provide a diverse and changing set of responses to the problems and challenges thrown up by multicultural Britain in the 1980s.

Conclusion: A National Cinema? _____

The book began with some consideration of whether, in the 1980s, British cinema could still, because of its growing involvement with television, be regarded as cinema. By way of conclusion, it might also be asked whether it is a cinema that may still usefully be regarded as 'British', at least as conventionally understood. For, traditionally, the idea of national cinema has been associated with a clear unified version of national identity and national preoccupations. Thus, writing in the context of Australian cinema, Susan Dermody and Elizabeth Jacka suggest that 'the *true* national cinema' (my italics) is characterized by a strong bond or 'feedback loop' between films and audiences.[1] In a similar fashion, Raphael Samuel suggests that, in comparison to other periods, British cinema in the 1940s was a genuinely 'national cinema' in the way that it addressed the shared 'preoccupations of the time'.[2] While it is, of course, possible to query whether, at an empirical level, national cinemas were ever truly 'national', in this sense of addressing unified 'national' interests, it would certainly not be possible to discuss British cinema of the 1980s in these terms.[3]

For it is clear that the certainties concerning the 'nation' upon which many earlier British films relied no longer prevailed in films of the period. British films, as various chapters have indicated, may, in many cases, have continued to address national concerns, or employ a strategy of national allegory. However, in the main, they did so not to project a unified notion of national identity and national culture but in order to offer a much more fluid, hybrid, and plural sense of 'Britishness' than earlier British cinema generally did. In this respect, while the British cinema of the 1980s failed to assert the myths of 'nation' with its earlier confidence it was nevertheless a cinema that could be regarded as representing the complexities of 'national' life more fully than ever before.

This acknowledgement of complexity was associated, moreover, with a growing sense of the variety of 'national' identities co-existing within the British

---

[1] Susan Dermody and Elizabeth Jacka, *The Screening of Australia, Vol. 1 Anatomy of a Film Industry* (Sydney: Currency Press, 1987), 4.

[2] Raphael Samuel, 'Introduction: Exciting to be English', in Raphael Samuel (ed.), *Patriotism: The Making and Unmaking of British National Identity, Vol. 1 History and Politics* (London: Routledge, 1989), p. xxviii.

[3] In the case of wartime Britain, for example, both the unity of the national community and the inclusiveness of the representations of national identity provided by the cinema have been queried. See, for example, Graham Dawson and Bob West, 'Our Finest Hour?: The Popular Memory of World War II and the Struggle Over National Identity', in Geoff Hurd (ed.), *National Fictions* (London: British Film Institute, 1984) and Jeffrey Richards, 'National Identity in British Wartime Films', in Philip M. Taylor (ed.), *Britain and the Cinema in the Second World War* (Basingstoke: Macmillan, 1989).

state. As Jeffrey Richards has observed in relation to British wartime films, the strong sense of 'national identity' which they contained 'derived almost entirely from England, which was often used interchangeably with Britain to describe the nation'.[4] During the 1980s, however, not only did British cinema articulate a much more inclusive sense of Englishness than hitherto but there was also a growing recognition of the differing (Scottish and Welsh) forms of national affiliation which co-existed within Britain.

Writing of Australian cinema in the 1990s, Graeme Turner notes the suspicion which has often accompanied discussion of both the nation and national cinema due to the socially conservative versions of national identity which these tend to imply. He argues, however, that the post-colonial status of Australia means that its discourses of the nation are much less settled and that it is possible for Australian films to provide 'a critical . . . body of representations within mainstream Western cinema'.[5] In the same way, the peculiar historical circumstances of Scotland and Wales—which may have gained economically from the British colonial enterprise but none the less encountered a degree of cultural subordination—provided a further opening for a negotiation of the discourses around the 'nation'. Thus, while it was possibly the 1990s when Scottish cinema (following the successes of *Shallow Grave* (1994) *Small Faces* (1995), and *Trainspotting* (1995)) and Welsh cinema (in the wake of *Hedd Wyn* (1992), *Gadael Lenin/Leaving Lenin* (1993) and *Twin Town* (1997)) acquired a particular prominence, it was developments in the 1980s, as Chapter 3 indicates, which laid the basis for their emergence.

In this respect, there is a certain historical irony that when *Chariots of Fire* was rereleased in the aftermath of its Oscar successes, and in the midst of the Falklands war, that it was as a part of a double-bill with the Scottish film *Gregory's Girl* (1980). While this was probably intended as a celebration of the range of British films constituting the 'renaissance', there was also something of a touch subversive in the showing of these films together. For while both are British films, they also represent very different kinds of British cinema. This was not simply an issue of cost and scale but also of the differing ways in which they articulated ideas of 'identity'. Thus, while *Chariots of Fire* is focused on the past, *Gregory's Girl* is resolutely of the present. The version of the past which *Chariots* constructs, moreover, is strongly identified with the English upper classes and male achievement (through sport). *Gregory's Girl*, on the other hand, is set amongst the suburban middle and working class and—by reversing conventional sporting roles—gently subverts traditional stereotypes of 'masculinity' and 'femininity'. And, while *Chariots* is very much an 'English' film, *Gregory's Girl* is decidedly 'Scottish'.

Chariots is, of course, partly set in Scotland but, as was argued in Chapter 1, it tends to look at Scotland from the outside (that is, from the metropolitan

    [4] 'National Identity in British Wartime Films', 44.
    [5] Graeme Turner, 'The End of the National Project?: Australian Cinema in the 1990s', in Wimal Dissanayake (ed.), *Colonialism and Nationalism in Asian Cinema* (Bloomington: Indiana University Press, 1994), 203.

English centre), associating it with the 'natural' and the 'primitive'. _Gregory's Girl_, on the other hand, is firmly rooted in contemporary Scottish realities and avoids the conventional signifiers of 'Scottishness'. Thus, it is set neither in the Highlands, the Lowlands small town nor Clydeside but in the conspicuously 'ordinary' 'new town' of Cumbernauld.[6] In this way, the film also implies a sense of the complexity of contemporary Scottish 'identities'. There are two aspects to this. On the one hand, it is clear that while the film speaks with a firm Scottish accent, it is not a film specifically about 'national concerns'. As Paul Willemen suggests, a national cinema may be 'nationally specific' without necessarily demonstrating any overt set of 'preoccupations with national identity'.[7] In this sense, one of the achievements of _Gregory's Girl_ is its confidence to speak from within Scottish culture without turning its 'Scottishness' into an overt 'issue'.

This relates, in turn, to the film's sense of the plural character of contemporary Scottish 'identities' (and, indeed, of all identities). As Cairns Craig argues, it is often the case that cultural practices which seek to combat non-Scottish images of Scotland end up constructing an 'essentializing' and 'reductive' Scottish 'identity' which simply opposes the supposed unity of English/British culture.[8] The way in which _Gregory's Girl_ challenges conventional Scottish imagery, therefore, is not by seeking to reveal an 'essential', or even distinctive, Scottish identity but by suggesting some of the different ways in which 'Scottishness' may be inhabited. Indeed, one of the key sources of pleasure in the film is precisely its play with identities in the form of characters who fail to occupy their social roles in the expected ways. Adults behave like children, children behave like adults, boys behave like girls, and girls behave like boys. While this has a certain link with the theme of 'escape' characteristic of British social realism, it is also the case that the desire for escape is not, in this case, motivated by poverty or hardship but by a wish to break free of the fixities of conventional social roles and identities (and especially those of gender).[9]

In many ways, it is these questions of identity—not just of nation but class, gender, sexual orientation, and ethnicity—with which this book has been concerned. In all cases, these have been discussed not in terms of 'essences' but in terms of plurality and hybridity. National identities, as with all identities, are not fixed and static, therefore, but are subject to historical change and redefinition.

---

[6] In an influential essay, Colin McArthur distinguishes three main discursive fields which have structured the representation of Scotland: tartanry, kailyard, and, to a lesser extent, Clydesidism. As McArthur indicates, _Gregory's Girl_ succeeded in sidestepping all of these. See 'Scotland and Cinema: The Iniquity of the Fathers', in McArthur (ed.), _Scotch Reels: Scotland in Cinema and Television_ (London: BFI, 1982), 66.

[7] Paul Willemen, 'The National' in _Looks and Frictions_ (London: BFI, 1994), 210.

[8] Cairns Craig, 'Visitors from the Stars: Scottish Film Culture', _Cencrastus_, no. 11 (1983), 8.

[9] Andrew Higson argues that the film is ultimately conservative in the way that it places 'faith in the family'. See 'Gregory's Girl', in Nicholas Thomas (ed.), _International Dictionary of Films and Filmmakers—1: Films_ (Chicago and London: St James Press, 1990), 367. This seems to ignore, however, that there are no conventional representations of family life within the film and that in the case of the main character, Gregory (John Gordon Sinclair), we never see his mother, his father is unable to effect paternal control, and it is his younger sister (in a reversal of roles typical of the film) who occupies the role of confidante and surrogate parent.

Nor are they, in some way, 'pure' and 'authentic' but are also involved in on-going transcultural dynamics. They do not, moreover, provide an exclusive form of identification but one which is interwoven with other forms of identity (and which may vary in degrees of importance for different social groups and individuals). As such the 'Britishness' of the British cinema in the 1980s was neither unitary nor agreed but depended upon a growing sense of the multiple national, regional, and ethnic identifications which characterized life in Britain in this period. So while it is *Chariots of Fire* which is conventionally taken to be the landmark in the revival of British cinema, it may, in fact, have been *Gregory's Girl* which was to prove the more reliable indicator of the way in which British filmmaking was moving.

Appendix: Industry Statistics

Numbers of UK film features produced	
1979	61
1980	31
1981	24
1982	40
1983	51
1984	53
1985	54
1986	41
1987	55
1988	48
1989	30
1990	60
1991	59

Source: *Screen Digest*/BFI

UK Cinema Admissions	
	Millions
1979	111.9
1980	101
1981	86
1982	64
1983	65.7
1984	54
1985	72
1986	75.5
1987	78.5
1988	84
1989	94.5
1990	97.37
1991	100.29

Source: *Screen Digest*/BFI

Select Bibliography

This is not a comprehensive bibliography of all works cited in the main text but a selection of key works.

AHMAD, AIJAZ, *In Theory: Classes, Nations, Literatures* (London: Verso, 1992).

ARROYO, JOSÉ, 'Look Back and Talk Black: The Films of Isaac Julien', *Jump Cut*, no. 36 (1991).

AUTY, MARTYN and RODDICK, NICK (eds.), *British Cinema Now* (London: BFI, 1985).

BAKER, JR., HOUSTON, A., *Modernism and the Harlem Renaissance* (Chicago: University of Chicago Press, 1987).

BALL, MICHAEL, GRAY, FRED, and McDOWELL, LINDA, *The Transformation of Britain: Contemporary Social and Economic Change* (London: Fontana, 1989).

BARKER, ADAM, 'Business as Usual? British Cinema in an Enterprise Culture', *Monthly Film Bulletin* (August 1989).

BARR, CHARLES (ed.), *All Our Yesterdays: 90 Years of British Cinema* (London: BFI, 1986).

BERRY, DAVID, *Wales and Cinema: The First Hundred Years* (Cardiff and London: University of Wales Press and BFI, 1994).

BORDWELL, DAVID, 'The Art Cinema as a Mode of Film Practice', *Film Criticism*, vol. 4 no. 1 (Fall 1979).

—— *Narration in the Fiction Film* (London: Routledge, 1985).

BRAVMANN, SCOTT, 'Isaac Julien's *Looking for Langston*: Hughes, Biography and Queer(ed) History', *Cultural Studies*, vol. 7 no. 2 (May 1993).

BROOK, PETER, *The Melodramatic Imagination: Balzac, Henry James, Melodrama and the Mode of Excess* (New York: Columbia University Press, 1984, orig. 1976).

CARTER, ED, '*Chariots of Fire*: Traditional Values/False History', *Jump Cut*, no. 28 (1988).

CAUGHIE, JOHN, 'Progressive Television and Documentary Drama', *Screen*, vol. 21 no. 3 (1980).

CHAM, MBYE B. and ANDRADE-WATKINS, CLAIRE (eds.), *Blackframes: Critical Perspectives on Black Independent Cinema* (Cambridge, Mass.: MIT Press, 1988).

CLIFFORD, JAMES, 'On Ethnographic Allegory', in Steven Seidman (ed.), *The Postmodern Turn: New Perspectives on Social Theory* (Cambridge: Cambridge University Press, 1994).

COHEN, ROBIN, *Global Diasporas: An Introduction* (London: UCL Press, 1997).

COOK, PAM, 'Melodrama and the Women's Picture', in Sue Aspinall and Robert Murphy (eds.), *Gainsborough Melodrama* (London: BFI, 1983).

CORNER, JOHN, 'Presumption as Theory: "Realism", in Television Studies', *Screen*, vol. 33 no. 1 (Spring 1992).

—— and Sylvia Harvey (eds.), *Enterprise and Heritage: Crosscurrents of National Culture* (London: Routledge, 1991).

CORRIGAN, TIMOTHY, *A Cinema Without Walls: Movies and Culture after Vietnam* (London: Routledge, 1991).

COVENEY, MICHAEL, *The World According to Mike Leigh* (London: HarperCollins, 1977).

DAVIS, FRED, *Yearning for Yesterday: A Sociology of Nostalgia* (New York: Free Press, 1979).

DE LAURETIS, TERESA, 'Guerrilla in the Midst: Women's Cinema in the 80s', *Screen*, vol. 31 no. 1 (Spring 1990).

DENT, GINA (ed.), *Black Popular Culture*, A Project by Michele Wallace (Seattle: Bay Press, 1992).

Department of National Heritage, *The British Film Industry*, Cm. 2884 (London: HMSO, 1995).

Department of Trade, *Film Policy*, Cmnd. 9319 (London: HMSO, 1984).

DICK, EDDIE (ed.), *From Limelight to Satellite: A Scottish Film Book* (Glasgow and London: Scottish Film Council and BFI, 1990).

DONALDSON, LAURA E., *Decolonizing Feminisms: Race, Gender and Empire-building* (London: Routledge, 1992).

DOTY, ALEXANDER, *Making Things Perfectly Queer: Interpreting Mass Culture* (Minneapolis: University of Minnesota Press, 1993).

DYER, RICHARD, *White* (London: Routledge, 1997).

EBERTS, JAKE and ILOTT, TERRY, *My Indecision is Final: The Rise and Fall of Goldcrest Films* (London: Faber and Faber, 1990).

EDGELL, STEPHEN and DUKE, VIC, *A Measure of Thatcherism: A Sociology of Britain* (London: HarperCollins, 1991).

ELEY, GEOFF, '*Distant Voices, Still Lives*, The Family is a Dangerous Place: Memory, Gender, and the Image of the Working Class', in Robert A. Rosenstone (ed.), *Revisioning History: Film and the Construction of a New Past* (Princeton, NJ: Princeton University Press, 1995).

FINCH, MARK and KWIETNIOWSKI, RICHARD, 'Melodrama and "Maurice": Homo is Where the Het Is', *Screen*, vol. 29 no. 3 (1988).

FINNEY, ANGUS, *The Egos Have Landed: The Rise and Fall of Palace Pictures* (London: Heinemann, 1996).

FRANKLIN, SARAH, LURY, CELIA, and STACEY, JACKIE (eds.), *Off-Centre: Feminism and Cultural Studies* (London: HarperCollins, 1991).

FRIEDMAN, LESTER (ed.), *British Cinema and Thatcherism: Fires Were Started* (London: UCL Press, 1993).

FUSCO, COCO, *Young British and Black: The Work of Sankofa and Black Audio Film Collective* (Buffalo, NY: Hallwalls/Contemporary Arts Center, 1988).

GAMBLE, ANDREW, *The Free Economy and the Strong State: The Politics of Thatcherism* (Basingstoke: Macmillan, 1988).

—— 'The Thatcher Decade in Perspective', in Patrick Dunleavy, Andrew Gamble, and Gillian Peele (eds.), *Developments in British Politics 3* (Basingstoke: Macmillan, 1990).

GILROY, PAUL, *There Ain't No Black in the Union Jack: The Cultural Politics of Race and Nation* (London: Hutchinson, 1987).

—— *Small Acts* (London: Serpent's Tail, 1993).

—— *The Black Atlantic: Modernity and Double Consciousness* (London: Verso, 1993).

HACKER, JONATHAN and PRICE, DAVID, *Take 10: Contemporary British Film Directors* (Oxford: Clarendon Press, 1991).

HALL, STUART, *The Hard Road to Renewal: Thatcherism and the Crisis of the Left* (London: Verso, 1988).

—— 'Old and New Identities, Old and New Ethnicities', in Anthony D. King (ed.), *Culture, Globalization and the World-System: Contemporary Conditions for the Representation of Identity* (Basingstoke: Macmillan, 1991).

—— 'The Question of Cultural Identity', in Stuart Hall and Tony McGrew (eds.), *Modernity and its Futures* (Cambridge: Polity Press, 1992).

HAMNETT, CHRIS, MCDOWELL, LINDA, and SARRE, PHILIP (eds.), *The Changing Social Structure* (London: Sage, 1990).

HARVEY, DAVID, *The Condition of Postmodernity* (Oxford: Basil Blackwell, 1989).

HARVEY, SYLVIA, 'Channel 4 Television: From Annan to Grade', in Stuart Hood (ed.), *Behind the Screens: The Structure of British Television in the Nineties* (London: Lawrence and Wishart, 1994).

HEWISON, ROBERT, *The Heritage Industry: Britain in a Climate of Decline* (London: Methuen, 1987).

HIGSON, ANDREW, *Waving the Flag: Constructing a National Cinema in Britain* (Oxford: Clarendon Press, 1995).

—— (ed.), *Dissolving Views: Key Writings on British Cinema* (London: Cassell, 1996).

HILL, JOHN, *Sex, Class and Realism: British Cinema, 1956–1963* (London: British Film Institute, 1986).

—— MCLOONE, MARTIN and HAINSWORTH, PAUL (eds.), *Border Crossing: Film in Ireland, Britain and Europe* (Belfast and London: Institute of Irish Sudies/BFI, 1994).

—— —— (eds.), *Big Picture, Small Screen: The Relations Between Film and Television* (Luton: John Libbey Media/University of Luton Press, 1996).

—— and CHURCH GIBSON, PAMELA (eds.), *The Oxford Guide to Film Studies* (Oxford: Oxford University Press, 1998).

HIPSKY, MARTIN A., 'Anglophil(m)ia: Why Does America Watch Merchant-Ivory Movies?', *Journal of Popular Film and Television*, vol. 22 no. 3 (Fall 1994).

HOOKS, BELL, *Yearning: Race, Gender and Cultural Politics* (London: Turnaround, 1991).

—— *Black Looks: Race and Representation* (Boston, MA: South End Press, 1992).

HUTCHINGS, PETER J., 'A Disconnected View: Forster, Modernity and Film', in Jeremy Tambling (ed.), *E. M. Forster* (Basingstoke: Macmillan, 1995).

ISAACS, JEREMY, *Storm Over 4: A Personal Account* (London: Weidenfeld & Nicolson, 1989).

JAMESON, FREDRIC, 'Postmodernism, or The Cultural Logic of Late Capitalism', *New Left Review*, no. 146 (July–August 1984).

—— 'Third-World Literature in the Era of Multinational Capitalism', *Social Text*, 15 (Fall 1986).

—— *Postmodernism, or the Cultural Logic of Late Capitalism* (London: Verso, 1991).

JARMAN, DEREK, *The Last of England* (London: Constable, 1987).

JESSOP, BOB, BONNETT, KEVIN, BROMLEY, SIMON, and LING, TOM, *Thatcherism* (Oxford: Polity Press, 1988).

JULIEN, ISAAC and MACCABE, COLIN, *Diary of a Young Soul Rebel* (London: BFI, 1991).

KAVANAGH, DENNIS and SHELDON, ANTHONY (eds.), *The Thatcher Effect* (Oxford: Clarendon Press, 1989).

KING, BARRY, 'Articulating Stardom', *Screen* vol. 26 no. 5 (September–October 1985).

KIPNIS, LAURA, ' "The Phantom Twitchings of an Amputated Limb": Sexual Spectacle in the Post-Colonial Epic', *Wide Angle*, vol. 11 no. 4 (1989).

KUREISHI, HANIF, *My Beautiful Laundrette and The Rainbow Sign* (London: Faber and Faber, 1986).

—— *Sammy and Rosie Get Laid: The Script and the Diary* (London: Faber and Faber, 1988).

LEIGH, MIKE, *Naked and Other Screenplays* (London: Faber and Faber, 1995).

LEMAHIEU, D. L., 'Imagined Contemporaries: Cinematic and Televised Dramas about the Edwardians in Great Britain and the United States, 1967–1985', *Historical Journal of Film, Radio and Television*, vol. 10 no. 3 (1990).

LEYS, COLIN, *Politics In Britain: From Labourism to Thatcherism* (London: Verso, 1989).

LINDLEY, ARTHUR, 'Raj as Romance/Raj as Parody: Lean's and Forster's Passage to India', *Literature/Film Quarterly*, vol. 20 no. 1 (1992).

LIPPARD, CHRIS (ed.), *By Angels Driven: The Films of Derek Jarman* (Trowbridge: Flicks Books, 1996).

MCARTHUR, COLIN (ed.), *Scotch Reels: Scotland in Cinema and Television* (London: BFI, 1982).

MCCRONE, DAVID, *Understanding Scotland: The Sociology of a Stateless Nation* (London: Routledge, 1992).

MACKINNON, KENNETH, *The Politics of Popular Representation: Reagan, Thatcher, AIDS and the Movies* (London: Associated University Presses, 1992).

MCKNIGHT, GEORGE (ed.), *Agent of Challenge and Defiance: The Films of Ken Loach* (Trowbridge: Flicks Books, 1997).

MASON, DAVID, *Race and Ethnicity in Modern Britain* (Oxford: Oxford University Press, 1995).

MEDHURST, ANDY, 'Mike Leigh: Beyond Embarrassment', *Sight and Sound* (November 1993).

MELLOR, ADRIAN, 'Whose Heritage?', *Journal of the North West Labour History Group*, Bulletin 14 (1989–90).

MERCER, KOBENA (ed.), *Black Film, British Cinema* (London: ICA, 1988).

—— 'Black Art and the Burden of Representation', *Third Text*, no. 10 (Spring 1990).

—— 'Dark and Lovely: Notes on Black Gay Image-Making', *Ten 8*, vol. 2 no. 1 (Spring 1991).

—— 'Black Gay Men In Independent Film', *Cineaction*, no. 32 (Fall 1993).

MILIBAND, RALPH, PANITCH, LEO, and SAVILLE, JOHN (eds.), *The Socialist Register 1987* (London: Merlin Press, 1987).

MONK, CLAIRE, 'The British "Heritage Film" and its Critics', *Critical Survey*, vol. 7 no. 2 (1995).

—— 'Sexuality and the Heritage', *Sight and Sound* (October 1995).

Monopolies and Mergers Commission, *Films: A Report on the Supply of Films for Exhibition in Cinemas in the UK*, Cm. 2673 (London: HMSO, 1994).

MURPHY, ROBERT (ed.), *The British Cinema Book* (London: BFI, 1997).

NEALE, STEVE, 'Art Cinema and the Question of Independent Film', in Rod Stoneman and Hilary Thompson (eds.), *The New Social Function of Cinema: Catalogue: British Film Institute Productions '79/80* (London: BFI, 1981).

O'PRAY, MICHAEL, *Derek Jarman: Dreams of England* (London: BFI, 1996).

PEARSON, ROBERTA E., *Eloquent Gestures: The Transformation of Performance Style in the Griffith Biograph Films* (Berkeley and Los Angeles: University of California Press, 1992).

PETRIE, DUNCAN, *Creativity and Constraint in the British Film Industry* (Basingstoke: Macmillan, 1991).

PINES, JIM and WILLEMEN, PAUL (eds.), *Questions of Third Cinema* (London: British Film Institute, 1989).

PYM, JOHN, *Film on Four: A Survey 1982/1991* (London: BFI, 1992).

QUART, LEONARD, 'The Politics of Irony: The Frears-Kureishi Films', *Film Criticism*, vol. xvi nos. 1–2 (Fall/Winter 1991–2).

RIDDELL, PETER, *The Thatcher Era And its Legacy* (Oxford: Blackwell, 1993).

ROBERTSON, ROLAND, *Globalization: Social Theory and Global Culture* (London: Sage, 1992).

ROCKETT, KEVIN, GIBBONS, LUKE, and HILL, JOHN, *Cinema and Ireland* (London: Routledge, 1988).

ROSENSTONE, ROBERT A., *Visions of the Past: The Challenge of Film to Our Idea of History* (Cambridge, Mass.: Harvard University Press, 1995).

RUSHDIE, SALMAN, *Imaginary Homelands: Essays and Criticism, 1981–1991* (London: Penguin, 1991).

RUTHERFORD, JONATHAN (eds.), *Male Order: Unwrapping Masculinity* (London: Lawrence and Wishart, 1988).

RYAN, MICHAEL and KELLNER, DOUGLAS, *Camera Politica: The Politics and Ideology of Contemporary Film* (Bloomington and Indianopolis: Indiana University Press, 1988).

SAID, EDWARD, *Orientalism* (Harmondsworth: Penguin, 1985, orig. 1978).

SAMUEL, RAPHAEL, *Theatres of Memory: vol. 1 Past and Present in Contemporary Culture* (London: Verso, 1994).

SHOHAT, ELLA, 'Notes on the "Post-Colonial" ', in Padmini Monga (ed.), *Contemporary Postcolonial Theory* (London: Arnold, 1996).

—— and STAM, ROBERT, *Unthinking Eurocentrism* (London: Routledge, 1994).

VAN WERT, WILLIAM F., '*The Cook, The Thief, His Wife and Her Lover*', *Film Quarterly*, vol. 44 no. 2 (Winter 1990/1).

WILLEMEN, PAUL, *Looks and Frictions* (London: BFI, 1994),

WILLIAMS, CHRISTOPHER (ed.), *Cinema: the Beginnings and the Future* (London: University of Westminster Press, 1996).

WILLIAMS, RAYMOND, 'A Lecture on Realism', *Screen* vol. 18 no. 1 (Spring 1977).

WILLIAMS, TONY, '*The Ploughman's Lunch*: Remembering or Forgetting History', *Jump Cut*, no. 36 (1991).

WILLIAMSON, JUDITH, 'The Lust For Truth and The Secret State', *New Socialist* (February 1986).

WOLLEN, PETER, *Readings and Writings: Semiotic Counter-Strategies* (London: Verso, 1982).

YOUNG, HUGO, *One of Us: A Biography of Margaret Thatcher* (London: Pan Books, 1990).

Index

£14.95   8009
Hallswoot